HTML, XHTML, CSS and XML by Example

HTML, XHTML CSS and XML by EXAMPLE

A Practical Guide

by Teodoru Gugoiu

Teora
Chevy Chase, Maryland, USA

2 Wisconsin Circle, Suite 870
Chevy Chase, MD 20815
USA

Stylistic Editor: Rob Couvillon

051

ISBN 1-59496-037-2

Printed in Romania

10 9 8 7 6 5 4 3 2 1

Library of Congress Cataloging-in-Publication Data

Gugoiu, Teodoru, 1959-
HTML,XHTML,CSS and XML by example : a practical guide / by Teodoru Gugoiu
Teora.
376 p. 18,5x23 cm.
Includes bibliographical references and index.
ISBN 1-59496-037-2
1. HTML (Document markup language) 2. XML (Document markup language) 3. Cascading style sheets. 4. XHTML (Document markup language) I. Title.

QA76.76.H94G83 2005
006.7'4--dc22

2005005766

Dedication

For my dear wife, Iulia,
whom I shall love eternally

Contents

Acknowledgments

I am grateful to my wife, Iulia and my son, Theo for their continuous support, encouragement and supreme patience through all the long nights and weekends I spent working on this book.

I would like to thank Teodor Raducanu, General Manager, and Diana Rotaru, Editorial Director, at Teora USA Publishing House for offering me the chance to write this book, and for their guidance and excellent collaboration.

I want to use this opportunity to thank all my university professors for the privilege I had to be one of their students and to attend courses that positively affected my professional development and my career. Special thanks must go to Irina Athanasiu, Nicolae Tapus, Cristian Giumale, Valeriu Cristea, Marian Dobre, and Valeriu Iorga.

Rob Couvillon did an excellent job by carefully editing this book, with his constructive comments and incisive questions. Without his help, this book would still exist only in my mind.

I also want to thank all my readers, who trust me by buying this book. Please send any comments, criticisms, ideas, or requests to teodoru_gugoiu@yahoo.com.

Preface

HTML, XHTML, CSS and XML by Example – A Practical Guide explains how to manually create web pages using HTML, XHTML, CSS, and XML technologies. This book is based on W3 Consortium specifications and details how the most commonly used browsers implement these recommendations.

Designed as a useful reference and guide, this book provides complete code sources, high-resolution screen captures and more than 300 descriptive examples to aid the developer. Each feature of HTML, XHTML, CSS, and XML is presented, analyzed and exemplified by emphasizing the purpose for which that each feature was designed and implemented. As well, the full range of possible attribute and property values is detailed with complete examples.

This book also presents detailed solutions explaining how the developer can integrate HTML, XHTML, CSS, and XML to create professional web pages using these complementary Internet technologies.

You can download all the files with code sources at www.teora.com.

Chapter 1

The First Web Page

1.1 The design cycle for a web page

A web page has the following design cycle:

1. Edit the file using a text editor.
2. Save the file using the extension `.html` or `.htm`
3. View the page using a browser (e.g. Internet Explorer or Netscape Navigator).

1.2 The first page

The following example shows the simplest web page.

Example 1_1. The first page (file e1_1.html)

```
The first page!
```

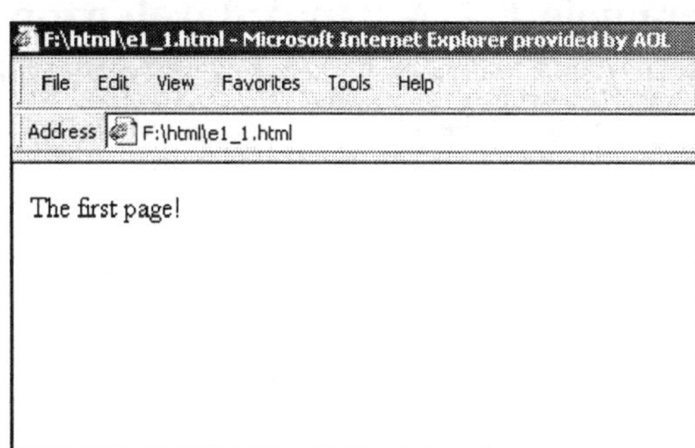

Figure 1.1

To create this example, follow these steps:

1. Open a text editor (e.g. Notepad) and type `The first page!`.
2. Save the file with the name `e1_1.html`.

Figure 1.2

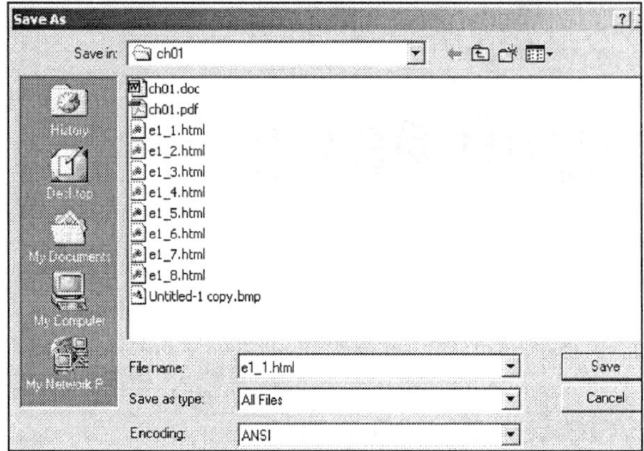

3. Open the file in your favorite browser.

Note

◆ Although this page doesn't adhere to any standards, the browser does its best to render it correctly.

1.3 Standard elements of an HTML document

Let's change the previous example to get a standard HTML document. To do this, enter the content into the text editor as illustrated in Example 1_2 and save it as `e1_2.html`, then open it in the browser.

Example 1_2. A standard web page (file e1_2.html)

```
<html>
        <head></head>
        <body>
        The first standard page!
        </body>
</html>
```

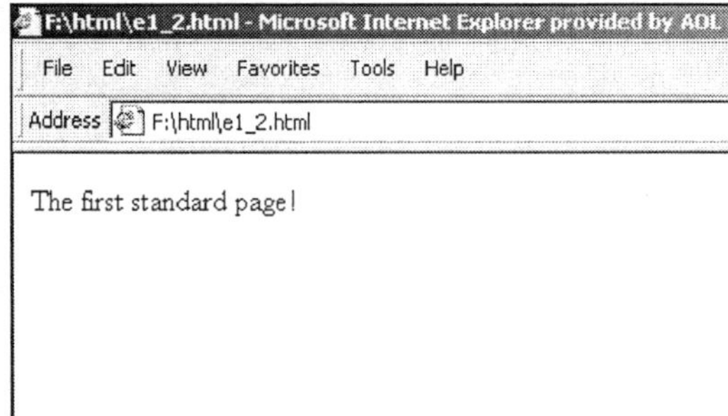

Figure 1.3

Notes

- The symbols <...> and </...> are used to identify the **tags** (markup elements in an HTML document). They represent **commands** to the browser for rendering the document.
- An HTML document consists of a sequence of **blocks**.
- The outermost block is `<html>...</html>` and represents the entire HTML document.
- A block has an opening tag (e.g. `<html>`) and a corresponding ending tag (e.g. `</html>`).
- Blocks can be nested. Inside the `<html>` block there are two other standard blocks: `<head>...</head>` and `<body>...</body>`.
- The words **html**, **head**, **body**, etc. are **reserved words** in HTML and cannot be used in brackets <...> or </...> for any other reason.
- No spaces are allowed between < or </ and the reserved words and between the reserved words and > (e.g. `< html /  >` is written incorrectly).
- The `<body>...</body>` block is the main block in an HTML document, and it contains the real content of the web page.
- HTML is case insensitive. This means that tags can be written in lower-case or upper-case characters and produce the same effects.

The following HTML documents are equivalent to the previous example 1_2:

```
<HTML>
      <HEAD></HEAD>
      <BODY>
      The first standard page!
      </BODY>
</HTML>
```

```
      <HtMl>
      <HEAD></head>
            <body>
      The first standard page!
      </BodY>
</htML>
```

1.4 White spaces

White spaces are the space, TAB, and CR/LF characters. The browser ignores all these white spaces. Only the first white space character in a sequence is considered. Therefore, the following HTML documents will produce the same effect as example 1_2:

Example 1_3. White spaces (file e1_3.html)

```
<html><head></head><body>The first standard page!</body></html>
```

```
<html>                                              <head>
            </head>
      <body>
            The
            first                   standard
            page!
      </body>       </html>
```

1.5 Web page titles

You can attach a *title* to a web page. This title will appear in the *title bar* of the browser. To do this, insert a new <title>...</title> block inside the <head>...</head> block. The content of this block will be the title of the web page.

Example 1_4. The title (file e1_4.html)

```
<html>
      <head>
            <title>
            This is the title!
            </title>
      </head>
      <body>
      This is the content!
      </body>
</html>
```

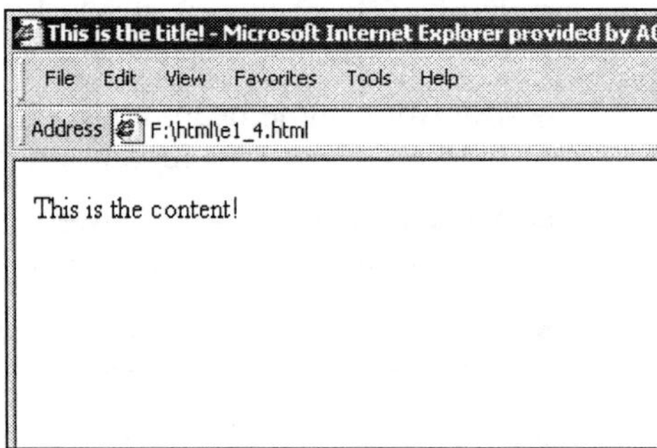

Figure 1.4

Note

- If the <title>...</title> block is missing, the path and the file name will appear in the title bar (see previous examples).

1.6 Line breaks

As mentioned earlier, browsers ignore the CR/LF character. Therefore, if you format the source document (the file with extension .html), as in the following example, the browser will render the document as shown in the Figure 1.5.

Example 1_5. The line break (file e1_5.html)

```
<html>
      <head></head>
      <body>
      First line.
      Second line.
      Third line.
      </body>
</html>
```

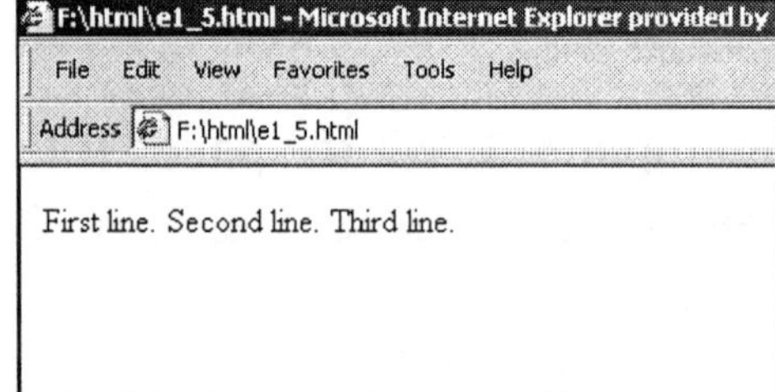

Figure 1.5

To force the browser to render an element from the beginning of the next line, you must enter the command using the <br> tag:

Example 1_6. The line break (file e1_6.html)

```
<html>
      <head></head>
      <body>
      First line.<br>
      Second line.<br>
      Third line.<br>
      </body>
</html>
```

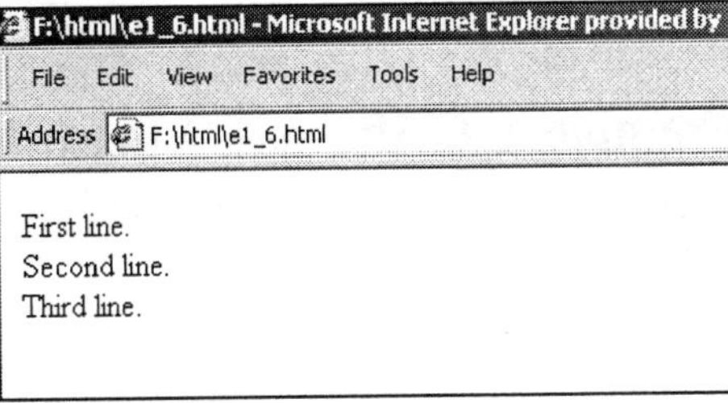

Figure 1.6

Notes

- The tag <br> is an empty element (i.e. it doesn't have an ending tag </br> and a content).
- In XHTML this tag must be replaced with the <br/> tag.

1.7 The <pre> tag for preformatted text

As mentioned earlier, the browser replaces any white space character (space, TAB, CR/LF) or sequence of these characters with one single space character. To preserve the formatting you used in editing the source document, use the <pre> element as illustrated below:

Example 1_7. Preformatted text (file e1_7.html)

```
<html>
<head></head>
<body>
<pre>

  _ _
|_| | |\/||
| | | ||||__
</pre>
</body>
</html>
```

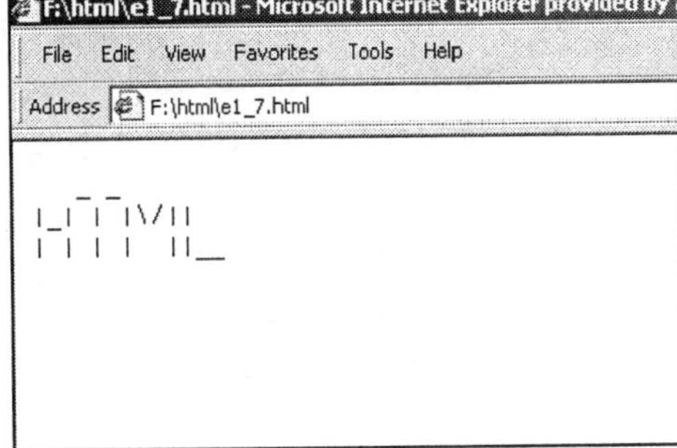

Figure 1.7

Note

- Most browsers render the <pre>...</pre> block using a mono-spaced font.

1.8 The <nobr> tag

If you want text to be rendered on a single line, include the text inside a <nobr>...</nobr> element. If the line of text is too long to fit in the browser window, a horizontal navigation bar will appear to allow the user to see the complete line.

Example 1_8. The <nobr> tag (file e1_8.html)

```
<html>
<head></head>
<body>
<nobr>
This text will be rendered on a single
long line. This text will be rendered on
a single long line. This text will be
rendered on a single long line.
</nobr>
</body>
</html>
```

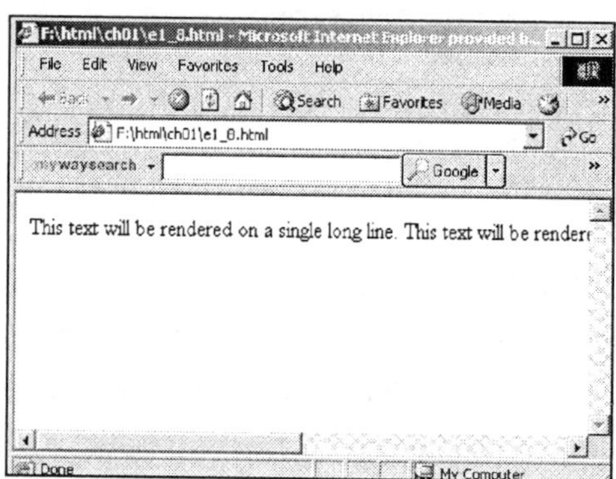

Figure 1.8

1.9 Review of Chapter 1

At the end of Chapter 01 you should know:

- A web page is an HTML document (a text file) with the extension .html or .htm.
- A standard HTML document contains an <html>...</html> block, inside of which are two other blocks: the <head>...</head> and <body>...</body> blocks.
- The title of a web page is what is contained within the <title>...</title> block that appears inside the <head>...</head> block.
- The content of the web page is what is contained within the <body>...</body> block.
- The browser replaces a sequence of white spaces characters (space, TAB, CR/LF) with a single space character.
- The <br> tag forces the browser to render the content that follows starting on a new line.
- To render text on a single line, include the text in a <nobr>...</nobr> block.
- To preserve the formatting that exists in the source document, use the <pre>...</pre> element.

Chapter 2

The physical styles of text

2.1 The default settings of the browser

If no style is specified for the text contained by the <body>…</body> block of a web page, the text will be rendered using the browser's default settings. The following example shows the default settings for Internet Explorer and how this browser will render a very simple web page that uses no text styles.

Example 2_1. Default settings of browsers (file e2_1.html)

```
<html>
<head></head>
<body>
Text with no styles!
</body>
</html>
```

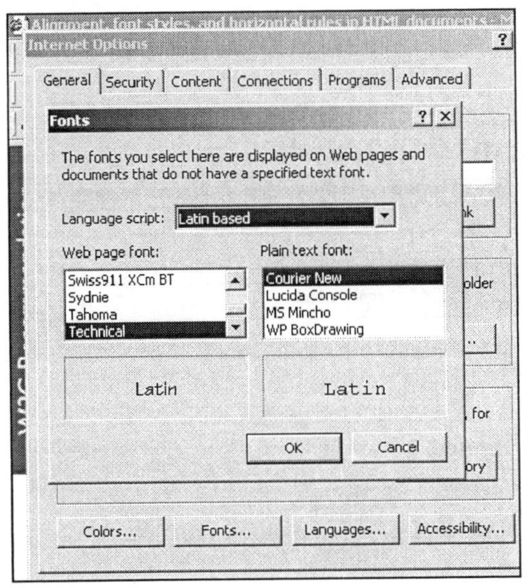

Figure 2.1

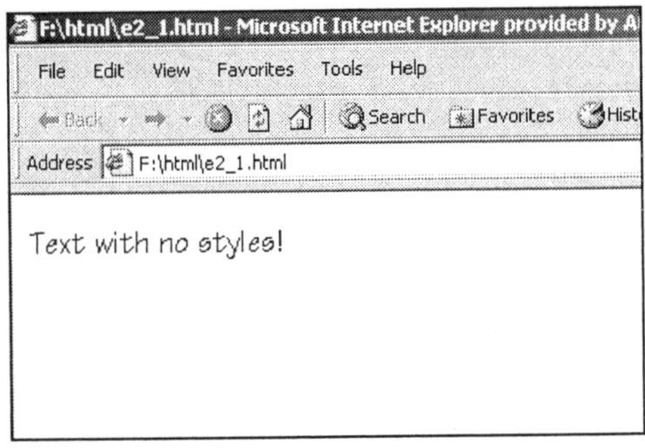

Figure 2.2

2.2 The physical styles of the text

You can change the text style using the following physical styles:

- `tt` (teletype)
- `i` (italic)
- `b` (bold)
- `big`
- `small`
- `strike` or `s`
- `u` (underlined)
- `sub` (subscript)
- `sup` (superscript)

Notes

- Most of these styles are considered deprecated in favor of Cascading Sheets of Styles (CSS) for defining text style.
- How exactly these styles will be rendered depends on the browser used.

Let's analyze each style.

2.3 The <tt> style

The `<tt>...</tt>` block allows you to render text in the *teletype* or *mono-spaced* text style.

Example 2_2. The teletype text style (file e2_2.html)

```
<html>
<head></head>
<body>
Initial text.
<tt>Teletype text.</tt>
Final text.
</body>
</html>
```

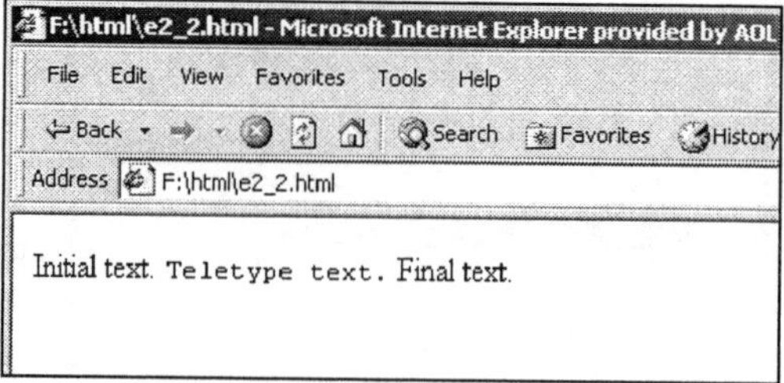

Figure 2.3

Notes

- The tags for physical styles of text are *inline* elements (i.e. they can be inserted at any point on a line).

- The CR/LF characters in the source file are replaced by a single space character when the document is rendered.

2.4 The <i>...</i> element

The <i>...</i> block is used to render text in the *italic* text style.

Example 2_3. The italic text style (file e2_3.html)

```
<html>
<head></head>
<body>
Initial text.
<i>Italic text.</i>
Final text.
</body>
</html>
```

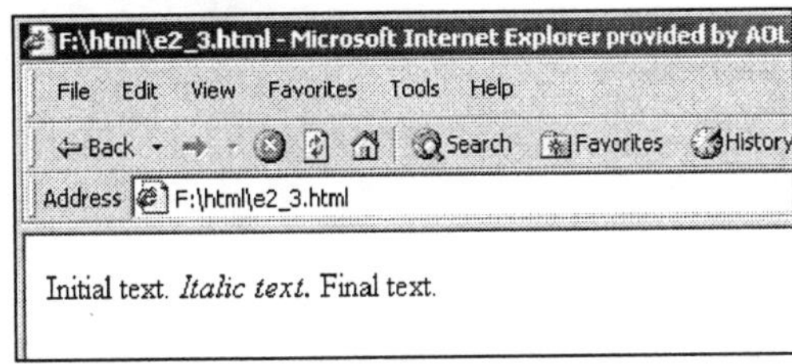

Figure 2.4

Note that the physical styles of text can be *nested* (i.e. one block can be completely inside of another block).

Example 2_4. Nested text styles (file e2_4.html)

```
<html><head></head><body>
Normal.
<i>
Italic.
<tt>Italic and teletype.</tt>
Italic again.
</i>
Normal
</body></html>
```

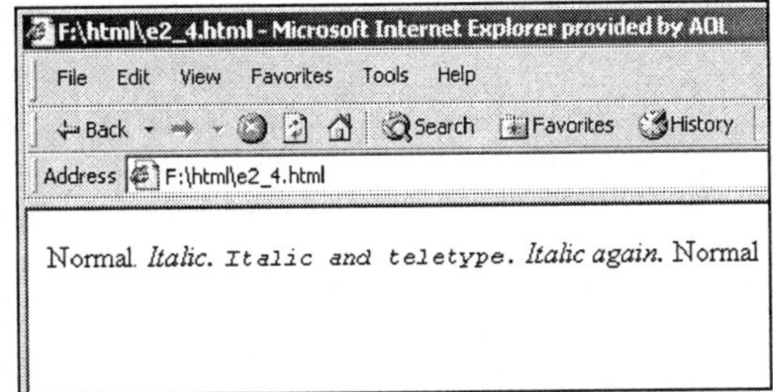

Figure 2.5

2.5 The <b> element

The text inside a <b>...</b> block is rendered in the **bold** text style.

Example 2_5. The bold text style (file e2_5.html)

```
<html><head></head><body>
Normal.
<b>Bold.</b>
<b><i>Bold and Italic.</i></b>
Normal
</body></html>
```

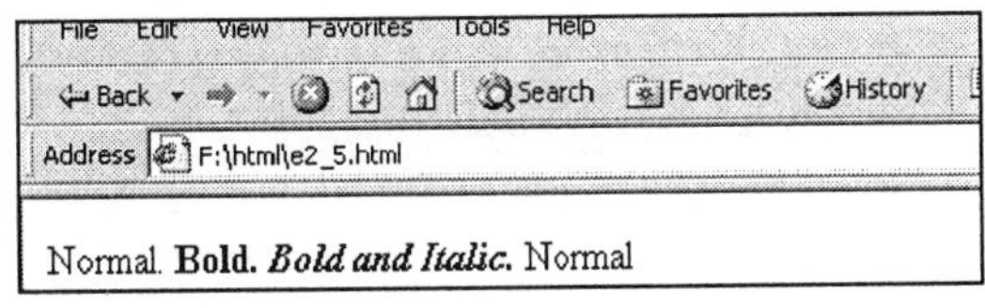

Figure 2.6

2.6 The <big> element

The text inside a <big>...</big> element is rendered with a *bigger* font than the current font.

Example 2_6. The bigger text style (file e2_6.html)

```
<html><head></head><body>
Normal.
<big>Bigger Text.</big>
<big><big>
Bigger than bigger.</big></big>
Normal
</body></html>
```

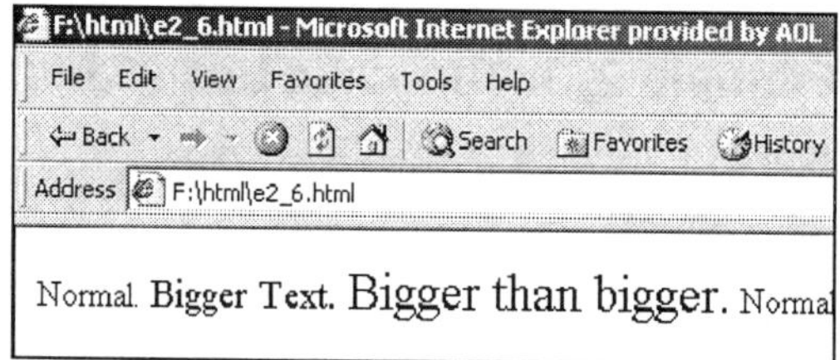

Figure 2.7

Note

- As you can see, <big> elements can be nested one inside of another.

2.7 The <small> element

The text inside a <small>...</small> block is rendered with a *smaller* font than the current font.

Example 2_7. The smaller text style (file e2_7.html)

```
<html><head></head><body>
Normal Text
<small>Smaller Text <small>smaller than
smaller </small></small>
<br><b><i><small>Bold, Italic, and
Small</small></i></b><br>
Normal Text again.
</body></html>
```

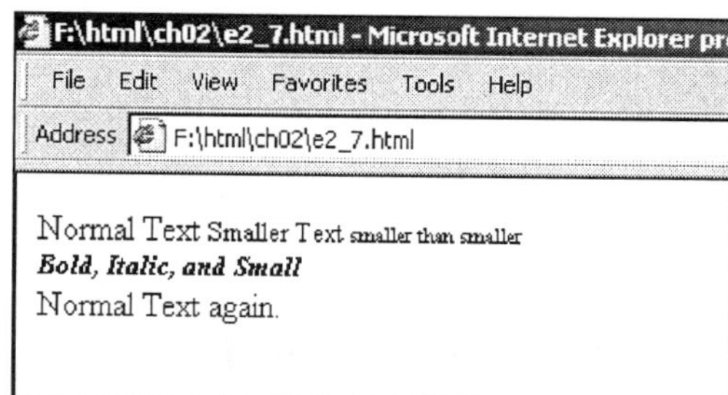

Figure 2.8

2.8 The <strike> or <s> element

The text inside a <strike>...</strike> block or inside a <s>...</s> block is rendered as *strike-through* style text.

Example 2_8. The strike text style (file e2_8.html)

```
<html><head></head><body>
Normal Text.<br>
<strike> Strike Text.</strike><br>
<s>Strike text again.</s><br>
Normal Text again.
</body></html>
```

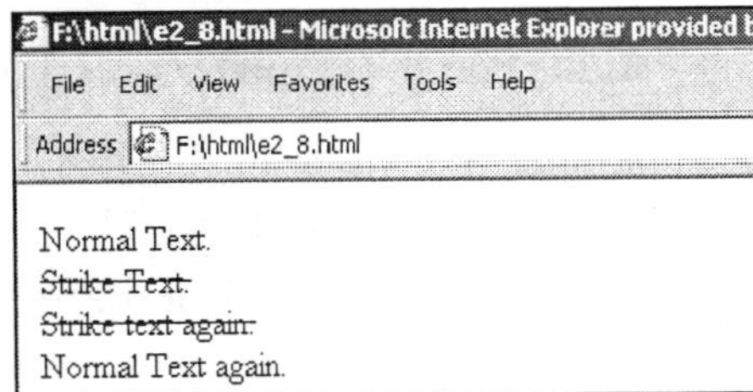

Figure 2.9

2.9 The <u> element

The text inside a <u>...</u> element is rendered with the *underlined* text style.

Example 2_9. The underlined text style (file e2_9.html)

```
<html><head></head><body>
Normal Text.
<u> Underlined Text.</u>
Normal Text.
</body></html>
```

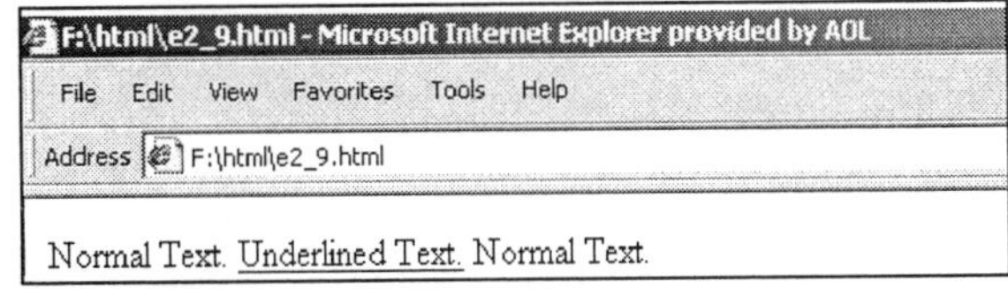

Figure 2.10

Note

- <strike>, <s>, and <u> elements are considered deprecated in favor of CSS.

2.10 The <sub> and <sup> elements

The text inside a _{...} element is rendered with the *subscript* text style. The text inside a ^{...} element is rendered with the *superscript* text style.

Example 2_10. The sub-script and super-script elements (file e2_10.html)

```
<html><head></head><body>
The 3-D surfacez
<sup>2</sup><sub>(x,y)</sub>=
R<sup>2</sup>-x<sup>2</sup>-
y<sup>2</sup> represents a sphere.
</body></html>
```

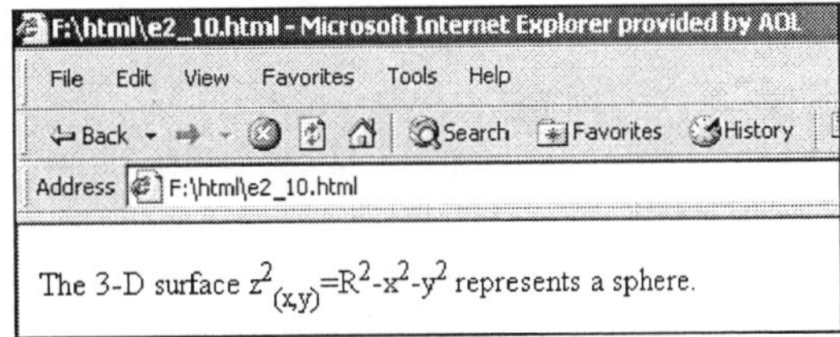

Figure 2.11

Note

- <sub> and <sup> elements can be nested.

2.11 Review of Chapter 2

At the end of Chapter 2 you should know:

- The text inside of the <body>...</body> element is rendered with the browser's default settings if no styles are specified for that text.
- To change the style of the text, you can use the physical styles: <tt> for teletype text, <i> for italic text, <b> for bold text, <big> for bigger text, <small> for smaller text, <strike> or <s> for strike-through text, and <u> for underlined text.
- The physical text styles can be nested.
- The element for super-script text is <sup> and for sub-script text is <sub>.
- Some of the physical text styles are considered deprecated, and it is recommended that you use CSS instead.

Chapter 3

The logical styles of text

3.1 The logical styles

The *logical styles* of text are used to add a specific destination to a specific block of text. The logical styles are:

- Paragraphs (`p`)
- Headings (`h1`, `h2`, `h3`, `h4`, `h5`, and `h6`)
- Quotations elements (`blockquote` and `q`)
- Horizontal rules (`hr`)
- The center element
- Grouping elements (`div` and `span`)
- Preformatted text blocks (`pre`, `plaintext`, and `xmp`)
- Phrase elements (`em`, `strong`, `dfn`, `code`, `samp`, `kbd`, `var`, `cite`, `abbr`, `acronym`)

Let's analyze each of these elements in detail.

3.2 The <p> element

If you have a long text, you generally need to split it into paragraphs. The <p> element lets you do that.

Notes

- The <p> element can have an attribute called `align`, which is used to define an alignment for the text of the paragraph. This attribute can have the values `"left"`, `"center"`, `"right"`, or `"justify"` (the default value is `"left"`).

- To specify a value for the `align` attribute, use the syntax:
  `<p align="center">...`
- An extra space is added between the <p> element and the previous block of text.
- Double quotes used to give a value to the align attribute are optional in HTML but required in XHTML.
- An ending tag </p> for <p> elements is optional in HTML but required in XHTML.

Example 3_1. The paragraph element (file e3_1.html)

```
<html>
<head></head>
<body>
First line.
<br>The second line is generated by a line break
<p>This is the first paragraph. It is by default aligned to the left. This is the
first paragraph. It is by default aligned to the left. This is the first paragraph.
It is by default aligned to the left.</p>
<p align="right">This is the second paragraph. It is aligned to the right. This is
the second paragraph. It is aligned to the right. This is the second paragraph. It
is aligned to the right.</p>
<p align="center">This is the third paragraph. It is aligned to the center. This is
the third paragraph. It is aligned to the center.</p>
</body>
</html>
```

Figure 3.1

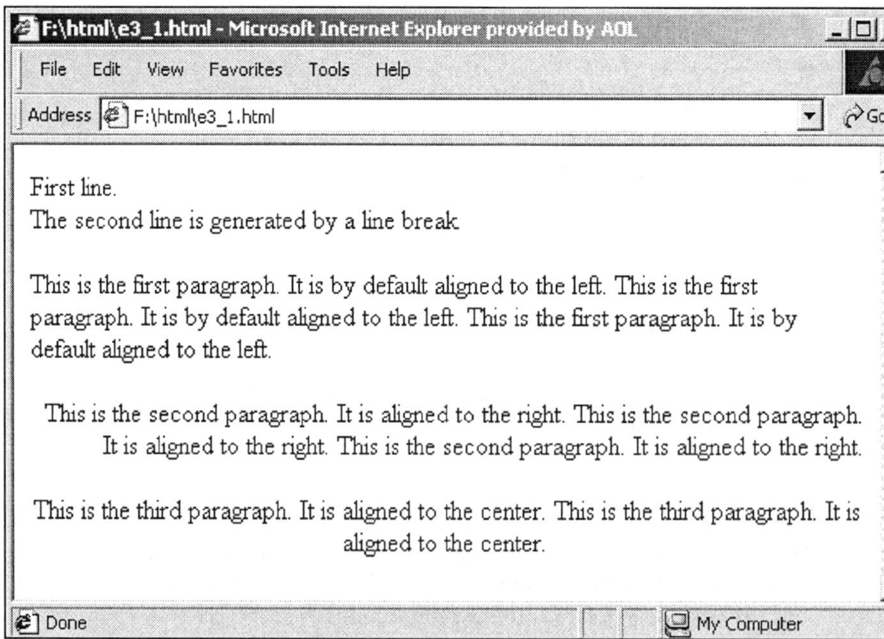

3.3 Headings

HTML allows you to insert headings into a web page. The rendering for headings is different from the rest of the page and depends on which browser a client is using.

There are six types of predefined headings: `<h1>…</h1>`, `<h2>…</h2>`, `<h3>…</h3>`, `<h4>…</h4>`, `<h5>…</h5>`, and `<h6>…</h6>`.

Notes

- All headings are blocks of text, so the ending tags are required.
- All headings are rendered starting on a new line and with an extra space after the previous block.
- The `<h1>…</h1>` heading is rendered using the biggest and strongest font, and the `<h6>…</h6>` heading is rendered with the smallest and weakest font.

All headings accept the `align` attribute, with possible values `"left"`, `"center"`, `"right"`, or `"justify"` (the default value is `"left"`).

Example 3_2. The heading elements (file e3_2.html)

```
<html><head></head><body>
<h1 align="center">Heading 1 aligned in the center</h1>
<h2>Heading 2 aligned by default on the left</h2>
<h3><h3 align="right">Heading 3 aligned on the right</h3>
<h4>Heading 4</h4>
<h5>Heading 5</h5>
<h6>Heading 6</h6>
</body></html>
```

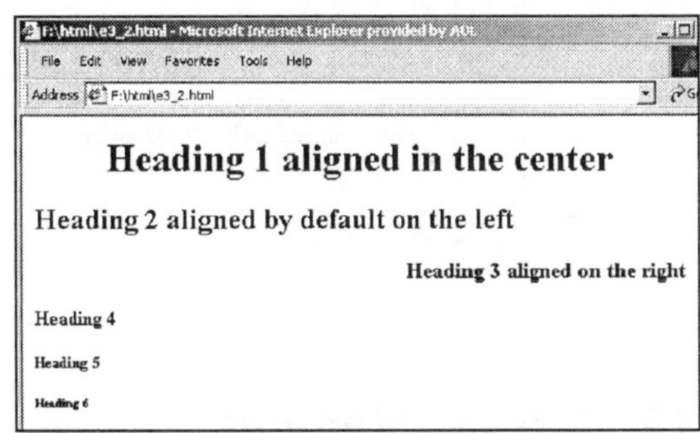

Figure 3.2

3.4 The <block-quote> element

The `<blockquote>…</blockquote>` element is designed for inserting long *quotations* into a web page.

Notes

- The block-quote element is a block element, so the ending tag `</blockquote>` is required.

- The block-quote element is rendered starting on a new line, with extra white space before and after the element and on the left and on the right of the element.
- HTML 4.01 recommends an attribute called `cite`, but most browsers do not implement this attribute. The value of this attribute should be the URL (Internet addresses) of the source from where the quotation was borrowed.

Example 3_3. The <block-quote> element (file e3_3.html)

```
<html><head>
</head><body>
Tate Collections:
<blockquote cite="http://www.tate.org.uk ">Constantin Brancusi (1876-1957) was one
of the founding figures of modern sculpture and one of the most original artists of
the twentieth-century. His groundbreaking carvings introduced abstraction and
primitivism into sculpture for the first time, and were as important as Picasso's
paintings to the development of modern art.</blockquote>
Visit http://www.tate.org.uk
</body></html>
```

Figure 3.3

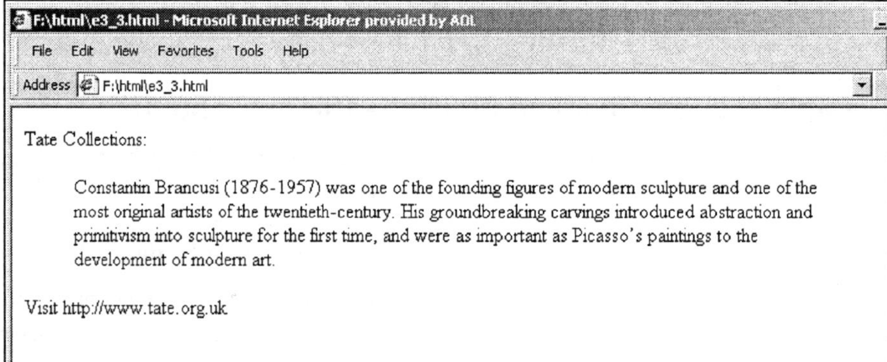

3.5 The <q> element

The <q>...</q> element is designed for *inline quotations* (when rendered, the <q> element doesn't start on a new line).

Notes

- The <q> element is recommended by HTML 4.01 but is not implemented by Netscape Navigator.
- The <q> element can accept the `cite` attribute (just like the block-quote element).

Example 3_4. The inline quote element (file e3_4.html)

```
<html>
<head></head><body>
Constantin Brancusi used to say:
<q>"I give you pure joy!"<q>
</body></html>
```

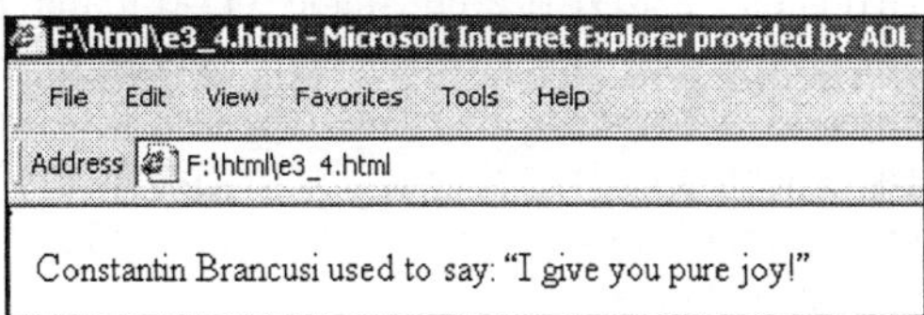

Figure 3.4

3.6 Horizontal Rules

To make a distinction between different sections of a web page, you can use the *horizontal rule* element <hr>.

Notes

- The horizontal rule tag <hr> doesn't require an ending tag. In XHTML it is replaced by <hr/>.
- A horizontal rule always starts on a new line.
- A horizontal rule can have more than one attribute.

The horizontal rule element can have the following attributes:

- `align` The possible values are `"left"`, `"center"`, and `"right"`; the default value is `"left"`.
- `width` The possible values are:
  - A positive integer that represents the width of the line in pixels
  - A percentage that represents a fraction of the width of the parent block (is a positive integer between `1` and `100` followed by `%`; the default value is `"100%"`)
- `size` The possible values are positive integers that represent the thickness of the rule in pixels; the default value is `"2"`.
- `noshade` If present, the rule is a flat rule and doesn't have a shadow; if absent the rule is a 3-D rule with a shadow.
- `color` For the possible values, see Section 4.1 Colors. The default value is `"black"`. Internet Explorer implements this attribute and changes the style of the rule to `noshade`.

Example 3_5. The <hr> element (file e3_5.html)

```
<html><head></head><body>
This is a horizontal rule with default settings:
<hr>
```

```
This is a horizontal rule, aligned on center, with a width equal to 50% of a page,
thickness 5 pixels, no shade (flat) and red color:
<hr align="center" width="50%" size="5" noshade color="red">
This is a horizontal rule with right alignment, width equal to 200 pixels,
thickness 10 pixels, and with shade (3-D):
<hr align="right" width="200" size="10">
</body></html>
```

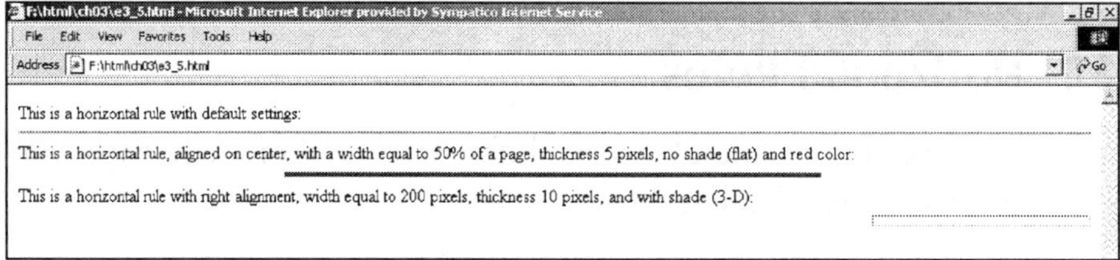

Figure 3.5

3.7 The <center> element

The <center> element is used to center content (e.g. text, images, horizontal rules). The following example shows how to center a bundle of consecutive horizontal lines of differing widths.

Example 3_6. The <center> element (file e3_6.html)

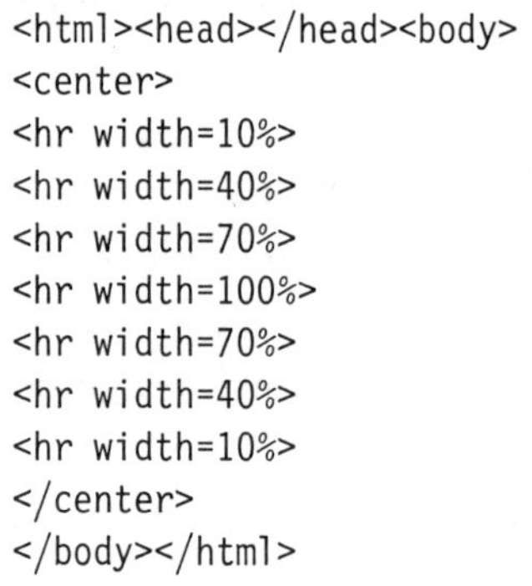

```
<html><head></head><body>
<center>
<hr width=10%>
<hr width=40%>
<hr width=70%>
<hr width=100%>
<hr width=70%>
<hr width=40%>
<hr width=10%>
</center>
</body></html>
```

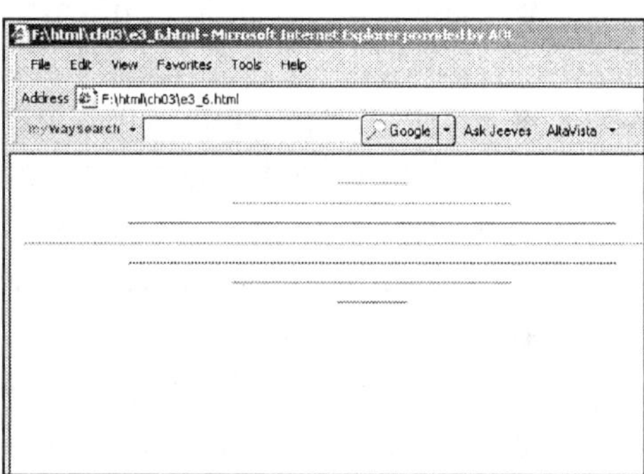

Figure 3.6

Note

- The <center> element is considered deprecated, and it is recommended that you use the <div align="center">...</div> element or CSS instead.

3.8 The <div> element

There are two kinds of elements in HTML:

- *Block-level* elements, which are rendered starting on a new line (e.g. <p> or <hr> elements).
- *In-line* elements, which are rendered on the same line (e.g. <b> or <q> elements).

The <div> element is the *most generic block-level element*, and it can be used in a variety of ways. This element is the best to attach a CSS to a section of a web page.

Notes

- The <div> element accepts the `align` attribute (possible values: `"left"`, `"center"`, `"right"`, or `"justify"`; the default value is `"left"`).
- The <div> element accepts attributes recommended by HTML 4.01 but not yet implemented (`charset`, `href`, `hreflang`, `media`, `rel`, `rev`, `target`, `title`, and `type`) as well as attributes that are implemented by Internet Explorer (`datafld`, `dataformatas`, `datasrc`, and `title`).
- The `title` attribute (Internet Explorer and HTML 4.01) causes the browser to display a tooltip when the mouse remains over the content of the <div> block for a few seconds.

Example 3_7. The <div> element (file e3_7.html)

```
<html><head></head><body>
<div align="right">
This is a right aligned division block.
</div>
<div align="center">
This is a centered division block.
</div>
<div title="This is a tooltip!">
This is a division block with a tooltip.<br>
Please move the cursor over this block to see the content<br>
of the title attribute appearing in a small yellow box.
</div>
</body></html>
```

Figure 3.7

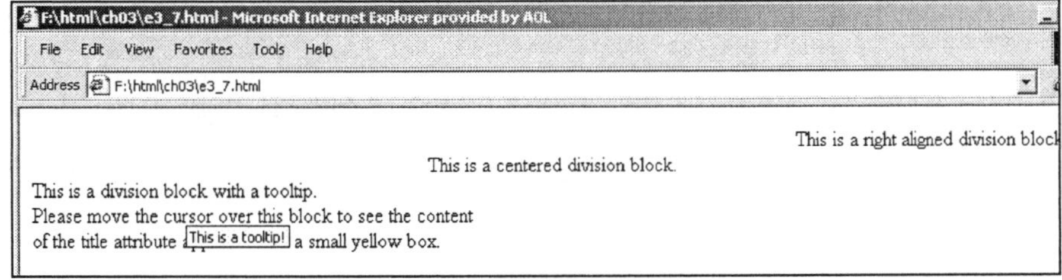

3.9 The <span> element

The <span> element is the *most generic inline element*, and it can be used in a variety of cases. This element is the best to attach a CSS to a small section of a line in a web page.

All the notes presented for the <div> element also apply to the <span> element. The big difference between these two elements is that the <div> element is a block-element and the <span> element is an *inline* element. The <span> element doesn't accept the `align` attribute, as it is an in-line element.

Example 3_8. The <span> element (file e3_8.html)

```
<html><head></head><body>
A complete documentation about
<span title="http://www.w3.org">
the specifications of HTML</span>
can be found on the Internet.
</body></html>
```

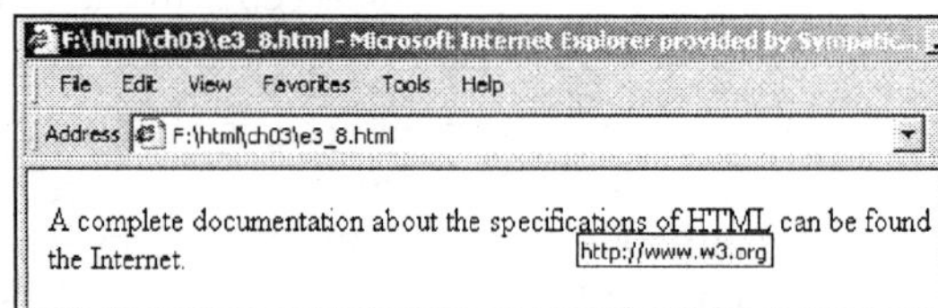

Figure 3.8

3.10 Preformatted text blocks

There are three text blocks related to preformatted text <pre>, <xmp>, and <plaintext>. The following table summarizes the differences and similarities between them:

	HTML	IE & NN
<pre>...</pre>	• Highly recommended Attributes: • `cols` • `width` • `wrap`	• Implemented • Rendered in monospace font • The white spaces are preserved • The HTML tags are not ignored (are interpreted by the browser)
<xmp>...</xmp>	• removed from HTML 4.01	• Implemented • Rendered in monospace font • The white spaces are preserved • The HTML tags are rendered as-is (i.e. are not interpreted by the browser)

	HTML	IE & NN
<plaintext> …</plaintext>	• removed from HTML 4.01	• Implemented • Rendered in monospace font • The white spaces are preserved • All the HTML tags that follow after a <plaintext> tag are rendered as-is (i.e. are not interpreted by the browser)

Notes

- If you need to insert a preformatted text block, it is recommended that you use the <pre>…</pre> block.
- To insert tags into a block of text that will not be interpreted by the browser, use < for the < character and > for the > character. For example, <h1> would be coded as <h1> and be rendered as <h1> but still not be interpreted as an HTML tag.

Example 3_9. The <pre> element (file e3_9.html)

```
<html><head></head><body>
To insert a division element use the
syntax:
<pre>
&lt;div align="right"&gt;
A block of right aligned text.
&lt;/div&gt;
</pre>
</body></html
```

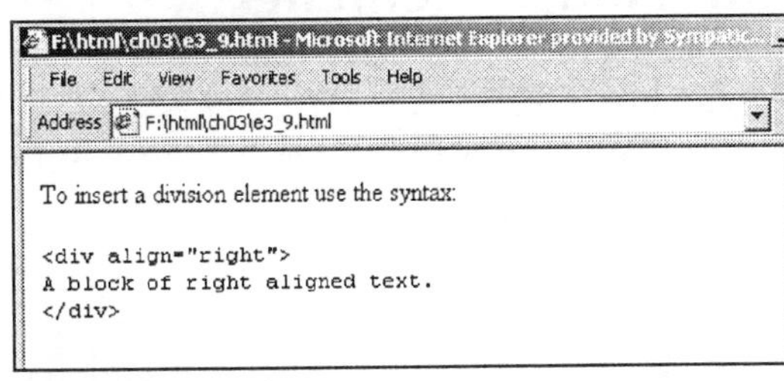
F:\html\ch03\e3_9.html - Microsoft Internet Explorer provided by Sympatic...
File Edit View Favorites Tools Help
Address F:\html\ch03\e3_9.html
To insert a division element use the syntax:
<div align="right">
A block of right aligned text.
</div>

Figure 3.9

Example 3_10. The <xmp> element (file e3_10.html)

```
<html><head></head><body>
To insert a division element use the
syntax:
<xmp>
<div align="right">
A block of right aligned text.
</div>
</xmp>
</body></html>
```

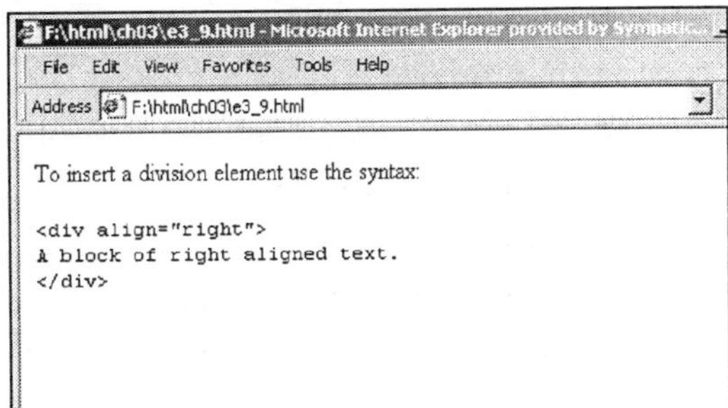
F:\html\ch03\e3_9.html - Microsoft Internet Explorer provided by Sympatic...
File Edit View Favorites Tools Help
Address F:\html\ch03\e3_9.html
To insert a division element use the syntax:
<div align="right">
A block of right aligned text.
</div>

Figure 3.10

Example 3_11. The <plaintext> element (file e3_11.html)

```
<html>
<head></head><body>
To insert a division element use
the syntax:
<plaintext>
<div align="right">
A block of right aligned text.
</div>
</plaintext>
</body></html>
```

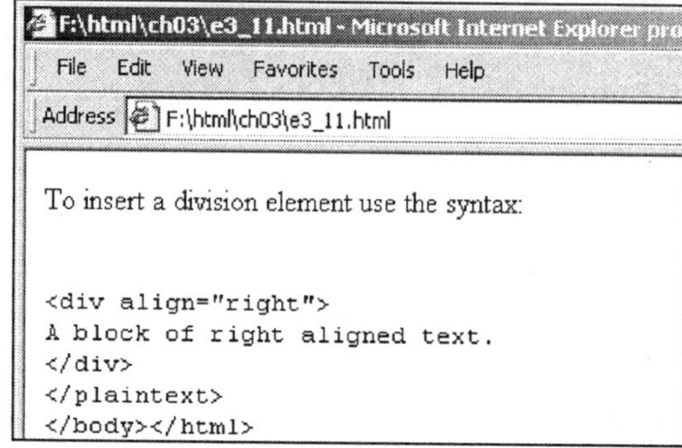
F:\html\ch03\e3_11.html - Microsoft Internet Explorer pro
File Edit View Favorites Tools Help
Address F:\html\ch03\e3_11.html
To insert a division element use the syntax:
<div align="right">
A block of right aligned text.
</div>
</plaintext>
</body></html>

Figure 3.11

Note

◆ All tags that follow the <plaintext> tag are rendered as-is, including </plaintext>, </body>, and </html> tags, but still are not interpreted as HTML tags.

3.11 Phrase elements

The *phrase elements* allow you to add a specific meaning to a section of the document. These phrase elements are implemented and rendered differently by different browsers.

The phrase elements are:

- <em>...</em> to emphasize; rendered in the italic text style
- <strong>...</strong> to emphasize; rendered in the bold text style
- <dfn>...</dfn> to emphasize the first appearance of a concept; rendered by Internet Explorer in the italic text style
- <code>...</code> to insert a fragment of computer program code; rendered in the monospace font style
- <samp>...</samp> to insert the output of an application; rendered in the monospace font style
- <kbd>...</kbd> to insert a computer command that the user should type; rendered in the monospace font style
- <var>...</var> to insert variables of a computer program; rendered in the italic text style
- <cite>...</cite> to insert a reference to its source document; rendered in the italic text style

- <abbr>…</abbr> to insert an abbreviation; recommended by HTML 4.01 but not implemented
- <acronym>…</acronym> to insert an acronym; recommended by HTML 4.01 but not implemented

Example 3_12. The phrase elements (file e3_12.html)

```
<html>
<head></head><body>
<dfn>HTML</dfn> stands for <em>HyperText Markup Language</em>.<br>
To find the date on your computer type on command prompt:<br>
<kbd>date</kbd><br>
and you will receive an answer like:<br>
<samp>The current date is: Sat 02/07/2004</samp><br>
This is a very simple function in C:<br>
<code>int sum (int x, int y) {return x+y;}</code><br>
The variables <var>x</var>, and <var>y</var> have a local scope inside of the
function body.<br>
<strong>Don't forget to add a <cite>return</cite> statement!</strong>
</body></html>
```

Figure 3.12

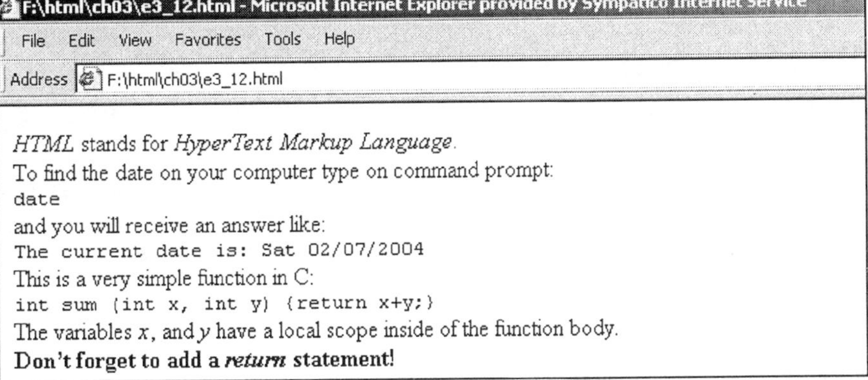
F:\html\ch03\e3_12.html - Microsoft Internet Explorer provided by Sympatico Internet Service
File Edit View Favorites Tools Help
Address F:\html\ch03\e3_12.html
HTML stands for HyperText Markup Language.
To find the date on your computer type on command prompt:
date
and you will receive an answer like:
The current date is: Sat 02/07/2004
This is a very simple function in C:
int sum (int x, int y) {return x+y;}
The variables x, and y have a local scope inside of the function body.
Don't forget to add a return statement!

3.12 Review of Chapter 3

At the end of Chapter 3 you should know:

- In a web page, headings can be inserted with the <h1>, <h2>, <h3>, <h4>, <h5>, and <h6> elements.
- You can insert paragraphs by using <p> elements and quotations by using <blockquote> elements (for block-level quotations) and <q> elements (for in-line quotations).

- To insert horizontal rules, use the <hr> element.
- To insert generic division blocks, use the <div> element for block-level divisions and the <span> element for in-line divisions.
- Preformatted text blocks can be inserted using the <pre>, <plaintext>, or <xmp> elements.
- There a special tags for phrase elements like <em>, <strong>, <dfn>, <code>, <samp>, <kbd>, <var>, <cite>, <abbr>, and <acronym>
- The <center> element can be used to center any content.

Chapter 4

Fonts

4.1 Colors

Colors can be used to define the color of a background or the color of a font.

A color can be defined by:

- *A color name.* There are 16 standard color names recommended by HTML 4.01 Specifications and implemented by all browsers: `aqua`, `black`, `blue`, `fuchsia`, `gray`, `green`, `lime`, `maroon`, `navy`, `olive`, `purple`, `red`, `silver`, `teal`, `white`, and `yellow`. In Appendix C, you can find a more complete list of color names.
- *The RGB color model.* According to this model, a color can be obtained by mixing three fundamental colors: Red, Green, and Blue. The syntax is `"#rrggbb"` where `r`, `g`, and `b` are the hexadecimal digits: 0, 1, 2, 3, 4, 5, 6, 7, 8, 9, a or A, b or B, c or C, d or D, e or E, f or F. Examples:
  - `white` is `#ffffff` (a mixture of all colors)
  - `black` is `#000000` (the absence of all colors)
  - `gray` is `#808080` (the mixture of three color with the same weight)
  - `red` is `#ff0000`
  - `green` is `#00ff00`
  - `blue` is `#0000ff`

Note that it is recommended that the color definition always be quoted. Examples: `"black"` or `"#abcdef"`.

4.2 Font names

To specify a font you can use:

- *The name* of a recommended generic font: "serif", "sans-serif", "cursive", "fantasy", or "monospace"
- *A list of font names* separated by commas. In this case, the browser will use the first recognized font name or its default settings. The last name in the list should be a recommended generic font name. Examples:
  - "Times New Roman, serif"
  - "Arial, Helvetica, Courier New, fantasy"

4.3 The <body> attributes

The <body> element has two very useful attributes that relate to color. They are:

- bgcolor=*color* defines the background color of the web page
- text=*color* defines the text color for the web page

Example 4_1. The <body> color attributes (file e4_1.html)

```
<html><head></head>
<body bgcolor="yellow" text="#ff0000">
This page has a yellow background and
the color of the text is red.
</body></html>
```

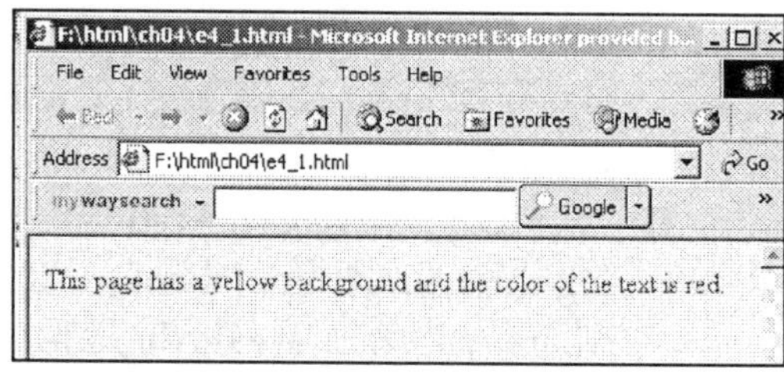

Figure 4.1

4.4 The margin attributes

Internet Explorer and Netscape Navigator use different margin attributes.

In Internet Explorer, the <body> element has 4 margin attributes:

- leftmargin (default value: 10 pixels)
- rightmargin (default value: 10 pixels)
- topmargin (default value: 15 pixels)
- bottommargin (default value: 0 pixels)

The value of each margin attribute is an integer (including 0) representing the distance in pixels between the content and the edge of the browser window.

Example 4_2. The margin attributes in Internet Explorer (file e4_2.html)

```
<html><head></head>
<body leftmargin="100" rightmargin="50" topmargin="0">
This page has the leftmargin attribute set to 100 pixels, the rightmargin attribute
set to 50 pixels, and the topmargin attribute set to 0 pixels.
</body></html>
```

Figure 4.2

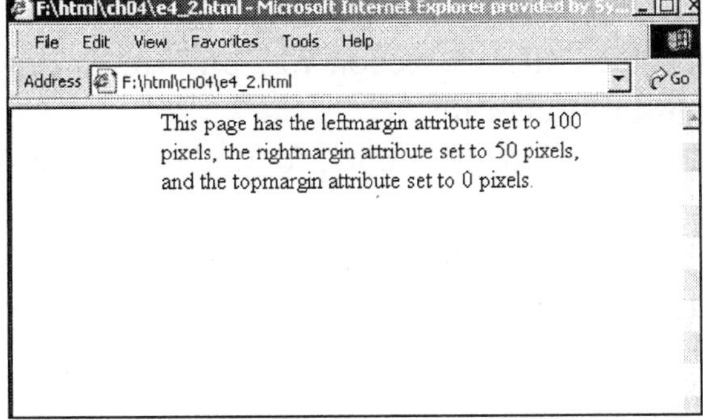

In Netscape Navigator, the `<body>` element has 2 margin attributes:

- `marginwidth`
- `marginheight`

The value of each margin attribute is an integer (including 0) representing the distance in pixels between the content and the edge of the browser window.

Example 4_3. The margin attributes in Netscape Navigator (file e4_3.html)

```
<html>
<head>
</head>
<body marginwidth="50"
marginheight="100">
This page has the marginwidth attribute
set to 50 pixels and the marginheight
attribute set to 100 pixels.
</body>
</html>
```

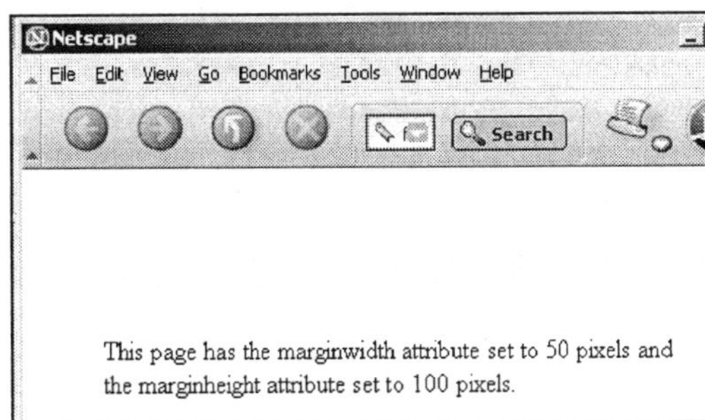

Figure 4.3

4.5 The <basefont> element

The browser will render the text in a document according to the default settings. These settings can be overridden with the <basefont> element or the <font> element.

To set the characteristic of the text with the <basefont> use its attributes:

- color=*color* For possible values see section 4.1 Colors, above.
- face=*font* For possible values see section 4.2 Font names, above.
- size=*size* The possible values are:
  - 1, 2, 3, 4, 5, 6, 7 (1 for the smallest font, 7 for the largest font; the default value is 3)
  - +1, +2, +3, … or -1, -2, -3, … (to increase or decrease the default value of the browser in the range 1 to 7)

Notes

- ◆ It is recommended that you use double quotes when you express these values (e.g. color="red" face="Times New Roman, serif" size="+2").
- ◆ The <basefont> element doesn't have an ending tag. The effect of the element remains active until another <basefont> element appears or until the end of the web page.

Example 4_4. The <basefont> element (file e4_4.html)

```
<html><head></head>
<body>
This text will be rendered with the default settings.
<basefont color="blue" face="Arial, sans-serif">
This text will be rendered with blue color and Arial font style.
<basefont size="+5" face="fantasy" color="#00ff00">
This text will be rendered with green color, fantasy font and the font size 5 units
greater than the default value of the browser.
</body></html>
```

Figure 4.4

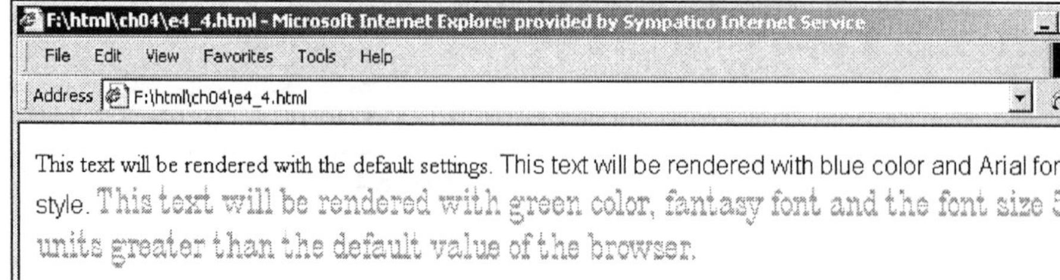
F:\html\ch04\e4_4.html - Microsoft Internet Explorer provided by Sympatico Internet Service
File Edit View Favorites Tools Help
Address F:\html\ch04\e4_4.html
This text will be rendered with the default settings. This text will be rendered with blue color and Arial fo
style. This text will be rendered with green color, fantasy font and the font size 5
units greater than the default value of the browser.

4.6 The <font> element

To change the characteristics for a block of text, use the <font>...</font> element. To do this, use the attributes of the <font> element:

- `color=`*`color`* For possible values, see section 4.1 Colors, above.
- `face=`*`font`* For possible values, see section 4.2 Font names, above.
- `size=`*`size`* The possible values are:
  - 1, 2, 3, 4, 5, 6, 7 (1 for the smallest font, 7 for the greatest font; the default value is 3)
  - +1, +2, +3, ... or -1, -2, -3, ... (to increase or decrease the default value of the browser in the range 1 to 7)
- `point-size` (Netscape Navigator only; possible values are positive integers, representing the size of the font in typographic points)

Example 4_5. The <font> element (file e4_5.html)

```
<html><head></head>
<body>
This text is rendered with the default settings of the browser.
<br><font color="blue" face="Arial, serif">
This text is rendered blue and with the Arial font style.</font>
<br><font color="#aaaaaa" point-size="50">
This text is rendered gray and in the 50 typographic points size.</font>
</body></html>
```

Figure 4.5

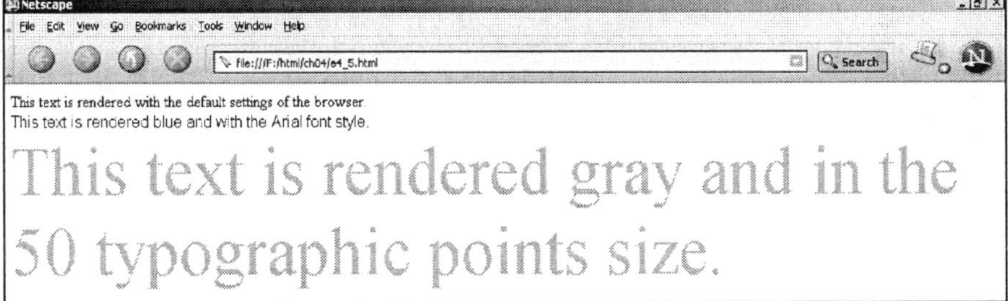

Note

- The <font>...</font> element is an in-line element.

4.7 Review of Chapter 4

At the end of Chapter 4 you should know:

- To define a color in HTML, you can use a standard color name or an RGB specification.
- To specify the background color for a web page, use the bgcolor attribute of the <body> element.
- To specify the text color of a web page, use the text attribute of the <body> element.
- To specify the margins for the web page in Internet Explorer, use the leftmargin, rightmargin, topmargin, and bottomargin attributes of the <body> element.
- To specify the margins for the web page in Netscape Navigator, use the marginwidth and marginheight attributes of the <body> element.
- The <basefont> element allows you to specify a font for the next section of the web page using the color, face, and size attributes.
- The <font> element allows you to specify a font for a block of text using the color, face, and size attributes.
- The font and face attributes accept lists of comma-delimited names of fonts.

Chapter 5

Lists

5.1 Types of lists

A list is a sequence of items. There are several kinds of lists that can be inserted into a web page:

- Unordered lists
- Ordered lists
- Definition lists
- Menu lists
- Directory lists

Let's analyze each of them.

5.2 Unordered lists

In an *unordered list*, each item has the same leading symbol. The items in the list will be rendered in the same order that they are entered. To insert an unordered list, use the `<ul>...</ul>` block. To insert an item into the list, use the `<li>` element.

Notes

- The `<ul>...</ul>` is a block-level element and will be rendered starting on a new line.
- The ending tag `</li>` is optional in HTML but required in XHTML.
- The list accepts a header (the text that follows immediately after the `<ul>` tag and before the first `<li>` element).
- The browsers insert an extra space before the list and indent the list a few spaces to the right.

- Before each item in the list, there is a leading symbol that shows that a list item follows. This symbol can be:
  - A disc (the default value)
  - A circle
  - A square

Example 5_1. The unordered list (file e5_1.html)

```
<html><head></head><body>
This is a normal text before the list.
<ul>This is the header of the list.
<li>The first item
<li>The second item
<li>The third item
</ul>
</body></html>
```

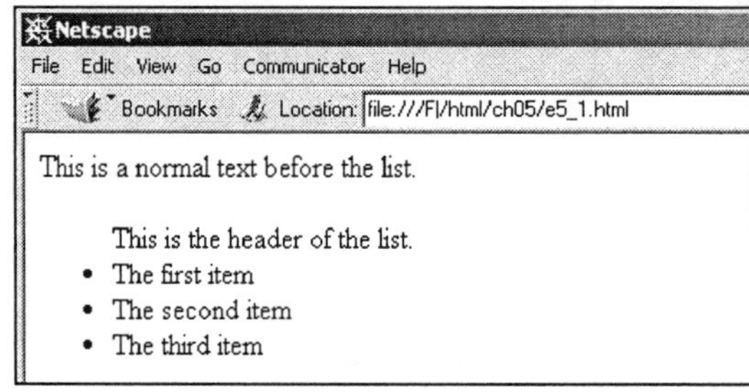

Figure 5.1

5.3 The type attribute of the unordered list

If you want to change the leading symbol for each item in the unordered list, assign a value to the type attribute of the <ul> element. The possible values are:

- "disc" (the default value)
- "circle"
- "square"

Example 5_2. The type attribute of the unordered list (file e5_2.html)

```
<html><head></head><body>
<ul type="square">This is a list with
square leading symbols.
<li>The first item in the list
<li>The second item
<li>The last item in the list
</ul>
</body></html>
```

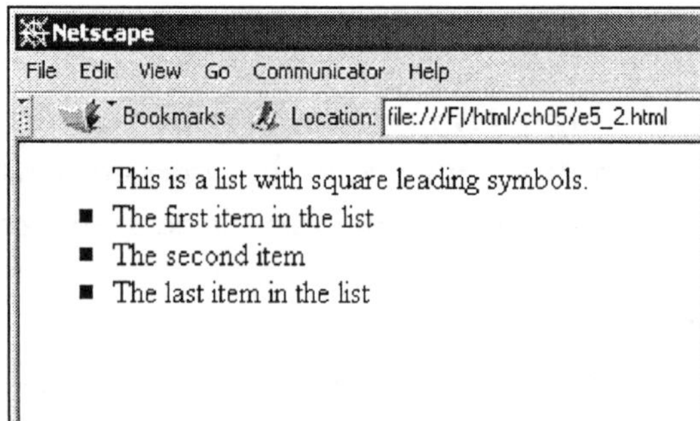

Figure 5.2

5.4 The empty list

If a list doesn't have any items, it is an empty list. The header text of the list will be rendered indented. This is another way to insert indented text (we learned already about the <blockquote> element that indents its content).

Example 5_3. The empty list (file e5_3.html)

```
<html><head></head><body>
This is a normal text.
<ul>This is an empty list.
<br>There are no items in this list.
<br>You can use an empty list to insert
a fragment of text that will be indented.
</ul>
</body></html>
```

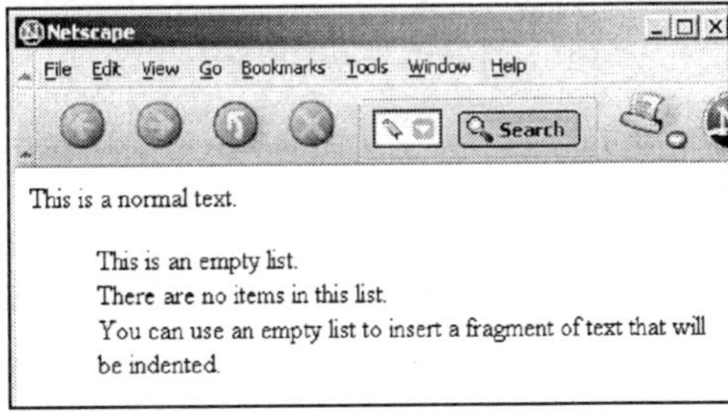

Figure 5.3

Note

- In this example, we used the <br> tag to start each new line.

5.5 Nested lists

Lists can be nested one inside of another. To do this, use a second (nested) list as an item of the first (outer) list. Here is an example:

Example 5_4. The nested list (file e5_4.html)

```
<html><head></head><body>
Normal text
<ul>A few elements and attributes in HTML:
<li>body    <ul>Attributes:
            <li>bgcolor
            <li>text
            </ul>
<li>font    <ul>Attributes:
            <li>face
            <li>size
</ul>
</ul>
</body></html>
```

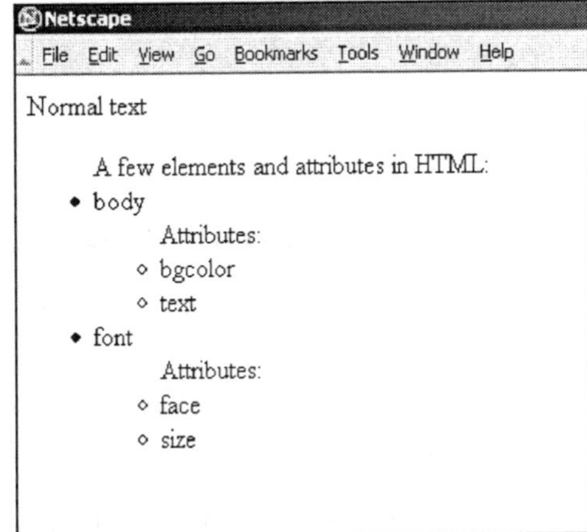

Figure 5.4

Notes

- The innermost list is double indented.
- The items of the innermost list are rendered with a different leading symbol.

5.6 Ordered lists

In an ordered list, each item has a sequential leading symbol. The browser assigns this sequence automatically. To insert an ordered list, use the `<ol>...</ol>` block. To insert items into the list, use `<li>` elements.

Notes

- The block <ol>...</ol> is a block-level element and will be rendered starting on a new line.
- The ending tag </li> is optional in HTML but required in XHTML.
- The list accepts a header (the text that follows immediately after <ol> tag and before the first <li> element).
- The browser inserts an extra space before the list and indents the list a few spaces to the right.

Example 5_5. The ordered list (file e5_5.html)

```
<html><head></head><body>
Normal text
<ol>This is an ordered list.
<li>First item in the list
<li>Second item
<li>The last item in the list
</ol>
</body></html>
```

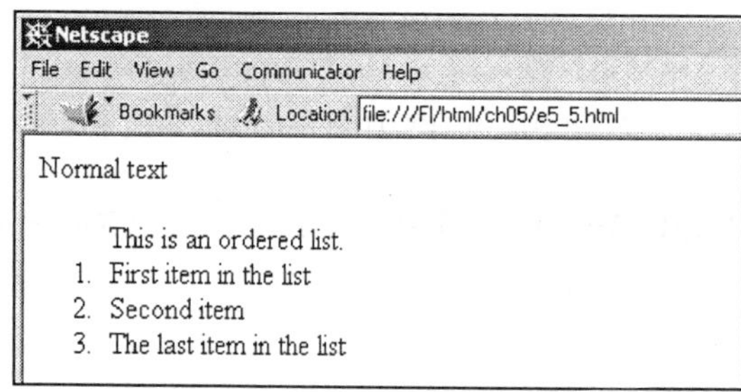

Figure 5.5

5.7 The type attribute of the ordered list

As you can see from the previous example, the leading symbols used for the items of an ordered list are Arabic numerals: 1, 2, 3, etc. You can change this default setting by assigning a value to the type attribute of the <ol> element. The possible values are:

- 1 (for Arabic numerals: 1, 2, 3, etc; the default value)
- a (for lowercase letters: a, b, c, etc.)

- A (for uppercase letters: A, B, C, etc.)
- i (for lowercase Roman Numerals: i, ii, iii, iv, v, etc.)
- I (for uppercase Roman Numerals: I, II, III, IV, V, etc.)

Example 5_6. The type attribute of the ordered list (file e5_6.html)

```
<html><head></head><body>
Normal text
<ol type="I">To create a web page
you should:
<li>Edit the source file
<li>Save the file with .html extension
<li>Publish the file on a web server
</ol>
</body></html>
```

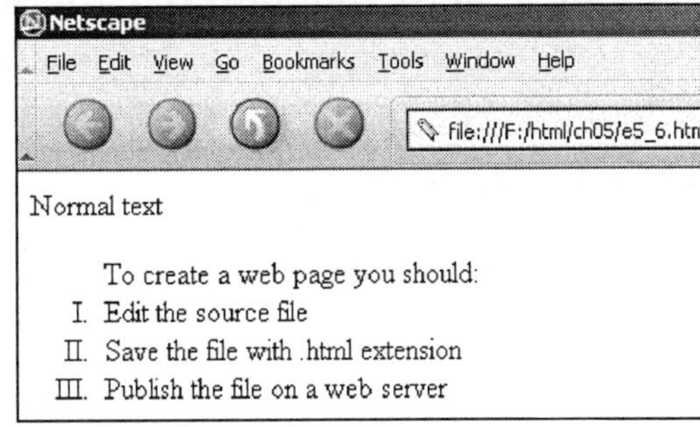

Figure 5.6

5.8 The start attribute of the ordered list

By default, the first symbol in sequence is 1, a, A, i, or I. You can change this default setting by assigning a value to the start attribute of the <ol> element. The possible values are positive integers (the default value is 1).

Note

- ◆ If you assign a value of "5" to the start attribute and a value of "A" to the type attribute, the first symbol in the sequence will be E (see the following example).

Example 5_7. The start attribute of the ordered list (file e5_7.html)

```
<html><head></head><body>
Normal text
<ol type="A" start="5">The final steps
in the development of a software
application are:
<li>testing
<li>deployment
<li>training
<li>maintenance
</ol>
</body></html>
```

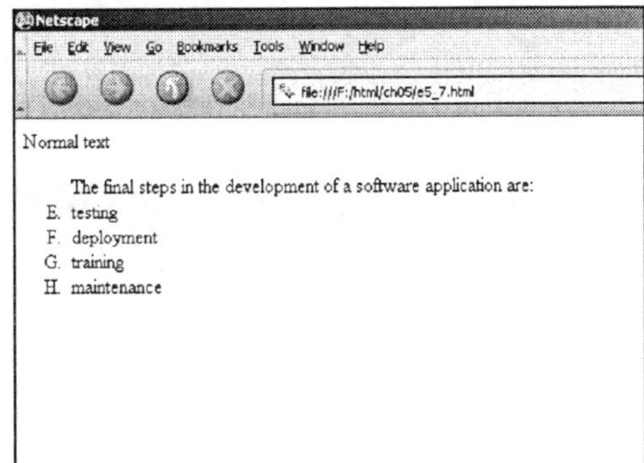

Figure 5.7

5.9 Nested ordered and unordered lists

Ordered and unordered lists can be nested one inside of another. To do this, use a second (nested) list as an item of the first (outer) list. Here is an example:

Example 5_8. Nested ordered and unordered lists (file e5_8.html)

```
<html><head></head><body>
Nested lists
<ol type="a" start="3">A few elements
and attributes in HTML:
<li>body     <ul type="square">
             Attributes:
             <li>bgcolor
             <li>text
             </ul>
<li>font     <ul type="circle">
             Attributes:
             <li>face
             <li>size
</ul>
</ol>
</body></html>
```

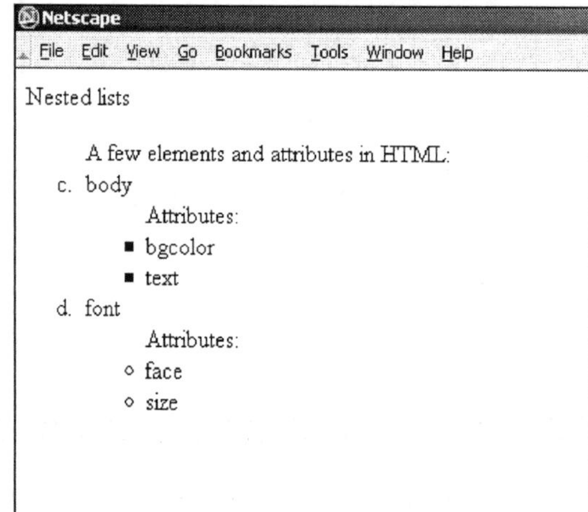

Figure 5.8

5.10 The attributes of the <li> element

To improve the appearance of a list, you can add attributes to the <li> elements. These attributes are:

- value (ordered lists only; possible values are positive integers; the default value is 1)
- type (both ordered or unordered lists; the possible values are the same as the values for type attributes defined for <ol> and <ul> elements, respectively)

Example 5_9. The attributes of the <li> element (file e5_9.html)

```
<html><head></head><body>
The item attributes
<ol type="I">A few elements and attributes in HTML:
<li>head
<li value="3">body
<ul type="square"> Attributes:
             <li>bgcolor
             <li type="disc"> text
```

```
           </ul>
<li>font   <ul> Attributes:
           <li type="disc">face
           <li type="circle">size
</ul>
</ol>
</body></html>
```

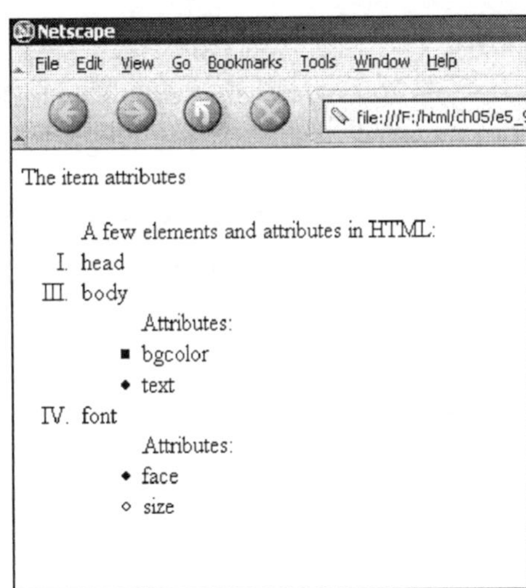

Figure 5.9

Notes

- After assigning a new number to the value attribute of the <li> element, the following items continue in sequence starting from that number.
- The settings defined for the <li> element override the settings defined for the <ol> or <ul> elements.

5.11 Definition lists

A definition list is a sequence of terms and descriptions of these terms. To implement a definition list, use a <dl>...</dl> block to incorporate the definition list. Inside the <dl> element you can insert:

- A definition term, using the <dt> tag.
- A definition description, using the <dd> tag.

All browsers may not render a definition list in the same way, but all browsers render the terms and the descriptions on a new line and indent the descriptions.

Example 5_10. The definition list (file e5_10.html)

```
<html><head></head><body>
A definition list
<dl>This is a glossary of Internet terms
<dt>Internet
<dd>The biggest public inter-net
<dt>Browser
<dd>A client application capable of
rendering an HTML file
<dt>HTML
<dd>HTML stands for HyperText Markup Language
</dl>
</body></html>
```

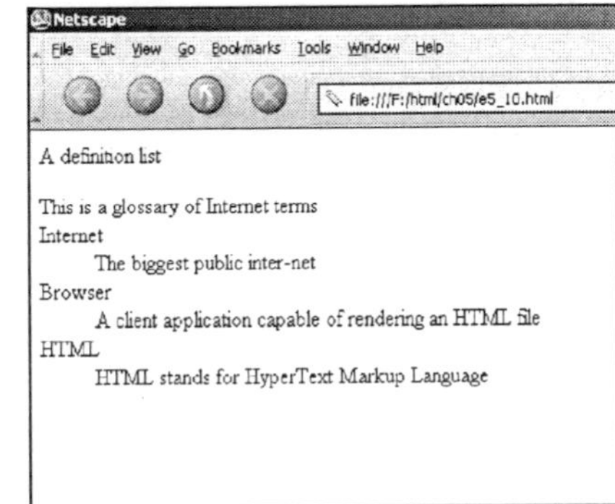

Figure 5.10

Note

- You can include more than one term or more than one description in the definition list (see the following example).

Example 5_11. A custom-made definition list (file e5_11.html)

```
<html><head></head><body>
<dl>Business hours:
<dt>Monday
<dt>Tuesday
<dd>9AM to 6PM
<dt>Wednesday
<dt>Thursday
<dd>1PM to 9PM
<dt>Friday
<dd>8AM to 11AM
<dd>4PM to 8PM
</dl>
</body></html>
```

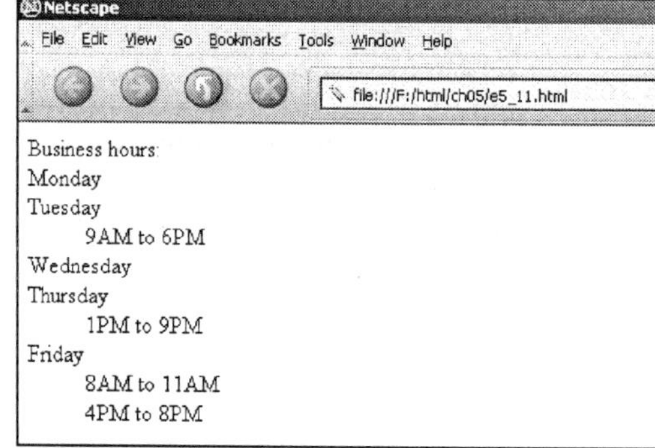

Figure 5.11

5.12 The `compact` attribute of a definition list

A definition list can be rendered compactly if you add the `compact` (space-saving) attribute to the `<dl>` element. In this case, the description starts on the same line as the associated term. To obtain this effect, the term (the content of the `<dt>` element) should consist of few characters.

Example 5_12. A compacted definition list (file e5_12.html)

```
<html><head></head><body>
<dl compact>Business hours:
<dt>Mon
<dt>Tue
<dd>9AM to 6PM
<dt>Wed
<dt>Thu
<dd>1PM to 9PM
<dt>Fri
<dd>8AM to 11AM
<dd>4PM to 8PM
</dl>
</body></html>
```

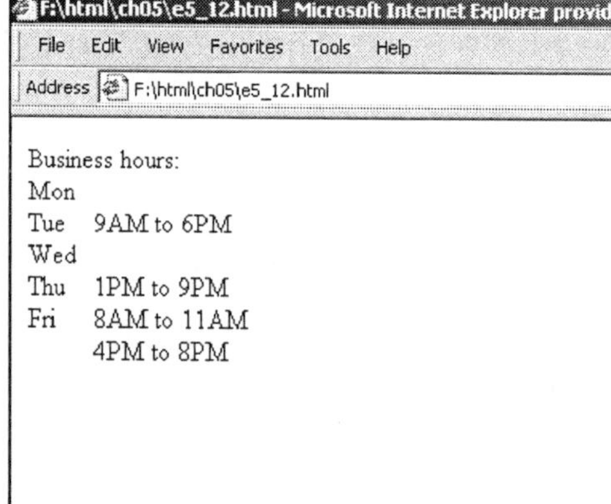

Figure 5.12

5.13 The <dir> and <menu> lists

In HTML 4.01, the <dir> and <menu> lists are considered deprecated in favor of the <ul> element, to which they are similar. The <dir> and <menu> lists contain items defined by <li> elements. Browsers implement the <dir> and <menus> lists and render them similarly to unordered lists.

Example 5_13. A <dir> list (file e5_13.html)

```
<html><head></head><body>
The directory list.
<dir>This is the header of the list.
<li>The first item
<li>The second item
<li>The third item
</dir>
</body></html>
```

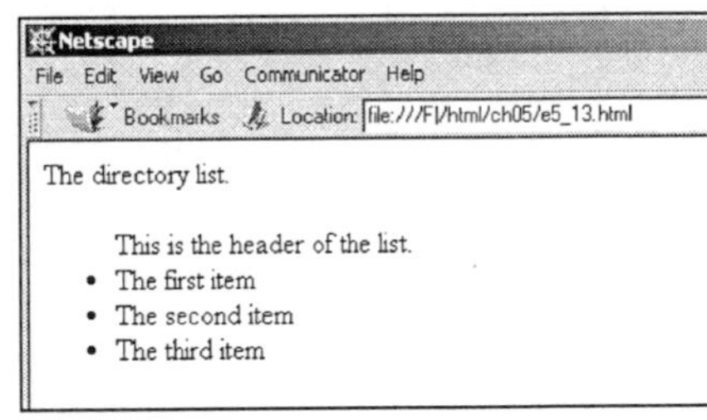

Figure 5.13

5.14 Review of Chapter 5

At the end of Chapter 5 you should know:

- To insert lists into a web page, use the <ol> element for ordered lists and the <ul> element for unordered lists.
- To insert an item into a list, use the <li> element.
- The leading symbols for the unordered list can be set using the type attribute to disc, circle, or square
- The leading symbols for the ordered lists can be set using the type attribute set to Arabic numerals, lower orand upper-case letters, or lower or upper-case Roman numerals.
- Lists can be nested.
- You can set properties for <li> elements individually using the value and type attributes.
- The definition list (<dl>) is formed by definition term <dt> and definition description <dd> elements.
- Other kinds of lists are the directory list (<dir>) and the menu (<menu>) list.

Chapter 6

Tables

6.1 Tables

One of the most complex elements in HTML is the `<table>...</table>` element. It is used both for positioning other elements (layout) and for organizing information into rows and columns.

Any table consists of:

- A `<table>...</table>` element (this is the container for all the other elements).
- Rows defined by `<tr>` (table row) tags. The ending tag `</tr>` is optional in HTML and required in XHTML.
- Cells defined by `<td>` (table data) tags. The ending tag `</td>` is optional in HTML and required in XHTML.

Example 6_1. A simple table (file e6_1.html)

```
<html><head></head><body>
This is the text before the table.
<table>
<tr><td>c11<td>c12<td>c13
<tr><td>c21<td>c22<td>c23
</table>
This is the text after the table.
</body></html>
```

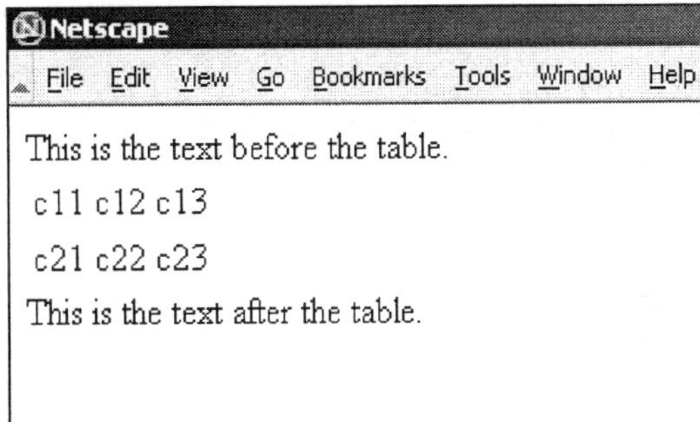

Figure 6.1

Notes

- By default, a table is rendered without borders.
- By default, a table is rendered starting on a new line and aligned to the left.

6.2 The borders of a table

As you see in the previous example, a table and its cells are rendered by default without borders. A border can easily be added by including the `border` attribute for the `<table>` element.

Example 6_2. A table with a border (file e6_2.html)

```
<html><head></head><body>
This is the text before the table.
<table border>
<tr><td>c11<td>c12<td>c13
<tr><td>c21<td>c22<td>c23
</table>
This is the text after the table.
</body></html>
```

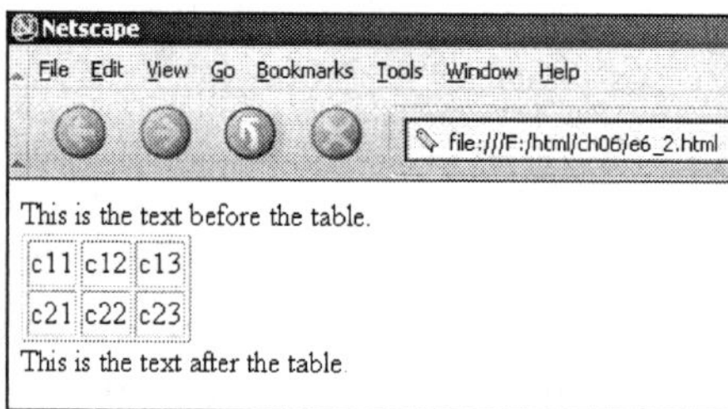

Figure 6.2

Notes

- The table and each cell of the table have a border with a thickness equal to the default value (1 pixel).
- You can assign a different value to the `border` attribute. This value can be any positive integer.
- A value of `0` for the border attribute is possible and indicates a table without borders.
- When the value of the `border` attribute is not `0`, the border has a 3-D style.

Example 6_3. A table with a thick border (file e6_3.html)

```
<html><head></head><body>
This is the text before the table.
<table border="5">
<tr><td>c11<td>c12<td>c13
<tr><td>c21<td>c22<td>c23
</table>
This is the text after the table.
</body></html>
```

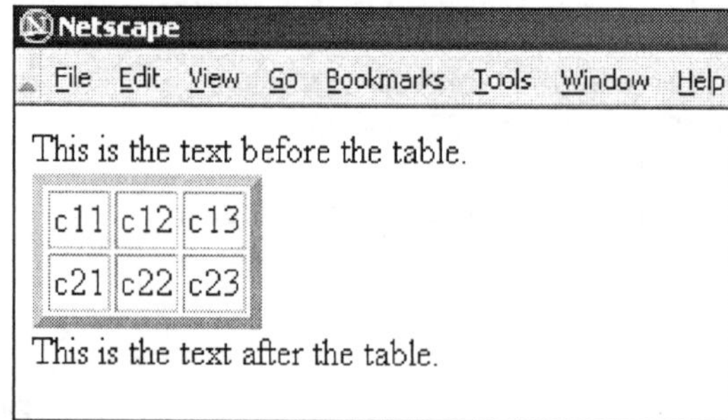

Figure 6.3

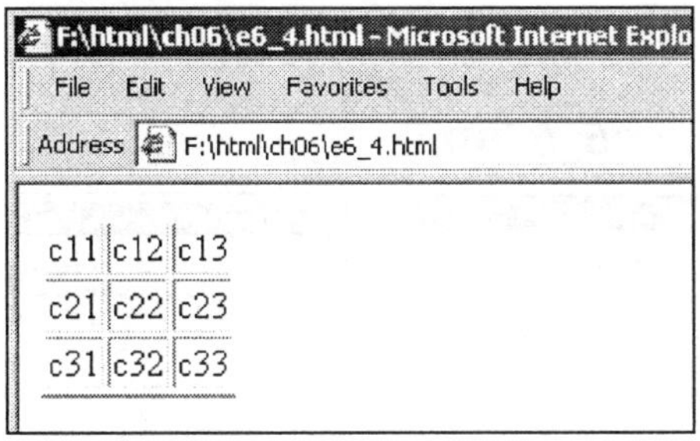

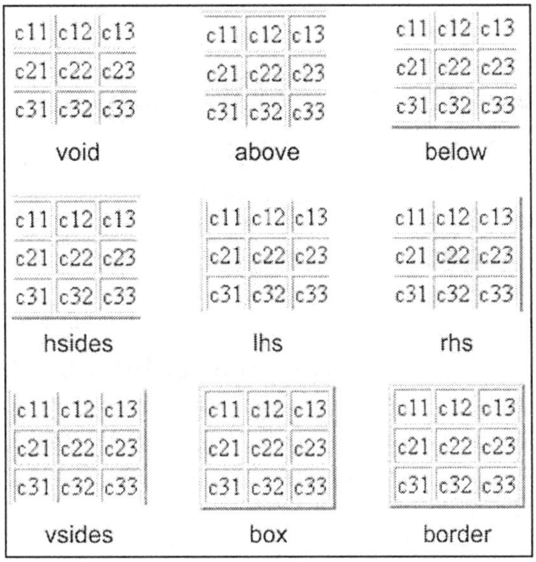

6.3 The `frame` attribute of the `<table>` element

The `frame` attribute of the table element allows you to specify which parts of the border will be rendered. The possible values for this attribute are presented in Figure 6.5, along with the effect each value will have on rendering the table.

Example 6_4. The `frame` attribute of the `<table>` element (file e6_4.html)

```
<html><head></head><body>
<table border="2"
frame="below">
<tr><td>c11<td>c12<td>c13
<tr><td>c21<td>c22<td>c23
<tr><td>c31<td>c32<td>c33
</table>
</body></html>
```

F:\html\ch06\e6_4.html - Microsoft Internet Explo
File Edit View Favorites Tools Help
Address F:\html\ch06\e6_4.html

c11 c12 c13
c21 c22 c23
c31 c32 c33

Figure 6.4

void above below
hsides lhs rhs
vsides box border

Figure 6.5

6.4 The `rules` attribute of the `<table>` element

The `rules` attribute of the `<table>` element allows you to specify how the borders for the cells of the table will be rendered. The possible values for this attribute are presented in Figure 6.6, together with the effect that each value will have on rendering the cells of the table.

Figure 6.6 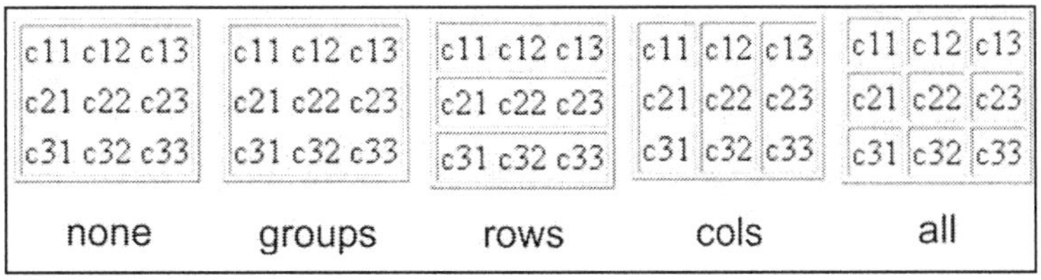

none groups rows cols all

Example 6_5. The `rules` attribute of the `table` element (file e6_5.html)

```
<html><head></head><body>
<table border rules="cols">
<tr><td>c11<td>c12<td>c13
<tr><td>c21<td>c22<td>c23
<tr><td>c31<td>c32<td>c33
</table>
</body></html>
```

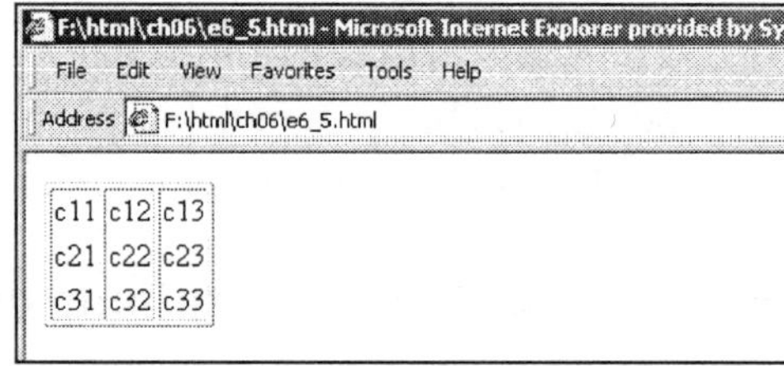

Figure 6.7

6.5 The color of the border of a table

To specify a color for the border of a table, you have to assign a value to the `bordercolor` attribute. The possible values are:

- A color name (e.g. `"red"`)
- An RGB triplet (e.g. `"#12ef74"`)

Example 6_6. The color of the border (file e6_6.html)

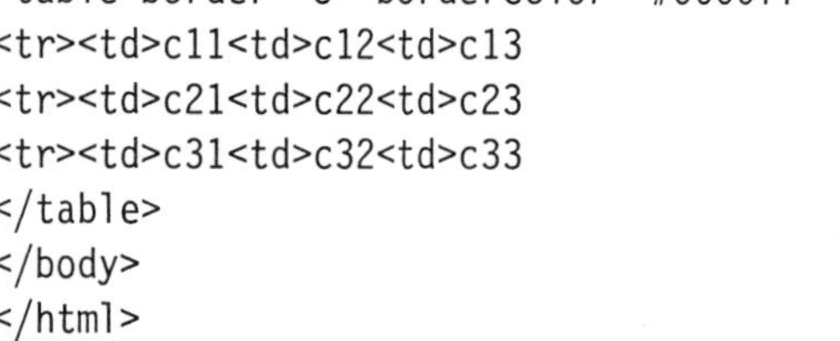

```
<html><head></head><body>
<table border="5" bordercolor="#0000ff">
<tr><td>c11<td>c12<td>c13
<tr><td>c21<td>c22<td>c23
<tr><td>c31<td>c32<td>c33
</table>
</body>
</html>
```

Figure 6.8

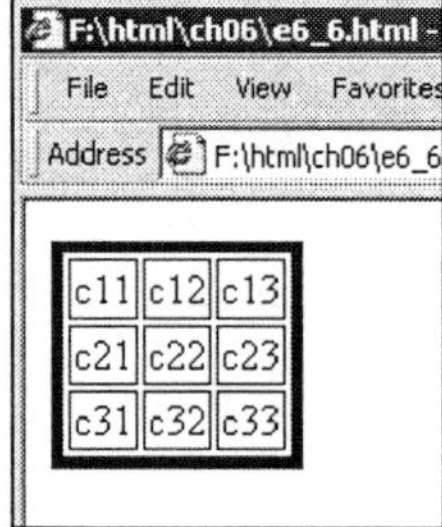

Figure 6.9

Notes

- Netscape Navigator renders the table border in 3-D style and leaves the color of the cell borders unchanged (black).
- Internet Explorer renders both the table border and cell borders in color and renders the table border in a flat (non 3-D) style.
- To keep the 3-D border style in Internet Explorer, set the value of these attributes:
  - `bordercolordark`
  - `bordercolorlight`

Example 6_7. The Internet Explorer attributes for the border (file e6_7.html)

```
<html><head></head><body>
<table border="5"
bordercolordark="#00ff00"
bordercolorlight="#ff0000">
<tr><td>c11<td>c12<td>c13
<tr><td>c21<td>c22<td>c23
<tr><td>c31<td>c32<td>c33
</table>
</body></html>
```

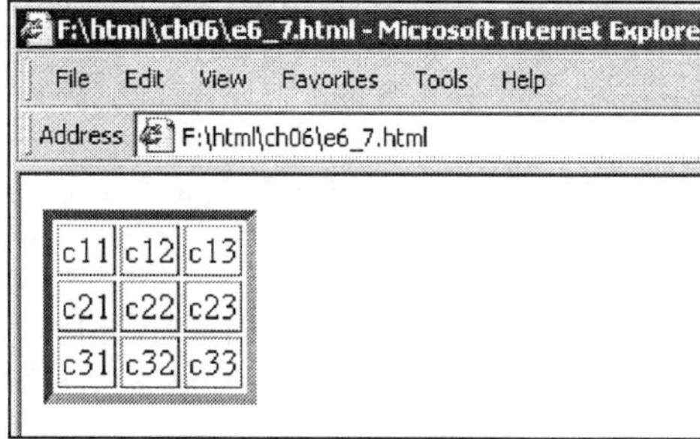

Figure 6.10

6.6 Table alignment

To specify the position of a table relative to the margins of the parent block (usually the HTML document), you can use the `align` attribute. The possible values are:

- `left` (the default value)
- `center`
- `right`

In the following example, you can see the interference between the rendering of tables and text before and after these tables.

Example 6_8. The alignment of a table (file e6_8.html)

```
<html><head></head><body>
This is the text before Table 1. This is the
text before Table 1.This is the text before
Table 1.This is the text before Table 1.This
is the text before Table 1.
<table align="right" border>
<tr><td>c11<td>c12<td>c13
<tr><td>c21<td>c22<td>c23
</table>
This is the text after Table 1 and before
Table 2.This is the text after Table 1 and
before Table 2.This is the text after Table 1
and before Table 2.This is the text after
Table 1 and before Table 2.
<table border>
<tr><td>c11<td>c12<td>c13
```

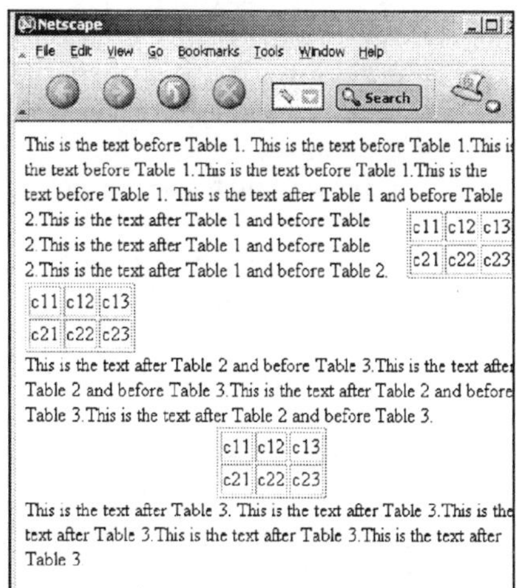

Figure 6.11

```
<tr><td>c21<td>c22<td>c23
</table>
This is the text after Table 2 and before Table 3.This is the text after Table 2
and before Table 3.This is the text after Table 2 and before Table 3.This is the
text after Table 2 and before Table 3.
<table align="center" border>
<tr><td>c11<td>c12<td>c13
<tr><td>c21<td>c22<td>c23
</table>
This is the text after Table 3. This is the text after Table 3.This is the text
after Table 3.This is the text after Table 3.This is the text after Table 3.
</body></html>
```

6.7 The white space around a table

In Netscape Navigator, the `<table>` element accepts two attributes that allow you to set the white space around a table. These attributes are:

- `hspace`
- `vspace`

The possible values for these attributes are positive integers (the size of the white space in pixels).

Example 6_9. The white space around a table (file e6_9.html)

```
<html><head></head><body>
This is the text before the table. This is the
text before the table.This is the text before
the table.This is the text before the
table.This is the text before the table.This
is the text before the table.This is the text
before the table.
<table align="right" border hspace="100"
vspace="50">
<tr><td>c11<td>c12<td>c13
<tr><td>c21<td>c22<td>c23
</table>
This is the text after the table.This is the
text after the table.This is the text after
the table.This is the text after the
table.This is the text after the table.This is
the text after the table.This is the text
after the table.
</body></html>
```

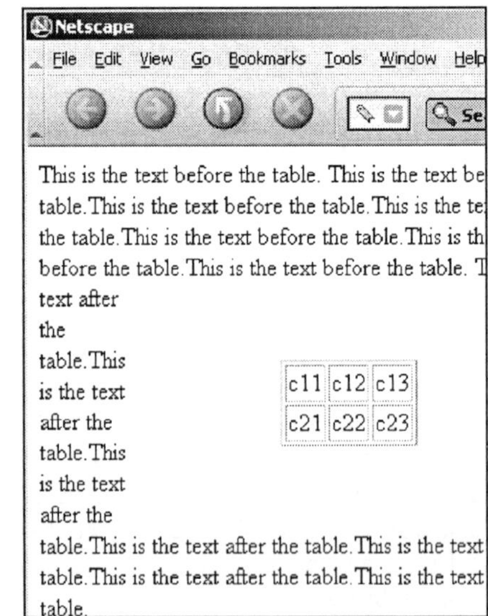

Figure 6.12

6.8 The cellpadding and cellspacing attributes

The cellpadding attribute of the <table> element defines the white space between the cell edge and the content of the cell. The default value is 0.

The cellspacing attribute of the <table> element defines the white space between the edges of adjacent cells. The default value is 0 (for tables without borders) or 2 (for tables with borders).

The values of these two attributes can be:

- Positive integers including 0 (representing the size in pixels)
- Percentages (representing a percentage of the size of the parent block).

Example 6_10. The cellpadding and cellspacing attributes (file e6_10.html)

```
<html>
<head>
</head><body>
<table border cellpadding="30"
cellspacing="0">
<tr><td>c11<td>c12<td>c13
<tr><td>c21<td>c22<td>c23
</table>
</body>
</html>
```

Figure 6.13

6.9 The width and the height of a table

By default, the browser calculates the width and the height of a table so that the content of each cell will be rendered correctly. The designer can define the dimensions of a table using the width and height attributes.

The possible values of these two attributes are:

- Positive integers (representing the size in pixels)
- Percentages (representing a percentage of the size of the width or height of the parent block).

Example 6_11. The `width` and the `height` attributes (file e6_11.html)

```
<html><head></head><body>
<table border width="50%" height="120">
<tr><td>c11<td>c12<td>c13
<tr><td>c21<td>c22<td>c23
</table>
</body></html>
```

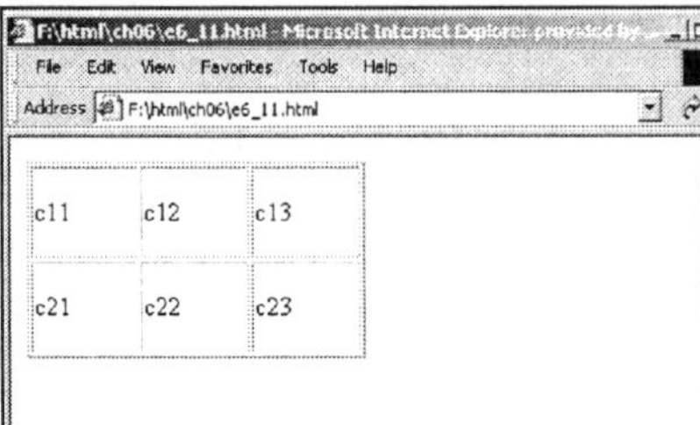

Figure 6.14

Notes

- The `height` attribute is not included in HTML 4.01 Specifications.
- If necessary, the browser will override the specified dimensions of the table.

6.10 The background color

The background color can be set by defining the `bgcolor` attribute. This attribute can be applied to the entire table by using the `<table>` element, to a row by using the `<tr>` element, or to a single cell by using the `<td>` or `<th>` element (for the `<th>` element, see Section 6.12 The `<th>` element, later in this chapter).

Notes

- If there are many `bgcolor` attributes, the order of priority is the `<td>` or `<th>` element first, then the `<tr>` element, and finally the `<table>` element.
- The possible values for the `bgcolor` attribute are presented in Section 4.1 Colors.

Example 6_12. The background color (file e6_12.html)

```
<html><head></head><body>
<table border bgcolor="ff0000">
<tr bgcolor="00ff00">
<td>row
<td>row
<td bgcolor="0000ff">cell
<tr><td>table
<td bgcolor="abcdef">cell
<td>table
</table>
</body></html>
```

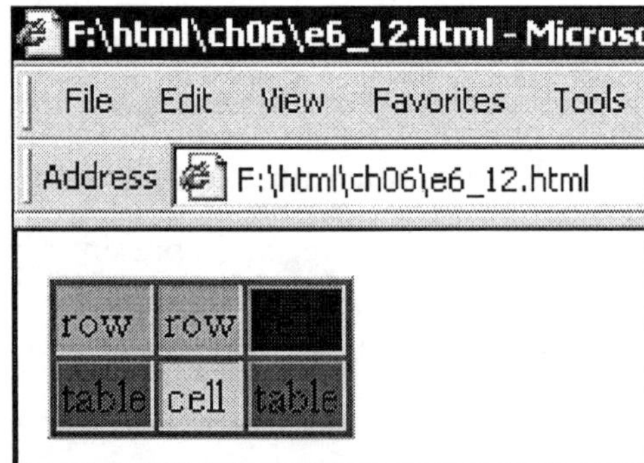

Figure 6.15

6.11 The background image

The background image can be set by defining the `background` attribute. This attribute can be applied to the entire table by using the <table> element, to a row by using the <tr> element, or to a single cell by using the <td> or <th> element.

Notes

- If there are many `background` attributes, the order of priority is first the <td> or <th> element, then the <tr> element, and finally the <table> element.
- The value of the `background` attribute is a reference to an image file (for a complete discussion about referencing images over the Internet, see Chapter 7 Images).

Example 6_13. The background image (file e6_13.html)

```
<html><head></head><body>
<table border background="bg1.jpg">
<tr background="bg2.gif">
<td>row
<td>row
<td background="bg3.jpg">cell
<tr><td>table
<td background="bg3.jpg">cell
<td>table
</table>
</body></html>
```

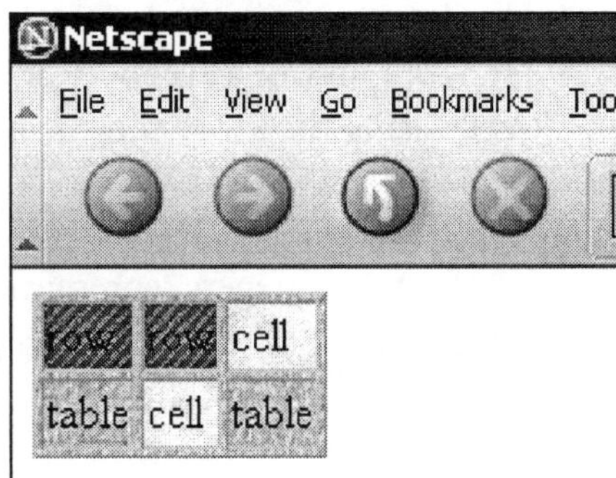

Figure 6.16

Notes

- The `background` attribute is not defined for the <tr> element in HTML 4.01 Specifications and is not implemented by Internet Explorer.
- Files `bg1.jpg`, `bg2.gif`, and `bg3.jpg` must be in the same directory as file `e6_13.html`.

6.12 The <th> element

The <th> element is similar to the <td> element used to display a cell. It is rendered in the bold style (if the content of the cell is text) and is used to create headings for the table.

Example 6_14. The <th> element (file e6_14.html)

```
<html><head></head><body>
<table border>
<tr><th>Sales 2004<th>Quarter
1<th>Quarter 2
<tr><th>USA<td>$1.2 mil<td>$1.5 mil
<tr><th>Europe<td>$2.2 mil<td>$1.2 mil
</table>
</body></html>
```

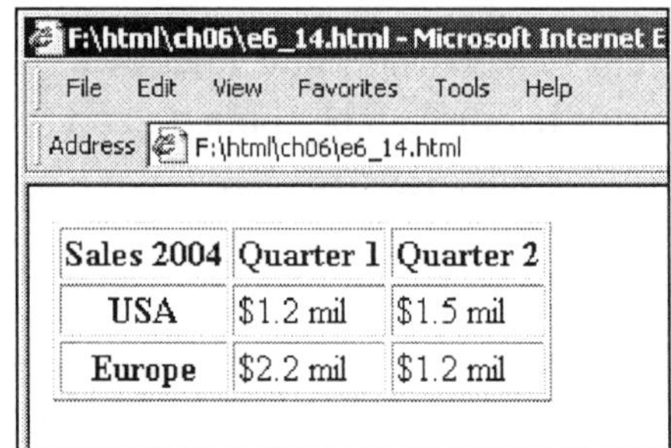

Figure 6.17

6.13 The width and height of a cell

By default, the browser calculates the width and height of each cell in a table so all the content can be rendered correctly. The designer can define the dimensions of cells using the `width` and the `height` attributes of the `<td>` or `<th>` elements.

The possible values of these two attributes are:

- Positive integers representing the size in pixels
- Percentages representing a percentage of the size of the width or height of the table

Example 6_15. The width and the height of a cell (file e6_15.html)

```
<html><head></head><body>
<table border>
<tr>
<td width="50" height="100">c11
<td width="75%">c12
<td width="30">c13
<tr>
<td height="50">c21
<td>c22
<td>c23
</table>
</body></html>
```

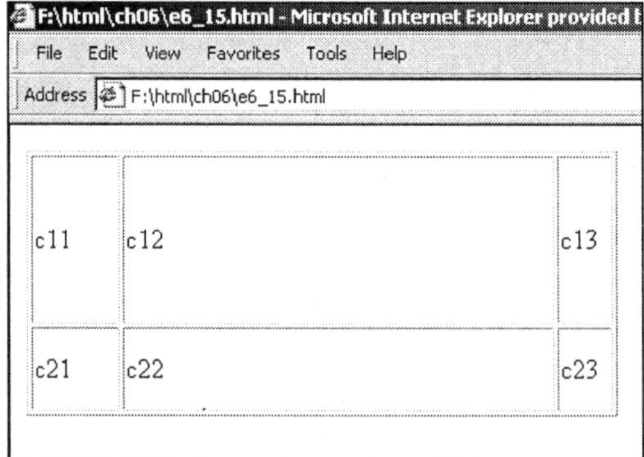

Figure 6.18

Note that changing one cell's height automatically changes the height of every other cell in the row. Similarly, changing one cell's width automatically changes the width of every other cell in the column.

6.14 The alignment of cell content

There are two attributes that govern the alignment of the cell content. These attributes can be attached to the `<tr>`, `<td>`, or `<th>` elements. They are:

- `align` Possible values are: `left` (default), `center`, `right`, `justify`, and `char`
- `valign` Possible values are: `top`, `middle` (default), `bottom`, and `baseline`

Example 6_16. The alignment of the cell data (file e6_16.html)

```
<html><head></head><body>
<table border>
<tr><td>here<td>the<br>alignment<br>
is<td>default<td>left<td>and middle
<tr align="right" valign="bottom">
<td>here<td>the alignment<td>is
<td>right<br>and<br>bottom
<td>$1.3<br>$100.234
<tr><td valign="middle" height="100">
middle<td valign="bottom">
bottom<td>left<td align="right">right
<td align="right" valign="top">top
<br>right
</table>
</body></html>
```

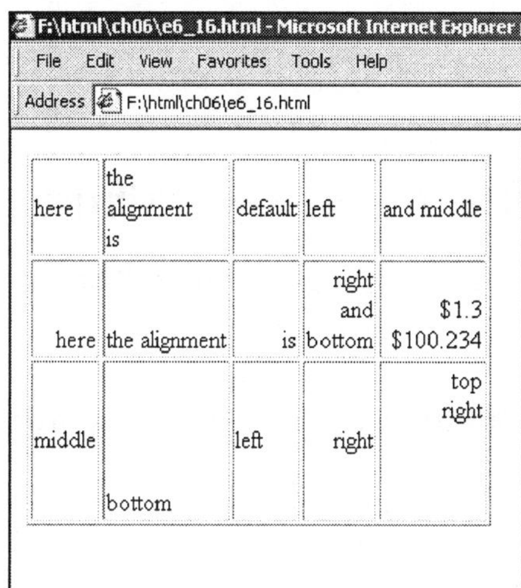

Figure 6.19

6.15 The `colspan` and `rowspan` attributes

A table is a rectangular grid with rows and columns. The content of a cell can be extended over the content of the adjacent cells using the `colspan` and `rowspan` attributes of the `<td>` or `<th>` elements.

The possible values for the `colspan` and `rowspan` attributes are positive integers, representing the number of columns or rows occupied by the extended cell.

Note

- When using an extended cell, only one `<td>` or `<th>` element is required to define the content of the cell.

Example 6_17. The colspan and rowspan attributes (file e6_17.html)

```
<html><head></head><body>
<table border>
<tr><td rowspan="3">c11<br>c21<br>c31
<td>c12<td colspan="2" rowspan="3">
c13 c14<br>c23 c24<br>c33 c34
<tr><td>c22
<tr><td>c32
<tr><td>c41
<td colspan="3">c42 c43 c44
</table>
</body></html>
```

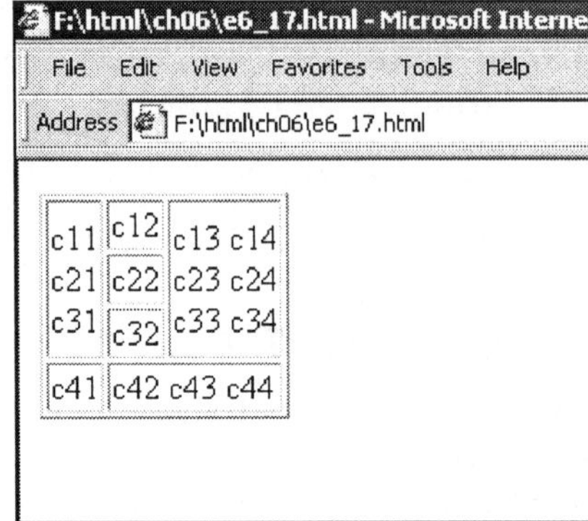

Figure 6.20

6.16 The nowrap attribute

To render text in a cell on a single line, use the nowrap attribute of the <td> or <th> element.

Example 6_18. The nowrap attribute (file e6_18.html)

```
<html><head></head><body>
<table border>
<tr><td>c11<td nowrap>
This is a very long line. This is a
very long line. This is a very long
line. This is a very long line.
This is a very long line. This is a
very long line.
<tr><td>c21<td>c22
</table>
</body></html>
```

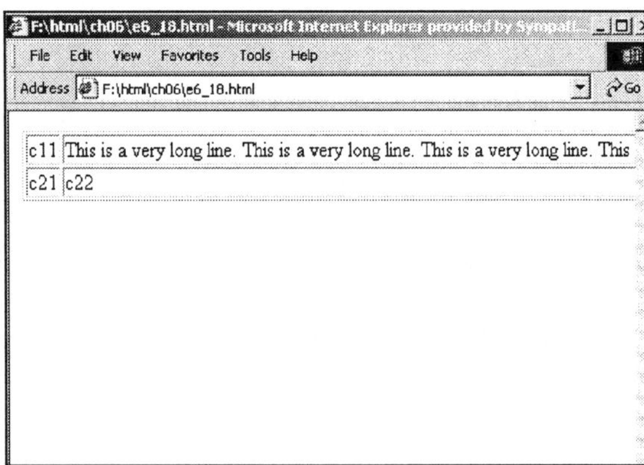

Figure 6.21

6.17 Empty cells

An empty cell is a <td> or <th> element without any content. By default, browsers do not display a border for these cells. To add a border, insert the character sequence   as the content. This character sequence is used to insert a blank space.

Example 6_19. The empty cells of a table (file e6_19.html)

```
<html><head></head><body>
<table border>
<tr><td>c11<td>c12<td>c13
<tr><td>c21<td><td>c23
<tr><td>c31<td> <td>c33
</table>
</body></html>
```

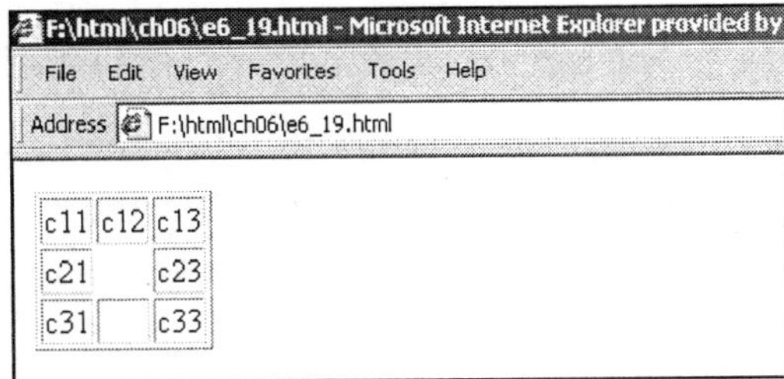

Figure 6.22

6.18 The <caption> element

To add a caption to a table, insert a `<caption>...</caption>` element inside the `<table>...</table>` element immediately after the `<table>` tag. The content of this element can be a short description of the table. The `<caption>` element accepts the `align` attribute to set the position of the caption relative to the table. The possible values are:

- `bottom`
- `top` (the default value)
- `left`
- `right`

Example 6_20. The caption of a table (file e6_20.html)

```
<html><head></head><body>
<table border>
<caption align="top">Fruits</caption>
<tr><td>apple<td>orange
<tr><td>peach<td>lemon
</table>
</body></html>
```

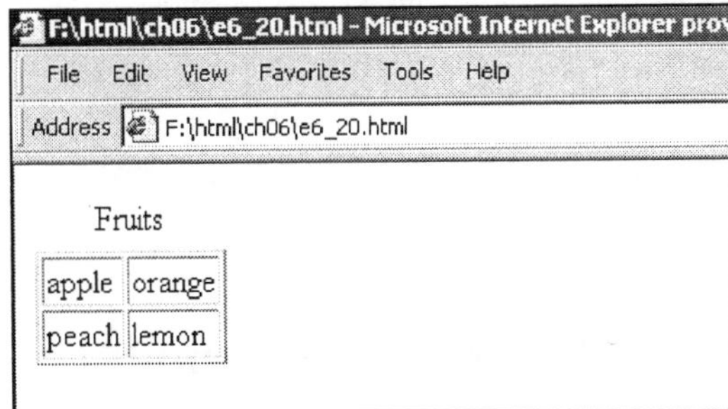

Figure 6.23

6.19 The structure of a table

The content of a table can be divided into sections. These sections are:

- <thead>...</thead> to define the head section
- <tfoot>...</tfoot> to define the foot section
- <tbody>...</tbody> to define a body section

Notes

- These blocks are included in the <table> block.
- Each <table> element may have only one <thead> section and one <tfoot> section.
- The <thead> and <tfoot> blocks must be defined before the <tbody> section.
- Each of these sections contains regular <tr> elements.
- These elements accept attributes like `align`, `bgcolor`, and `valign`.

Example 6_21. The structure of a table (file e6_21.html)

```
<html><head></head><body>
<table border>
<thead align="right" bgcolor="red">
<tr><td>h1<td>h2
</thead>
<tfoot bgcolor="#aabbcc">
<tr><td>f1<td>f2
</tfoot>
<tbody bgcolor="cyan">
<tr><td>c11<td>c12
<tr><td>c21<td>c22
</tbody>
</table>
</body></html>
```

Figure 6.24

6.20 The <colgroup> element

To set a common style for all the cells in a column, use the <colgroup>...</colgroup> element. Insert <col> elements describing each column into the <colgroup> block.

Both <colgroup> and <col> elements accept the following attributes to describe a style:

- `align`
- `valign`
- `width`

Notes

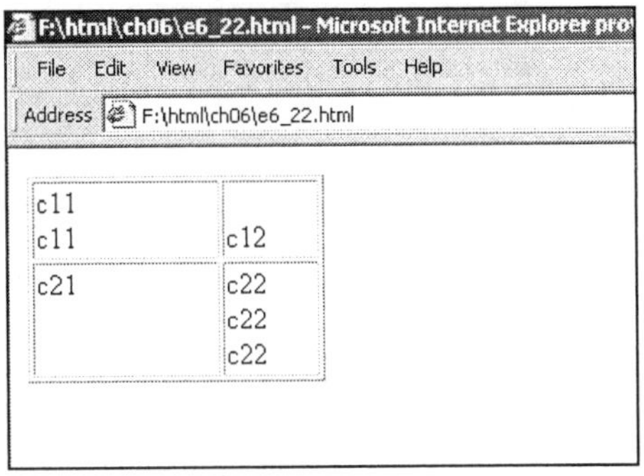

- The <colgroup> element must be inside the <table> element.
- The <col> element doesn't have an ending tag (i.e. it is an empty element and is replaced by <col/> in XHTML).
- You should insert a <col> element for each column in the table.

Example 6_22. The <colgroup> element (file e6_22.html)

```
<html><head></head><body>
<table border>
<colgroup valign="top">
<col width="100">
<col width="50" valign="bottom">
</colgroup>
<tr><td>c11<br>c11<td>c12
<tr><td>c21<td>c22<br>c22<br>c22
</table>
</body></html>
```


c11 c11	c12
c21	c22 c22 c22

Figure 6.25

6.21 Review of Chapter 6

At the end of Chapter 6 you should know:

- Tables can be inserted into a web page using the <table> element.
- A table is composed of rows (the <tr> elements) and cells (the <td> elements).
- To add a border to a table, use the `border` attribute of the <table> element.
- To assign a color to the border, use the `bordercolor` attribute.
- The `frame` and `rules` attributes of the <table> element allow you to design the borders for the rows, columns, and the cells of a table.
- A table can be aligned using the `align` attribute.
- The white space around a table can be set using the `hspace` and `vspace` attributes of the <table> element.
- The `cellspacing` attributes determines the distance between adjacent cells, and the `cellpadding` attribute determines the distance between the content of the cell and the cell's border.
- Fixed dimensions for a table or for a cell can be set using the `width` and `height` attributes.
- You can set a background color for a table using the `bgcolor` attributes and a background image using the `background` attribute.

- To define headers for a table, use the <th> element.
- To align data in a table, use the align and valign attributes attached to <tr>, <td>, or <th> elements.
- To extend a cell over adjacent cells, use the colspan and rowspan attributes of the <td> or <th> elements.
- To add a caption to a table, use the <caption> element inside the <table> element.
- To add a structure to a table, use the <thead>, <tfoot>, and <tbody> elements.
- To set the properties for the columns of the tables, use the <colgroup> element.

Chapter 7

Images

7.1 Image formats on the web

The web was designed to be a multimedia environment. To achieve this goal, HTML allows you to insert images, sounds, animations, movies, and other multimedia content into a web page. The image formats accepted on the web are:

- GIF (Graphic Interchange Format) has the extension `.gif`
- JPEG (Joint Photographic Experts Group) has the extension `.jpg` or `.jpeg`
- PNG (Portable Network Graphics) has the extension `.png`
- TIFF (Tagged Image File Format) has the extension `.tif` or `.tiff`
- BMP (BitMaP format) has the extension `.bmp`

Notes

- GIF, JPEG, and PNG are accepted by most browsers.
- BMP is accepted by Internet Explorer.
- TIFF is displayed correctly if the browser has a plug-in or a helper application to handle it.

7.2 A comparison of image formats

The following table presents a comparison of different image formats accepted on the web:

	GIF	JPEG	PNG
Colors	8 bit pixel (256 colors)	24 bit pixel	32 bit pixel
Transparency	Yes	No	Yes
Interlacing (rough previous)	Yes	Yes	Yes
Animation	Yes	No	Yes
Compression	Yes	Yes	Yes
Notes	Recommended for drawings	Recommended for pictures (photographs)	Recommended for drawings and pictures

7.3 The `<img>` element

Use the `<img>` element to insert an image into a web page.

Notes

- The `<img>` element is an inline element. This means you can insert an image anywhere (e.g. inside a block of text, inside a table cell, inside a list item, etc.)
- The `<img>` element doesn't require an ending element. It is an empty element and is replaced by the `<img/>` tag in XTHML.
- The `<img>` element requires an `src` attribute to define the name and the location of the image file. The possible values are valid URLs (see next section).

Example 7_1. The `<img>` element (file e7_1.html)

```
<html>
<head>
</head>
<body>
An image is following:
<img src="casa_loma.jpg">
Text after the image.
</body>
</html>
```

Figure 7.1

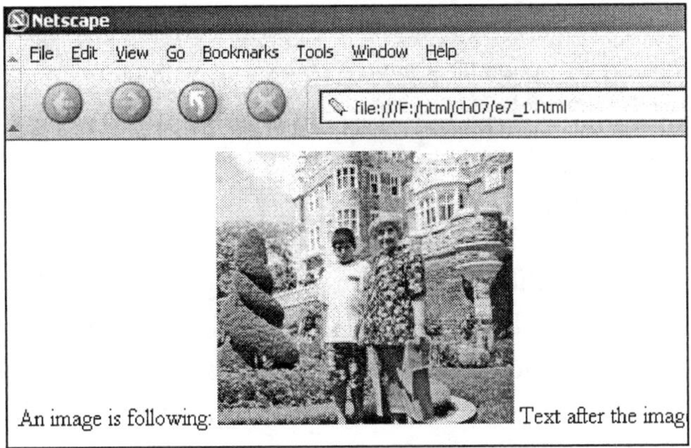

Note

◆ In order for this example to work properly, both `e7_1.html` and `casa_loma.jpg` must be in the same directory.

7.4 The absolute URL

URL stands for Uniform Resource Locator. The URL is a standard to identify resources (e.g. files) over the Internet. The URL can be absolute or relative.

An example of an absolute URL is:

`http://www.google.ca/intl/en_ca/images/logo.gif`

The absolute URL contains:

- *The Internet protocol, e.g.* `http://`
- *The computer name, e.g.* `www.google.ca`
- *The path, e.g.* `intl/en_ca/images/`
- *The file name, e.g.* `logo.gif`

Example 7_2. The absolute URL (file e7_2.html)

```
<html><head></head><body>
An image is following:
<img src="
http://www.teora.com/img/
TopBar.gif">
Text after the image.
</body></html>
```

Figure 7.2

Note

- The HTML file and the image file can be on the same computer or on different computers connected to the Internet.

7.5 The relative URL

The relative URL identifies the location of the image by describing a path relative to the current directory where the HTML file is located. For example, let's suppose we have the directory structure presented in Figure 7.3. The HTML file into which we want to insert an image is "test.html" located in the "html" directory. The relative URLs presented below reference images located in the other directories:

- /im0.gif
- ../../../im0.gif
- ../../im1.jpg
- /projects/im1.jpg
- ../../project2/im5.png
- /projects/project2/im5.png
- ../../project2/html/im6.gif
- ../im2.png
- /projects/project1/im2.png
- /projects/project2/html/im6.gif
- im3.gif
- /projects/project1/html/im3.gif
- draft/im4.jpg
- /projects/project1/html/draft/im4.jpg

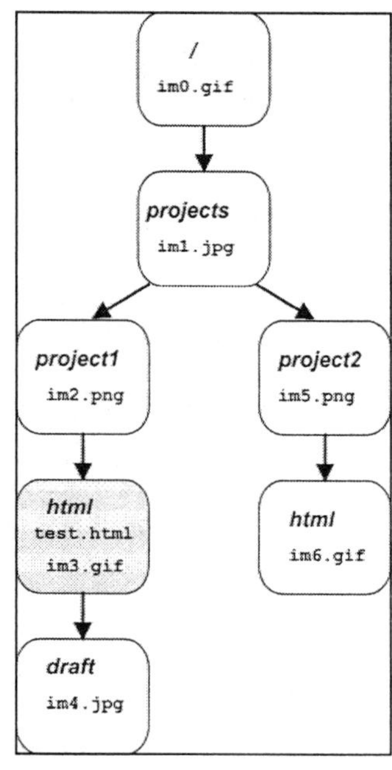

Figure 7.3

Note that

- ../ stands for the parent directory
- / stands for the root directory

Example 7_3. The relative URL (file test.html)

```
<html><head></head>
<body>
<img src="../../project2/im5.png">
</body>
</html>
```

Figure 7.4

7.6 The image border

By default, the browser will render an image as-is (without a border). To add a black border to the image, set a value to the border attribute of the `<img>` element. The possible values are `0` (the default value) and any positive integer, indicating the thickness of the border in pixels .

Example 7_4. The image border (file e7_4.html)

```
<html>
<head></head>
<body>
No border
<img src="happy.gif">
With border
<img src="happy.gif" border="5">
</body>
</html>
```

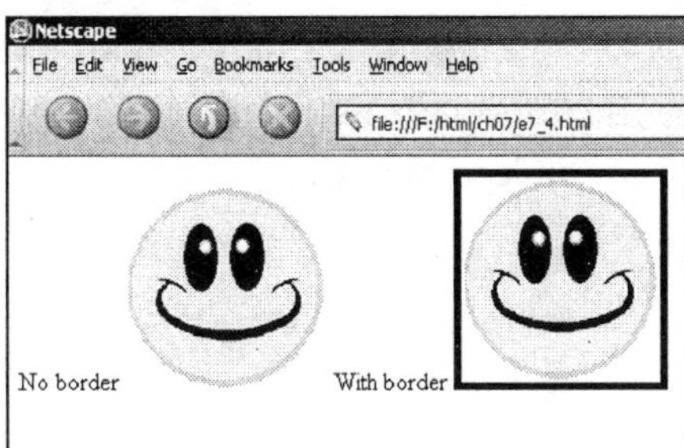

Figure 7.5

7.7 The `width` and `height` attributes of the image

By default, the browser renders images with their actual width and height. If you want to scale an image to a different width or height, set values to the `width` and/or `height` attributes of the `<img>` element. The possible values are:

- Positive integers (indicating the size in pixels)
- Percentages (indicating the percentage of the width or height of the parent block)

Example 7_5. The `width` and the `height` of the image (file e7_5.html)

```
<html><head></head>
<body>
Actual
<img src="babele.jpg">
Half width
<img src="babele.jpg" width="200">
<br>Scaled unproportionally
<img src="babele.jpg"
width="200" height="100">
</body></html>
```

Figure 7.6

Notes

- The image "babele.jpg" has an actual size of 400 pixels wide by 273 pixels high.
- If you change only one dimension, the browser will render the image proportionally.
- If you set both the width and the height, the image will be rendered disproportionately and therefore be distorted.

7.8 The image vertical alignment

The alignment between an image relative to other inline elements of a web page (especially text) can be set using the align attribute of the <img> element. The possible values are:

- top
- texttop (Netscape Navigator only)
- middle
- absmiddle
- center
- bottom (the default value)
- baseline
- absbottom

Example 7_6. The image vertical alignment (file e7_6.html)

```
<html><head></head>
<body><table border>
<tr height="150">
<td><font size="6">Bottom</font><img src="grid.gif" align="bottom">
<font size="6">jpg</font>
<font size="6"> Baseline</font><img src="grid.gif" align="baseline">
<font size="6">jpg </font>
<font size="6">Absbottom</font><img src="grid.gif" align="absbottom">
<font size="6">jpg</font>
<tr height="150">
<td><font size="6">Middle</font><img src="grid.gif" align="middle">
<font size="6">jpg</font>
<font size="6"> Absmiddle</font><img src="grid.gif" align="absmiddle">
<font size="6">jpg </font>
<font size="6">Center</font><img src="grid.gif" align="center">
<font size="6">jpg</font>
<tr height="150">
<td><font size="6">Top</font><img src="grid.gif" align="top">
<font size="6">jpg</font>
```

```
<font size="6"> Texttop</font><img src="grid.gif" align="texttop">
<font size="6">jpg</font>
</table></body></html>
```

Figure 7.7

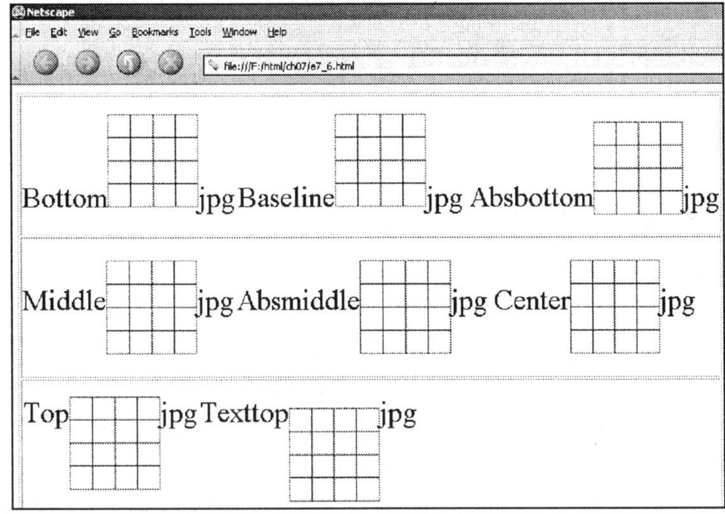

Notes

- Various browsers may align images differently than how they are presented here.
- In the previous example, the alignment is between the image and the other content (in this case text) of the parent block (in this case the table cell).

7.9 Horizontal image alignment

To set the horizontal alignment of an image relative to the parent block, use the `align` attribute with these values:

- `left`
- `right`
- `center`

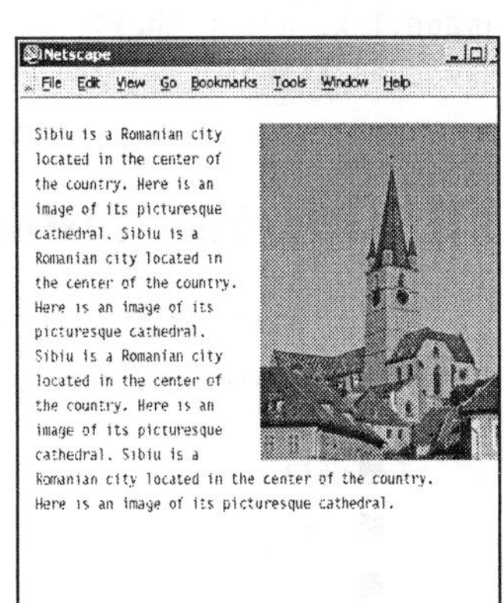

Figure 7.8

Example 7_7. The image horizontal alignment (file e7_7.html)

```
<html><head></head>
<body>
<img src="cathedral.png" align="right">
Sibiu is a Romanian city located in the center of the
country.
```

```
Here is an image of its picturesque cathedral.
Sibiu is a Romanian city located in the center of the country.
Here is an image of its picturesque cathedral.
Sibiu is a Romanian city located in the center of the country.
Here is an image of its picturesque cathedral.
Sibiu is a Romanian city located in the center of the country.
Here is an image of its picturesque cathedral.
</body></html>
```

7.10 White space around an image

There are two attributes that define the size of the white space between an image and the other content of the web page: `hspace` and `vspace`.

The possible values for these attributes are:

- Positive integers, indicating the size of the white space in pixels
- Percentage of the size of the parent block

Example 7_8. The white space around an image (file e7_8.html)

```
<html><head></head><body>
Text before the image. Text before the image. Text before
the image. Text before the image. Text before the image.
Text before the image. Text before the image. Text before
the image. Text before the image. Text before the image.
<img src="tree.bmp" hspace="30" vspace="50" align="right">
Text after the image. Text after the image. Text after the
image.Text after the image.Text after the image.
Text after the image. Text after the image.Text after the
image.Text after the image. Text after the image.
</body></html>
```

Figure 7.9

7.11 The `clear` attribute of the <br> element

To clear the left or right side of an image of text, use a <br> element having the `clear` attribute set to:

- `all`
- `left`
- `none`
- `right`

Let's change the previous example. Insert `<br clear="right">` before the first appearance of the sentence `"Text after the image."` and see the effect of this change.

Example 7_9. The `clear` attribute of the `<br>` element (file e7_9.html)

```
<html><head></head>
<body>
Text before the image. Text before the image. Text before
the image. Text before the image. Text before the image.
Text before the image. Text before the image. Text before
the image. Text before the image. Text before the image.
<img src="tree.bmp" hspace="30" vspace="50"
align="right">
<br clear="right">Text after the image. Text after the
image. Text after the image.Text after the image.Text
after the image.
Text after the image. Text after the image.Text after the
image.Text after the image. Text after the image.
</body></html>
```

Figure 7.10

7.12 The `alt` attribute

Although not required, it is strongly recommended that you add the `alt` attribute to the `<img>` element. The `alt` attribute allows you to attach a description to an image. The value of the `alt` attribute can be any double-quoted string of less than 1024 characters (e.g. `alt="London, Aug 2004. The Tower Bridge"`).

Notes

- If the browser cannot download an image or is set to not download the images, the browser will render the value of the `alt` attribute instead of the image.
- If you hover the mouse over an image, a tool tip will appear containing the value of the `alt` attribute.
- The value of the `alt` attribute is important for tools to aid vision-impaired people and for speaking browsers.
- For descriptions with more than 1024 characters, use the `longdesc` attribute of the `<img>` element.

Example 7_10. The `alt` attribute (file e7_10.html)

```
<html>
<head>
</head>
<body>
<img src="newyork.jpg"
alt="August 2002, New York">
<br>
<img src="london.jpg"
alt="London, Aug 2004.
The Tower Bridge">
</body>
</html>
```

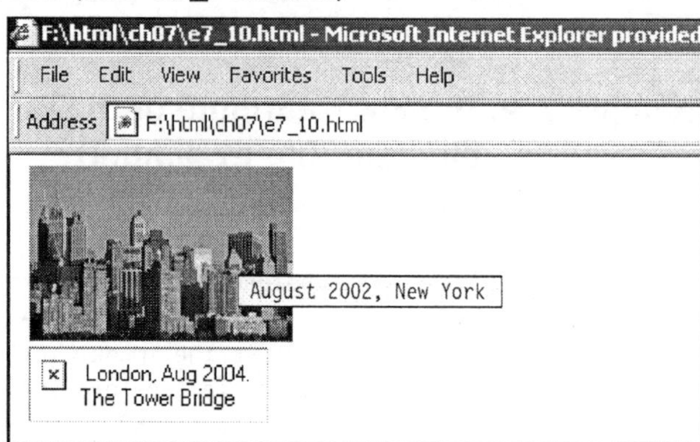

Figure 7.11

7.13 The `lowsrc` attribute

Using the `lowsrc` attribute, you can attach a second URL to an `<img>` element. This URL identifies an image similar to the one indicated by the `src` attribute but in low-resolution format.

Notes

- The images indicated by `src` and `lowsrc` can be different images.
- The low-resolution image (indicated by the `lowsrc` attribute) will be downloaded first (useful for low-speed connections), and later the actual image (indicated by the `src` attribute) will be downloaded.
- It is recommended that you use the same size for both images, so the browser does not have to render the web page again after the high-resolution image is downloaded.

Example 7_11. The `lowsrc` attribute (file e7_11.html)

```
<html><head></head>
<body>
<img src="newyork.jpg"
lowsrc="newyork_low.jpg">
</body></html>
```

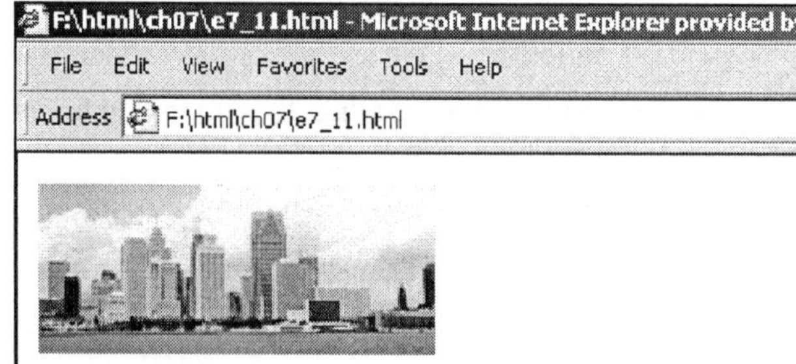

Figure 7.12

7.14 The background image

The designer can attach a background image to a web page. To do this, use the background attribute of the <body> element. The value of the background attribute is the URL that indicates the desired image file.

Example 7_12. The background image (file e7_12.html)

```
<html>
<head></head>
<body background="bg.jpg">
This is a web page with a background
defined by an image.
</body></html>
```

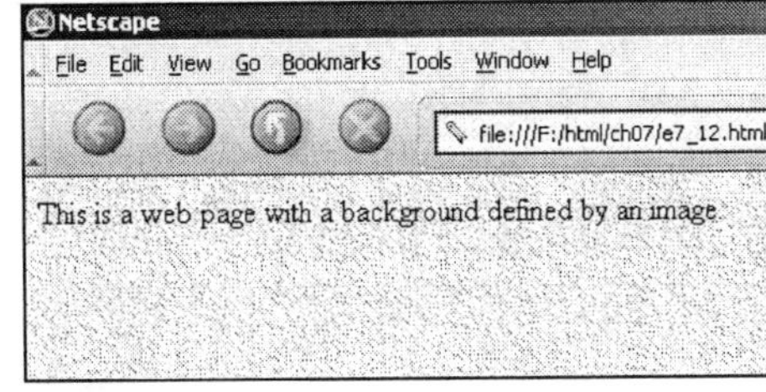

Figure 7.13

Notes

- The image is tiled horizontally and vertically to fill the entire page.
- Internet Explorer accepts an additional attribute called bgproperties, which can be set to "fixed" so the background image will stay in the same position when a user scrolls the page content using the navigation tools (Vertical Navigation Bars or Up/Down Keys).

7.15 Using images to create custom-made lists

The following example shows how you can use images to create a custom-made list in which the leading symbols of items are images. Note that this method doesn't use the <li> element. Rather, it is simply an assembly of images accompanied by text and formatted with <br> elements.

Example 7_13. A custom-made list using images (file e7_13.html)

```
<html>
<head></head>
<body>
<ul>A Custom-made List:
<br><img src="cross.gif"> First item
<br><img src="cube.gif"> Second item
<br><img src="square.gif"> Third item
<br><img src="star.gif"> Last item
</ul>
</body></html>
```

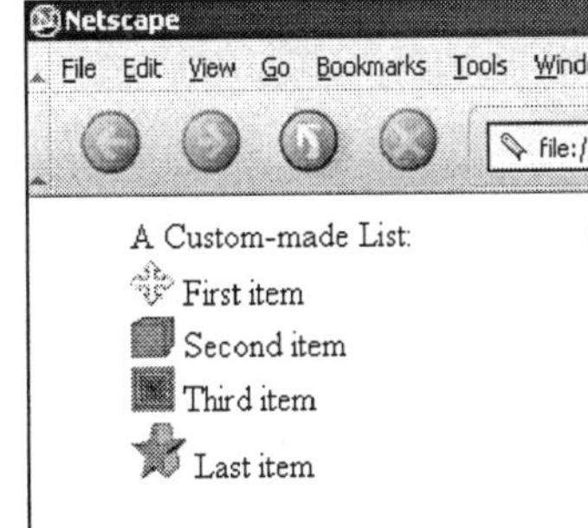

Figure 7.14

7.16 Review of Chapter 7

At the end of Chapter 7 you should know:

- There are a several kinds of images that you can insert into a web page (GIF format recommended for drawings, JPEG recommended for pictures, PNG and TIFF for general purpose images, and BMP for Internet Explorer).
- To insert an image, use the `<img>` element.
- The Internet address of the image is set by the `src` attribute, which accepts any valid URL as its content.
- To add a border to an image, set the `border` attribute of the `<img>` element.
- To set fixed dimension for the image, use the `width` and `height` attributes.
- The image can be aligned horizontally or vertically with the `align` attribute.
- Use the `hspace` and the `vspace` attributes to set the white space around an image.
- Additional attributes for the `<img>` elements are `alt` (for alternative text) and `lowsrc` (for low resolution replacement image).
- To set an image background for a web page, use the `background` attribute of the `<body>` element.

Chapter 8

Metadata

8.1 Metadata

Metadata is data about data (i.e. data that describes other data). Metadata is information you can insert into an HTML file to supplement information about the content and the goals of a specific page or web site.

Notes

- Metadata is not rendered by the browser.
- Metadata can transfer useful information to browsers, servers, and users.
- Metadata can be read and organized by Internet robots and search engines.

8.2 The <meta> tag

To insert metadata into an HTML file (web page), insert <meta> tags inside the <head>...</head> element.

Notes

- The <meta> tag doesn't have an ending tag (i.e. it is an empty element).
- You can insert as many <meta> tags inside the <head>...</head> element as you like.

8.3 The attributes of the <meta> tag

The <meta> tag has attributes that allow you to store the metadata. These attributes are:

- `content` This attribute is used to store the actual metadata content. The possible values are double quoted strings.
- `name` The possible values are:
  - `description`
  - `keywords`
  - `author`
- `http-equiv` The possible values are:
  - `creation-date`
  - `expires`
  - `from`
  - `replay-to`
  - `content-type`
  - `refresh`
  - `pragma`
- `scheme` This attribute is used to refine the information given by the other attributes. The possible values are double quoted strings.
- `lang` This attribute is used to specify the language. The possible values are language identifiers (e.g. `en`, `uk`, `ca`, `ro`, etc).

Note

- Generally, the metadata consists of a pair of attributes:
  - `name=`value `content=`value (e.g. `name="author" content="Robert Adams, Julia McGill"`)
  - `http-equiv=`value `content=`value (e.g. `http-equiv="refresh" content="5"`)

A <meta> element may have other attributes, but they are rarely used.

All examples in this chapter refer to a fictitious web database application development company named IT&D Group.

8.4 The description of a web page

To insert a description of a web page or a web site, use a <meta> tag with these attributes:

- name="description"
- content=a descriptive, double-quoted string

Example 8_1. The description of a web page (file e8_1.html)

```
<html>
<head>
<meta name="description"
content="IT&D Group is a web database applications development company. Our company
has successfully implemented cross-platform multi-tier e-commerce applications for
many clients. Using an Oracle Database on a Linux Operating System, our business
relies on professional applications at affordable prices">
</head>
<body>
<center><img src="logo.gif"></center>
</body>
</html>
```

Figure 8.1

8.5 Keywords

Keywords are frequently used by Internet search engines like Google, Yahoo, and Altavista. Therefore, the keywords must be carefully defined to exactly describe the purpose the web site has been designed for.

To insert the keywords of a web page or a web site, use a <meta> tag with these attributes:

- name ="keywords"
- content=list of keywords separated by commas

Example 8_2. The keywords of a web page (file e8_2.html)

```
<html>
<head>
<meta name="keywords"
content="IT&D, Group, web, database, applications, development, company,
cross-platform, multi-tier, e-commerce, Oracle, Linux, professional, affordable,
prices">
</head>
<body>
Welcome to the IT&D Group web site!
</body>
</html>
```

8.6 Author and copyright

To insert information about the author (or authority) and copyright, insert two `<meta>` elements with their `name` attributes set to `"author"` and `"copyright"`, respectively. Since this information is not directly visible to users, it is recommended that you include clear copyright and contact details in the `<body>...</body>` element of the web page.

Example 8_3. The author and the copyright (file e8_3.html)

```
<html>
<head>
<meta name="author" content="Robert Adams, Julia McGill">
<meta name="copyright" content="IT&D Group. All Rights Reserved">
</head>
<body>
Copyright &copy; 2004, IT&D Group. All Rights Reserved.
</body>
</html>
```

Figure 8.2

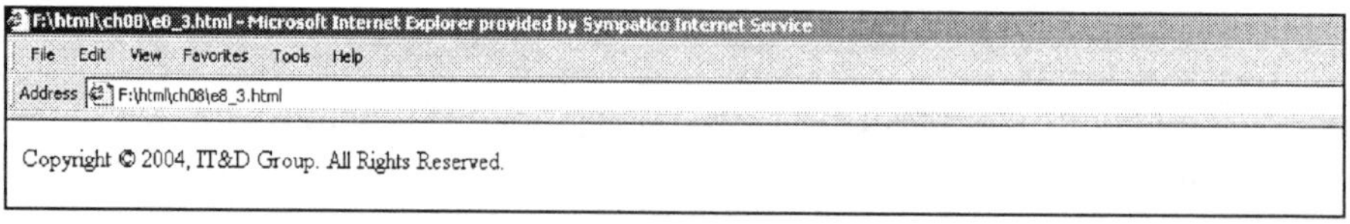

F:\html\ch08\e8_3.html - Microsoft Internet Explorer provided by Sympatico Internet Service
File Edit View Favorites Tools Help
Address F:\html\ch08\e8_3.html

Copyright © 2004, IT&D Group. All Rights Reserved.

Note

- To insert the Copyright symbol © into a web page, use this special sequence of characters: `©`

8.7 Creation and updating date

To transmit information about the creation and updating date of a page to Internet search engines, insert two `<meta>` elements with their `http-equiv` attributes set to `"creation-date"` and `"expires"`, respectively. The value of each `content` attribute should be a date that satisfies the default format `"ddd, dd mmm yyyy hh:mm:ss ttt"`, where:

- `ddd` represents the first three letters of the day name (Mon, Tue, Wed, Thu, Fri, Sat, or Sun)
- `dd` represents the day number (01, 02, ..., 31)
- `mmm` represents the first three letters of the month name (Jan, Feb, Mar, Apr, May, Jun, Jul, Aug, Sep, Oct, Nov, or Dec)
- `yyyy` represent the year (e.g. 2004)
- `hh:mm:ss` represents the hour, minute, and second (e.g. 11:23:45)
- `ttt` represents the time standard (e.g. GMT)

Example 8_4. The creation and updating date (file e8_4.html)

```
<html>
<head>
<meta http-equiv="creation-date" content=" Sun, 19 Sep 2003 12:00:00 GMT">
<meta http-equiv="expires" content="Sun, 25 Jul 2004 12:00:00 GMT">
</head>
<body>
Welcome to the IT&D Group web site!
</body>
</html>
```

Note

◆ To use a different date format, set the `scheme` attribute as in the following example:

```
<html>
<head>
<meta http-equiv="creation-date" content="03-07-2001"
scheme="Month-Day-Year">
</head>
<body>
Welcome to the IT&D Group web site!
</body>
</html>
```

8.8 The contact person

To add the name and email address of the person responsible for the design of the web page or site, insert two `<meta>` elements with the `http-equiv` values set to `"from"` and `"reply-to"`, respectively. The associated content should contain the contact person's email address in both cases.

Example 8_5. The contact person (file e8_5.html)

```
<html>
<head>
<meta http-equiv="from" content="robert.adams@itd-group.com">
<meta http-equiv="reply-to" content="Julia.mcgill@itd-group.com">
</head>
<body>
Welcome to the IT&D Group web site!
</body>
</html>
```

8.9 The file details

To insert information about the type of HTML file (by default set to `text/html`) and about the character set used in the file, use a `<meta>` element and set the `http-equiv` value to `"content-type"`. The value of the associated `content` attribute should contain the file type and the character set used.

Example 8_6. The file details (file e8_6.html)

```
<html>
<head>
<meta http-equiv="content-type"
content="text/html; charset=ISO-8859-5">
</head>
<body>
Welcome to the IT&D Group web site!
</body>
</html>
```

8.10 The `lang` attribute

The designer can add metadata in different languages. To specify which language is used, add a `lang` attribute to the `<meta>` element. The possible values for this attribute are:

- A 2-character language identifier (e.g. "ro")
- A 5-character language-dialect identifier (e.g. "en-us")

Example 8_7. The `lang` attribute (file e8_7.html)

```
<html>
<head>
<meta name="keywords" content="aplicatie, programare" lang="ro">
<meta name="keywords" content="application, programing" lang="en-us">
</head>
<body>
Welcome to the IT&D Group web site!
</body>
</html>
```

8.11 Refreshing a web page

If your web page contains information that you wish to change or update regularly (e.g. stock market information), you can give the browser a directive to update the page after a specified time interval. To do this, insert a `<meta>` tag, and set the `http-equiv` attribute to `"refresh"` and the `content` attribute to the number of seconds after which the page will be updated.

Example 8_8. Refreshing a web page (file e8_8.html)

```
<html>
<head>
<meta http-equiv="refresh" content="5">
</head>
<body>
This page will automatically be updated every 5 seconds!
</body>
</html>
```

Figure 8.3

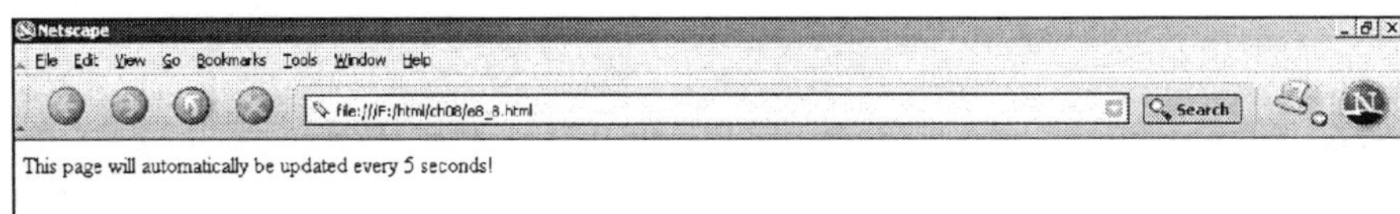

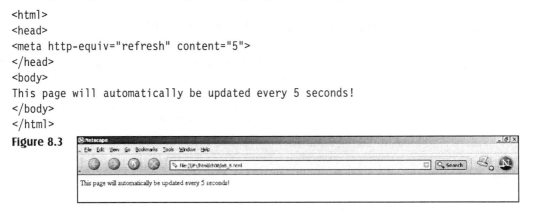

8.12 Forwarding a web page

To automatically redirect to another web page after a number of seconds, use the syntax:

```
http-equiv="refresh" content="5; url='www.teorausa.com'"
```

where `url` points to the new web page that will be loaded after a number of seconds (twenty seconds in this case).

Example 8_9. Forwarding a web page (file e8_9.html)

```
<html>
<head>
<meta http-equiv="refresh" content="20; url=http://www.teorausa.com">
</head>
<body>
This page will automatically be redirected to the Teora USA website after 20 seconds!
</body>
</html>
```

Figure 8.4

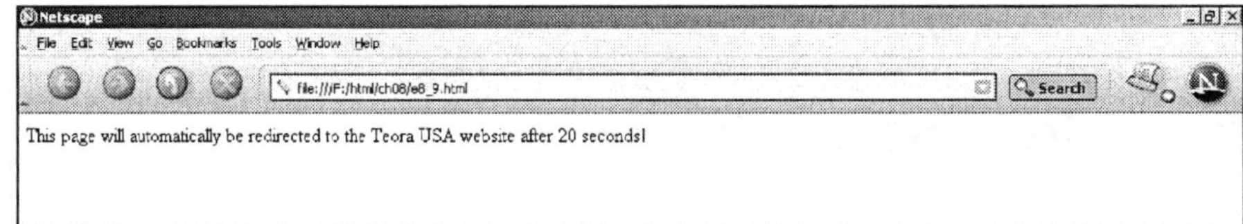

8.13 The `pragma` directive

To force the browser to download a web page each time a user accesses it, use the syntax:

```
http-equiv="pragma" content="no-cache"
```

Example 8_10. The `pragma` directive (file e8_10.html)

```
<html>
<head>
<meta http-equiv="pragma"
content="no-cache">
</head>
<body>
This page will be downloaded again
each time it is accessed.
</body>
</html>
```

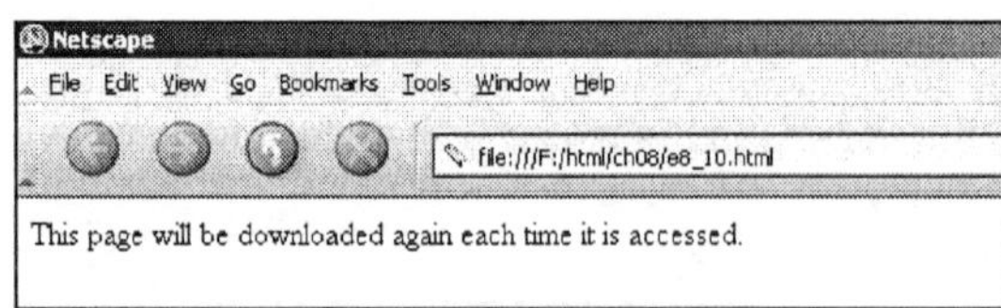

Figure 8.5

8.14 The comment block

To insert a comment into a web page (HTML file), use the syntax:

```
<!--Your comment here-->
```

Notes

- The comment block can be placed anywhere inside the HTML file.
- The comment block can extend over many lines.
- The comment block is not rendered by the browser.

Example 8_11. The comment block (file e8_11.html)

```
<html>
<head>
<body>
<!--this block is a comment.
This block will not be rendered by the browser. -->
Welcome to the IT&D Group web site!
</body>
</html>
```

Figure 8.6

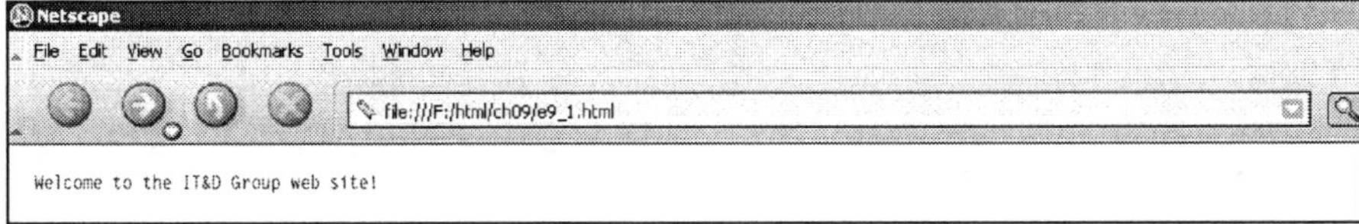

8.15 Review of Chapter 8

At the end of Chapter 8 you should know:

- Metadata is information inserted into the `<head>` element used to document the web page and send information to Internet robots and search engines.
- Metadata is not rendered by browsers.
- To insert metadata, use a pair of attributes: `name` and `content` or `http-equiv` and `content`
- The `content` attribute contains the actual data.
- The `name` attribute is used to insert data like the `description` (to insert a description), `keywords` (to define a set of keywords), `author` (to add information about the authority) and `copyright` (to define the copyright details).

- The `http-equiv` attribute is used to insert data like `creation-date` (the date of creation), `expires` (the updating date), `from` and `reply-to` (to insert an e-mail address to communicate with the authority), `content-type` (to describe the file type), `refresh` and `pragma` (to automatically refresh the browser).
- To add a comment into a web, page use the `<!--…-->` element.

Chapter 9

Links

9.1 Links

WWW stands for World Wide Web. The Web was designed to be a globally shared set of resources, stored on different servers, connected to the Internet (the biggest public computer network in the world). A user can access any of these resources and can easily navigate between them using the basic commands generated by the mouse or/and the keyboard.

Links are the elements of a web page that make the navigation between Internet resources possible. A link is a property attached to a block of text or image that makes it able to accept commands from the mouse and/or keyboard.

9.2 Client-server technology

When a link is clicked with the left mouse button (or is active and the user presses the <ENTER> key), the following events occur:

1. The browser identifies the URL of the Internet resource that is called.
2. The browser sends a request to the web server that hosts the required resource.
3. The web server reads the request and identifies the location of the required resource.
4. The web server sends back a response to the client browser, including the required resource.
5. The browser gets the resource and loads it into the browser window.

9.3 The first link

To create a link, use the <a>...</a> element (the anchor element). The <a> element must have an src attribute that identifies the URL (absolute or relative) of the resource. The content of the <a>...</a> element is rendered by the browser as a link and is able to accept commands from the mouse and/or the keyboard.

When the user moves the mouse pointer over a link, the image appears informing the user that the browser is ready to accept the command to download the Internet resource that is attached to that link.

The <TAB> key can be used to navigate between the links on a web page. Only one link will be highlighted (active) at a time. A rectangle is rendered around the active link. The user can then press the <ENTER> key to open that link without using a mouse (see the image below).

Figure 9.1

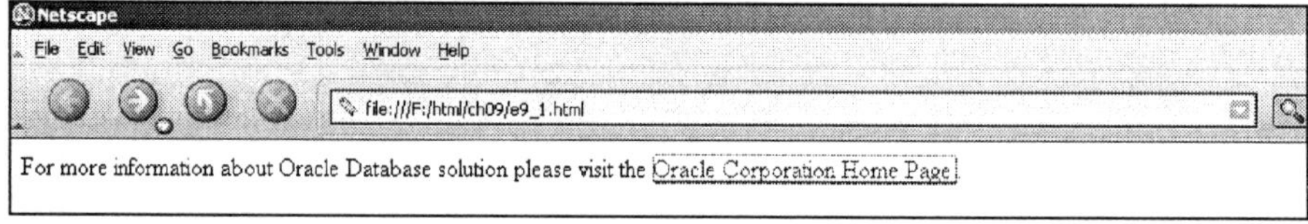

Example 9_1. The first link (file e9_1.html)

```
<html><head></head><body>
For more information about Oracle Database solution please visit the
<a href="http://www.oracle.com"> Oracle Corporation Home Page.</a>
</body></html>
```

Figure 9.2

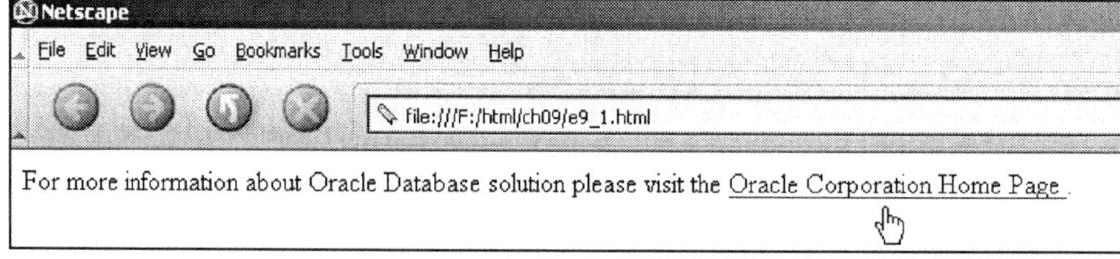

Notes

- By default, the browser will render the links colored and in the underlined style (see Section 9.9 Link Colors, below, to learn how to override these setting).
- The previous example used an absolute URL to define the address of the new resource.

9.4 Using an image to define a link

As mentioned earlier, the content of the <a>...</a> element can be either a block of text or an image. In the next example, an image is used to define a link to a web page.

Example 9_2. Using an image to define a link (file e9_2.html)

```
<html><head></head><body>
For more information about Oracle Database solution please visit the Oracle
Corporation Home Page.
<a href="http://www.oracle.com">
<img src="oracle.gif">
</a>
</body></html>
```

Figure 9.3

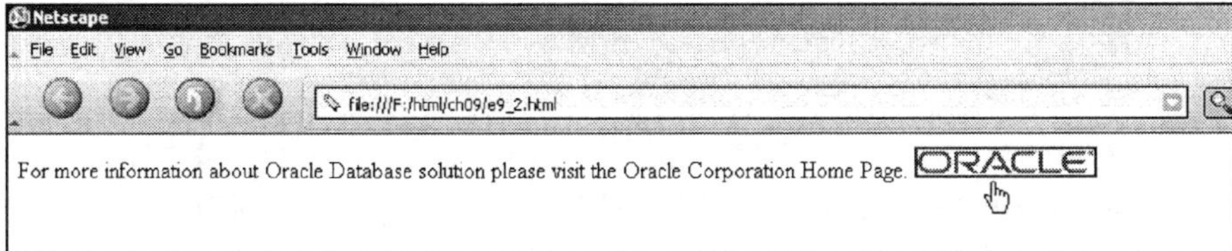

By default, browsers render each image used to define a link with a colored border (see the example above). To eliminate this border, set the border attribute of the <img> element to "0".

Example 9_3. An image link without a border (file e9_3.html)

```
<html><head></head><body>
For more information about Oracle Database solution please visit the Oracle
Corporation Home Page.
<a href="http://www.oracle.com">
<img src="oracle.gif" border="0">
</a>
</body></html>
```

Figure 9.4

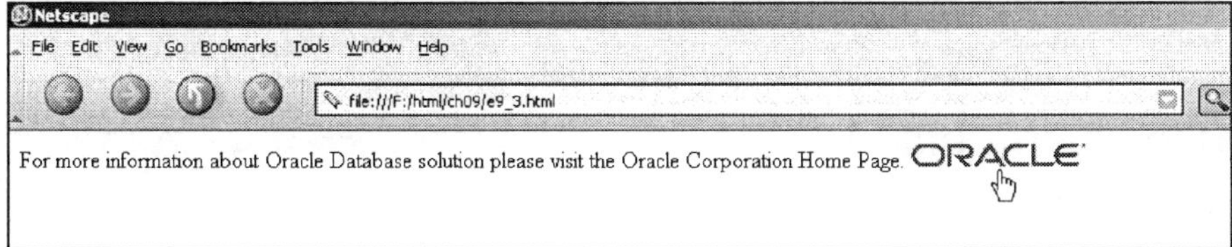

9.5 Links defined by relative URLs

Let's suppose we have the directory structure presented in Figure 9.5. From the page "page11.html" stored in the directory "/projects/project1/html/", access the other pages using a relative reference using the syntax below:

- /page0.html
- ../../../page0.html
- ../../page1.html
- /projects/page1.html
- ../../project2/page2.html
- /projects/project2/page2.html
- ../../project2/html/page21.html
- /projects/project2/html/page21.html
- page12.html
- /projects/project1/html/page12.html
- draft/page.html
- /projects/project1/html/draft/page.html

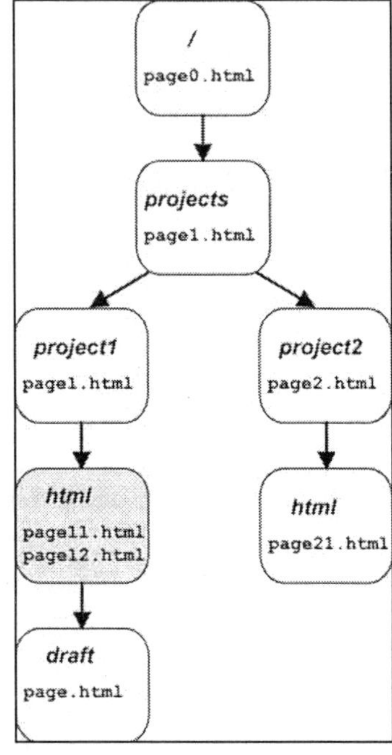

Figure 9.5

Note that

- ../ stands for the parent directory
- / stands for the root directory

Example 9_4. Links between two pages located in the same directory (file page11.html)

```
<html><head></head><body>
<a href="page12.html">
Link to page 12
</a>
</body></html>
```

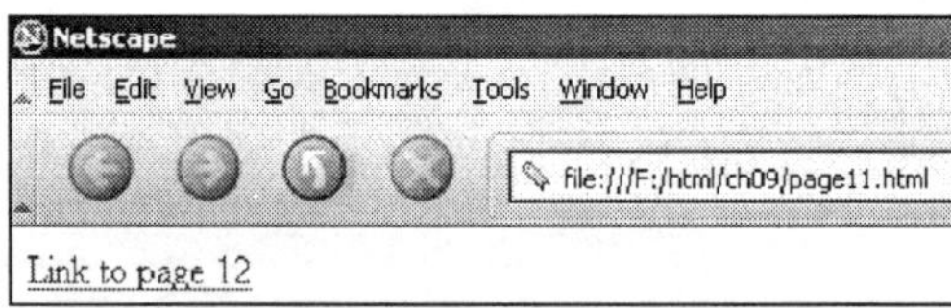

Figure 9.6

(file page12.html)

```
<html><head></head><body>
<a href="page11.html">
Link to page 11
</a>
</body></html>
```

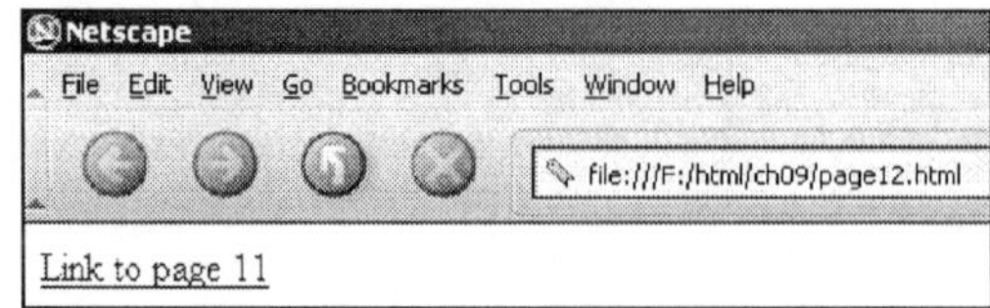

Figure 9.7

9.6 Linking to a web page located on the local system

In the case of an application that runs locally (i.e. not on the Internet), a link can be defined to a local HTML file. To do this, use the `href` attribute as in the following example:

```
href="file:///c:/test/page.html"
```

where:

- `file:///` is the protocol to access the local system
- `c:/test/` is the path to the directory where is located the resource
- `page.html` is the name of the resource

Example 9_5. A link to a local system file (file e9_5.html)

```
<html>
<head>
</head>
<body>
<a href="file:///c:/test/page.html">
This is a link to a local system file
</a>
</body>
</html>
```

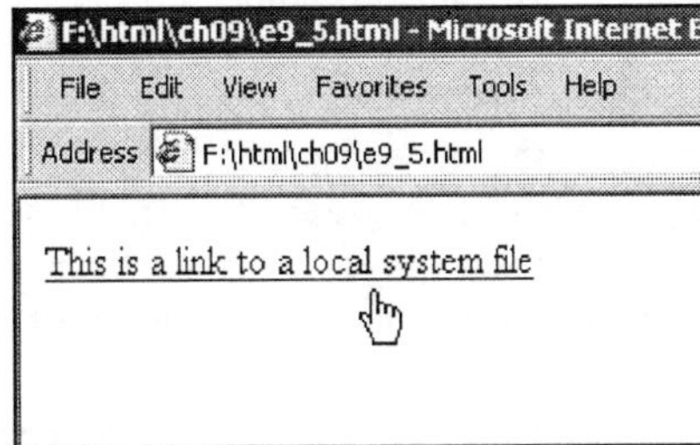

Figure 9.8

Note

- ◆ When the user moves the mouse pointer over a link, the content of the `href` attribute appears in the status bar of the browser window (see `file:///c:/test/page.html` in the previous example).

9.7 Anchors

Anchor can be used to navigate to different sections of a page that is too long to be displayed on a single computer screen or to navigate to a specific section of another web page. The anchor is an identifier for the beginning of an element that belongs to the web page. After you define the anchor (identifier), you can create links to that anchor.

There are two ways to define an anchor:

- Using the `<a>...</a>` element together with the name attribute. The content of the `<a>` element can be empty or not.
  Example: `<a name="name_value">any text</a>`

- Using any HTML element together with the universal attribute `id`. Example: `<p id="id_value">`

To link to an anchor defined on the a web page, use the `<a>...</a>` element together with the `href` attribute set to an *anchor reference* as either:

- `#name_value`
- `#id_value`

Example 9_6. Anchors (file e9_6.html)

```
<html><head></head><body>
<a href="#p1" id="p0">link to paragraph 1</a><br>
<a href="#p2">link to paragraph 2</a><br>
<a href="#p3">link to paragraph 3</a>
<p id="p1">paragraph 1. line 1.<br>paragraph 1. line 2.<br>paragraph 1. line
3.<br>paragraph 1. line 4.<br>paragraph 1. line 5.
<p><a name="p2">paragraph 2.</a> line 1.<br>paragraph 2. line 2.<br>paragraph 2.
line 3.<br>paragraph 2. line 4.<br>paragraph 2. line 5.
<p id="p3">paragraph 3. line 1.<br>paragraph 3. line 2.<br>paragraph 3. line
3.<br>paragraph 3. line 4.<br>paragraph 3. line 4.
<br><a href="#p0">up to the list of links</a>
</body></html>
```

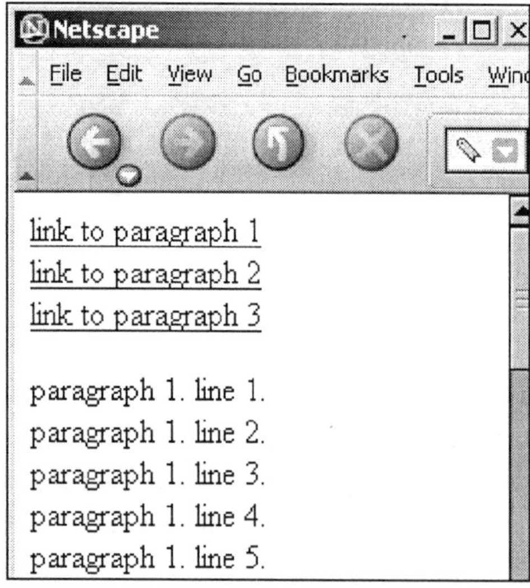

Figure 9.9

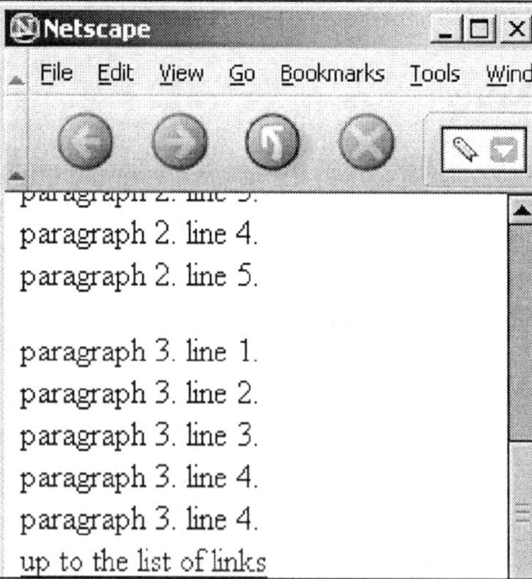

Figure 9.10

To define a link to an anchor defined on another web page, add the *anchor reference* to the end of the URL of that page (e.g. `<a href="e9_6.html#p3">Any text</a>`).

Example 9_7. Referencing anchors defined in an external file (file e9_7.html)

```
<html>
<head>
</head>
<body>
<a href="e9_6.html#p3">
This is a link to an anchor defined in
an external file
</a>
</body>
</html>
```

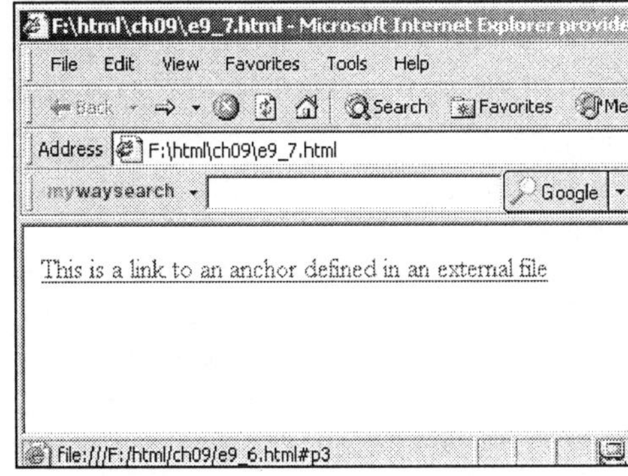

Figure 9.11

9.8 Target Windows

When the user activates a link, by default the browser replaces the page containing that link with the new page pointed to by the link. To change this behavior, attach a new attribute named `target` to the `<a>` element. This attribute defines the *name* of the window in which the new page will be loaded. If no window with that name exists, a new window will be created. The possible values are:

- Any double-quoted string that defines a name for a new window
- The following constant values (more about them in the Chapter 13 Frames):
  - `_self` (the default value)
  - `_blank`
  - `_parent`
  - `_top`

Example 9_8. Loading a new page into a new window (file e9_8.html)

```
<html>
<head></head>
<body>
<a href="page11.html" target="nw">
This link opens page 11 into a window
named "nw".
</a>
</body></html>
```

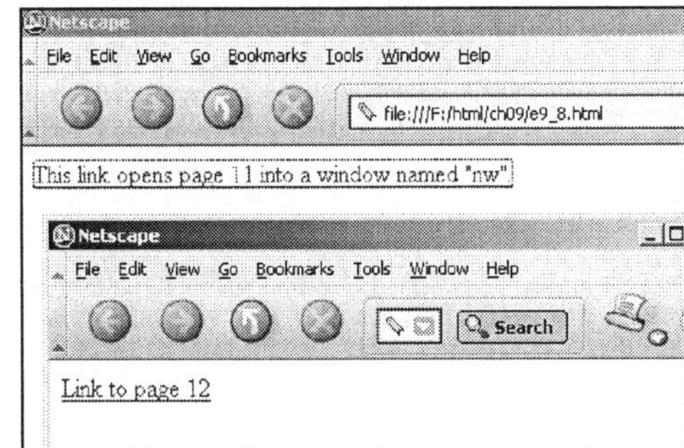

Figure 9.12

It is possible for many links to load their target pages into the same named window if the target attribute of each link is set to the same value.

Example 9_9. Links sharing a target (file e9_9.html)

```
<html>
<head></head>
<body>
<a href="page11.html" target="nw">
Load 11 into "nw" window.</a><br>
<a href="page12.html" target="nw">
Load 12 into "nw" window.</a><br>
<a href="page11.html">
Load 12 into the same window.</a>
</body></html>
```

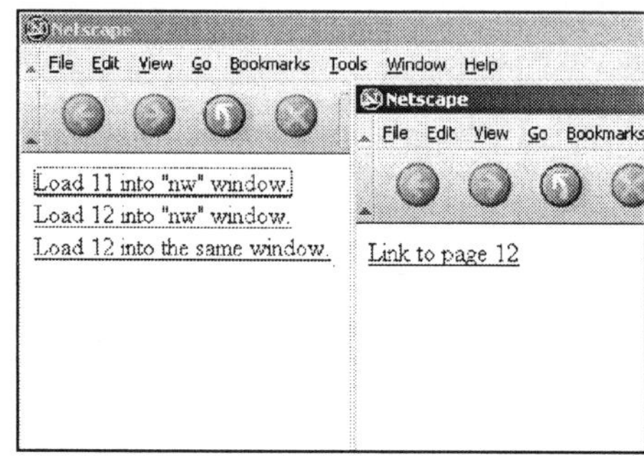

Figure 9.13

9.9 Link colors

There are three *states of a link*. Each state has a particular color associated with it by default. These default values can be overridden by setting specific attributes of the `<body>...<body>` element. These states of a link are:

- The active state. The properties of this state are:
  - Only one link on a page can be active at a time.
  - The active link is rendered with a rectangle around it.
  - The default color is `"#ff0000"`(red).
  - To override the default value, use the `alink` attribute.
- The non-visited state. The properties of this state are:
  - The default color is `"#0000ff#` (blue).
  - To override the default value, use the `link` attribute.
- The visited state. The properties of this state are:
  - The default value is `"#551ab8"` (Netscape Navigator) or `"#800080"` (Internet Explorer).
  - To override the default value, use the `vlink` attribute.
  - The visited state of a web page is permanently recorded by a browser and is maintained over multiple sessions.

Example 9_10. Custom-made colors for links (file e9_10.html)

```
<html>
<head></head>
<body link="#ff00ff" alink="orange"
vlink="00ffff">
<a href="page_1.html">
page 11</a><br>
<a href="page_2.html">
page 12</a><br>
<a href="page_3.html">
page 13</a><br>
</body></html>
```

Figure 9.14

9.10 Links to other kinds of files

You can define links to any kind of files, not only to HTML files. What happens after a user clicks on the link (or presses the <ENTER> key if the link is active) depends on the capabilities of the browser. There are two possibilities

Case 1: If the browser can handle that type of file (using a helper application or a plug-in), it correctly renders the file in the browser window (this happens, for example, with images, text, PDF files, and other similar files).

Example 9_11. Links to regular files (file e9_11.html)

```
<html><head></head><body>
<a href="f1.txt" target="one">text file</a><br>
<a href="f2.jpg" target="two">image file</a><br>
<a href="f3.pdf" target="three">PDF file</a>
</body></html>
```

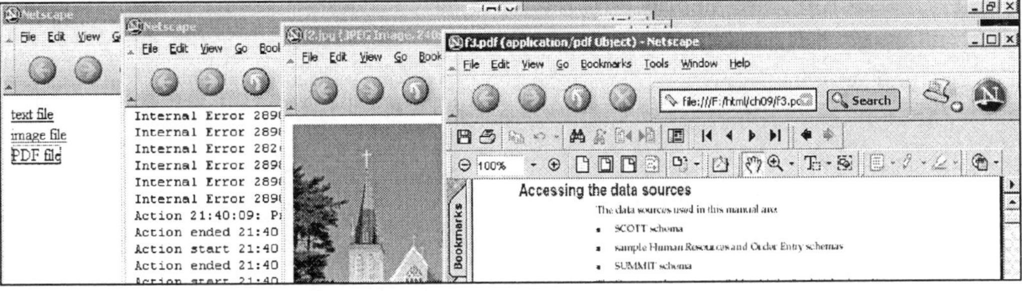

Figure 9.15

Case 2: If the browser cannot handle the new type of file, it will try to download the file to the client system (a File Download Window will appear, as shown in Figure 9.16).

Example 9_12. Downloading files (file e9_12.html)

```
<html>
<head></head>
<body>
<a href=" http://download.microsoft.
com/download/win2000platform/SP/
SP3Express/NT5/EN-US/sp3express.exe">
Windows 2000 Professional, Service
Pack 3, Download
</a>
</body></html>
```

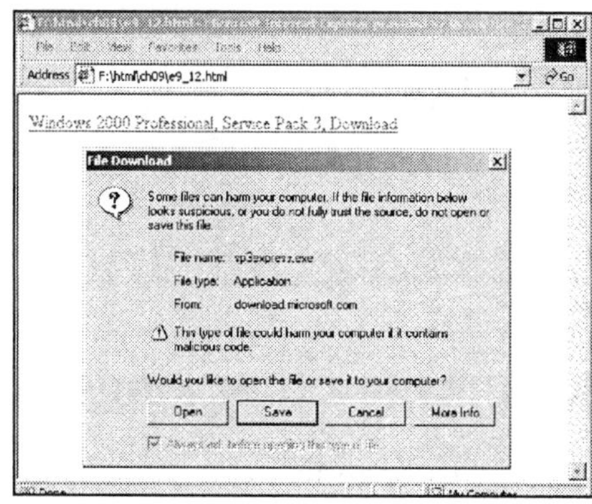

Figure 9.16

9.11 Links to ftp web sites

It is possible to define a link not only to a specific file but also to a specific directory located on a server connected to the Internet. What happens in this case depends on the server's settings:

- If the link contains the http protocol, the server will try to return a default document (e.g. `default.htm` for an IIS Server, or `index.html` for an Apache Sever).
- If a default document doesn't exist or the server is not configured to return it, the server can be configured to return the directory structure for that Internet directory (see Figure 9.18 for Microsoft Internet Information Server).

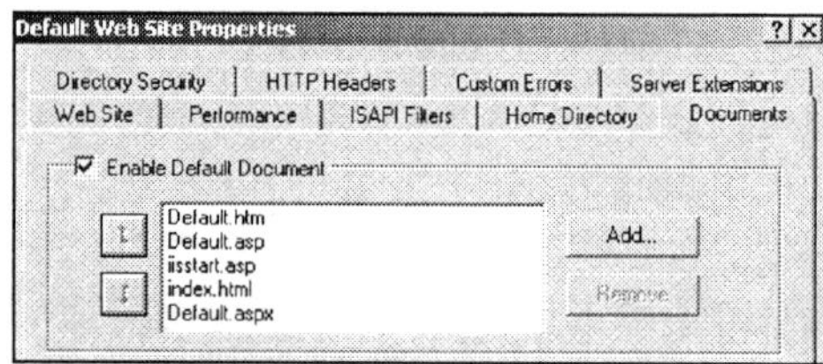

Figure 9.17

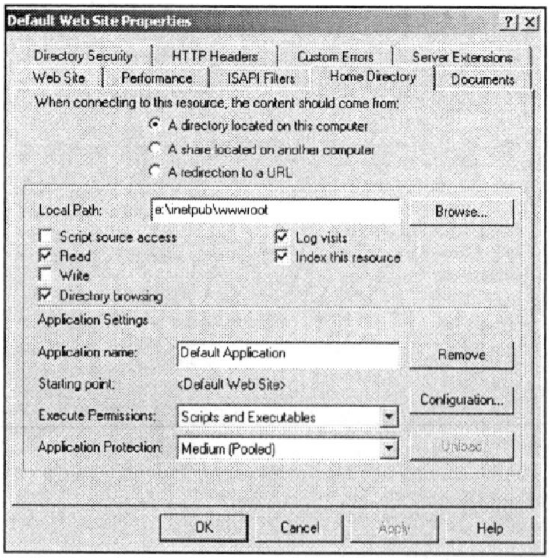

Figure 9.18

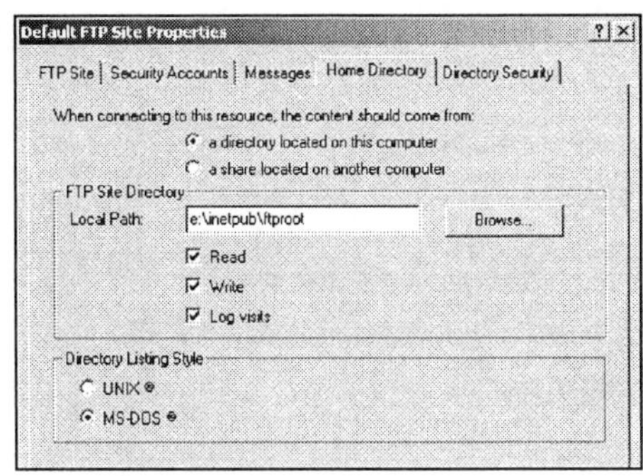

Figure 9.19

- If the link contains an ftp protocol, the server will return a directory structure for that Internet directory (if permitted by the server's security settings). Then, the user can execute operations (read, write to and delete files and directories), depending on the level of access granted by the server. The server may be configured to require a user name and password or employ other security measures (see Figure 9.19 for Microsoft IIS).

To create a link to an ftp server, use an <a> element with the `href` attribute set for `ftp` protocol instead of `http` protocol (e.g. `href="ftp://ftp.arsc.edu/"`).

Example 9_13. Links to FTP servers (file e9_13.html)

```
<html>
<head></head>
<body>
<a href="ftp://ftp.arsc.edu/"
</a>
</body></html>
```

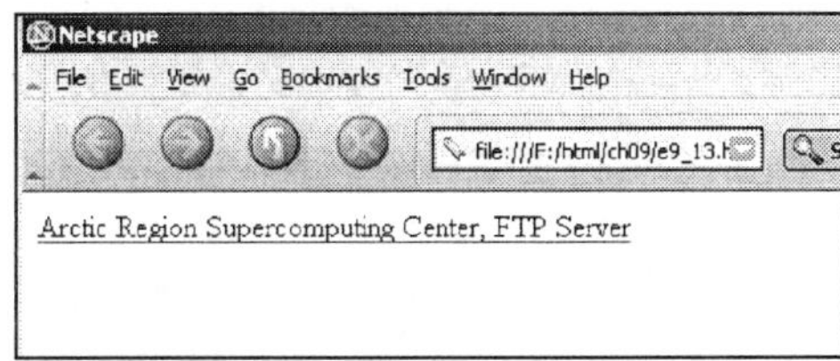

Figure 9.20

Figure 9.21

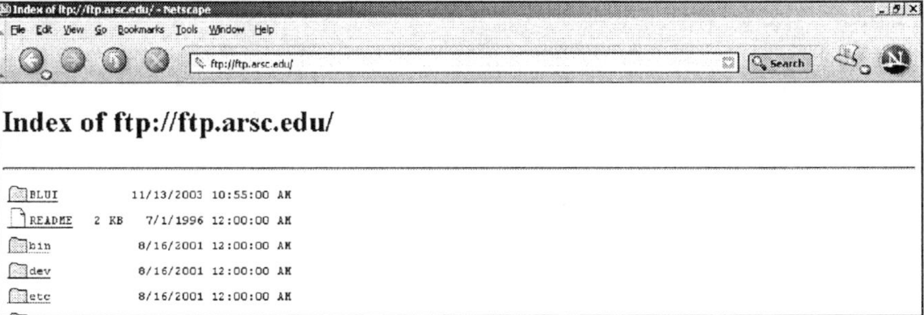

9.12 Links to e-mail addresses

To create a link to an e-mail address, use an <a> element with the `href` attribute set for the `mailto` protocol (the Internet mail protocol) and pointing to a valid email address (e.g. `href="mailto:theo@yahoo.com"`).

Example 9_14. Links to e-mail addresses (file e9_14.html)

```
<html>
<head></head>
<body>
<a href="mailto:theo@yahoo.com">
Send an e-mail to us!</a>
</body></html>
```

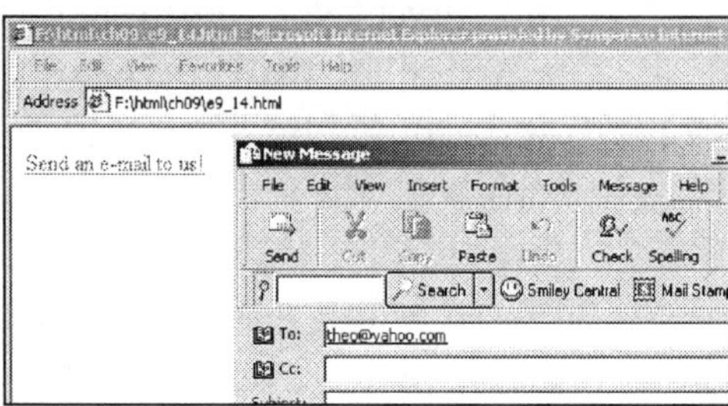

Figure 9.22

Note

- When a user clicks on an e-mail link, a client e-mail application will be opened (e.g. Microsoft Outlook Express) that allows the user to compose and send a message to the e-mail address pointed to by the link.

9.13 The `title` attribute of the <a> element

The `title` attribute is a universal attribute and can be attached to any HTML element. When the user places the mouse pointer over the element, a *tooltip* will appear, rendering the content of the `title` attribute.

Example 9_15. The title attribute of the <a> element (file e9_15.html)

```
<html><head></head><body>
<a href="page1.html"
title="this is a tooltip">
Link to page 1</a>
</body></html>
```

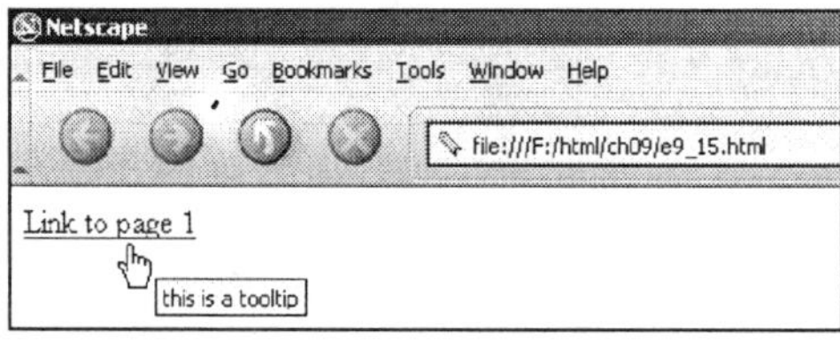

Figure 9.23

9.14 The <base> element

The `<base>` element allows you to set a prefix that will automatically be attached to the URL indicated by any link on that page, allowing you to avoid repetitive code if all links on a page point to the same server.

Notes

- The <base> element is an empty element (i.e. it doesn't require an ending tag).
- The <base> element requires an `href` attribute set to the absolute URL of an Internet directory (e.g. `href="http://www.itdgroup.com/projects/project1/"`).
- The <base> element must be placed inside the <head>...</head> element.

The following example refers to the hypothetical directory structure presented in Section 9.5 *Links defined by relative URLs* (Figure 9.5). The file `e9_16.html` can be placed anywhere under the Root Directory "/" of the web site.

Example 9_16. The <base> element (file e9_16.html)

```
<html><head>
<base href="http://www.itdgroup.com/projects/
project1/">
</head><body>
<a href="page1.html">page 1</a><br>
<a href="html/page11.html">page 11</a><br>
<a href="html/draft/page.html">page</a><br>
<a href="../project2/page2.html">page 2</a>
</body>
</html>
```

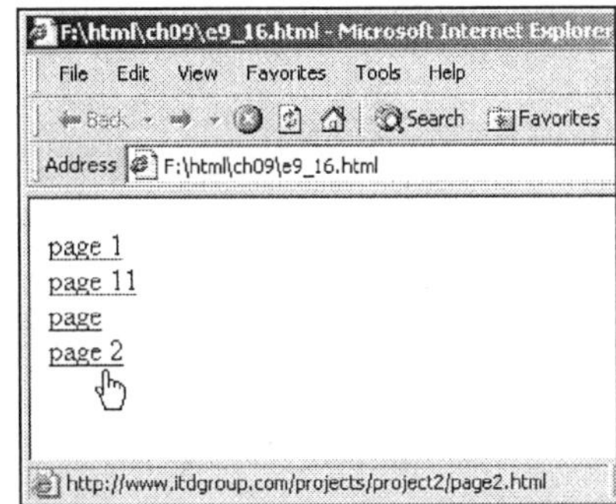

Figure 9.24

Note

- When using the <base> element in a web page, the actual URL of a link is a concatenation of the value of the `href` attribute from <base> element and the value of the `href` attribute of the <a> element. The actual URL is shown in the status bar of the window (see Figure 9.24).

9.15 Review of Chapter 9

At the end of Chapter 9 you should know:

- Links are used to navigate between Internet resources.
- A link can be inserted using the <a> element.
- The Internet resource pointed to by the link is specified by the `href` attribute of the <a> element.
- Links are defined using relative or absolute URLs.
- To define a link using an image, insert the <img> element inside of the <a> element.

- To define a link to a local system resource, use the `file:///` protocol.
- To define a link to a FTP site, use the `ftp://` protocol.
- To define a link to an e-mail address, use the `mailto:` protocol.
- To navigate inside of a web page, use the `<a>` element in conjunction with the `name` attribute.
- To define the window where the new resource pointed to by a link will be loaded, attach the `target` attribute to the `<a>` element.
- To customize the link color, use the `link`, `alink`, and `vlink` attributes of the `<body>` element.
- To define a prefix for the `href` attributes of a web page, insert the `<base>` element, in conjunction with the `href` attribute, into the `<head>` element.

Chapter 10

Multimedia

10.1 Multimedia

One of the most appealing concepts related to computers today is Multimedia. Multimedia refers to data and applications in any format or media. This chapter presents how the browser deals with multimedia files.

10.2 Applications files

Applications are stored as files and are executed by the computer's operating system. Generally, the extension for these files is `.exe`, and each application is designed for a specific use.

Some applications are professional applications (e.g. text editors, sound editors, image editors) and some applications are small and dedicated to a very specific task (e.g. readers, viewers, and players).

Some applications are independent and some are used to help other applications (e.g. plug-ins, ActiveX Controls, DLL).

To see if a file is an application (in the Windows operating system), right click on the file icon and chose Properties from the pop-up menu. If that file is an application, the `Type of file` will be Application (see Figure 10.1).

Figure 10.1

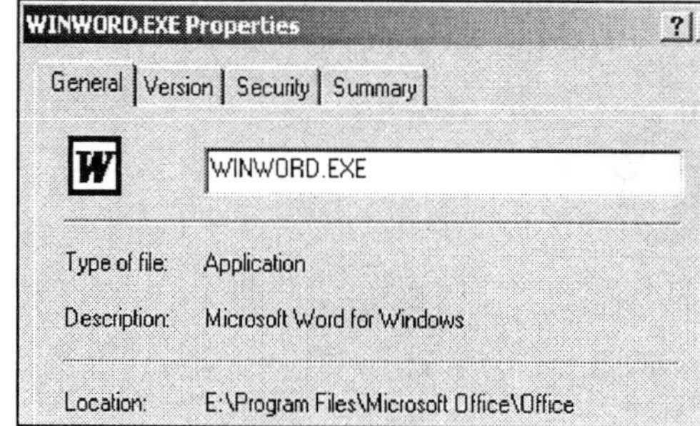

10.3 Data files

Data is stored in files. To read, edit, save, preview, or print this data you need an appropriate application, so data files are related to and dependant upon their specific applications. Generally, the data file's extension gives you an idea about what kind of data is stored in that file and what applications you can use to read, edit, save, preview, or print the data.

The operating system allows you to attach a default link between a data file extension and an application.

To see which applications you can use to open a data file (in the Windows operating system), right click on the file icon and chose Properties from the pop-up menu. The `Open with:` label indicates the default application (e.g. Notepad as illustrated in Figure 10.2). The user can change this default behavior using the `Change...` button.

Figure 10.2

10.4 MIME

MIME stands for Multipart Internet Mail Extensions. MIME map data files' extensions to file types and subtypes. The following table lists some useful examples (see `ftp://ftp.isi.edu/in-notes/iana/assignments/media-types/` for a more complete list).

DESCRIPTION	FILE EXTENSION	MIME TYPE/SUBTYPE
HTML text	html, htm	text/html
Plain text	txt	text/plain
CSS files	css	text/css
GIF images	gif	image/gif
JPEG files	jpg, jpeg, ipe	image/jpeg
PNG files	png	image/x-png
TIFF files	tiff, tif	image/tiff
Microsoft Bitmap files	bmp	image/x-ms-bmp
Basic audio files	au, snd	audio/basic
Microsoft Video files	avi	video/x-msvideo
Macintosh audio format	aif, aiff, aifc	audio/x-aiff
Microsoft audio format	wav	audio/x-wav
MPEG audio	mpa, mpega	audio/x-mpeg
MPEG-1 audio	mp2a, mpa2	audio/x-mpeg-2
Real audio	ra, ram	application/x-pn-realaudio
MIDI	mmid	x-music/x-midi
MPEG video	mpeg, mpg, mpe	video/mpeg
MPEG-2 video	mpv2, mp2v	video/mpeg-2
Macintosh QuickTime	qt, mov	video/quicktime
Microsoft video	avi	video/x-msvideo
Microsoft Rich Text	rtf	application/rtf
Adobe Acrobat PDF	pdf	application/pdf
Microsoft Word files	doc	application/msword
Microsoft Excel	xls	application/ms-excel
Microsoft Power Point	ppz	application/mspowerpoint
Microsoft Power Point	ppt	application/vnd.ms-powerpoint
VRML files	wrl, vrml	x-world/x-vrml

10.5 Helper Applications

MIME types and file extensions are important when you add multimedia files to your web page. They make it possible for the browser to identify a helper application to handle the data file you refer to on the web page.

These two examples show how you can define a connection between a file extension (e.g. gug) and/or a MIME type and a helper application (e.g. Notepad) that can access it.

Case 1: Internet Explorer 6 on Windows 2000 Professional. Follow these steps:

1. Open Explorer.
2. Choose Tools, Folder Options...
3. Click on File Types and then on the New button.
4. In the File Extension box, type gug and click on the OK button.
5. Select the file extension gug from the list, and then click on the Change... button.
6. Select Notepad, and then click on the OK button.
7. Finally, click on the Close button.

Figure 10.3

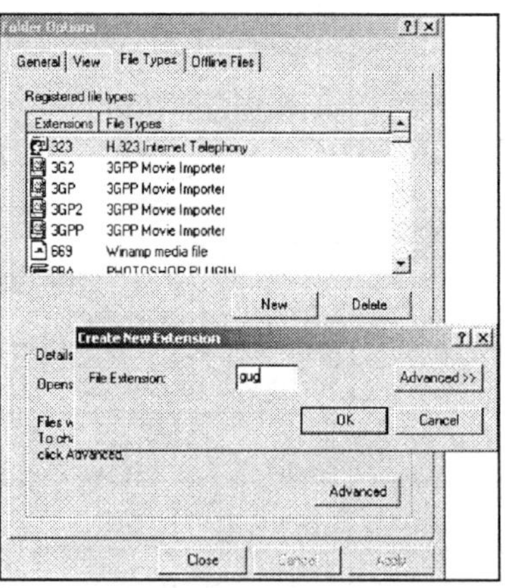

Figure 10.4

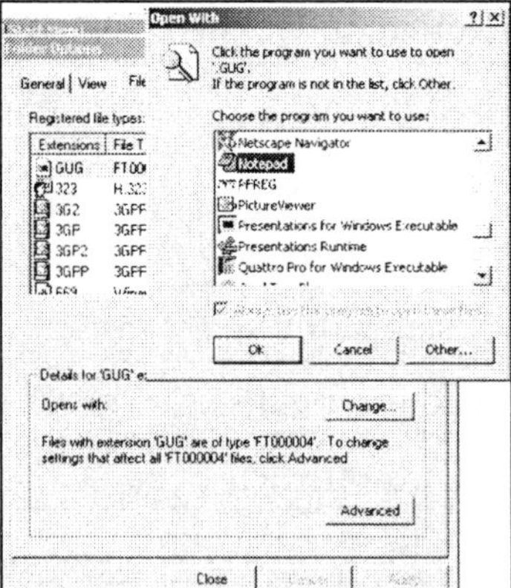

To test if the association works, open Notepad, edit a text file, and save the file with extension `.gug`. Next, open the text file with the extension `.gug` in Internet Explorer. If you can see the content of the file, the test was successful, and Internet Explorer will handle this kind of file properly.

Case 2: Netscape Navigator 7. Follow these steps:

1. Open Netscape Navigator.
2. Choose Edit, Preferences.
3. Select Helper Applications, then click on the New Type… button.
4. Fill the text fields as illustrated below.
5. Click on the `Choose...` button and find Notepad.exe.
6. Click on the OK button.

Figure 10.5

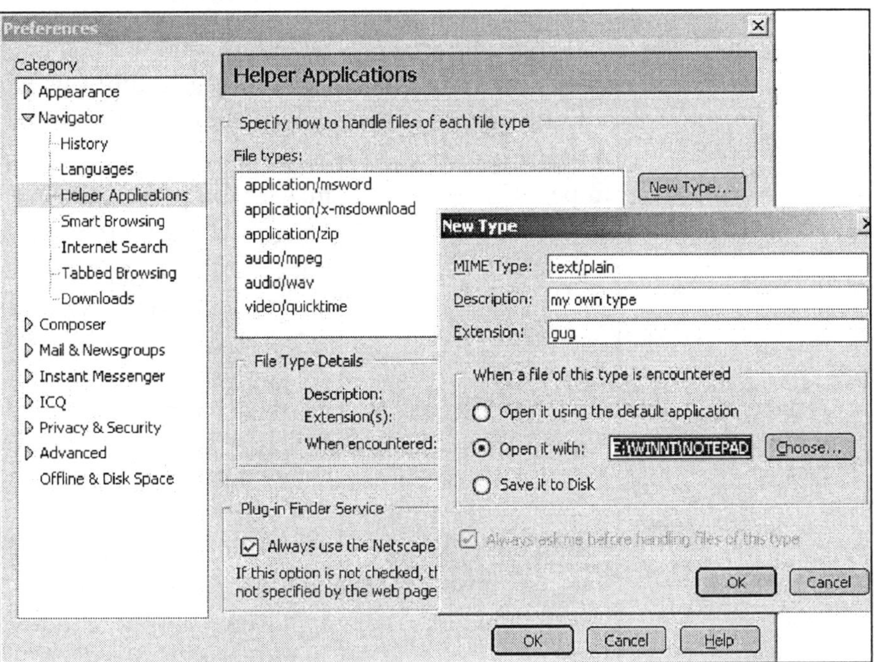

To test if the association works, open Notepad, edit a text file, and save the file with the extension `.gug`. Next, open the text file with the extension `.gug` in Netscape Navigator. If you can see the content of the file, the test was successful, and Netscape Navigator will handle this kind of file properly.

10.6 Plug-ins

Plug-ins are small applications that help browsers correctly render data files inside the browser window. Each is created to handle a very specific range of file extensions and/or MIME types. Generally, these applications are free to download and install.

The following table lists some useful plug-ins:

PLUG-IN NAME	SUPPORTED FILE EXTENSIONS	SUPPORTED MIME TYPES
Windows Media Player	.asf, .asx, .wma, .wax, .wmv, .wvx	application/x-mplayer2, application/asx, video/x-ms-asf-plugin, video/x-ms-asf, video/x-ms-wm, audio/x-ms-wma, audio/x-ms-wax, video/x-ms-wmv, video/x-ms-wvx
Apple QuickTime	.aiff, .au, .mpeg, .wav, .aif, .mid, .png, .tif, .tiff, .bmp, .ptng, .png, .targa, .avi, .flc, .mpe	audio/aiff, audio/basic, audio/midi, audio/mpeg, audio/wav, audio/x-aiff, audio/x-midi, audio/x-mpeg, audio/x-wav, image/png, image/tif, image/x-bmp, image/x-macpaint, image/x-photoshop, image/x-png, image/x-sgi, image/x-targa, image/x-tiff, video/avi, video/flc, video/mpeg, video/quicktime, video/x-mpeg, video/x-msvideo
Winamp MP3 Player	.mp3, .mp2, .mp1, .wma, .voc, .wav, .cda, .it, .xm, .s3m, .stm, .mod, .dsm, .far, .ult, .mtm, .669, .mid, .m3u, .pls, .mjf	audio/mid, application/x-msdownload, audio/mpeg, audio/mpg, audio/mp3, audio/x-mpg, application/x-winamp-plugin, interface/x-winamp-skin, application/x-mpeg, audio/x-mp3, audio/x-scpls, audio/x-mpegurl, audio/mpegurl, audio/scpls, audio/x-vnd.AudioExplosion.Mjuide Media
Flash Player	.spl, .swf	application/futuresplash, application/x-shockwave-flash
Shockwave	.aam, .dir, .dxr, .dcr	application/x-director
Adobe Acrobat	.pdf	application/pdf

10.7 Links to external multimedia files

The simplest way to add multimedia files to a web page is to insert links using the <a>...</a> element. The `href` attribute is set to the URL of the multimedia file you want to attach. When a user clicks on the link, one of the following four cases will apply:

1. The browser can handle the file by itself, and renders it correctly in the browser window (e.g. HTML, GIF, JPG, and PNG files).
2. The browser can handle the file using a plug-in, and renders it correctly in the browser window (e.g. text files, PDF files, some images, sounds, and movies).
3. The browser cannot handle the file but has access to a helper application that can handle it. In this case, the browser opens the helper applications and the file is loaded in that application (e.g. Word, Excel, and PowerPoint documents; some images, sounds, and movies).
4. The browser cannot identify a helper application and asks the user to download the file to the local file system.

Example 10_1. Links to external multimedia files (file e10_1.html)

```
<html><head></head><body>
<a href="f1.html" target="w1">Link to a .html file</a><br>
<a href="f2.txt" target="w2">Link to a .txt file</a><br>
<a href="f3.gug" target="w3">Link to a .gug file</a><br>
<a href="f4.rtf" target="w4">Link to a .rtf file </a><br>
<a href="f5.pdf" target="w5">Link to a .pdf file</a><br>
<a href="f6.swf" target="w6">Link to a .swf file</a><br>
<a href="f7.doc" target="w7">Link to a .doc file </a><br>
<a href="f8.xls" target="w8">Link to a .xls file </a><br>
<a href="f9.au" target="w9">Link to a .au file </a><br>
<a href="f10.wav" target="w10">Link to a .wav file </a><br>
<a href="f11.mp3" target="w11">Link to a .mp3 file </a><br>
<a href="f12.avi" target="w12">Link to a .avi file </a><br>
<a href="f13.mov" target="w13">Link to a .mov file </a><br>
<a href="f14.ra" target="w14">Link to a .ra file </a><br>
</body></html>
```

Here is how Internet Explorer 6 rendered the resources pointed to by the links on the above web page:

Figure 10.6

Notes

- Some files are handled directly by the browser (`.html`, `.txt`, `.gug`).
- Some files are handled by plug-ins (`.pdf`, `.swf`).
- Some files are handled by helper applications (`.rtf`, `.doc`, `.xls`, some audio and video files). Some helper applications are so powerful they allow the user to edit and save those changes to the files (e.g. `.rtf`, `.doc`, `.xls`).
- In order for this example to work properly, you must make the proper associations between each file extension and either Windows (if you are using Internet Explorer) or Netscape Navigator. You must also have all the plug-ins and/or helper applications installed on your computer.

10.8 Embedding multimedia files with the `<embed>` element

The designer of a web page can insert multimedia content directly into the browser window using the `<embed>...</embed>` element. This element was initially proposed by the Netscape community and was also implemented by Internet Explorer. Despite this, the `<embed>` element is not accepted by the W3 Consortium. Instead, the W3 Consortium recommends the `<object>` element (see Section 10.9).

Several attributes can be used with the <embed> element:

- src determines the multimedia file that should be rendered internally by the browser. Possible values are *valid URLs*.
- type determines the MIME type associated with the multimedia file. The possible values are valid *MIME type/subtype* expressions. It is not necessary to include this attribute because the browser will use the multimedia file's extension to determine what type of file it is.
- width and height define the width and height of the space the browser will allocate to the multimedia file. The possible values are:
  - *positive integers* (representing the dimensions in pixels)
  - *percentages* (representing the dimensions as a percentage of the parent frame)
- align defines the alignment used to render the content of the multimedia file relative to the other elements rendered on the page. The possible values vary from browser to browser but generally are : "left", "center", and "right".
- hidden defines whether or not controls will be shown on the web page. The possible values are "true" and "false".

Example 10_2. The <embed> element (file e10_2.html)

```
<html><head></head><body>
<table cellspacing=30>
<tr><td><embed src="f1.tif" width=100 height=100></embed><br>type="image/tiff"
<td><embed src="f2.png" width=100 height=100></embed><br>type="image/x-png"
<td><embed src="f6.swf" width=100 height=100></embed><br>
type="application/futuresplash"
<tr><td><embed src="f5.pdf" width=300 height=300></embed><br>
type="application/pdf"
<td><embed src="f12.avi" width=300 height=300></embed><br>type="video/x-msvideo"
<td><embed src="f13.mov" width=300 height=300></embed><br>type="video/quicktime"
<tr><td><embed src="f9.au" width=200 height=50></embed><br>type="audio/basic"
<td><embed src="f10.wav" width=200 height=50></embed><br>type="audio/x-wav"
<td><embed src="f11.mp3" width=200 height=50></embed><br>type="audio/mp3"
<td><embed src="f14.ra" width=200
height=50></embed><br>type="application/x-pn-realaudio"
</table>
</body></html>
```

Here is how Internet Explorer 6 rendered the above code. Embedded elements may be rendered differently depending on the browser and plug-ins installed.

Figure 10.7

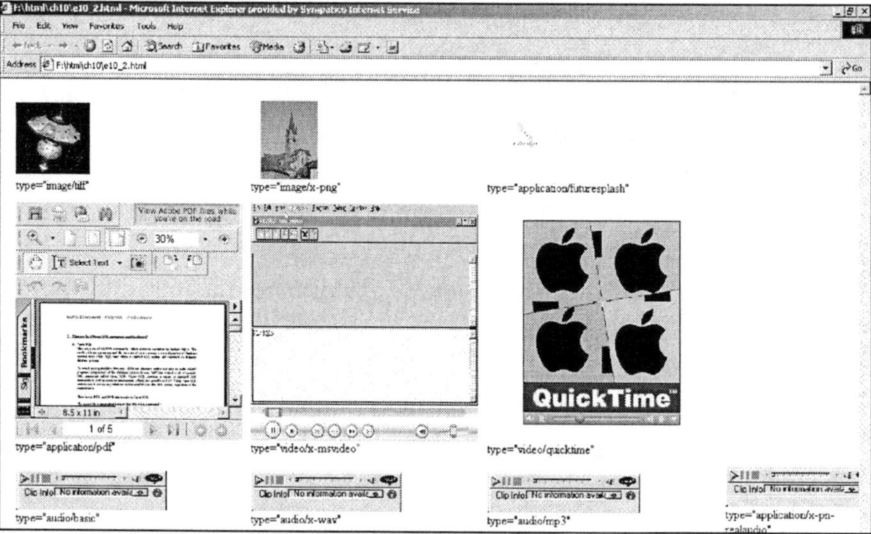

10.9 Embedding multimedia files with the `<object>` element

The designer of a web page can insert multimedia content directly into the browser window using the `<object>`...`</object>` element. The W3 Consortium recommends using this element, and both Internet Explorer and Netscape Navigator implement it.

Several attributes can be used with the `<object>` element:

- `data` determines the multimedia file that should be rendered internally by the browser. Possible values are *valid URLs*.
- `type` determines the MIME type associated with the multimedia file. The possible values are valid *MIME type/subtype* expressions. This attribute is required.
- `classid` is used by Internet Explorer to identify the ActiveX control that will be used to render the object. The possible values depend on the developer of the control. All `classid` values can be found in the Registry Editor (e.g. `"CFCDAA03-8BE4-11cf-B84B-0020AFBBCCFA"`).
- `width` and `height` define the width and height of the space the browser will allocate to the multimedia file. The possible values are:
  - *positive integers* (representing the dimensions in pixels)
  - *percentages* (representing the dimensions as a percentage of the parent frame)

- `align` defines the alignment used to render the content of the multimedia file relative to the other elements rendered on the page. The possible values vary from browser to browser but generally are: `"left"`, `"center"`, `"right"`, `"top"`, and `"bottom"`
- `hspace` and `vspace` define the white space around the object. The possible values are *positive integers* (representing the dimensions in pixels).
- `border` defines the *thickness* of the border around the object. The possible values are *positive integers* (representing the thickness in pixels).

Example 10_3. The `<object>` element (file e10_3.html)

```
<html><head></head><body>
<table cellspacing=20>
<tr><td><object data="f1.tif" width=100 height=100></object><br>TIF
<td><object data="f3.gif" width=100></object><br>GIF
<td><object data="f3.bmp" width=100></object><br>BMP
<td><object data="f1.jpg" width=100></object><br>JPG
<tr><td><object data="f2.txt" width=300 height=200></object><br>TXT
<td><object data="f3.html" width=300 height=200></object><br>HTML
<td><object data="f5.pdf" width=300 height=200></object><br>PDF
<tr><td><object data="f6.swf" width=300 height=200></object><br>SWF
<td><object data="f13.mov" width=300 height=300></object><br>MOV
<td><object data="f12.avi" width=300 height=300></object><br>AVI
<tr><td><object data="f9.au" width=300 height=50></object><br>AU
<td><object data="f10.wav" width=300 height=50></object><br>WAV
<td><object data="f11.mp3" width=300 height=50></object><br>MP3
</table>
</body></html>
```

This is how Netscape Navigator 7.1 rendered the above code. Embedded elements may be rendered differently depending on the browser and plug-ins installed.

Figure 10.8

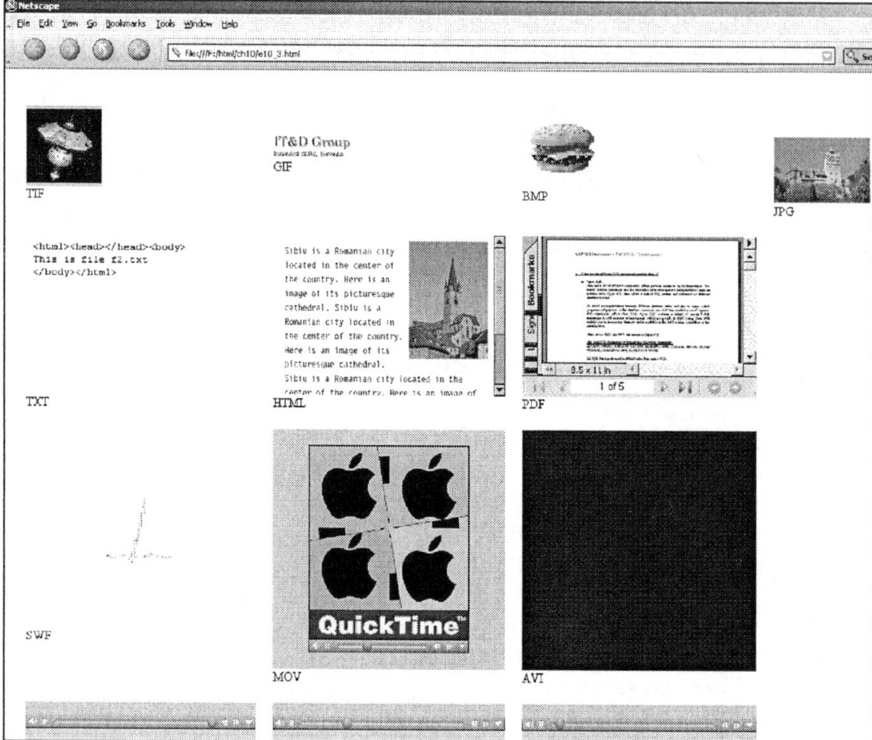

10.10 Embedding applets

HTML allows you to embed applets directly into a web page. To do this, use the `<applet>` element and its attributes:

- `width` - specifies the width of the applet window. The possible values are integers (size in pixels) or percentages (relative to the parent width).
- `height` - specifies the height of the applet window. The possible values are integers (size in pixels) or percentages (relative to the parent width).
- `code` - specifies the URL to the applet class file.
- `archive` - specifies the applet archive. The possible values are comma separated lists of archive files.
- `object` - specifies a serialized applet file.
- `alt` - specifies a short description.
- `align` - specifies a horizontal or vertical alignment.

- hspace - specifies the horizontal distance between the applet and other elements. The possible values are integers representing the horizontal distance in pixels.
- vspace - specifies the vertical distance between the applet and other elements. The possible values are integers representing the vertical distance in pixels.

Note that only the width and height attributes are required.

Example 10_4. The <applet> element (file e10_4.html)

```
<html>
<body>
Java 2 SDK!<br>
The Tic-Tac-Toe Example<br>
<applet code="TicTacToe.class" width="120"
height="120">
</applet>
</body>
</html>
```

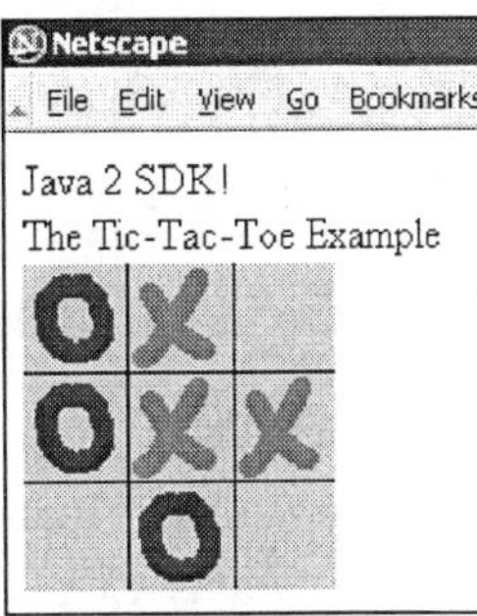

Figure 10.9

10.11 Embedding applets with parameters

If the applet can accept parameters, you can transmit parameters to an applet using the empty <param> element as a child of the <applet>...</applet> element. The <param> element has two useful attributes:

- name - represents the *name* of the parameter. The possible values are valid identifiers.
- value - represents the *value* of the parameter. The possible values are strings of characters.

Example:

```
<applet code="NervousText.class" width="400" height="100">
      <param name="text" value="Hello from Java!">
</applet>
```

The developer of the applet uses a statement similar to:

```
s = getParameter("text");
```

to extract the value of the parameter.

Example 10_5. The <param> element (file e10_5.html)

```
<html>
<body>
Java 2 SDK!<br>
Nervous Text Example<br>
<applet code="NervousText.class" width="400"
height="100">
<param name="text" value="Hello from Java!">
</applet>
</body>
</html>
```

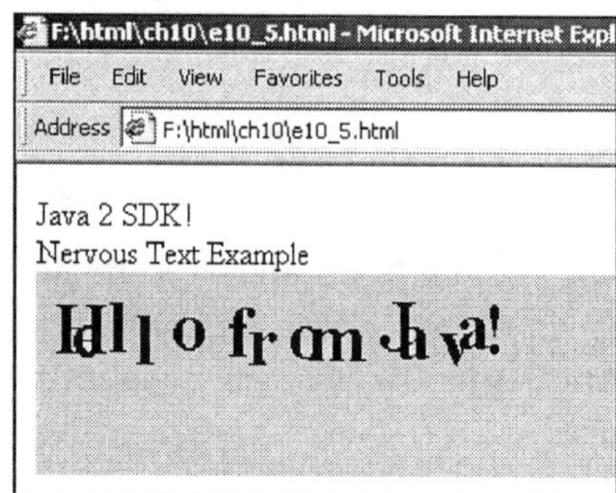

Figure 10.10

10.12 Embedding applets using the <object> element

The HTML 4.01 Specifications consider the <applet> element deprecated in favor of the <object> element. To embed an applet using the <object> element, HTML 4.01 recommends this syntax:

```
<OBJECT codetype="application/java" classid="class_file_name" width="400"
height="100">
<PARAM name="text" value="Hello from Java!">
</OBJECT>
```

Unfortunatley, Netscape doesn't support embedding applets using the <object> element, while Internet Explorer requires this syntax:

```
<OBJECT codetype="application/java" code="class_file_name" width="400"
height="100">
<PARAM name="text" value="Hello from Java!">
</OBJECT>
```

Example 10_6. Embedding an applet with the <object> element (file e10_6.html)

```
<html><body>
Java 2 SDK!<br>
Nervous Text Example<br>
<object codetype="application/java"
code="NervousText.class" width="400" height="100">
<param name="text" value="Hello from Java!">
If your browser doesn't support embedding applets with
&lt;object&gt; element,
```

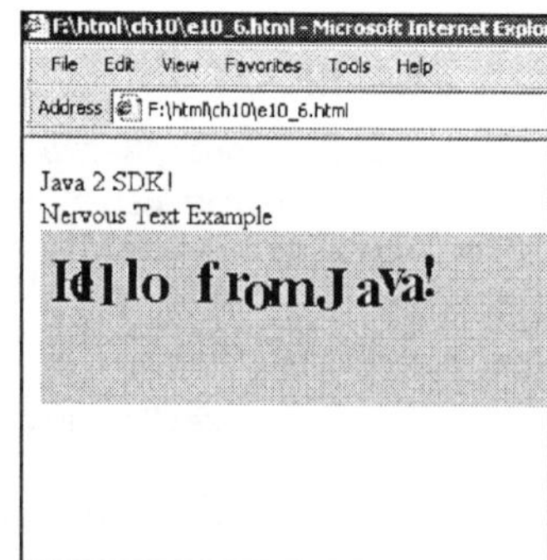

Figure 10.11

```
then this text will appear instead of the applet!
</object>
</body></html>
```

Note that Netscape renders only the content of the <object> element.

Figure 10.12

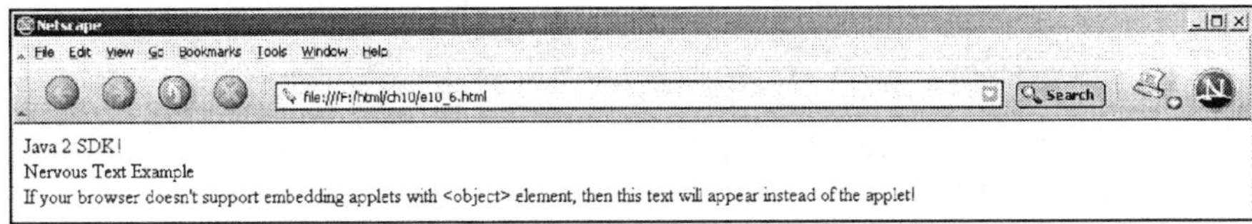

10.13 ActiveX Controls

ActiveX Controls are a Microsoft technology that allows you to include COM objects in other applications (for example, in a web page). Before using an ActiveX Control, you must know its `classid` (from the Registry Editor or from the documentation) and how to set its parameters. The following table presents some ActiveX Controls together with `classids` as you can find them on the most Windows platforms:

DESCRIPTION	CLASSID
button	D7053240-CE69-11CD-A777-00DD01143C57
label	978C9E23-D4B0-11CE-Bf2D-00AA003f40D0
textfield	8BD21D10-EC42-11CE-9E0D-00AA006002f3
graphic	369303C2-D7AC-11d0-89D5-00A0C90833E6
calendar	8E27C92B-1264-101C-8A2F-040224009C02
avi	05589FA1-C356-11CE-BF01-00AA0055595A
excel	0002E510-0000-0000-C000-000000000046

To embed an ActiveX Control, use the syntax:

```
<object id="identifier" width="…" height="…"
classid="clsid:978C9E23-D4B0-11CE-Bf2D-00AA003f40D0">
<param name="param_name" value="param_value">
…
</object><br>
```

Example 10_7. ActiveX Controls (file e10_7.html)

```
<html><body>
ActiveX Controls!<br>
<object id="textfield" width="200" height="30"
classid="clsid:8BD21D10-EC42-11CE-9E0D-00AA006002f3">
```

```
</object>
<object width="200" height="30"
classid="clsid:D7053240-CE69-11CD-A777-00DD01143C57">
<param name="caption" value="This is a button!">
</object>
<object id="label" width="200" height="30"
classid="clsid:978C9E23-D4B0-11CE-Bf2D-00AA003f40D0">
<param name="Caption" value="This is a Label!">
<param name="Size" value="3000;1000">
<param name="FontCharSet" value="0">
<param name="FontPitchAndFamily" value="2">
<param name="FontWeight" value="0">
</object><br>

<object ID = "shapes" style = "background-color: #abcdef; width: 300; height: 300"
classid = "clsid:369303C2-D7AC-11d0-89D5-00A0C90833E6">
<param name = "Line0001" value = "SetLineColor( 0, 0, 0 )">
<param name = "Line0002" value = "SetLineStyle( 1, 1 )">
<param name = "Line0003" value = "SetFillColor( 255, 0, 0 )">
<param name = "Line0004" value = "SetFillStyle( 1 )">
<param name = "Line0005" value = "SetFont( 'TimesRoman', 65, 400, 0, 0, 0 )">
<param name = "Line0006" value = "Text( 'This is Text!', -120, -120 , 45 )">
<param name = "Line0007" value = "SetFillColor(0, 0, 255 )">
<param name = "Line0008" value = "Oval( 50, -100, 50, 100, 0 )">
<param name = "Line0009" value = "Arc( -100, -100, 200, 150, 45, 135, 0 )">
<param name = "Line0010" value = "Pie( -100, 0, 50, 100, 90, 120, 0 )">
<param name = "Line0011" value = "Polygon(4,50,50,100,100,0,100,-100,-100)">
<param name = "Line0012" value = "SetFillColor(0, 255, 0 )">
<param name = "Line0013" value = "Rect( -100, 100, 60, 30, 90 )">
<param name = "Line0014" value = "RoundRect( 200, 100, 35, 60, 10, 10, 25 )">
<param name = "Line0015" value = "SetLineStyle( 2,1 )">
<param name = "Line0016" value = "PolyLine( 3, -100, 100, 100, -100, 0, 100">
</object>

<object ID="Calendar" classid="clsid:8E27C92B-1264-101C-8A2F-040224009C02">
<param name="day" value="1">
</object>
<object id="m1" classid="clsid:05589FA1-C356-11CE-BF01-00AA0055595A" width="200"
height="200">
<param name="ShowDisplay" value="0" />
<param name="ShowControls" value="0" />
<param name="AutoStart" value="1" />
<param name="PlayCount" value="3" />
<param name="Filename" value="f12.avi" />
</object>
<object ID="Spreadsheet" classid="clsid:0002E510-0000-0000-C000-000000000046">
</object></body></html>
```

Figure 10.13

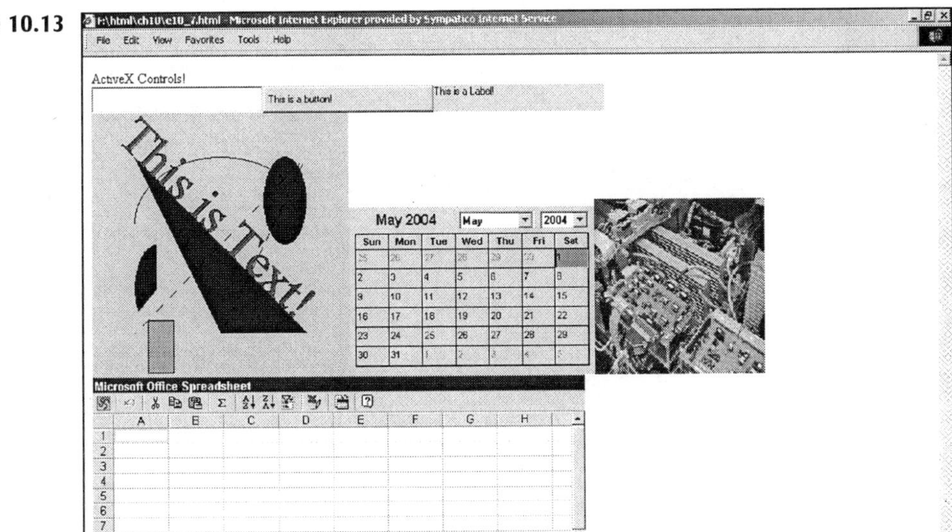

10.14 Review of Chapter 10

At the end of Chapter 10 you should know:

- HTML has the ability to embed multimedia files.
- Browsers deal with multimedia files using plug-ins or helper applications.
- The type of a multimedia file is determined by the file extension or by the attached MIME type.
- You can create a link to a multimedia file using the `<a>` element in conjunction with the `href` attribute.
- A multimedia resource can be embedded in a web page using the `<embed>` element in conjunction with specific attributes: `src` (to specify the multimedia file), `type` (to specify the associated MIME type), `width` and `height` (to specify the space allocated to the multimedia resource in the web page).
- A general method to include any type of resource (including multimedia files, ActiveX controls, and Java applets) is the `<object>` element in conjunction with specific attributes: `data` (to specify the URL of the resource), `type` (to specify the associated MIME type), `classid` (to specify the `id` of the ActiveX control), `width` and `height` (to specify the space allocated to that resource in the web page), `align` (to align the resource), `hspace` and `vspace` (to define the white space around the resource), and `border` (to define a border).

Chapter 11

Image Maps

11.1 Using images to define links

As presented in Chapter 9 Links, an image can be used to define a link. To do this, use syntax as in the following example:

```
<a href="new_page.html">
<img src="image_name.gif">
</a>
```

Example 11_1. A favorite collection (file e11_1.html)

```
<html><head></head><body>
<a href="http://www.oracle.com">
<img src="ora.gif" border="0"></a><br>
<a href="http://www.macromedia.com">
<img src="mac.jpg" border="0"></a><br>
<a href="http://www.google.com">
<img src="gog.gif" border="0"></a><br>
<a href="http://www.itdgroup.com">
<img src="itd.gif" border="0"></a>
</body></html>
```

Figure 11.1

Note

- ◆ In this way, a single link to a new page is attached to each image.

11.2 The image map

The image map allows you to define *multiple links* using a single image. This is a three-step process:

1. Insert the image as a map: To do this, use the usemap attribute of the image element. The value of this attribute starts with # and is followed immediately by a *map identifier*. For example:

   ```
   <img src="image_name.gif" usemap="#map_name">
   ```

2. Insert the map: To describe a map, use the <map>...</map> element. A required attribute for the <map> element is name. The value of this attribute must be the same as the *map identifier*. For example:

   ```
   <map name="map_name">...</map>
   ```

3. Insert the links: To insert the links, use the <area> element inside the <map> element (the <map> element is a container for <area> elements). An <area> element has three important attributes:

   - href to define the URL of the new Internet resources you want to access. To indicate no link for a region, either do not add this attribute or use the nohref attribute instead.
   - shape to define the shape of a hotspot inside the image. The possible values are:
     - rect or rectangle to define a rectangular area
     - circle to define a circular area
     - poly or polygon to define a polygonal area
     - default for the other region(s) of the image for which no links are defined
   - coords to define the coordinates of the hotspot. The value is a list of comma-delimited positive integers (e.g. "100,100,200,200"). For details, see the next section.

Here is an example of an <area> element:

```
<area href="page1.html " type="rect" coords="100,100,200,200">
```

Combining the above elements, here is an example of an image map:

```
<img src="image_name.gif" usemap="#map_name">
<map name="map_name">
<area href="page1.html " shape="rect" coords="100,100,200,200">
<area href="page2.html " shape="rect" coords="200,200,300,300">
</map>
```

11.3 Describing the hotspots

Let's suppose we have a picture 500 pixels wide and 500 pixels high. We need to define hotspots for each colored region using coordinates expressed in pixels.

Figure 11.2

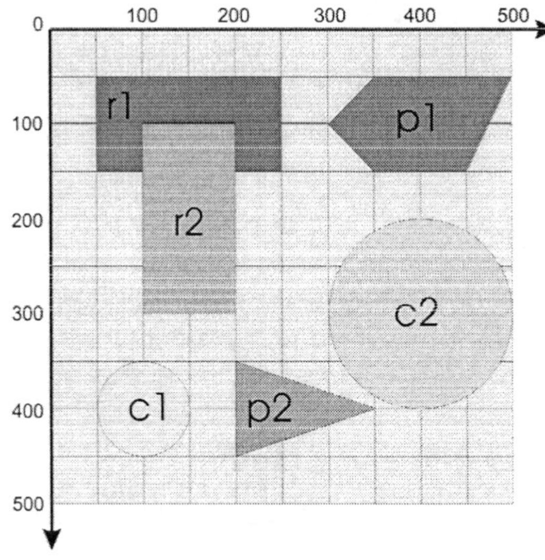

To define a rectangular hotspot, use the syntax:

```
coords="left, top, right, bottom"
```

where:

- `left` and `top` are the x and y coordinates of the top-left corner
- `right` and `bottom` are the x and y coordinates of the bottom-right corner

Examples:

For r1: `coords="50, 50, 250, 150"`

For r2: `coords="100, 100, 200, 300"`

To define a circular hotspot, use the syntax:

```
coords="center-x, center-y, radius"
```

where `center-x`, `center-y` are the coordinates of the center and `radius` is the size of the radius of the circle

Examples:

For c1: `coords="100, 400, 50"`

For c2: `coords="400, 300, 100"`

To define a polygonal hotspot, use the syntax:

```
coords="x1, y1, x2, y2, …, xn, yn"
```

where `xn` and `yn` are the x and y coordinates of point number `n` of the polygon.

Examples:

For p1: `coords="300, 100, 350, 50, 500, 50, 450, 150, 350, 150"`

For p2: `coords="200, 350, 350, 400, 200, 450"`

11.4 Putting it all together

In the following example, we use an image map to define different types of links. The image and the hotspots are identical to those we used as examples in the preceding section.

Example 11_2. An image map (file e11_2.html)

```
<html><head></head><body>
<img src="map1.jpg" usemap="#map_id">
<map name="map_id">
<area href="f1.html" shape="rect"
coords="50, 50, 250, 150">
<area href="f5.pdf" shape="rect"
coords="100, 100, 200, 300">
<area href="f8.xls" shape="circle"
coords="100, 400, 50">
<area href="f11.mp3" shape="circle"
coords="400, 300, 100">
<area href="f3.bmp" shape="poly"
coords="300, 100, 350, 50, 500, 50, 450,
150, 350, 150">
<area nohref shape="polygon" coords="200,
350, 350, 400, 200, 450">
<area href="desc.txt" shape="default">
</map></body></html>
```

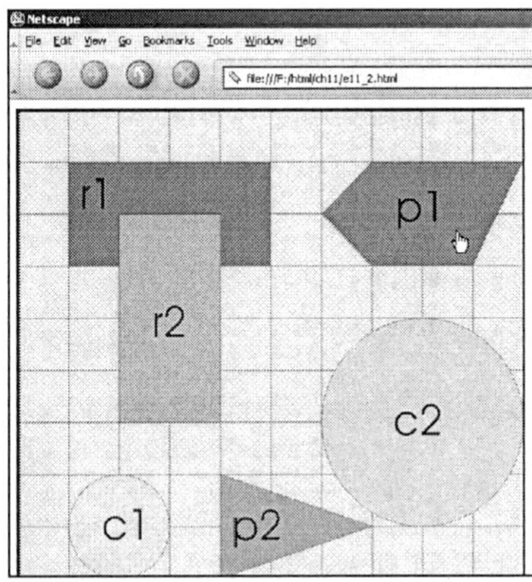

Figure 11.3

Notes

- If two areas are overlapped, as are the two rectangles in our example, the priority is determined by the order in which the `<area>` elements appear inside of the `<map>` element.
- The border for the image map can be eliminated if you set the `border` attribute of the `<img>` element to `"0"`.

11.5 Other attributes for <area> element

There are several other attributes that can be used with the <area> element:

- title and alt to insert *tooltips* that appear when the user hovers the mouse pointer over that region.
- target to define the browser window in which the new resource will be loaded (see Chapter 9.8 Target Windows for detail).

Example 11_3. Other attributes for <area> element (file e11_3.html)

```
<html><head></head><body>
<img src="map1.jpg" border="0"
usemap="#map_id">
<map name="map_id">
<area href=" f1.html" shape="rect"
coords="50, 50, 250, 150" title="this is
a title">
<area href=" f5.pdf" shape="rect"
coords="100, 100, 200, 300" alt="this is
a description">
<area href=" f8.xls" shape="circle"
coords="100, 400, 50"
target="new_window">
</map>
</body></html>
```

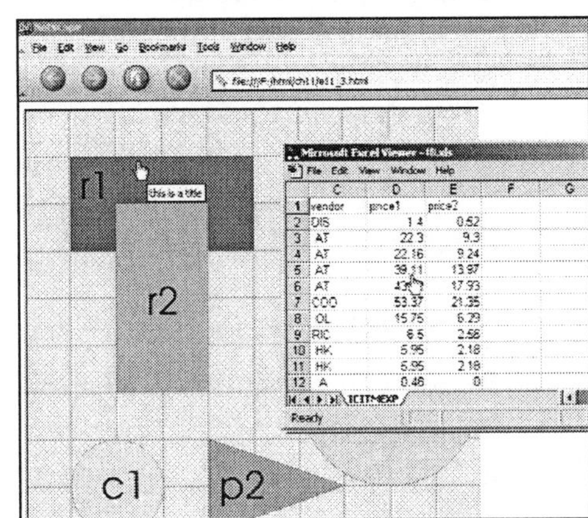

Figure 11.4

11.6 Image maps using the <object> element

The <object> element can be used to insert an image map. To do this, change the <img> element to the <object>...</object> element and the src attribute to the data attribute.

Example 11_4. Image map using the <object> element (file e11_4.html)

```
<html><head></head><body>
<object data="map1.jpg" border="0" usemap="#map_id" type="image/jpeg" width=500
height=498></object>
<map name="map_id">
<area href=" f1.html" shape="rect" coords="50, 50, 250, 150" title="this is a
title">
```

```
<area href=" f5.pdf" shape="rect"
coords="100, 100, 200, 300" alt="this is a
description">
<area href=" f8.xls" shape="circle"
coords="100, 400, 50" target="new_window">
</map>
</body>
</html>
```

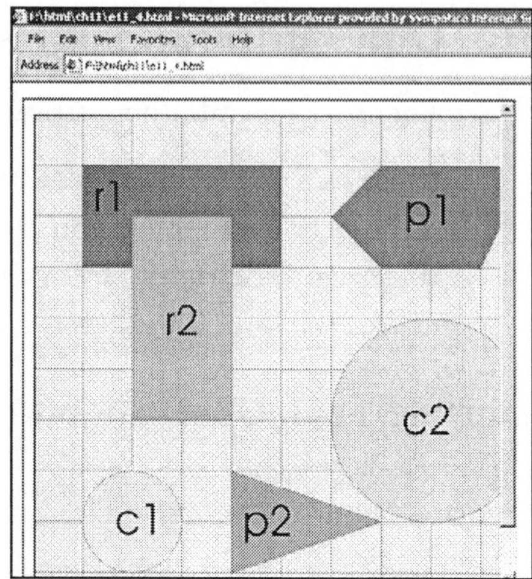

Figure 11.5

Note

- Remember to include `type`, `width`, and `height` attributes for the `<object>` element.
- Internet Explorer adds navigation bars to the embedded image.

11.7 Review of Chapter 11

At the end of Chapter 11 you should know:

- You can use an image map to define multiple links to different Internet resources.
- Inserting an image map is a multi-step process, including declaring the map, describing the map, and defining the links.
- To declare an image to be an image map, use the `<img>` element in conjunction with the `usemap` attribute, which creates an anchor to the *map id.*
- To describe a map, use the `<map>` element in conjunction with the `name` attribute set to a *map id* and insert `<area>` elements into it for each hotspot.
- The `shape` attribute of the `<area>` element is used to define the type of the spot (`rect`, `circle`, `poly`, or `default`).
- The `coords` attribute of the `<area>` element is used to define the actual coordinates of the hotspot.
- The `href` attributes of the `<area>` element is used to define the URL of the Internet resource pointed to by the hotspot.
- The `target` attribute of the `<area>` element is used to define the window in which the new resource will be loaded.
- You can also create an image map using the `<object>` element.

Chapter 12

Forms

12.1 The interactivity of web pages

From the beginning, the WWW (World Wide Web) was designed to be an interactive technology. The links we have learned about so far fulfill this purpose well. The user can see links to many other web pages and decide where to go next. However, links only allow access to static, predefined Internet resources.

Forms, on the other hand, allow users to enter parameters. The application installed on the server side will analyze the value of these parameters and take different actions accordingly. In this manner, we add a dynamic behavior to WWW technology (i.e. a comportment that is decided at the run time and not by default).

To be complete, this chapter should be followed by a discussion of the applications capable of analyzing the parameters entered into the forms. These applications decide what action the server will take in response to the data received. Although coding these applications is beyond of the scope of this book, we will present simple solutions for this matter. For more information, please consult documentation related to JavaScript, ASP, JAVA, JSP, PHP, and other web programming languages.

12.2 The text field element

To enter parameters into a web page, insert a text field element. To do this, use the `<input>` element with the type attribute set to `"text"`.

Example 12_1. The text field (file e12_1.html)

```
<html>
<head>
</head>
<body>
<input type="text">
</body>
</html>
```

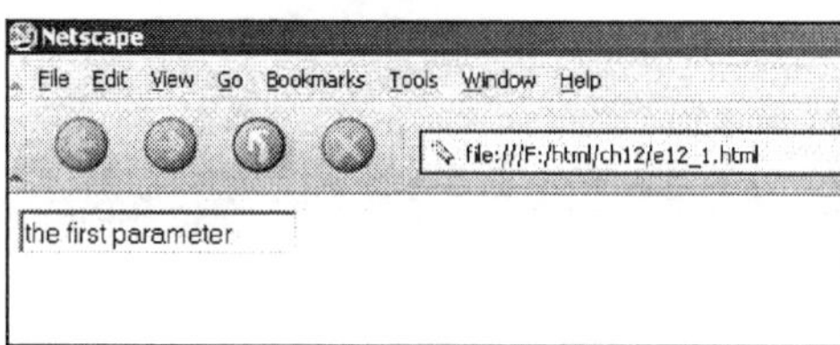

Figure 12.1

Notes

- The user can type any text into the text field.
- This text can be read and used by a client-side application coded in JavaScript (or another client-side application).

12.3 The <form> element

It is recommended that you use the <form>...</form> element to encapsulate related text fields and other form elements.

Notes

- The ending tag for the <form> element is required.
- You can include as many <form> elements as you like.
- <form> elements cannot be nested one inside of another.
- Each <form> element has a `name` attribute to distinguish it from other forms on the page.
- Each <input> element has a `name` attribute to distinguish it from other <input> elements included in the same <form> element. This attribute is required if you need its value to be sent.
- Insert various elements (e.g. text field elements, using the <input> element) into the <form>...</form> block.
- Since the <form> element doesn't have a formatting style associated with it, you can use either regular or formatted text to clarify the meaning of the fields. You can even insert the form(s) into a table element.

Example 12_2. Two <form> elements with multiple text fields (file e12_2.html)

```
<html><head></head><body>
<h3>Form 1</h3>
<form name="f1">
```

```
Element e11:<input type="text" name="e11">
Element e12=<input type="text" name="e12">
</form>
<h3>Form 2</h3>
<form name="f2">
Element e21<input type="text" name="e21">
Element e22<input type="text" name="e22">
</form></body></html>
```

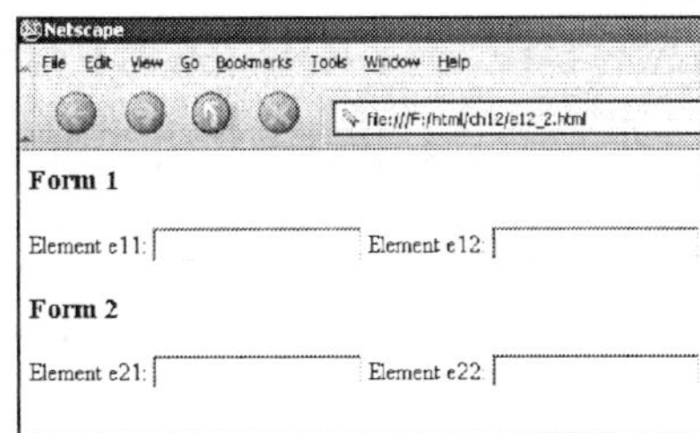

Figure 12.2

12.4 Other attributes of the text field element

The text field element has attributes other than `name` and `type` (the `type` attribute is set to `"text"` for a text field element). Some other useful attributes are:

- `disabled` to disable the text field; the user cannot select the text field, and the content of the field is not submitted to the server.
- `maxlength` to define the maximum number of characters that can be typed; the possible values are positive integers.
- `readonly` to prevent the user from changing the content of the text field.
- `size` to define the length of the text field in characters; if the size is less than `maxlength`, a horizontal scroll bar may appear; the possible values are positive integers.
- `value` to set the initial, or default, value of the text field; the possible values are double-quoted strings.

Example 12_3. The attributes of the text field element (file e12_3.html)

```
<html><head></head><body>
<form name="f1">
Regular <input type="text" name="f11"><br>
Disabled <input type="text" name="f12" disabled><br>
Default Value <input type="text" name="f13"
value="initial text"><br>
Read Only <input type="text" name="f14" readonly
value="constant"><br>
Size <input type="text" name="f15" size="5"><br>
Maxlength <input type="text" name="f16"
maxlength="10"><br>
All <input type="text" name="f17" value="ini" size="5"
maxlength="10">
</form></body></html>
```

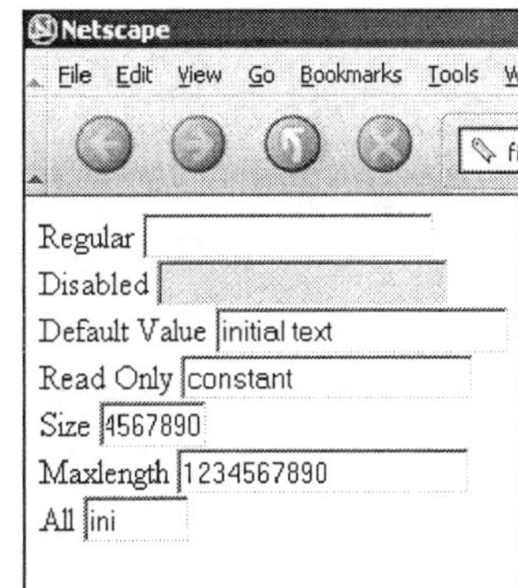

Figure 12.3

12.5 The attributes of the <form> element

The `<form>` element can be used by client-side or server-side applications to read data entered by the user and write the results from the web applications.

Some attributes of the `<form>` element are necessary to achieve this goal:

- `action` to define the *receiver* of the form data. If this attribute is missing, the web page itself is considered to be the receiver. The possible values are:
  - The URL of the web application to process the data (e.g. `"http://www.itdgroup.com/scripts/test.asp"`)
  - A valid e-mail address to send the data via the mailto protocol (e.g. `"mailto:teodoru@sympatico.ca"`)
- `method` to define the method used to send the form data. The possible values are:
  - `GET` to attach data to the URL string using name/value syntax (this is the default setting)
  - `POST` to send data to the server in a separate transaction
- `enctype` to define the method used to encode data before sending it to the server (see the next section for details)
- `target` to define (if necessary) a new browser window in which the results will appear (the default setting is `"_self"`, causing the results to appear in the same window)

12.6 Encoding the Data

The browser encodes the form's data before sending it to the *receiver*. The technique used to encode depends on the value of the `enctype` attribute. The possible values of this attribute are:

- `"application/x-www-form-urlencoded"` used in conjunction with the `GET` method (the default settings). In this case:
  - The data is sent as a list of `name=value` pairs separated by `&` symbols.
  - Any white space is replaced by a + symbol.
  - Any non-alphanumeric character is replaced by `%` plus the ASCII code for that character.
  - Line breaks are replaced by `%0D%0A%` (CR/LF).

For example:

```
first=Julia+M.+P.&last=Smith+Kennedy&address=35+Warrender,Toronto%0D%0A%
Ontario,+Canada
```

- "text/plain" used in conjunction with the mailto action for sending data by e-mail. This case is similar to the preceding case, but the white spaces are not replaced by + symbols .
- "multiform/form-data" used in conjunction with the POST method to send images or other files to the server (i.e. for *up-loading*).

12.7 Sending form data by e-mail

After the user fills out the form fields, the data can be sent to the *receiver*. To do this, a *submit button* must be included in the <form> element. Use the syntax:

```
<input type="submit">
```

Example 12_4. Sending data by e-mail (file e12_4.html)

```
<html><head></head><body>
<form name="f1" method="POST" enctype="text/plain"
action="mailto:teodoru_gugoiu@yahoo.com">
First Name: <input type="text" name="first"><br>
Last Name: <input type="text" name="last"><br>
Click to send data: <input type="submit">
</form>
</body></html>
```

Figure 12.4

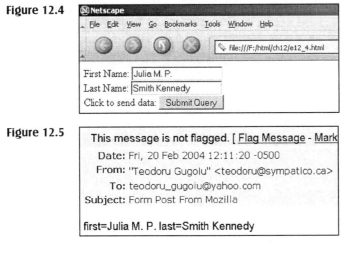

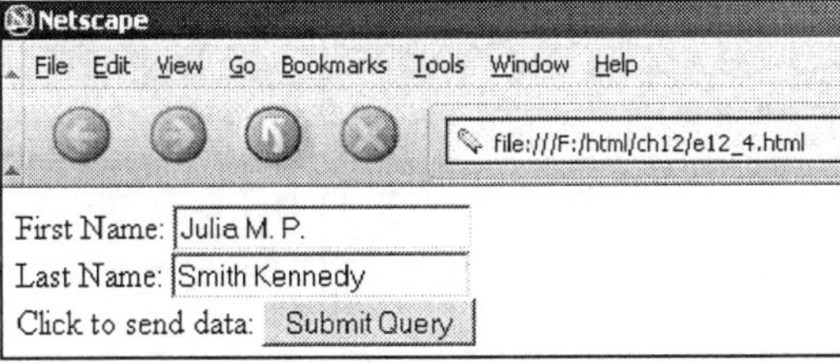

Figure 12.5

This message is not flagged. [Flag Message - Mark
Date: Fri, 20 Feb 2004 12:11:20 -0500
From: "Teodoru Gugoiu" <teodoru@sympatico.ca>
To: teodoru_gugoiu@yahoo.com
Subject: Form Post From Mozilla

first=Julia M. P. last=Smith Kennedy

Note

- The content of the message (rendered here in a Netscape Mail window) is a string with the syntax: `field_name1=field_value1 field_name2=field_value2 ...`

12.8 The attributes of the submit button element

The *submit button* has several attributes:

- `disabled` disables the submit button (i.e. the button cannot be used to send data).
- `name` is an *identifier* for the element (highly recommended).
- `value` represents the label (text) that will appear on the button (the default value is `"Submit Query"`).

More than one *submit button* can be attached to the same `<form>` element. To differentiate between them, use the `name` attribute.

Example 12_5. Customized submit button elements (file e12_5.html)

```
<html><head></head><body>
<form name="f1" method="POST" enctype="text/plain"
action="mailto:teodoru_gugoiu@yahoo.com">
First Name: <input type="text" name="first"><br>
Last Name: <input type="text" name="last"><br>
Default Submit Button: <input type="submit"><br>
Disabled Submit Button: <input type="submit" name="dis" disabled><br>
Customized Submit Button: <input type="submit" name="cus" value="Send Data">
</form></body></html>
```

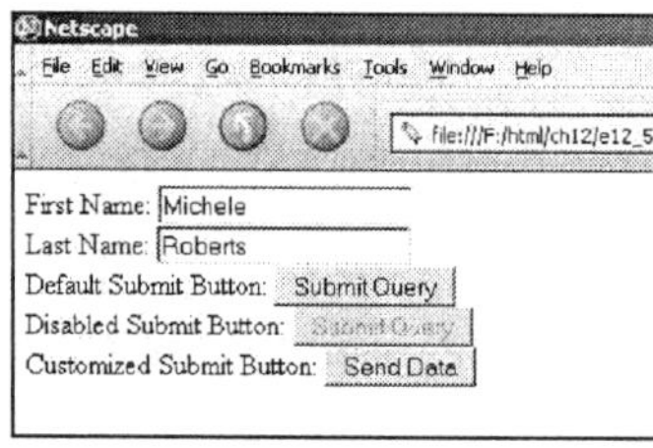

Figure 12.6

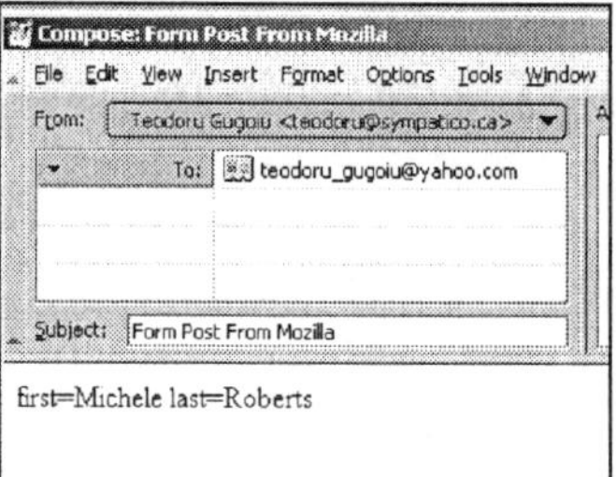

Figure 12.7
Using the default button

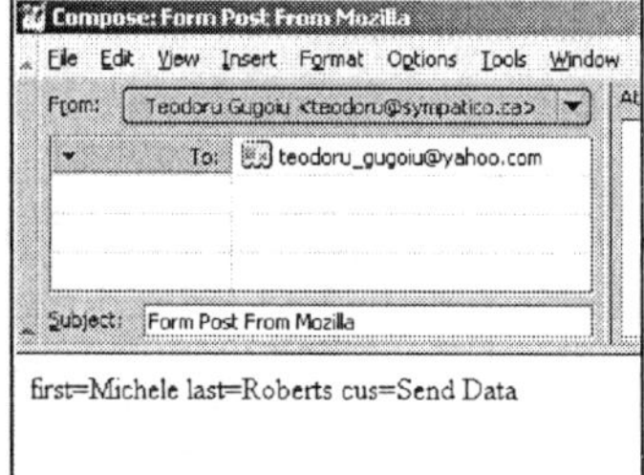

Figure 12.8
Using the named button

Note

- Different data will be sent depending on which button is clicked:
  - A **disabled button** doesn't send any data.
  - A **default button** sends the form data but does not send data about itself.
  - A **named button** sends the form data and includes data about itself (see `"cus=Send Data"` string in Figure 12.8).
- The form name `"f1"` doesn't appear anywhere in the sent data (only the values of the form elements are sent).

12.9 The password element

The password element is similar to the text field element and accepts the same attributes. The differences are:

- The value for the type attribute is "password".
- The value attribute of this element is *required.*
- When the user fills this field, the characters are not shown (a * symbol appears in the field for each character typed). When the data is submitted, the real string of characters typed by the user is sent.

Example 12_6. The password element (file e12_6.html)

```
<html><head></head><body>
<form name="f1" method="POST" action="mailto:teodoru_gugoiu@yahoo.com">
Username: <input type="text" name="user" value="guest">
<br>Old Password: <input type="password" name="old" value="test" readonly>
<br>New Password (maximum 10 characters):
<input type="password" name="new" maxlength="10">
<br>Retype New Password: <input type="password" name="new_copy" size="10">
<br>Click the button to update:: <input type="submit">
</form>
</body></html>
```

Figure 12.9

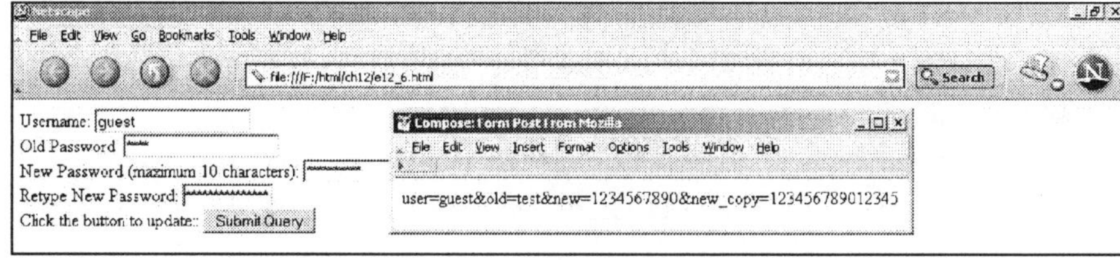

Notes

In this example, although the method of sending data is POST and the action is mailto, the value of the enctype attribute is not defined. Consequently, the default value "application/x-www-form-urlencoded" is used and the data is encoded using this method.

12.10 The hidden element

The hidden element is a special form element. It is special because it exists in the code of the page but is not rendered by the browser. There are at least two uses for this element:

1. To pass information between web application pages.

2. To add an *identifier* to the form the element belongs to (we already know that the `<form>` tag doesn't have an attribute to be sent together with other data from the form).

To insert a hidden element into a form, use the `<input>` element with the `type` attribute set to `"hidden"`. Two other attributes are required: the `name` and `value` attributes.

Example 12_7. The hidden element (file e12_7.html)

```
<html><head></head><body>
<form name="f1" method="POST" action="mailto:teodoru_gugoiu@yahoo.com">
<input type="hidden" name="form_id" value="f1">
<input type="hidden" name="transaction_no" value="1234567890">
<input type="hidden" name="user" value="Jacob_Spilberg">
<input type="hidden" name="password" value="jcbsplbrg">
<input type="text" name="id" value="Enter here your Driving Licence ID..." size="50">
<br><input type="text" name="plates" size="50" value="Enter here your License
Plates...">
<br><input type="submit" value="Send">
</form>
</body></html>
```

Figure 12.10

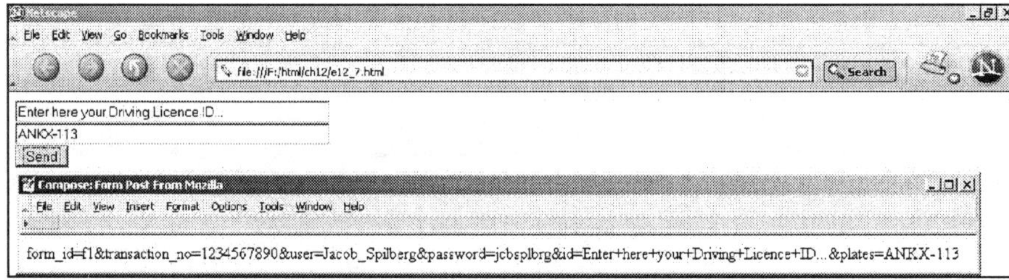

Note

- Data from hidden elements is included in the data submitted as **name=value** pairs, just like all other form elements.

12.11 The checkbox

The checkbox is an `<input>` element that can be selected or deselected by the user. Only the selected checkboxes are included in the data submitted by the browser. The submitted checkboxes follow the standard syntax `name1=value1&name2=value2` where:

- `name1` is the value of the `name` attribute of the checkbox `<input>` element, and
- `value1` is the value of the `value` attribute of the same checkbox `<input>` element

To insert a checkbox, use the `<input>` element with the `type` attribute set to `"checkbox"`. There is another attribute that can be used in conjunction with the checkbox element:

- `checked` for when the default *state* of the checkbox element is *selected*

Example 12_8. The checkbox element (file e12_8.html)

```
<html><head></head><body>
Searching for a house!<br>
<form name="f1" method="POST" action="mailto:teodoru_gugoiu@yahoo.com">
<ul>What kind of house are you looking for?
<li>Condominium:<input type="checkbox" name="kind" value="condominium">
<li>Townhouse:<input type="checkbox" name="kind" value="townhouse" checked>
<li>Detached:<input type="checkbox" name="kind" value="detached" checked>
</ul>
<ul>How much can you afford to pay?
<li>Less than $200,000:<input type="checkbox" name="money" value="less2">
<li>Between $200,000 and $400,000:<input type="checkbox" name="money"
value="between24" checked>
<li>More than $400,000:<input type="checkbox" name="money" value="more4">
</ul>
Are you OK?<input type="checkbox" name="OK" checked>
<br><input type="submit" value="Send">
</form>
</body></html>
```

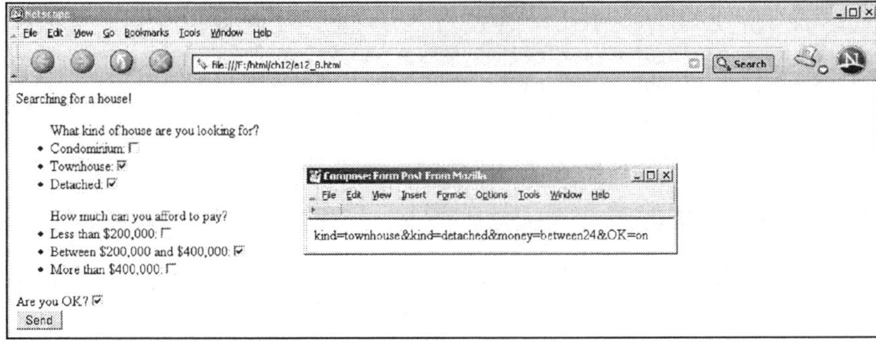

Figure 12.11

Notes

- It is possible to have more than one checkbox with the same `name`. All these elements are submitted if the user selects them.
- If the `value` attribute is not included, only the selected checkboxes will be submitted to the receiver, using a syntax like: `"checkbox_name=on"`. It is recommended that you avoid this situation.

12.12 The radio button element

The radio button is very similar to the checkbox. It uses the same syntax and attributes. There are three major differences between them:

- The value of the `type` attribute is `"radio"`.
- The user can select only one radio button in a group at a time (radio buttons are grouped according to the `name` attribute).
- The browser renders them in the radio button style.

Example 12_9. The radio button element (file e12_9.html)

```
<html><head></head><body>
Searching for a house!<br>
<form name="f1" method="POST" action="mailto:teodoru_gugoiu@yahoo.com">
<ul>What kind of house are you looking for?
<li>Condominium:<input type="radio" name="kind" value="condominium">
<li>Townhouse:<input type="radio" name="kind" value="townhouse">
<li>Detached:<input type="radio" name="kind" value="detached" checked>
</ul>
<ul>How much can you afford to pay?
<li>Less than $200,000:<input type="radio" name="money" value="less2">
<li>Between $200,000 and $400,000:<input type="radio" name="money"
value="between24" checked>
<li>More than $400,000:<input type="radio" name="money" value="more4">
</ul>
<ul>Are you OK?
<li>Of course!<input type="radio" name="OK" value="YES">
<li>Sorry, No!<input type="radio" name="OK" checked>
<br><input type="submit" value="Send">
</form>
</body></html>
```

Figure 12.12

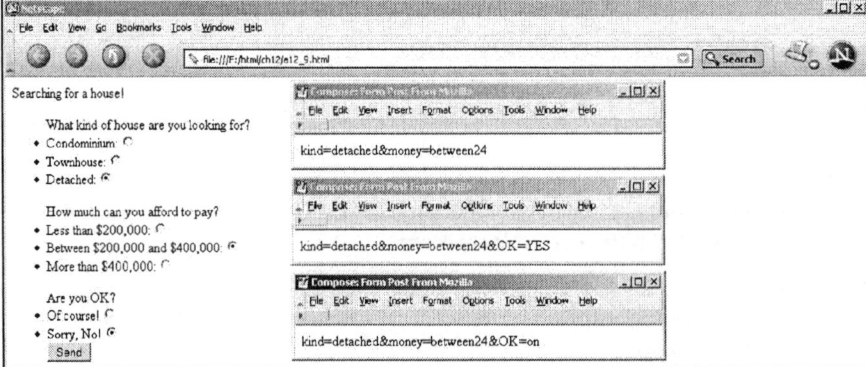

Notes

- If no radio button in a group (having the same `name`) is selected, no data is sent regarding that group.
- If an element in a group of radio button elements is selected and this element has a `value` attribute, data is submitted using the syntax: `"radio_button_name=radio_button_value"`
- If an element in a group of radio button elements is selected and this element doesn't have a value attribute, data is submitted using the syntax: `"radio_button_name=on"`. It is recommended that you avoid this scenario.

12.13 The <textarea> element

The <textarea> element allows you to attach a multi-line text field to a <form> block. To do this, include a <textarea>...</textarea> element inside the <form> block.

Notes

- The <textarea> element has a content (the ending tag </textarea> is required)
- A `name` attribute can be attached to the <textarea> element to be submitted with the form's data.
- The content of the <textarea> block is the initial value assigned to that element.

Example 12_10. The <textarea> element (file e12_10.html)

```
<html><head></head><body>
<form name="f1" method="POST" action="mailto:teodoru_gugoiu@yahoo.com">
<textarea name="message">
this is the initial value assigned to this textarea element...
</textarea>
<br><input type="submit" value="Send this Textarea">
</form>
</body></html>
```

Figure 12.13

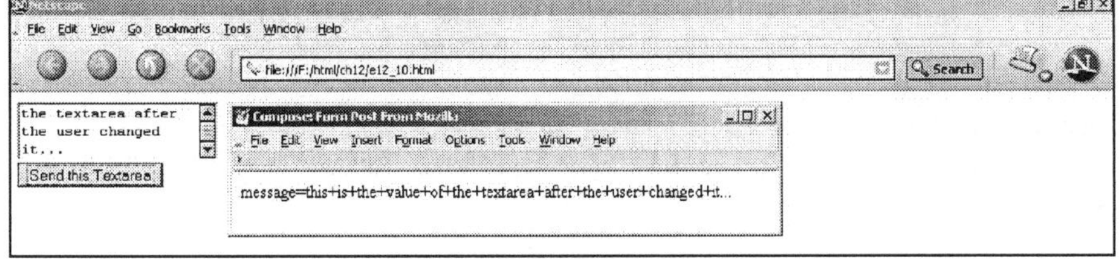

Note

- The browser allocates a size for the <textarea> element by default. If the text inside doesn't fit, the browser scrolls the text both vertically and horizontally.

12.14 Other attributes for the `<textarea>` element

There are a few more attributes of the <textarea> element that can be useful:

- `disabled` to disable the element, so the user cannot select it and the browser doesn't submit its value.
- `readonly` so the user cannot change its content.
- `cols` to determine the horizontal size (in characters) of the visible area allocated to the element (if the line typed doesn't fit, a horizontal scrolling appears).
- `rows` to determine the number of lines allocated to the element for the visible area (if the typed text doesn't fit, a vertical scroll bar will appear).
- `wrap` to determine how CR/LF characters (line breaks) are handled. The possible values are:
  - `off` so *only the user* can insert the CR/LF characters. These characters will be submitted as `%0D%0A%`
  - `soft` or `virtual` (the default value) so the text is visually (and automatically) wrapped inside the `textarea` element, but only the *user- entered* CR/LF characters will be submitted.
  - `hard` or `physical` so the text is visually (and automatically) wrapped and the CR/LF sequences are automatically inserted. These automatically inserted sequences *will* be submitted together with other similar sequences inserted by the user.

Example 12_11.Other attributes for the `<textarea>` element (file e12_11.html)

```
<html><head></head><body>
<form name="f1" method="POST" action="mailto:teodoru_gugoiu@yahoo.com">
<textarea name="def">default textarea</textarea>
<textarea name="dis" disabled>disabled textarea</textarea><br>
<textarea name="rea" readonly>readonly textarea</textarea>
<textarea name="colsrows" cols="10" rows="3">customized textarea</textarea><br>
<textarea name="sof" wrap="soft">soft textarea</textarea>
<textarea name="har" wrap="hard">hard textarea</textarea><br>
<textarea name="off" wrap="off">off textarea</textarea>
<br><input type="submit" value="Send all!">
</form>
</body></html>
```

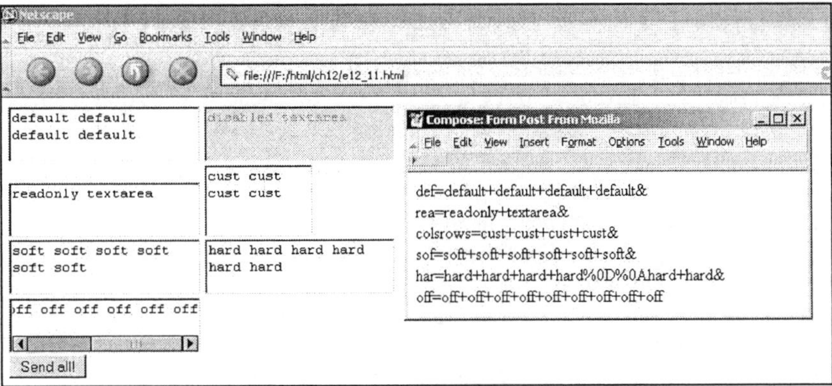

Figure 12.14

Notes

- The "disabled" <textarea> element is not sent.
- wrap="off" is the only case that produces a horizontal scroll.
- The text inside the Compose window was **manually arranged** to fit into the window for this example (i.e. the content of each line follows immediately after the preceding & character).

12.15 The reset button

In addition to the submit button used to submit the form's data, HTML allows you to add other kind of buttons to a form element. In the following sections, we will explain each of them in detail.

To clear the content of the form fields and reset them to their default values (removing any changes made by the user), use a reset button. This can be added to a form element by including an <input> element with the type attribute set to "reset".

There are several attributes for the *reset button* that can be set:

- disabled to disable the button so it cannot be used to reset to the default data
- name to *identify* the element (its use is recommended).
- value to set the label (text) that will appear on the button (the default value is "Reset").

More than one *reset button* can be attached to the same <form> element. To differentiate between them, use the name attribute.

Example 12_12. The reset button (file e12_12.html)

```
<html><head></head><body>
<form name="f1" method="POST" action="mailto:teodoru_gugoiu@yahoo.com">
TA: <textarea name="message">text area</textarea><br>
TF1: <input type="text" name="tf1">
TF2: <input type="text" name="tf2" value="text field"><br>
CB1: <input type="checkbox" name="cb1">
CB2: <input type="checkbox" name="cb2" checked><br>
RB1: <input type="radio" name="rb1">
RB2: <input type="radio" name="rb2" checked><br>
<br><input type="reset">
<input type="reset" value="Reset All!" name="res">
<input type="submit">
</form>
</body></html>
```

Figure 12.15

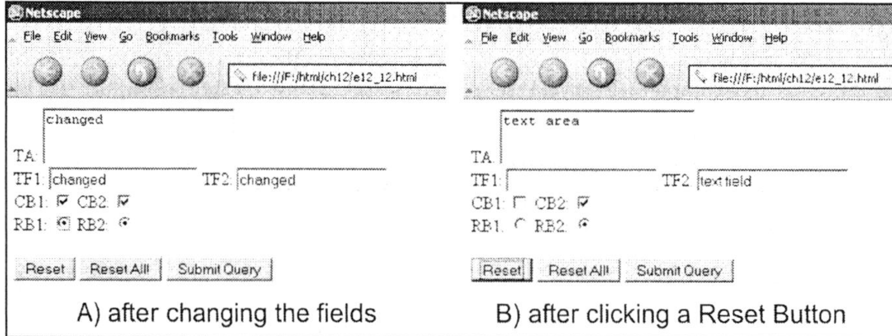

A) after changing the fields
B) after clicking a Reset Button

Note

◆ Reset buttons do not add name=value pairs to the form's data sent by the browser.

12.16 The generic <input> button

To attach a *generic* button without any default behavior to a form, use the <input> element with the type attribute set to "button".

Notes

◆ All the <input> button attributes (disabled, name, and value) apply to this button.

◆ More than one generic button can be attached to the same <form> element. To differentiate between them, use the name attribute.

◆ To add a specific behavior to an <input> button, use JavaScript or another client-side programming language (see next example).

Example 12_13. The <input> button (file e12_13.html)

```
<html><head></head><body>
<form name="f1" method="POST" action="mailto:teodoru_gugoiu@yahoo.com">
TA: <textarea name="ta">initial text</textarea><br>
TF: <input type="text" name="tf" value="initial value">
CB: <input type="checkbox" name="cb" checked>
<br>Simple button: <input type="button">
<br>Named button: <input type="button" name="b2">
<br>Nothing: <input type="button" name="b3" value="I can do nothing!">
<br>A customized Submit Button: <input type="button" name="b4" value="I can send
data!" onClick="submit()">
<br>A command button: <input type="button" name="b5" value="Click me!"
onClick="alert('Hello from JavaScript!')">
<br>A regular Submit Button: <input type="submit" name="b6" value="v6">
</form>
</body></html>
```

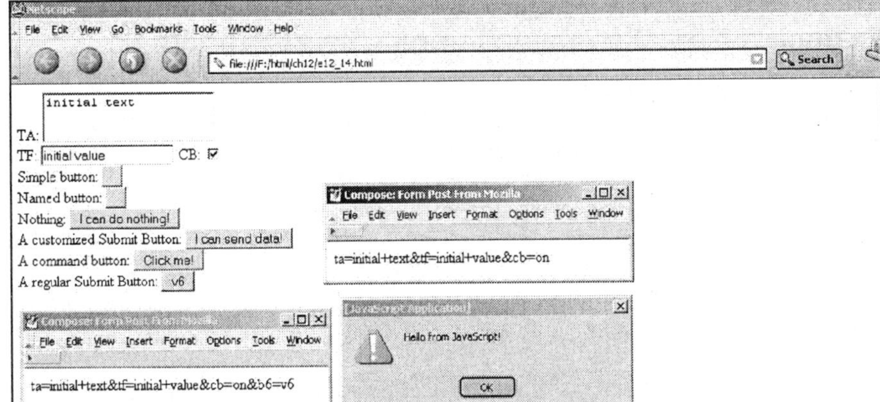

Figure 12.16

Note

- Generic `<input>` buttons do not add *name=value* pairs to the form's data sent by the browser, but submit buttons do (as you can see in Figure 12.16).

12.17 The image button

You can add an *image* button to a form by using the `<input>` element with the `type` attribute set to `"image"`. Other useful attributes for the image button are:

- `src` to specify the URL of the image
- `name` to identify the image
- `align` to align the image relative to other elements
- `disabled` to disable the element

Notes

- Each time a user clicks on the image, the form's data is submitted. In this way, you don't need a submit button.
- The data submitted by the image button element is in the format: *`element_name.x=x-coordinate&element_name.y=y-coordinate`* where:
  - `element_name` is the value of the `name` attribute element assigned to the image element, and
  - `x-coordinate` and *`y-coordinate`* are the x and y coordinates, respectively, of the point on the image where the user clicked. They are expressed in pixels relative to the top-left corner of the image.
- The image button is a server-side image map, and the server should have an application that reads and processes the data submitted.
- More than one image button can be attached to the same `<form>` element. To differentiate between them, use the `name` attribute.

Example 12_14. The image button (file e12_14.html)

```
<html><head></head><body>
<form name="f1" method="POST" action="mailto:teodoru_gugoiu@yahoo.com">
This is a Text Field: <input type="text" name="tf" value="initial value">
<input type="submit" name="sb" value="Send all!">
<p><input type="image" src="map1.jpg" name="im">
</form>
</body></html>
```

Figure 12.17

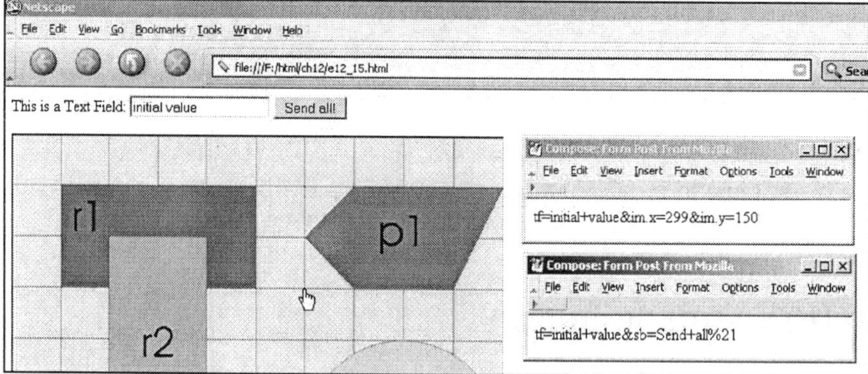

Notes

- If you click on the image, the coordinates of the clicked point are sent together with the name of the image, but no data about the submit button is sent.
- If you click on the default submit button, a *`name=value`* pair for this button is sent, but no data about the image is sent. The `!` character is replaced by the sequence `%21`.

12.18 The <button> button

The last kind of button you can add to a form element uses the <button>…</button> element instead of the <input> element.

Notes

- The <button> button has a content (i.e. has a body and an ending tag).
- The <button> button accepts the same attributes as the <input> button (name, value, type, disabled).
- The type attribute determines the behavior of the button. The possible values are:
  - button (the default value)
  - reset
  - submit
- You can add content (text, images, formatting styles, etc.) to the body of the <button> button to create custom-made buttons.

Example 12_15. The <button> button (file e12_15.html)

```
<html><head></head><body>
<form name="f1" method="POST" action="mailto:teodoru_gugoiu@yahoo.com">
TF: <input type="text" name="tf" value="initial value">
<br><button name="default_empty" value="default_empty_value"></button>
<br><button type="reset" name="reset_text" value="reset_text_value">reset
text</button>
<br><button type="submit" name="image_submit" value="image_submit_value"><img
src="arrow.gif"></button>
<br><button name="def_tex_ima_tex" value="def_tex_ima_tex_value">def text <img
src="star.gif"> def text</button>
<br><input type="submit" name="sb" value="sb_value">
</form>
</body></html>
```

The Netscape Mail window in Figure 12.18 shows the data the browser sends when each button shown is clicked.

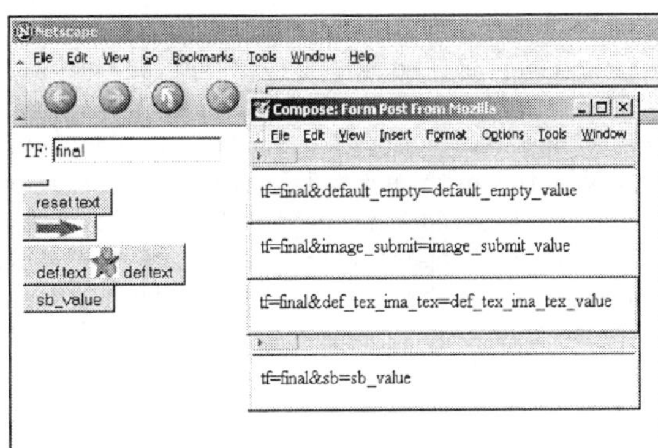

Figure 12.18

Notes

- Only the clicked button adds a **name=value** pair to the data submitted by the form.
- The reset button doesn't submit any data (it just resets the default values for the form's fields).
- Only the reset button doesn't submit the form's data.

12.19 Uploading a file

The `<input>` element allows you to attach a file from the local system to the form and submit it together with the form's field data. This process is called *uploading* from client to server. This can be done using an `<input>` element with the `type` attribute set to `"file"`.

Notes

- The file can be of any type (including image and executable formats).
- The form will render a text field (to enter a file name and associated path) and a **Browse** button (to navigate the directory structure to the file). Both allow you to identify which file will be uploaded.
- More than one file can be uploaded using a `<form>` element. To distinguish between them, attach a `name` attribute to each `<input>` element.
- The `<form>` element must have these attributes:
  - `method="POST"`
  - `enctype="multiform/form-data"`
  - `action`=URL of the server application that will get and process the file(s)

Example 12_16. Uploading a file (file e12_16.html)

```
<html><head></head><body>
<form name="f1" method="POST" action="http://www.itdgroup.com/scripts/upload.asp"
enctype="multiform/form-data">
TF: <input type="text" name="tf" value="initial value">
<p>Type the path and file name or use the Browse... button to navigate to the file!
<br>File 1: <input type="file" name="f1" value="Find the File 1">
<br>File 2: <input type="file" name="f2" value="Find the File 2">
<br>Click to submit: <input type="submit" name="sb" value="sb_value">
</form>
</body></html>
```

Figure 12.19

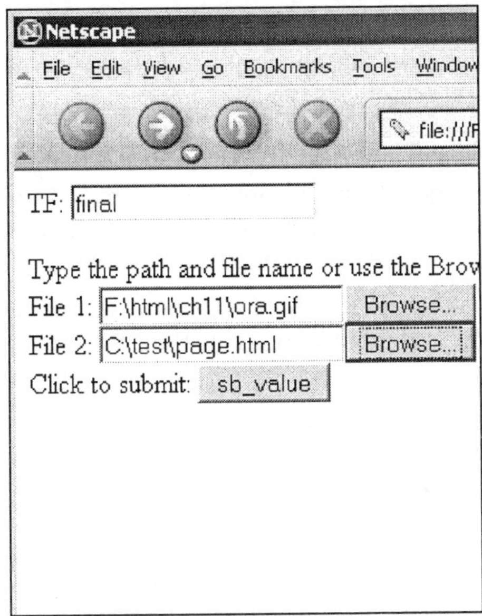

Note

- For this example to be completely functional, an application capable of retrieving and processing the uploaded files is needed on the server side.

12.20 The `<select>` list

The `<select>` list allows you to group related items into a list. In this way, the `<select>` list is similar to a group of check boxes or radio buttons. The main difference is in the way the browser renders it.

If only one list item is visible at a time, the `<select>` list is rendered similarly to a pop-up menu, and only one list item can be selected at a time (similar in behavior to a group of radio buttons).

If many list items are visible at a time, the `<select>` list is rendered similarly to a scrolling list. In this case, only one list item can be selected at a time (the default behavior; similar in behavior to a radio button group), or multiple items can be selected if the `multiple` attribute is attached (similar in behavior to a checkbox group, see below).

To define a `<select>` list, use the `<select>...</select>` element. To define list items, insert `<option>` elements into the body of the `<select>` element.

Notes

- To uniquely identify which list items are selected, add a `name` attribute to the `<select>` element and a `value` attribute to each `<option>` element.
- The ending tag for the `<option>` element is optional in HTML and required in XHTML.
- By default, a `<select>` list is rendered with a single item visible (similar to a pop-up menu). To change this setting, add a `size` attribute to the `<select>` element to define the number of visible items (in this case, the list is rendered as a scrolling list).
- For each item selected, a *name=value* pair is added to the form's data, where **name** is the value of the `name` attribute of the `<select>` list and **value** is the value of the `value` attribute of the selected list element.
- You can insert many `<select>` lists into the same `<form>` element.

Example 12_17. The `<select>` list (file e12_17.html)

```
<html><head></head><body>
<form name="f1" method="POST"
action="mailto:teodoru_gugoiu@yahoo.com">
TF: <input type="text" name="tf"
value="initial value">
<br><select name="s1">
<option value="v11">b11</option>
<option value="v12">b12</option>
<option value="v13">b13</option>
</select>
<br><select name="s2" size="2">
<option value="v21">b21</option>
<option value="v22">b22</option>
<option value="v23">b23</option>
<option value="v24">b24</option>
</select>
<br><input type="Submit">
</form>
</body></html>
```

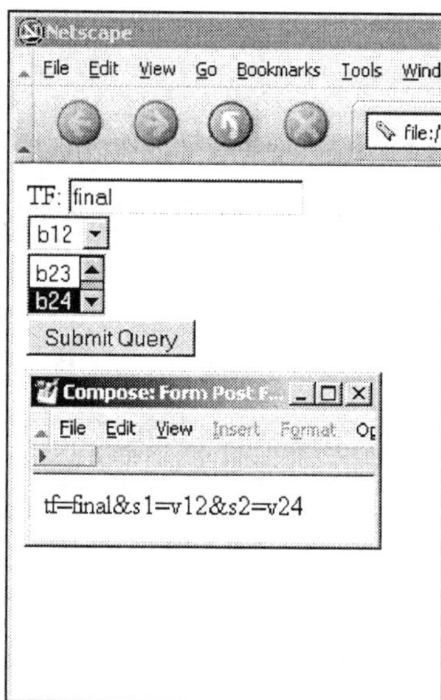

Figure 12.20

12.21 The multiple `<select>` list

By default, only one item on the `<select>` list can be selected at a time and submitted with the form's data. To change this setting, add the `multiple` attribute to the `<select>` tag. To select a range of list elements, the user must hold down the SHIFT key and click on the first and the last items in the range. To select discontinuous items, the user must hold down the CTRL key and click on each item to be included. Note the `multiple` attribute works only if the `size` attribute is set to a value greater than 1.

Example 12_18. The multiple <select> list (file e12_18.html)

```
<html><head></head><body>
<form name="f1" method="POST" action="mailto:teodoru_gugoiu@yahoo.com">
TF: <input type="text" name="tf" value="initial value">
<br>Select universities you want to apply for:
<select name="univ" size="3" multiple>
<option value="uoft">University of Toronto</option>
<option value="york">University of York</option>
<option>Ontario Institute of Technology</option>
<option value="brock">Brock University</option>
</select>
<br><input type="Submit"></form></body></html>
```

Figure 12.21

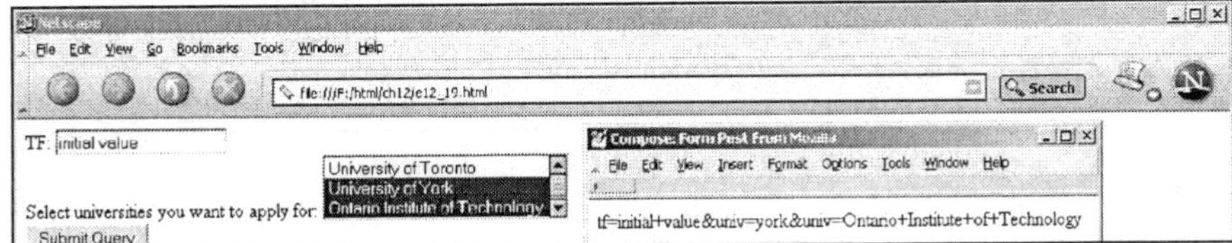

Notes

- For each selected item, a name=value pair is added to the form's data.
- If the `value` attribute for an item in the `<select>` list is not defined, the content of the `<option>...</option>` block is used in the submitted data (see the Ontario Institute of Technology case in Figure 12.21).

12.22 Other attributes related to forms

There are two other attributes that can be added to form elements:

- `accesskey` to define a shortcut to execute a command specific to that element and/or place the focus around that element. The possible values are any double-quoted character (e.g. `"t"`). To get the focus or execute the command, the user must hold down the ALT key and press the appropriate character (e.g. `ALT+t`).
- `tabindex` to define a different order of navigation between the form's elements when using the TAB key (the default order is given by the order in which the element are added to the form). The possible values are `"0"` or any positive integer.

Example 12_19. The `accesskey` and `tabindex` attributes (file e12_19.html)

```
<html><head></head><body>
<form name="f1" method="POST" action="mailto:teodoru_gugoiu@yahoo.com">
<table><tr><td>
(ALT+u)<input type="text" name="un" accesskey="u" tabindex="1">
<td>(ALT+c)<input type="checkbox" name="cb" accesskey="c" tabindex="4">
<tr><td>(ALT+p)<input type="password" name="pw" accesskey="p" tabindex="2">
<td>(ALT+t)<textarea name="ta" accesskey="t" tabindex="5">initial text</textarea>
<tr><td>(ALT+s)<input type="submit" tabindex="3" accesskey="s">
<td>(ALT+r)<input type="reset" accesskey="r" tabindex="6">
</table>
</form></body></html>
```

Figure 12.22

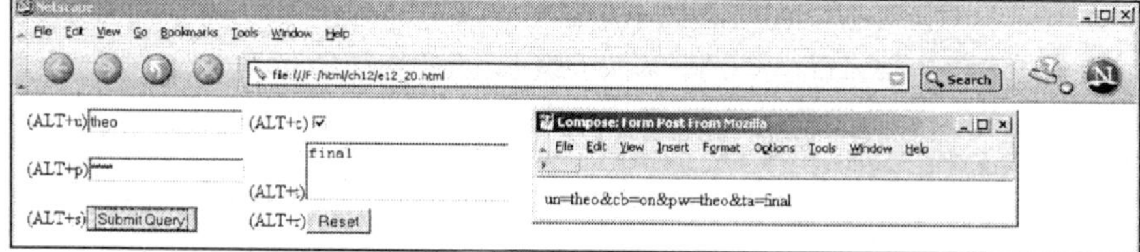

Notes

- Using the shortcut ALT+s, the form's data is automatically submitted.
- We used a table to make the form layout a grid.
- The navigation is set to follow the columns instead of the rows of the table.

12.23 Review of Chapter 12

At the end of Chapter 12 you should know:

- Forms are used to send data to a client-side or server-side application or to an e-mail address.
- To insert a form, use the `<form>` element together with specific attributes.
- The `action` attribute of the `<form>` element determines the receiver of the data sent by the form (server-side application or e-mail address).
- The `method` attribute of the `<form>` element determines the method by which the data is sent by the form (the `GET` method adds data to the URL, the `POST` method sends data using a separate transaction).
- The `enctype` attribute of the `<form>` element determines the encoding method used to send data.
- Insert the form's components inside the `<form>` element.

- You can add different types of form elements by setting different values for the type attribute of the <input> element: text for text fields, password for passwords, hidden for hidden fields, checkbox for checkboxes, radio for radio buttons, image for image-type buttons, file to upload files, button for generic buttons, submit for submit-type buttons, and reset for reset-type buttons).
- The <textarea> element allows you to add multi-line text fields.
- The <button> element allows you to add custom-made buttons.
- The <select> element allows you to add a list of options defined by the <option> element. The user will be only be able to select a single option unless the multiple attribute is added to the <select> element.
- There are several attributes with similar meanings for all the components of the <form> element, such as: name (a unique identifier), value (an initial value or the label on buttons), disabled (to disable an element), readonly (to disallow editing the element value), maxlength (to set the maximum number of characters), size (the size of the visible area in characters), checked (for checkboxes and radio buttons), selected (for selected options), cols and rows (for the size of the visible area for the <textarea> element), src and align (for the image-type element).
- The accesskey attribute allows you to move the focus to a form element using a shortcut.
- The tabindex attribute allows you to change the order of navigation between the form elements when using the TAB key.
- The data sent by a form using the GET method is added to the end of the URL after a ? symbol using an & separated list of *name=value* pairs.

Chapter 13

Frames

13.1 Frames

Frames allow the browser to simultaneously render multiple web pages. Many older browsers do not support this option. Also, be aware that frames require special treatment in XHTML because they are not standard web pages.

13.2 The <frameset> element

To define frames on a web page, replace the `<body>` block of a standard web page with a `<frameset>...</frameset>` block. For each web page you want to simultaneously insert, add a `<frame>` element inside of the `<frameset>` element. To define which page will be loaded in each frame set, use the `src` attribute of each `<frame>` element.

Note

- The examples presented in this chapter make reference to `p1.html`, `p2.html`, and other pages that you must first create in order for the examples to be functional.

13.3 Horizontal frames

Let's suppose we want to define a frameset containing 2 horizontal frames, the first frame 100 pixels high and the second filling the rest of the browser window. To do this, add a `rows` attribute set to `"100,*"` to the `<frameset>` element.

Example 13_1. Two horizontal frames (file e13_1.html)

```
<html>
<head>
<title>
Two Horizontal Frames
</title>
</head>
<frameset rows="100,*">
<frame src="p1.html">
<frame src="p2.html">
</frameset>
</html>
```

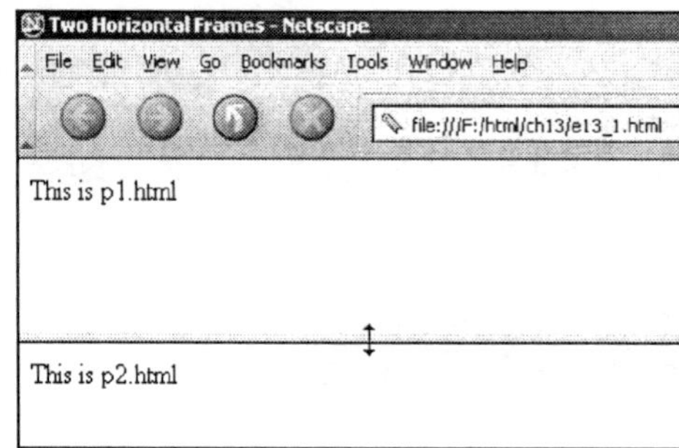

Figure 13.1

Notes

- The HTML file used to define a frameset must have an `<html>...</html>` block containing two blocks: the `<head>...</head>` block and the `<frameset>...</frameset>` block.
- To add a title to this page, insert a `<title>...</title>` block into the `<head>` element.
- You can adjust the frame size by placing the mouse cursor over the common border until it changes to a double arrow (see Figure 13.1) and then clicking and dragging the border to the new position.

13.4 Vertical frames

Now let's suppose we want to define a frameset containing three vertical frames, the left frame 150 pixels wide, the right frame covering 10% of the total width of the browser window, and the middle frame covering the rest of the space. To describe this, attach a `cols` attribute set to `"150, *, 10%"` to the `<frameset>` element.

Example 13_2. Three vertical frames (file e13_2.html)

```
<html><head></head>
<frameset cols="150,*,10%">
<frame src="p1.html">
<frame src="p2.html">
<frame src="p3.html">
</frameset>
</html>
```

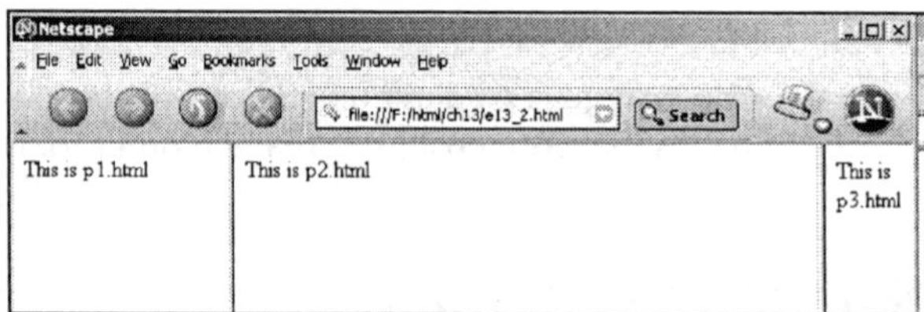

Figure 13.2

13.5 Grid of frames

To define a grid of frames, set both the `rows` and the `cols` attributes. For example: `rows="200, *, 2*" cols="30%,*"` means:

- A grid of frames 3 rows by 2 columns.
- The top row is 200 pixels high, and the rest of the vertical space is divided into 3 equal parts (1*+2*=3*), from which the middle row covers one third (* meaning one part) and the bottom row covers two thirds (2* meaning two parts).
- The left column will cover 30% of the width of the browser, and the right column will cover the rest.

Example 13_3. A grid of frames (file e13_3.html)

```
<html><head></head>
<frameset rows="200, *,
2*" cols="30%,*">
<frame src="p1.html">
<frame src="p2.html">
<frame src="p3.html">
<frame src="p4.html">
<frame src="p5.html">
<frame src="p6.html">
</frameset>
</html>
```

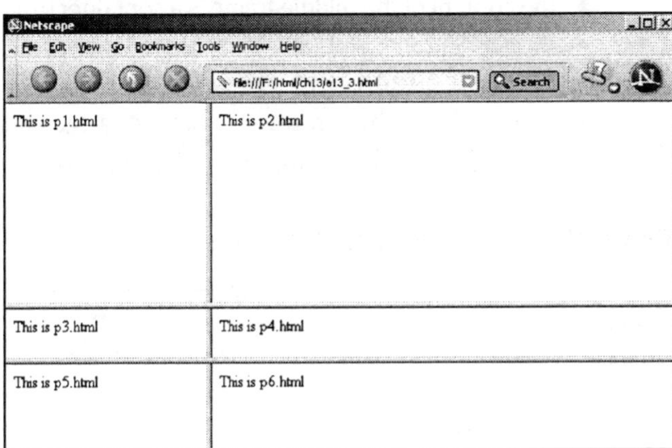

Figure 13.3

Note

◆ The frames fill the grid from left to right and from top to bottom.

13.6 Nested framesets

Framesets can be nested. There are two ways to obtain nested framesets.

The first option is to set the `src` attribute of a frame to a page containing the description of another frameset. For example, let's change the `src` value of the middle frame in Example 13_2 to `e13_1.html`.

Example 13_4. Nested framesets (file e13_4.html)

```
<html>
<head>
</head>
<frameset cols="150,*,10%">
<frame src="p1.html">
<frame src="e13_1.html">
<frame src="p3.html">
</frameset>
</html>
```

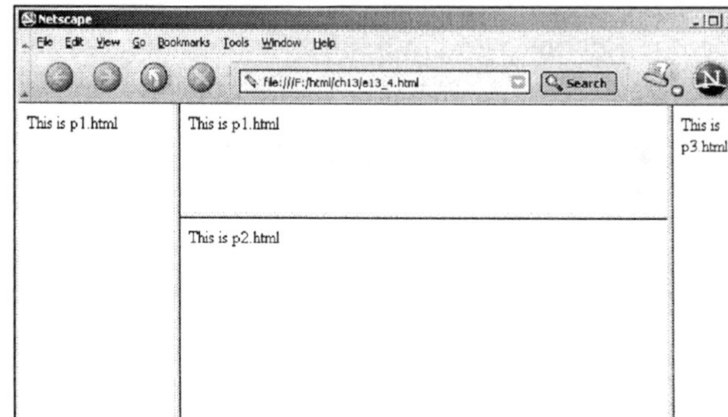

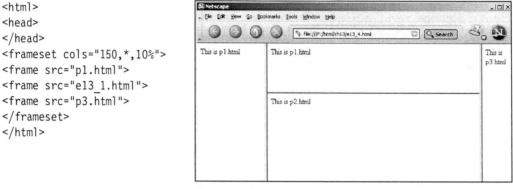

Figure 13.4

Note

◆ The content of the middle frame is a container (frameset) for the two horizontal frames.

The second option is to replace a frame element inside a frameset with the description of another frameset. Let's change the previous example in this way to obtain the same functionality and appearance.

Example 13_5. Nested framesets (file e13_5.html)

```
<html>
<head>
</head>
<frameset cols="150,*,10%">
<frame src="p1.html">
      <frameset rows="100,*">
      <frame src="p1.html">
      <frame src="p2.html">
      </frameset>
<frame src="p3.html">
</frameset>
</html>
```

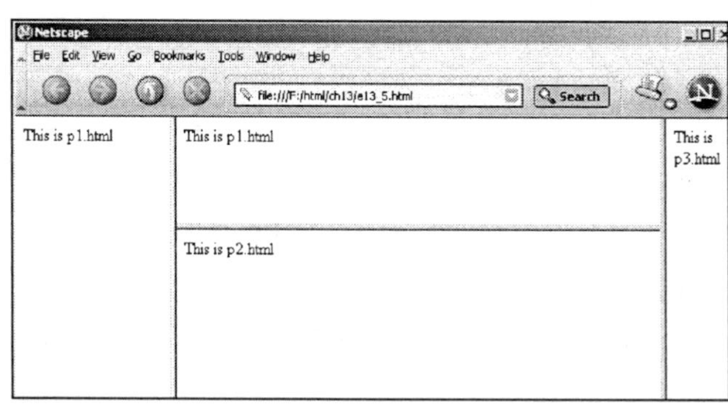

Figure 13.5

13.7 The <frameset> attributes

The `<frameset>` element accepts attributes to describe the content and the appearance of the frame. These attributes are:

- `cols` to describe the vertical division of the frameset. The value of this attribute is a *double-quoted, comma-delimited* list of any combination of the following:

- Positive integers defining an absolute size in pixels
- Percentages defining a size as a percentage of the size of the parent frame
- `n*` where `n` is a positive integer defining how many equal parts of the rest of the space (the `*` character represents all remaining space)

■ `rows` to describe the horizontal division of the frameset. The value of this attribute is a *double-quoted, comma-delimited list* (same possible values as `cols`).

■ `border` to define the thickness in pixels of the inter-frame borders. The possible values are 0 and positive integers (if set to 0, the inter-frame borders disappear).

■ `bordercolor` to define the color of the borders. The possible values are color names or RGB color descriptions.

■ `frameborder` to define whether or not the borders are visible. The possible values are `"yes"` (the default value) and `"no"`.

■ `framespacing` is identical to the `frameborder` attribute, but applies only to Internet Explorer.

Example 13_6. The `<frameset>` attributes (file e13_6.html)

```
<html><head></head>
<frameset rows="150,*,10%,100"
frameborder="no">
<frame src="logo.gif">
      <frameset cols="100,5*,*,10%"
border="15" bordercolor="#ff0000"
frameborder="yes">
      <frame src="p1.html">
      <frame src="p2.html">
      <frame src="p3.html">
      <frame src="p4.html">
      </frameset>
<frame src="p5.html">
<frame src="p6.html">
</frameset></html>
```

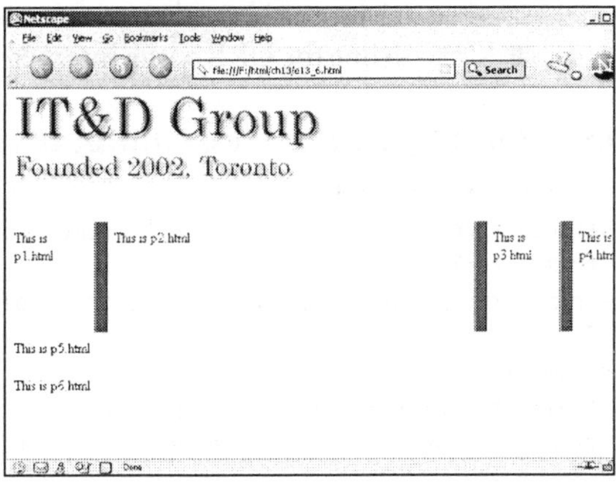

Figure 13.6

13.8 The `<frame>` attributes

The `<frame>` attributes allow you to specify the role and appearance of each frame. These attributes are:

■ `bordercolor` to define the color of the border. The possible values are color names or RGB color descriptions. The value of this attribute overrides the value of the `bordercolor` attribute of the `<frameset>` (if set).

- `frameborder` to define whether or not the borders are visible. The possible values are `"yes"` (the default value) and `"no"`. The value of this attribute overrides the value of the `frameborder` attribute of the `<frameset>` (if set).
- `marginheight` to define the white space between the content of the frame and the top and bottom margins. The possible values are 0 and positive integers defining the size in pixels.
- `marginwidth` to define the white space between the content of the frame and the left and right margins. The possible values are 0 and positive integers defining the size in pixels.
- `name` to add a unique identifier to the frame (used to define the target frames for links).
- `noresize` to make the frame non-resizable.
- `scrolling` to set the appearance of the horizontal and vertical scrollbars. The possible values are:
  - `"auto"` (the default value; the scrollbars appear only if necessary)
  - `"yes"` (the scrollbars appear at all times)
  - `"no"` (the scrollbars do not appear at all)
- src to define the URL of the Internet resource that will be loaded into the frame.

Example 13_7. The `<frame>` attributes (file e13_7.html)

```
<html><head></head>
<frameset rows="*,3*" cols="*,*,*" frameborder="yes" bordercolor="green">
<frame src="logo.gif" noresize>
<frame src="p2.html" marginwidth="100" scrolling="yes">
<frame src="p3.html" frameborder="no" longdesc="http://www.oracle.com">
<frame src="f3.pdf">
<frame src="p5.html" marginheight="100" marginwidth="100">
<frame src="p6.html" marginheight="100" bordercolor="blue">
</frameset></html>
```

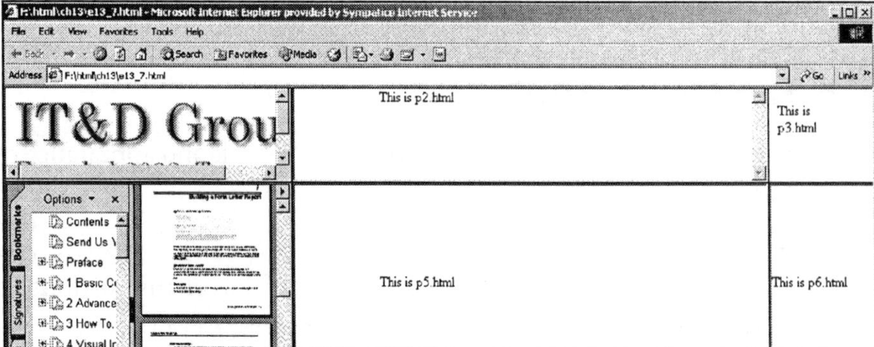

Figure 13.7

Note

- Different browsers may render these properties differently, so be aware and test your web pages before you deploy them.

13.9 Targets

The link target is the window or frame where a new Internet resource pointed to by a link will be loaded. By default, the target of a link is the same window or frame in which the link is placed. To change this default setting, you must assign a target to the link. This can be done in two ways:

1. By assigning a target for all links contained in a web page. To do this, set the `target` attribute of the `<base>` element and place this element in the `<head>...</head>` element of the page.
2. By assigning a `target` attribute to a specific link (i.e. to the `<a>` element).

The possible values for the `target` attribute are:

- The `name` of a window opened by the browser or the `name` of a frame loaded by the browser.
- One of these magic values:
  - `_self` (the new resource is loaded into the same window/frame)
  - `_blank` (the new resource is loaded into a new window)
  - `_parent` (the new resource is loaded into the parent window/frameset)
  - `_top` (the new resource is loaded into the browser window)

Example 13_8. Targets (files index.html, home.html, menu.html, logo.html and main.html)

```
<html><head>
<title>main.html
</title>
</head><body>
This is the Main Page!
</body></html>
```

```
<html><head>
<title>logo.html
</title>
</head><body>
<center>
<img src="logo.gif">
</center>
</body></html>
```

```
<html><head>
<title>home.html
</title>
</head><body>
<a href="index.html"
target="_top">Home<a>
</body></html>
```

```
<html><head>
<title>index.html
</title>
</head>
<frameset rows="150,*" cols="150,*"
frameborder="no">
<frame src="home.html" name="home">
<frame src="logo.html" name="logo">
<frame src="menu.html" name="menu">
<frame src="main.html" name="main">
</frameset>
</html>
```

```
<html><head>
<title>menu.html
</title>
<base target="main"></head>
<body>
HTML by Example
<br><a href="p1.html">1. First Page</a>
<br><a href="p2.html">2. Fonts and
Colors</a>
<br><a href="p3.html">3. Physical
Styles</a>
<br><a href="p4.html">4. Links</a>
</body></html>
```

Figure 13.8

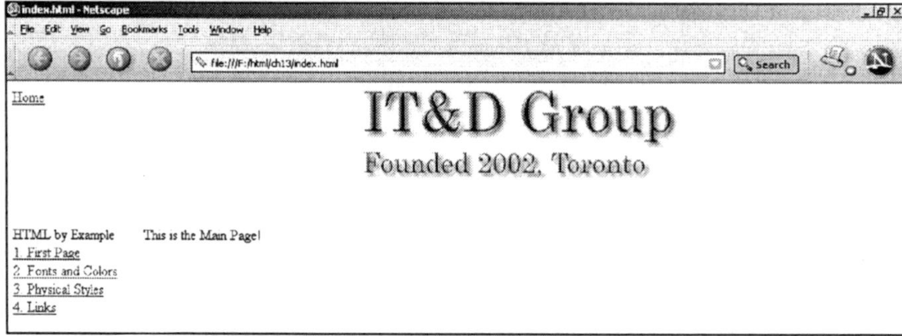

13.10 Older Browsers

Tags that a browser cannot interpret will be ignored by the browser and therefore not rendered. Therefore, a frameset block and all its frame elements would be ignored and not rendered by an older browser that does not support frames. In this case, the browser would display a blank page.

This problem can easily be solved by inserted a `<noframes>…</noframes>` element into the outermost `<frameset>…</frameset>` block. Of course, even this tag will be ignored by the older browser, but its content will be rendered *as-is*, allowing you to insert useful information for users surfing the web with older browsers.

You can insert regular HTML code into the `<noframes>…</noframes>` element, including a complete `<body>…</body>` block. Do not include the `<html>…</html>` block because this is normally already included in the page. Newer browsers will recognize and ignore the `<noframes>…</noframes>` tag, and in this way each user will see only one kind of content (i.e. only frames or noframes).

Example 13_9. Older browsers (file e13_9.html)

```
<html><head><title>index.html
</title></head>
<frameset rows="150,*" cols="150,*">
<frame src="home.html" name="home">
<frame src="logo.html" name="logo">
<frame src="menu.html" name="menu">
<frame src="main.html" name="main">
<noframes><body>
This page is designed for browsers capable of
supporting frames.
A version of this page without frames can be
visited at:
<br><a href="http://www.itdgroup.com/old">
No Frames Version</a>
</body></noframes></frameset></html>
```

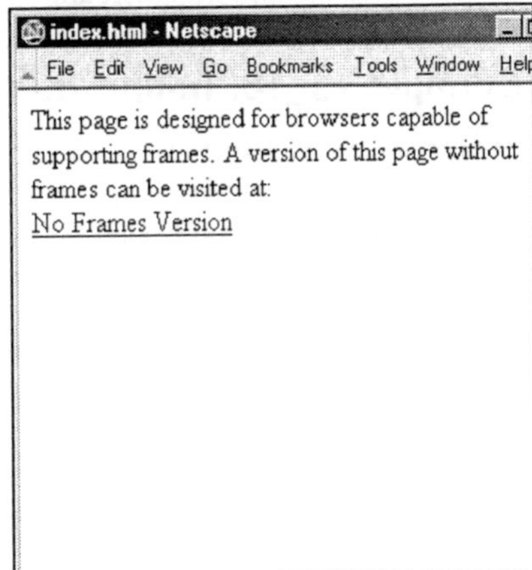

Figure 13.9

Note

- To get the screen capture in Figure 13.9, we used a trick in the code. We added an "x" to each tag related to frames (e.g. framesetx, framex, noframesx). In this way, Netscape 7.1 was not able to recognize a frame structure and rendered the content of the <noframesx>...<noframesx> element without interpreting it.

13.11 In-line frames

In-line frames (iframes) are frames that can be inserted anywhere inside a web page (similar to image elements). To insert an in-line frame, use the <iframe>...</iframe> element.

Notes

- The <iframe> element uses all the same attributes as the <frame> element to the same effects (i.e. frameborder, marginheight, marginwidth, name, scrolling, and src).
- There are several attributes, specific to image elements, that can be used with the <iframe> element to the same effect (width, height, align, hspace, and vspace). The default values for width and height are 300 pixels and 150 pixels, respectively.
- The name attribute of the <iframe> element can be used as a target for links.
- The src attribute of the <iframe> element defines the URL of the Internet resource that will be loaded into the frame.
- You can add as many <iframe> elements as you want to a web page. Use the name attribute to attach a unique identifier to each of them.

◆ If the browser doesn't support iframes, the content of the `<iframe>...</iframe>` element will be rendered instead.

Example 13_10. In-line frames (file e13_10.html)

```
<html><head></head><body>
This is the text before the first iframe. This is the text before the first iframe.
This is the text before the first iframe.
<iframe src="../ch12/e12_3.html" align="left">iframe 1</iframe>
This is the text between the iframes. This is the text between the iframes. This is
the text between the iframes. This is the text between the iframes.
<iframe src="../ch07/e7_7.html" align="right" width="350" height="200">iframe
2</iframe>
This is the text after the last iframe. This is the text after the last iframe.
This is the text after the last iframe. This is the text after the last iframe.
</body></html>
```

Figure 13.10

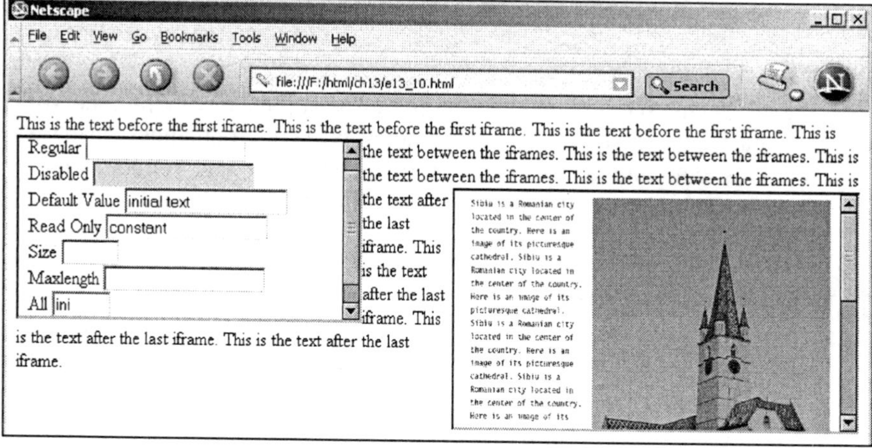

13.12 Review of Chapter 13

At the end of Chapter 13, you should know:

- Frames are used to render multiple web pages simultaneously in the same browser window.
- Frames are defined using the `<frame>` element inside the `<frameset>` element, which replaces the regular `<body>` element in an HTML file.
- The `cols` and `rows` attributes of the `<frameset>` element allow you to split the browser window into vertical (for `cols`) and horizontal (for `rows`) frames.

- There are other attributes of the <frameset> element, like border (to attach a border), bordercolor (to assign a color to the border), frameborder (to define if the borders are visible or not), and framespacing (for Internet Explorer).
- There are similar attributes for the <frame> element, like bordercolor and frameborder
- Other <frame> attributes for the <frame> element are marginheight and marginwidth (to define the white space between the content and the margin), name (to attach a unique identifier to the frame), noresize (to disable click and drag resizing of the frames), scrolling (to attach scroll bars), and src (to define the URL of the page that will be loaded in that frame).
- The <base> element, placed inside of the <head> element in conjunction with the target attribute, allows you to define a target for links placed in a web page.
- There are four magic values of the target attribute: _self, _blank, _parent, and _top
- The <noframes> element, placed into the <frameset> element, allows you to set a web page that can be rendered by older browsers.
- The <iframe> element allows you to insert in-line frames anywhere in a regular web page. The <iframe> element accepts all the attributes of a regular <frame> element in addition to some attributes specific to the <image> element, like width, height, align, hspace, and vspace

Chapter 14

Introduction to CSS

14.1 Cascading Style Sheets

CSS stands for *Cascading Style Sheets*. CSS is used to refine the presentation of a web page (i.e. the way the browser displays it). CSS allows you to set properties for HTML elements using a huge variety of values. Having more than 100 properties, CSS is an advanced tool for web designers to create professional web sites that cannot be made using regular HTML attributes.

14.2 Declarations

A style sheet is a *set of rules*. To define a *rule* you need a *selector* and a *declaration*. The selector allows you to choose which elements will use the settings defined by the declaration.

A declarations has the syntax:

```
property_name : property_value;
```

where the `property_name` is *a reserved word* that defines a *property* and the `property_value` is a valid *value* for that property.

Here are some examples of declarations we use in this chapter, including a short description. For full details related to them, please see Chapters 15-20.

`font-size : 12pt;`	used to set the size of the text to 12 pt
`font-style : italic;`	used to set the style of the text to italic style

`color : red;`	used to set the color of the text to red
`background : yellow;`	used to set the color of the background to yellow
`text-transform : uppercase;`	used to render text in upper-case style
`text-decoration : none;`	used to eliminate any decoration of the text
`cursor : move;`	used to set the mouse pointer to the move style

14.3 Declaration blocks

A *declaration block* is a list of declarations separated by semi-colons (;) and included in a {...} block. Here are some declaration blocks you can make using the declarations presented above:

```
{font-size : 12pt; font-style : italic;}
{color : red; text-transform : uppercase;}
{text-decoration : none; cursor : move;}
{background : yellow;}
```

Notes

- The last ";" symbol is optional in a declaration block.
- Black spaces can be added before and after the ":" or ";" symbols to increase the readability of the code.

14.4 The type selectors

To define a rule, use a *selector* followed by a *declaration block*. There are many different types of selectors, which we will describe in detail later in this chapter. For now, we will use HTML tags (the type selector). For example, the following code defines a rule for rendering all <p> element using a 12 pt, italic font. In this case `p` is the selector, so it applies to any <p> element.

```
p {font-size : 12pt; font-style : italic;}
```

14.5 Style sheets

Many rules can be added to define a *style sheet*. For example, the following fragment represents a *style sheet*:

```
p {font-size : 12pt; text-transform : uppercase;}
h3 {font-style : italic; background : cyan;}
div {color : red; font-size : 12pt;}
```

```
ol {background : yellow;}
il {font-style : italic;}
a {text-decoration : none; color : green;}
img {cursor : move;}
```

In this example, the *selectors* are regular HTML elements (type selectors).

14.6 Universal attributes for HTML elements

There are several attributes that can be attached to almost any HTML element included in the `<body>...</body>` element of a web page.

They are:

- `id` to attach a *unique identifier* to the element. The possible values are unique identifiers for the document (e.g. `id="id1"`).
- `class` to assign a *class* to the element. The possible values are space-separated lists of identifiers (e.g. `class="c1 c2 myclass yourclass"`).
- `style` to assign a *style* to the element. The possible values are sequences of declarations of styles (e.g. `style="font-style : italic; cursor : crosshair;"`).
- `title` to assign a *title* (tooltip) for the element. The possible values are double-quoted strings (e.g. `title="this is the title"`).
- `lang` to define the *language* for the content of the element. The possible values are double-quoted language identifiers (e.g. `lang="en"`).
- `dir` to define a *rendering direction* of the content for the element. The possible values are `"ltr"` (for left to right) or `"rtl"` (for right to left).

14.7 In-line styles

As mentioned above, you can add a `style` attribute to almost any HTML element (`BASE`, `BASEFONT`, `HEAD`, `HTML`, `META`, `PARAM`, `SCRIPT`, `STYLE`, and `TITLE` are exceptions). The value of the `style` attribute is a list of declarations separated by semi-colons (;).

For example:

```
style="font-style : italic; cursor : crosshair;"
```

creates an italic font style and a crosshair cursor style for the element to which it is attached.

Example 14_1. In-line styles (file e14_1.html)

```
<html><head></head><
body>
<h3 style="font-size : 24pt;">This Heading has a 12 pt Font Style</h3>
<p style="font-style : italic;">This Paragraph has an Italic Style</p>
<div style="color : cyan;">The Division Block has a Cyan Color</div>
<img src="logo.gif" style="cursor : move;">
<br><a href="p.html" style="text-decoration : none; font-style : italic;">
This is Just a Link! Isn't It?</a>
<ol style="background : yellow; "> An Ordered List:
<li> The First Item
<li style="text-transform : uppercase;"> Make Me UpperCase!
</ol></body></html>
```

Figure 14.1

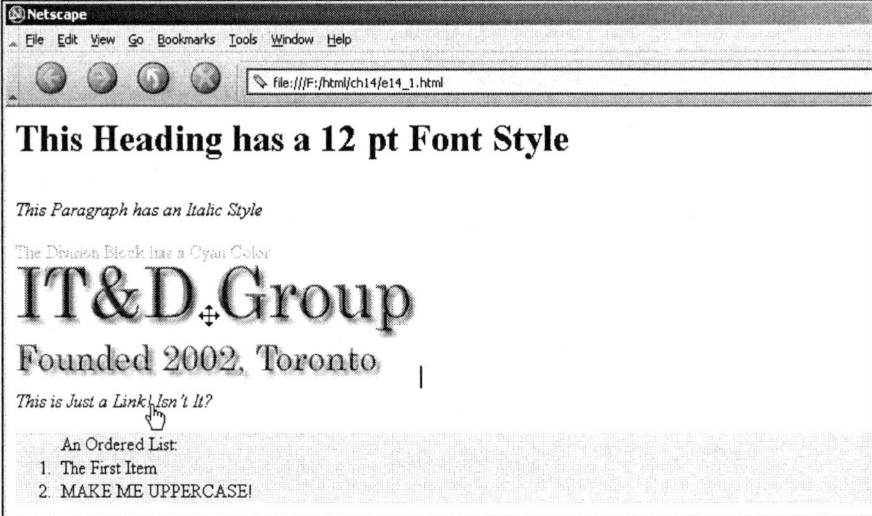

Notes

- The above screen shot was edited to show the appearance of the mouse pointer both when it is over the image and when it is over the link.
- Internet Explorer renders the background of the ordered list a little differently.

14.8 Style sheet defined inside the document

The style declared in the last section was an *in-line* style that you can attach directly to an element, using the `style` attribute of that element.

If you want to define a style and apply it to many elements that belong to a web page, use a style sheet. The style sheet can be place inside the document using a

<style>…</style> element, or it can be placed in an external file (see Section 14.9 for details).

To define a style sheet inside the document, place the style sheet rules inside a <style>…</style> element and insert that element into the <head>…</head> section of the web page. A required attribute of the <style> element is type. This attribute defines the style sheet syntax used to define the rules. Set this attribute to "text/css" for CSS (the default value). To be compatible with older browsers that cannot correctly interpret the <style> element, wrap the rules inside an HTML comment element:

```
<head>
<style type="text/css">
<!--
Insert the style sheet rules here…
-->
</style>
</head>
```

Example 14_2. Style sheet defined inside the document (file e14_2.html)

```
<html><head><style>
p {font-size : 12pt; text-transform : uppercase;}
h3 {font-style : italic; background : cyan;}
div {color : red; font-size : 16pt;}
ol {background : yellow;}
li {font-style : italic;}
a {text-decoration : none; color : green;}
img {cursor : move;}
</style></head><body>
<p>This paragraph has a 12 pt font size and uppercase characters
<h3>This heading has an italic style and a cyan background</h3>
<div>This division block has a red color and a 16 pt font size </div>
<ol>This List has a yellow background<li>italic item<li>another italic item</ol>
<a href="#">This link has a green color and is not underlined</a>
<br><img src="smile.gif">
</body></html>
```

Figure 14.2

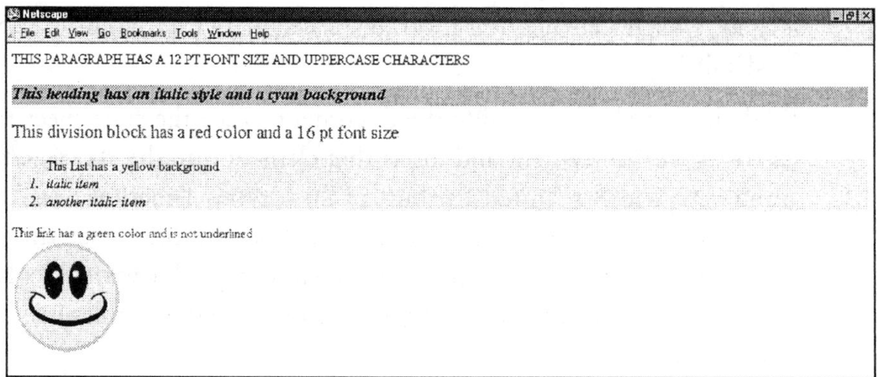

14.9 Style sheet defined in external files

You can define a style sheet in an external file and then link it to any web page you want to have the same appearance. In this way, the changes made in the style sheet file will affect all the web pages linked to that style sheet file. The style sheet file will be shared between many pages that belong to the same project or web site. This is the "*Write once, run anywhere*" philosophy.

To create a style sheet file, place the style sheet (the set of rules) inside a regular text file and attach the `.css` extension to that file.

To create a link between a web page and an external style sheet file, place a `<link>` element inside the `<head>...</head>` element of that web page. Three attributes of the `<link>` element are required:

- `type` set to `"text/css"`
- `rel` set to `"stylesheet"`
- `href` set to the URL of the external style sheet file (the `.css` file)

Example 14_3. External style sheets (files e14_3.html, styles.css)

```
<html><head>
<link rel="stylesheet" type="text/css" href="styles.css">
</head><body>
<h3>uppercase heading 3</h3>
<table border><tr><td>c11<td>c12
<tr><td>c21<td>c22</table>
<p>Italic paragraph
<div>The cursor type for this division block is "move"</div>
<a href="#">green link, normal style</a>
</body></html>
```

```
h3 {text-transform : uppercase;}
table {background : yellow; color : red;}
p {font-style : italic;}
div {cursor : move;}
a {text-decoration : none; color : green;}
```

Figure 14.3

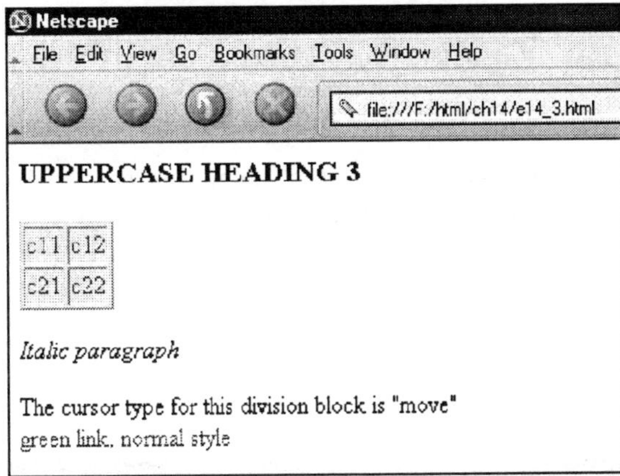

14.10 The cascading of styles

It is possible for many styles to apply simultaneously to an element. The Cascading Style Sheets define a rigorous priority of rules (the cascading of styles) that determine which style is applied to an element:

1. If an in-line style exists for that element, the in-line style is applied.
2. If an in-line style doesn't exist for that element, the styles defined inside of the document are applied.
3. If a style defined inside of the document doesn't exist for that element, the styles defined in external style sheets are applied.
4. If a style defined in external style sheets doesn't exist for that element, the default HTML styles are applied.

Example 14_4. The cascading of styles (files e14_4.html, styles2.css)

```
<html><head><title>e14_4.html</title>
<link rel="stylesheet" type="text/css" href="styles2.css">
<style>
h2 {text-transform : uppercase;}
tr {color : red;}
a {font-style : italic;}
</style>
```

```
</head><body>
<h1 style="font-size : 30pt;">h1, in-line, 30 pt</h3>
<h2>h2, inside document, uppercase</h2>
<h3>h3, external file, red</h3>
<h4>h4, HTML default style</h4>
<table border>
<tr><td style="background : yellow;">td, in-line, yellow background<td>tr, in
document, red color
<tr><td>table, external file, italic<td>default border style
</table>
<a href="#" style="text-decoration : none;">in-line none, inside italic, external
yellow background, and default hand mouse pointer</a>
</body></html>

/*styles2.css*/
h3 {color : red;}
table {font-style : italic;}
a {background : yellow;}
```

Figure 14.4

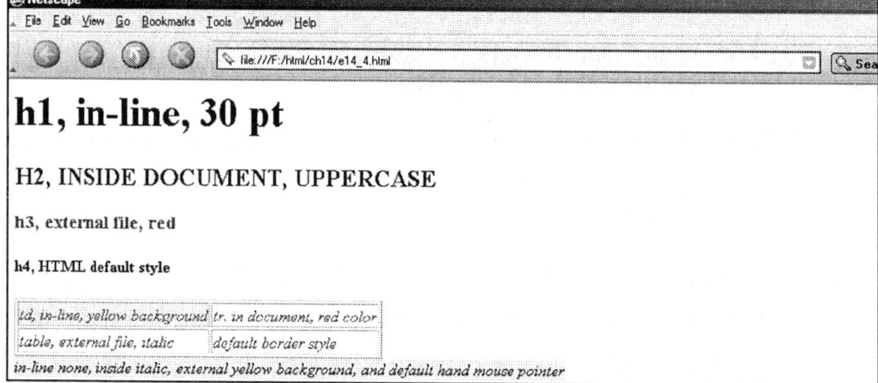

14.11 Selectors

Now that you understand how to define rules and create style sheets, we will explore the topic of *selectors*. As we presented above, selectors are used to determine the HTML elements to which the rules will apply. So far, we have defined selectors using the HTML elements (the type selector). In the following sections, we present other kinds of selectors used in CSS.

14.12 The universal selector

The *universal selector* matches any element and is denoted by the * symbol.

Example 14_5. The universal selector (file e14_5.html)

```
<html><head>
<style>
* {color : red; font-style : italic;
background : yellow;}
</style></head><body>
<ul>All elements on this page are
rendered with:
<li>a red color
<li>a yellow background
<li>an italic font style
</ul>
<h1>This is Heading 1</h1>
<p>This is a paragraph
<br><a href="#">This is a link</a>
</body></html>
```

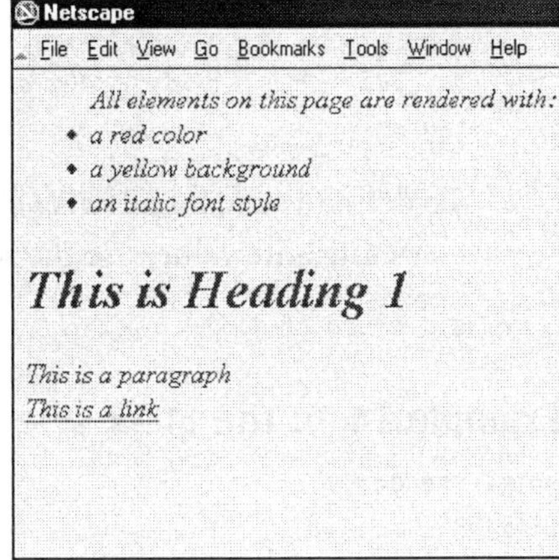

Figure 14.5

14.13 The `class` selector

As mentioned earlier in this chapter, almost any HTML element can accept the `class` attribute. The value of this attribute must be a list of identifiers separated by spaces (e.g. `class="c1 c2 myclass yourclass"`). In this way, you can create classes and assign the HTML elements to those classes.

You can define a style for elements that belongs to a class. First, let's define some `class` attributes:

```
<p class="c1">paragraph 1
<p class="c2">paragraph 2
<h1 class="c1 c2">heading 1
<div class="c3 c4">division block 1</div>
<div class="c2 c3 c5 c6">division block 2</div>
<a href="#" class="c2 c3 c4 c5 c6">a link</a>
```

To define a style for all elements with `"c1"` included in the `class` attribute value, use these selectors:

`*.c1 {…}` *These selectors match paragraph 1 and heading 1.*

`.c1 {…}`

To define a style for all <p> elements having "c2" included in the class attribute value, use the selector:

`p.c2 {…}` *This selector matches paragraph 2 only.*

To define a style for all elements having "c2" *and* "c3" included in the class attribute value, use these selectors:

`*.c2.c3 {…}` *These selectors match division block 2 and to the link.*
`.c2.c3 {…}`

To define a style for all <div> elements having "c2", "c3", and "c6" included in the class attribute value, use the selector:

`div.c2.c3.c6 {…}` *This selector matches division block 2 only.*

Example 14_6. The class selector (file e14_6.html)

```
<html><head>
<style>
*.c1 {color : red;}
p.c2 {font-style : italic;}
*.c2.c3 {background : yellow;}
div.c2.c3.c6 {text-transform : uppercase;}
</style></head><body>
<p class="c1">paragraph 1
<p class="c2">paragraph 2
<h1 class="c1 c2">heading 1
<div class="c3 c4">division block 1</div>
<div class="c2 c3 c5 c6">division block
2</div>
<a href="#" class="c2 c3 c4 c5 c6">a link</a>
</body></html>
```

Figure 14.6

14.14 The id selector

Another universal attribute is the id attribute. The value of this attribute must be a unique identifier for the entire HTML document. You can create selectors using the id attribute. For example:

`*#id1` *matches any elements with the* id *attribute equal to* "id1"

`p#id2` *matches a* <p> *element with the* id *attribute equal to* "id2"

`div#id3` *matches a* <div> *element with the* id *attribute equal to* "id3"

Example 14_7. The `id` selector (file e14_7.html)

```
<html><head>
<style>
*#id1 {color : red;}
p#id2 {font-style : italic;}
div#id3 {background : yellow;}
</style></head><body>
<h3 id="id1">heading with id1</h3>
<p>normal paragraph
<p id="id2">paragraph with id2
<div>normal division block</div>
<div id="id3">division block with id3</div>
</body></html>
```

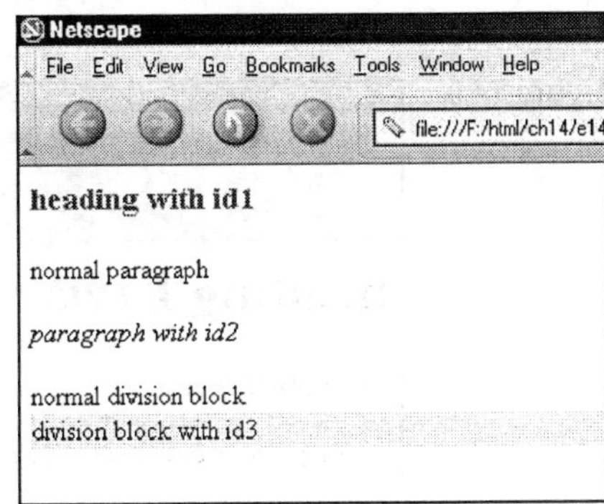

Figure 14.7

14.15 The descendent selectors

The descendent selectors match elements that are nested inside of other elements. The descendent selectors have the syntax:

```
A B {…}
```

and match any B element that is inside an A element (i.e. B is an arbitrary descendent of A).

For example:

`h1 i {…}`	*matches any `<i>` element that is inside an `<h1>` element*
`div b {…}`	*matches any `<b>` element that is inside a `<div>` element*
`p i b {…}`	*matches any `<b>` element that is inside an `<i>` element that is inside a `<p>` element*
`p * i {…}`	*matches any `<i>` element that is a descendant of a `<p>` element but not a direct child (is a grandchild)*

Example 14_8. The descendant selector (file e14_8.html)

```
<html><head>
<style>
h1 i {color : red;}
div b {font-style : italic;}
p i b {background : yellow;}
p * i { text-transform : uppercase;}
</style></head><body>
<h1>heading 1 <i>italic </i> heading 1</h1>
<div>division <b> bold </b>division</div>
```

```
<p>paragraph<i> italic <b> bold </b> italic </i> paragraph</p>
<p><span><i>italic in span in paragraph</i></span></p>
</body></html>
```

Figure 14.8

14.16 The child selector

Child selectors have the syntax:

```
A > B {…}
```

and match any B element that is immediately inside an A element (i.e. B is a direct descendent or child of A).

For example:

body > p {…}	*matches any <p> element that is child of the <body> element*
p > i {…}	*matches any <i> element that is a direct descendent of a <p> element*
table > td {…}	*cannot match any element because <td> is always a grandchild of the <table> element (between them is the <tr> element)*
p > i > b {…}	*matches any <b> element that is a child of a <i> element that is a child of a <p> element*

Example 14_9. The child selector (file e14_9.html)

```
<html><head><style>
body > p {color : red;}
p > i {font-style : italic;}
p > i > b {background : yellow;}
div > b { text-transform : uppercase;}
</style></head><body>
<p>paragraph, child of body
```

```
<p><i>italic, child of paragraph</i></p>
<p>paragraph<i> italic <b> bold, child of italic, child of paragraph </b> italic
</i> paragraph</p>
<div>division <b> bold, child of division </b>division</div>
</body></html>
```

Figure 14.9

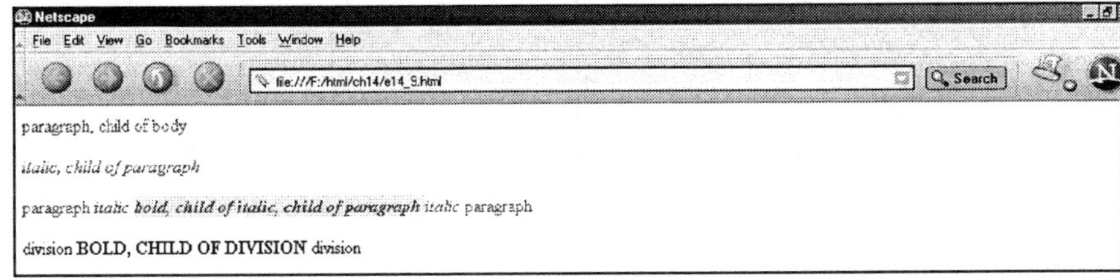

Note that all <p> elements are children of the <body> element and are rendered in a red color (using the first rule).

14.17 The adjacent sibling selector

The adjacent sibling selector has the syntax:

`A + B {...}`

and matches if the elements A and B both have the same parent and A immediately precedes B.

For example:

`h1 + h2 {...}`	*matches any <h2> element that follows immediately after an <h1> element where both have the same parent*
`p + ol {...}`	*matches any <ol> element that follows immediately after a <p> where both have the same parent*
`tr + tr {...}`	*matches any row of a table except the first row*

Example 14_10. The adjacent sibling selector (file e14_10.html)

```
<html><head><style>
h1 + h2 {font-style : italic; color : red;}
p + ol {background : yellow;}
tr + tr {text-transform : uppercase;}
</style></head><body>
<h1>Heading 1</h1>
<h2>Heading 2</h2>
<p>Paragraph
<ol>Ordered list<li>Item 1<li>Item2</ol>
```

```
<table><tr><td>cell 11<tr><td>cell 21<tr><td>cell 31</table>
</body></html>
```

Figure 14.10

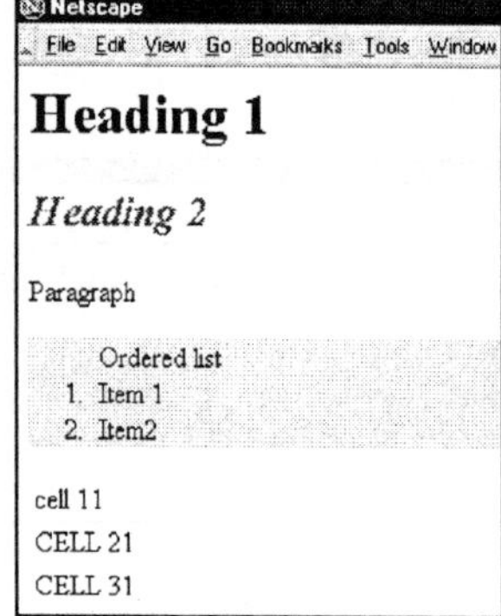

14.18 The attribute selector

The syntax for the attribute selector is:

- `E[attrib] {...}` — *matches if the element E has an attribute* `attrib`
- `E[attrib=val] {...}` — *matches if the element E has the attribute* `attrib=val`
- `E[atrib~=val] {...}` — *matches if the element E has an attribute* `attrib` *set to a list of space-separated values that includes* `val`
- `E[attrib|=val] {...}` — *matches if the element E has an attribute* `attrib` *set to a list of hyphen-separated values that starts with* `val`
- `E[attrib1=val1] [attrib2=val2] {...}` — *matches if the element E has an attribute* `attrib1=val1` *and an attribute* `attrib2=val2`

Example 14_11. The attribute selector (file e14_11.html)

```
<html><head><style>
p[id] {background : yellow;}
*[align="center"][id="id2"] {text-transform : uppercase;}
img[border][src="logo.gif"] {cursor : move;}
div[lang|="en"] {font-style : italic;}
</style></head><body>
<p>paragraph without id
<p id="id1">paragraph with id
<div lang="en-us">division block with lang en</div>
<h1 align="center" id="id2">heading center aligned</h1>
<img src="smile.gif">
<img border src="logo.gif">
</body></html>
```

Figure 14.11

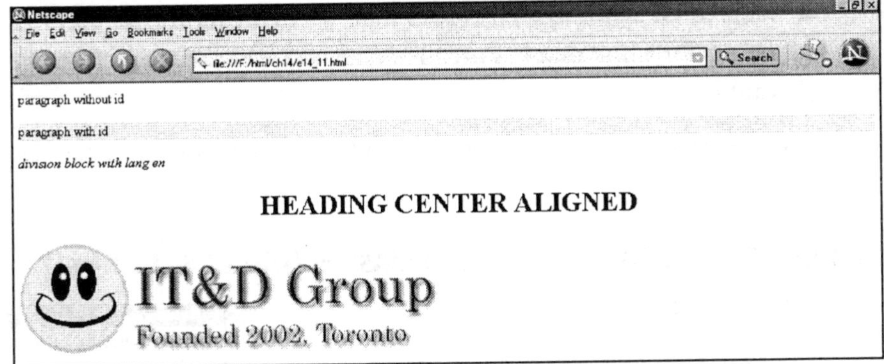

14.19 The :first-child pseudo-class

The :first-child pseudo-class has the syntax:

```
E: first-child {…}
```

and matches when the element E is the first child of the parent element.

Example 14_12. The :first-child pseudo-class (file e14_12.html)

```
<html><head><style>
p:first-child {background : yellow;}
td:first-child {font-style : italic; color : red;}
li:first-child {color : green;}
h3:first-child {text-transform : uppercase;}
</style></head><body>
<p>para 1</p>
<p>para 2</p>
<h3>heading 1</h3>
<h3>heading 2</h3>
<ol>ordered list<li>item 1<li>item2</ol>
<table><tr><td>c11<td>c12<tr><td>c21<td>c22<tr>
<td>c31<td>c32</table>
</body></html>
```

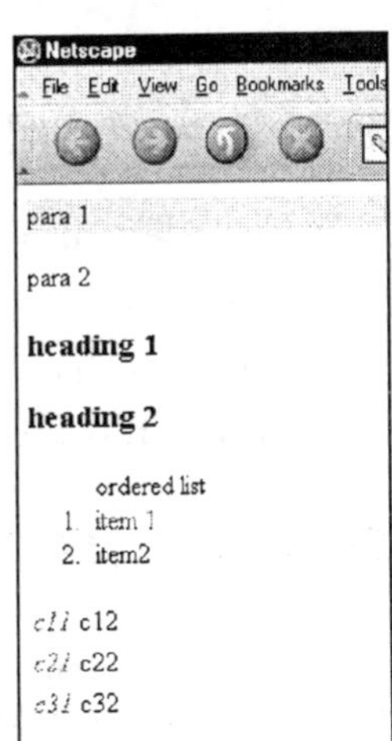

Figure 14.12

14.20 The link pseudo-classes

In CSS, a link has five states. There are five corresponding pseudo-classes:

- `:link` for links that have not yet been visited
- `:visited` for links that have been visited
- `:hover` for a link with the mouse pointer over it

- `:active` for a link when it is activated (when the mouse pointer is clicked on it)
- `:focus` for a link that has the focus (i.e. the user can use the <ENTER> key to activate it)

Use these pseudo-classes together with the <a> element, as in the following example.

Example 14_13. The link pseudo-classes (file e14_13.html)

```
<html><head><style>
a:link {color : blue;}
a:visited {color : red;}
a:hover {text-transform : uppercase;}
a:active {font-style : bold;}
a:focus {font-style : italic;}
</style></head><body>
<a href="e14_1.html">Example 1</a><br>
<a href="e14_2.html">Example 2</a><br>
<a href="e14_3.html">Example 3</a><br>
<a href="e14_40.html">Example 40</a><br>
<a href="e14_50.html">Example 50</a>
</body></html>
```

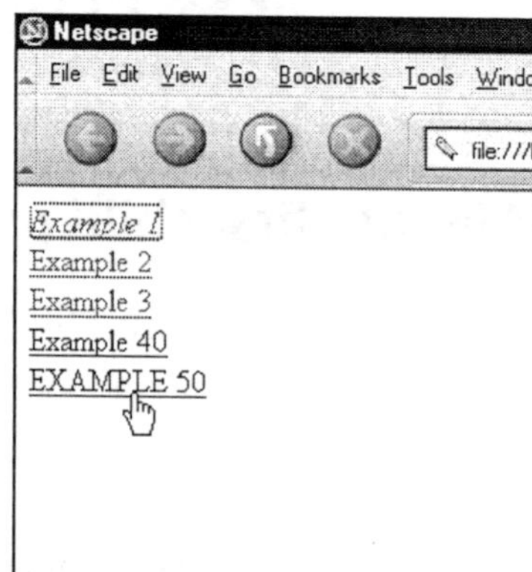

Figure 14.13

14.21 The :first-line pseudo-element

To select the first line of a block of text (e.g. paragraph, division text, etc.) use the selector:

```
E:first-line
```

where E is the element in which the first line is selected.

Example 14_14. The first-line pseudo-element (file e14_14.html)

```
<html><head><style>
p:first-line { font-style : italic;}
div:first-line { text-transform : uppercase;}
center:first-line {color : red;}
</style></head><body>
<p>This is a paragraph. This is a paragraph. This is a paragraph. This is a
paragraph. </p>
<div>This is a division block. This is a division block. This is a division block.
This is a division block. </div>
<center>This is a centered text. This is a centered text. This is a centered text.
This is a centered text. </center>
</body></html>
```

Figure 14.14

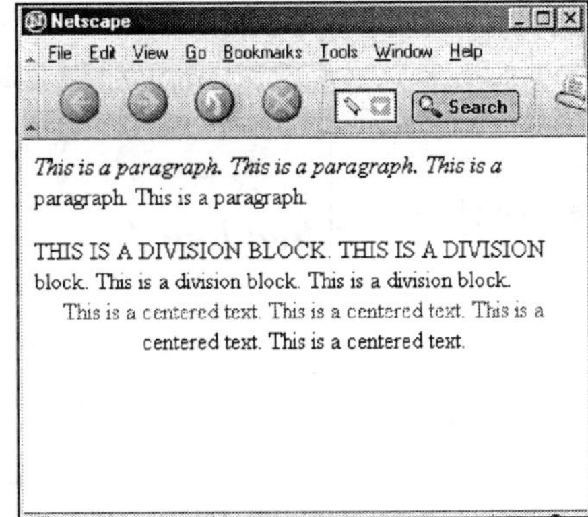

14.22 The :first-letter pseudo-element

To select the first letter of a block of text, use the selector:

```
E:first-letter
```

where E is the text element in which the first letter is selected.

Example 14_15. The first-letter pseudo-element (file e14_15.html)

```
<html><head><style>
p:first-letter {font-size : 300%;}
div:first-letter {color:red;font-size:20pt;}
center:first-letter {font-size : 30pt;
font-style : italic;}
</style></head><body>
<p>This is a paragraph.</p>
<div>Division block.</div>
<center>Centered text.</center>
</body></html>
```

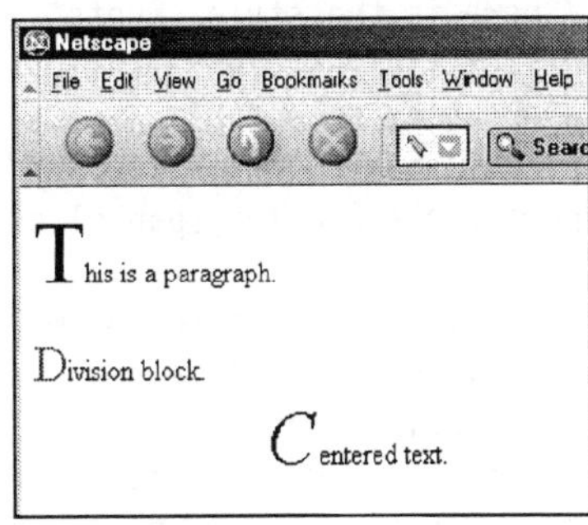

Figure 14.15

14.23 Grouping selectors

If the same style applies to many elements, you can group selectors in a list of selectors separated by commas:

```
S1, S2, S3, … {…}
```

For example, the rule

```
p, h1, div {color : red;}
```

defines a red color for all `<p>`, `<h1>`, and `<div>` elements.

Example 14_16. Grouping selectors (file e14_16.html)

```
<html><head><style>
h1, h2, p {font-style : italic;}
p, div {color : red;}
span, b, center {text-transform : uppercase;}
</style></head><body>
<h1>heading 1</h1>
<p>This is a <b>paragraph</b>.</p>
<div><span>Division</span> block.</div>
<center>Centered text.</center>
</body></html>
```

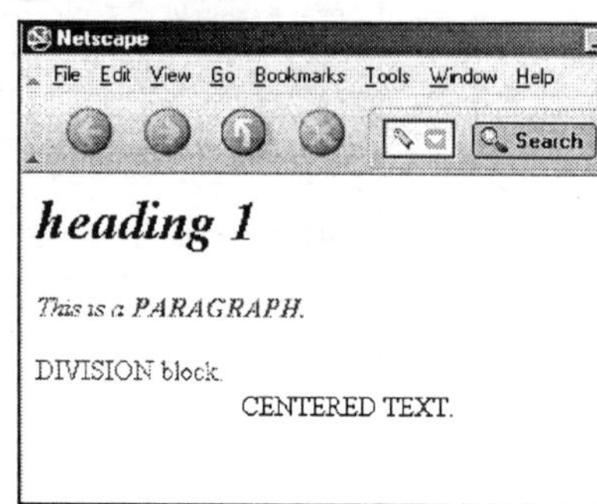

Figure 14.16

14.24 Comment blocks

You can use "/*" to start a comment block and "*/" to end it. Comment blocks cannot be nested one inside of another. Comment blocks are used to document style sheets and are ignored by the browser.

Example 14_17. The comment block (file e14_17.html)

```
<html><head><style>
/*here is the style sheets*/
h1, h2 {font-style : italic; color : red;} /*this is
a grouping selector*/
p, div span{color : blue;} /*this rule matches for
paragraphs and for span blocks inside a division
block*/
/* style sheet created on March 2004*/
</style></head><body>
<h1>heading 1</h1>
<p>This is a <b>paragraph</b>.</p>
<div>Division<span> Span </span> Division</div>
<h2>heading 2.</h2>
</body></html>
```

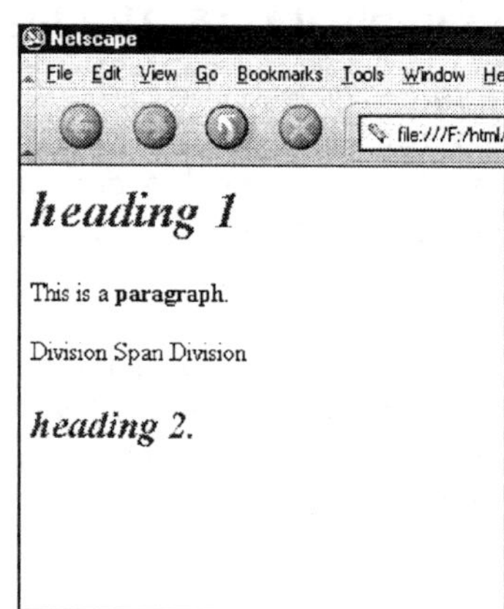

Figure 14.17

14.25 Values

Values are used to set properties. In CSS, the syntax for assigning values is very strict, so be careful.

Here are some categories of values you can use to set properties:

<number> stands for any real numbers (e.g. +3.14 or –0.01 or –123 or 400)

<integer>	stands for any integer numbers (e.g. 400 or -12)
<non-negative-integer>	stands for 0 or any positive integers (e.g. 10 or +12)
<relative-unit>	stands for: ■ `em` (relative to the `'font-size'`) ■ `ex` (relative to the `'x-height'`) ■ `px` (relative to the pixel size)
<absolute-unit>	stands for: ■ `in` (inches) ■ `cm` (centimeters) ■ `mm` (millimeters) ■ `pt` (points) ■ `pc` (picas; 1 pica = 12 pt = 1/6 inch)
<percentage>	stands for relative values expressed as percentages (e.g. +20% or –25% or +110%)
<length>	stands for horizontal or vertical measurements: ■ `<number><relative-unit>` ■ `<number><absolute-unit>`
<url>	stands for a valid URL (function notation): ■ `url`(e.g. `"http://www.itdgroup.com/e14_1.html"`)
<color>	stands for a color specification. The possible values are: ■ color name keywords (`aqua`, `black`, `blue`, `fuchsia`, `gray`, `green`, `lime`, `maroon`, `navy`, `olive`, `purple`, `red sil-ver`, `teal`, `white`, or `yellow`) ■ `#rgb` specification (e.g. `blue` corresponds to `#00f`) ■ `#rrggbb` specification (e.g `blue` corresponds to `#0000ff`) ■ `rgb(0,0,255)` for blue ■ `rgb(0%,0%,100%)` for blue

14.26 Review of Chapter 14

At the end of Chapter 14 you should know:

- CSS stands for Cascading Style Sheets and allows you to refine the presentation of a web page.
- A style sheet is a sequence of rules.

- A rule is a defined by a selector (to specify where the rule is applied) and a declaration (to specify a style).
- The declaration is a sequence of *property: value* pairs delimited by semi-colons.
- Properties are reserved words.
- Values use a very specific syntax.
- To define an in-line style, set the style property of an HTML element.
- To define a style inside of the HTML document, use a `<style>` element placed inside of the `<head>` element.
- To define a style in an external file, create a style sheet and make the browser rendering the document reference the style sheet by using a `<link>` element placed inside of the `<head>` element.
- The required attributes of the `<link>` element are: `rel` set to `"stylesheet"`, `type` set to `"text/css"`, and `href` set to the URL of the file containing the style sheet.
- Universal attributes can be attached to any HTML elements. They are: `id` (to define a unique identifier), `class` (to attach the element to a class), `style` (to attach a style), `title` (to attach a title), `lang` (to define a language), and `dir` (to define the direction of rendering).
- CSS defines a priority of styles that applies to rendering an element: first *in-line*, then *in document*, then *external files*, and finally *HTML style.*
- A selector can be defined by a universal, class, id, descendant, child, adjacent sibling, attribute, or grouping selector.
- To personalize links, use the pseudo-classes `:link`, `:visited`, `:hover`, `:active`, and `:focus`
- Other pseudo-classes include `:first-child`, `:first-line`, and `:first-letter`
- To insert a comment, use the C language syntax: /*...*/
- Be sure that when you assign a value to a property, the value is in the range of that property.

Chapter 15

Fonts in CSS

CSS allows you to refine font characteristics using a variety of properties and values.

15.1 Font family

The 'font-family' property allows you to specify the *font(s)* the browser uses to render a character.

The possible values are comma-separated lists of fonts:

- Family names (e.g. "Times New Roman", Arial, Symbol, "Courier New", etc). Font family names containing spaces should be quoted.
- Generic font names (e.g. serif, sans-serif, cursive, fantasy, and monospace). Generic fonts are keywords and must not be quoted.

For example:

```
font-family : "Times New Roman", Garamond, serif
font-family : "Arial", Verdana, Helvetica, sans-serif
font-family : "Adobe Poetica", cursive
font-family : "Alpha Geometrique", fantasy
font-family : "MS Courier New", Courier, monospace
```

Example 15_1. Font family (file e15_1.html)

```
<html><head>
<style>
p {font-family : "Times New Roman", Garamond, serif;}
div {font-family : "Arial", Verdana, Helvetica, sans-serif;}
```

```
h1 {font-family : "Adobe Poetica", cursive;color : red;}
h2 {font-family : "Alpha Geometrique", fantasy;}
span {font-family : "MS Courier New", Courier, monospace;color : blue;}
</style></head><body>
<p>"Times New Roman", Garamond, serif;
<div>"Arial", Verdana, Helvetica, sans-serif;</div>
<h1>"Adobe Poetica", cursive </h1>
<h2>"Alpha Geometrique", fantasy </h2>
<p>paragraph <span>"MS Courier New", Courier, monospace </span> paragraph
</body></html>
```

Figure 15.1

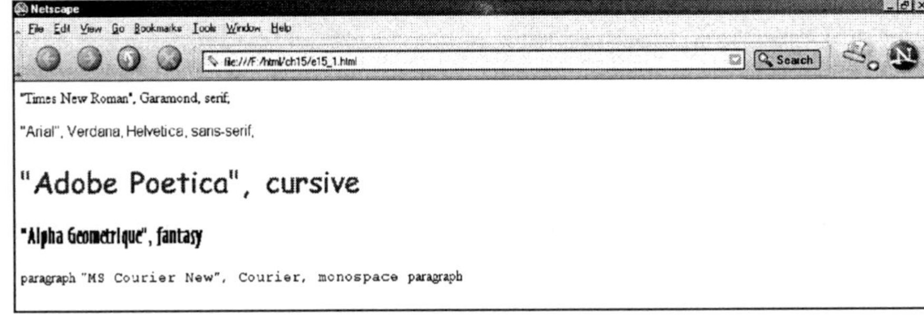

Notes

- The browser will use the first font it recognizes in the font set.
- It is recommended that the last font name in the list be a generic font name.

15.2 Font style

The 'font-style' property allows you to specify the *font style* the browser uses to render a character.

The possible values are:

- normal
- italic (similar to Cursive)
- oblique (similar to Slanted, Incline)
- inherit (the face will be inherited from the parent)

For example:

```
font-style : italic
font-style : normal
```

Example 15_2. Font style (file e15_2.html)

```
<html><head>
<style>
p {font-style : normal; color : red}
div {font-style : italic;}
h1 {font-style : oblique; color : green}
span {font-style : italic; color : blue;}
</style></head><body>
<p>this paragraph has font-style : normal;
<div>this division block has font-style : italic;</div>
<h1>this heading 1 has font-style : oblique; color : green </h1>
<p>paragraph <span>this span has font-style : italic; color : blue;</span>
paragraph
</body></html>
```

Figure 15.2

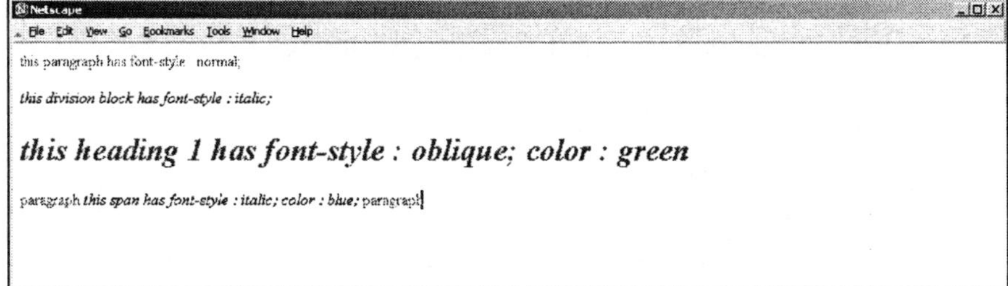

15.3 Font variant

The 'font-variant' property allows you to specify the *font variant* the browser uses to render lowercase characters.

The possible values are:

- normal
- small-caps (similar to uppercase characters but smaller in size)
- inherit (the face will be inherited from the parent)

For example:

```
font-variant : small-caps
font-variant : normal
```

Example 15_3. Font variant (file e15_3.html)

```
<html><head>
<style>
p {font-variant : normal; color : red}
```

```
table {font-variant : small-caps;font-style :
italic;}
ol {font-variant : small-caps; color : blue;}
</style></head>
<body>
<p> font-variant : NORMAL; color : RED;
<table border><tr><td>THIS<td>table<td>HAS
<tr><td>font-style<td>:<td> ITALIC</table>
<ol>ordered LIST<li>first ITEM<li>SECOND
item<li>last ITEM</ol>
</body></html>
```

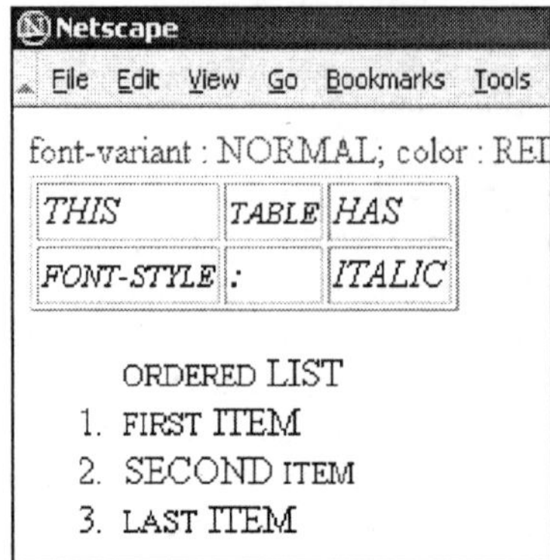

Figure 15.3

15.4 Font weight

The 'font-weight' property allows you to specify the *font weight* (boldness or lightness) the browser uses to render characters.

The possible values are:

- normal (similar to '400')
- bold (similar to '700')
- bolder (the next darker numerical value, up to '900')
- lighter (the next lighter numerical value, down to '100')
- 100 | 200 | 300 | 400 | 500 | 600 | 700 | 800 | 900
- inherit (the face will be inherited from the parent)

For example:

```
font-weight : bolder
font-weight : 900
```

Example 15_4. Font weight (file e15_4.html)

```
<html><head><style>
ol {font-family : "Times New Roman";}
ul {font-family : Arial;}
</style></head><body>
<ol>Ordered List
<li style="font-weight:lighter;">font-weight : lighter;
<li>inherit
<li style="font-weight : bolder;">font-weight : bolder;
</ol>
<ul>Un-ordered List
<li style="font-weight : 100;">font-weight : 100;
<li style="font-weight : 300;">font-weight : 300;
```

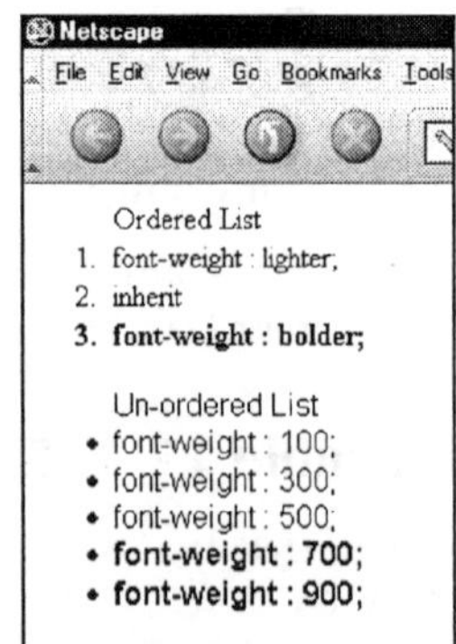

Figure 15.4

```
<li style="font-weight : 500;">font-weight : 500;
<li style="font-weight : 700;">font-weight : 700;
<li style="font-weight : 900;">font-weight : 900;
</ul></body></html>
```

Note that this style is not completely implemented by all browsers, as seen in the above example.

15.5 Font stretch

The 'font-stretch' property allows you to specify *the font stretch* (condensed or expanded) the browser uses to render characters.

The possible values are:

- normal
- wider (relative to the inherit value)
- narrower (relative to the inherit value)
- ultra-condensed | extra-condensed | condensed | semi-condensed
- semi-expanded | expanded | extra-expanded | ultra-expanded
- inherit (the face will be inherited from the parent)

For example:

```
font-stretch : extra-expanded
font-stretch : narrower
```

Example 15_5. Font stretch (file e15_5.html)

```
<html><head><style>
ol {font-family : "Times New Roman";}
ul {font-family : Arial;}
</style></head><body>
<ol>Ordered List
<li style="font-stretch : wider;">wider
<li style="font-stretch : normal;">normal
<li style="font-stretch : narrower;">narrower
</ol>
<ul>Un-ordered List
<li style="font-stretch : ultra-condensed;">ultra-condensed
<li style="font-stretch : condensed;">condensed
<li style="font-stretch : semi-condensed;">semi-condensed
<li style="font-stretch : semi-expanded;">semi-expanded
<li style="font-stretch : ultra-expanded;">ultra-expanded
</ul></body></html>
```

Note that neither Internet Explorer 6 nor Netscape 7.1 implements this style.

15.6 Font size

The 'font-size' property allows you to specify the *font size* (from baseline to baseline) the browser uses to render characters.

The possible values are:

- <absolute-size>:
  - xx-small | x-small | small | medium | large | x-large |xx-large
- <relative-size>
  - larger | smaller (relative to the parent value)
- <length>
- <percentage> (relative to the parent value)
- inherit (the face will be inherited from the parent)

For example:

```
font-size : xx-small
font-size : larger
font-size : 12pt
font-size : 120%
```

Example 15_6. Font size (file e15_6.html)

```
<html><head><style>
ol {color : red;}
ul {color : blue;}
</style></head><body>
<ol>Lenghts 1
<li>inherit
<li style="font-size : 1.2em;">1.2em;
<li style="font-size : 1.2ex;">1.2ex;
<li style="font-size : 20px;">bolder;
</ol>
<ul>Lengths 2
<li style="font-size : 0.5in;">0.5in;
<li style="font-size : 1cm;">1cm;
<li style="font-size : 5mm;">5mm;
<li style="font-size : 15pt;">15pt;
<li style="font-size : 2pc;">2pc;
</ul>
<ol>Absolute Size
```

```
<li style="font-size : xx-small;">xx-small
<li style="font-size : small;">small
<li>inherit
<li style="font-size : large;">large
<li style="font-size : xx-large;">xx-large
</ol>
<ul>Relative Size
<li style="font-size : larger;">larger
<li>inherit
<li style="font-size : smaller;">smaller
</ul>
<ol>Percentage
<li style="font-size : 50%;">50%
<li>inherit
<li style="font-size : 200%;">200%
</ol>
</body></html>
```

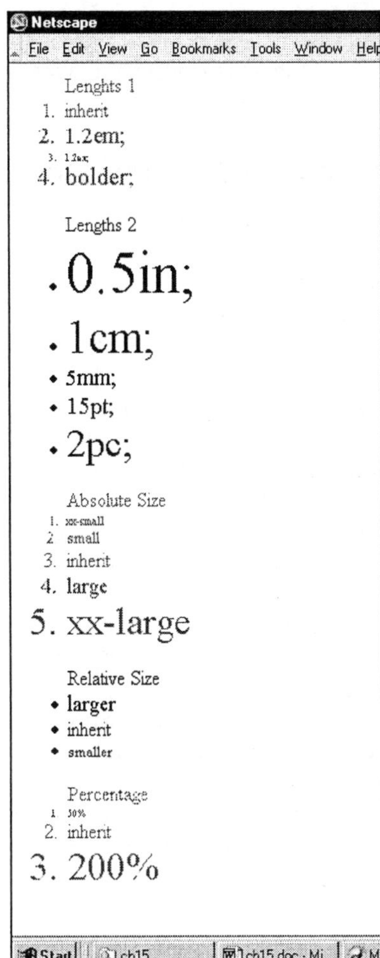

Figure 15.5

15.7 Font aspect value

The 'font-size-adjust' property allows you to specify the *font aspect value* (the ratio between the font-size value and the x-height) the browser uses to render characters. The normal values are 0.58 for Verdana and 0.46 for Times New Roman. Because of this parameter, the Verdana fonts remain legible at small sizes.

The possible values are:

- normal
- <number>
- inherit (the face will be inherited from the parent)

For example:

```
font-size-adjust : normal
font-size-adjust : 0.58
```

Example 15_7. Font aspect value (file e15_7.html)

```
<html><head><style>
ol {font-family : "Times New Roman";}
ul {font-family : Verdana;}
</style></head><body>
<ol>Times New Roman Fonts
<li style="font-size-adjust : 0.58;">0.58
(Verdana default value)
<li style="font-size-adjust : 0.46;">0.46 (Times
New Roman default value)
<li>inherit
<li style="font-size-adjust : 0.99;">0.99
<li style="font-size-adjust : 0.33;">0.33
</ol>
<ul>Verdana Fonts
<li style="font-size-adjust : 0.58;">0.58
(Verdana default value)
<li style="font-size-adjust : 0.46;">0.46 (Times
New Roman default value)
<li>inherit
<li style="font-size-adjust : 0.99;">0.99
<li style="font-size-adjust : 0.33;">0.33
</ul>
</body></html>
```

Figure 15.6

Note that Internet Explorer 6 doesn't yet implement this style.

15.8 The `'font'` property

The `'font'` property allows you to use a shorthand to specify the *font* the browser uses to render characters.

The possible values are:

- `<'font-style'><'font-variant'><'font-weight'><'font-size'>/<'line-height'> <'font-family'>`
- `caption | icon | menu | message-box | small-caption | status-bar`
- `inherit` (the face will be inherited from the parent)

For example:

```
font : italic small-caps 700 18pt/22pt Arial, serif
font : 120% "Times New Roman", Garamond, serif
font : 120%/150% "Courier New", fantasy
```

Example 15_8. The 'font' property (file e15_8.html)

```
<html><head></head><body>
<ul>The 'font' property
<li style="font : italic small-caps 700 18pt/22pt Arial, sans-serif">italic
small-caps 700 18pt/22pt Arial, sans-serif
<li style="font : oblique bolder 0.2in/0.3in Times New Roman, serif">oblique bolder
0.2in/0.3in Times New Roman, serif
<li style="font : 20px/25px fantasy">20px/25px fantasy
<li style="font : 150%/200% Verdana, Helvetica, monospace">150%/200% Verdana,
Helvetica, monospace
<li style="font : 1.1pc cursive">1.1pc cursive
</ul>
</body></html>
```

Figure 15.7

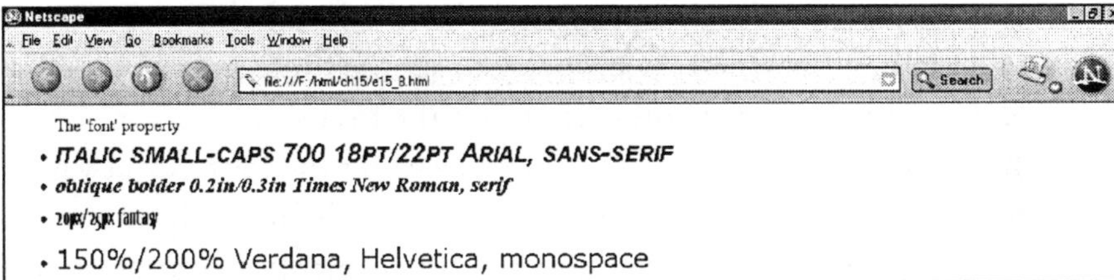

Note that you may omit some font properties, but the order in which they appear is important.

15.9 Font download

CSS2 allows the designer to describe and download custom-made fonts. This is made possible by a `@font-face` block inserted into the style sheet. The `@font-face` block contains rules that describe the font. One of these rules is:

```
src : <url>
```

where *url* defines the Internet address for the font that will be downloaded and used by the browser for rendering. The common fonts extensions are: `.pfr`, `.eot`, `.ttf`, `.pfb`, and `.pfa`

For example:

```
<style>
@font-face {font-family : choc;
           font-size : 15pt;
           src : http://www.itdgroup.com/fonts/chocolate.ttf;}
p {font : choc; color : red;}
</style>
```

15.10 Review of Chapter 15

At the end of Chapter 15 you should know:

- To define a font, use the `'font-family'` property and assign a list of comma delimited names of fonts as its value.
- There are five generic fonts: `serif`, `sans-serif`, `cursive`, `fantasy`, and `monospace`
- Use the `'font-style'` property to set the font style to `normal`, `italic`, or `oblique`
- Use the `'font-variant'` property to set the font variant to `normal` or `small-caps`
- Use the `'font-weight'` property to set the font boldness.
- Use the `'font-stretch'` property to set the font stretch.
- Use the `'font-size'` property to set the font size.
- Use the `'font-size-adjust'` property to set the font aspect value.
- Use the `'font'` property as a short-hand to define all the font properties using a space-delimited list of values: `<style> <variant> <weight> <size/height> <family>`
- To force the browser to download and use a specific font, insert a `@font-face` directive in conjunction with the src property set to the URL of the font.

Chapter 16

Text in CSS

CSS allows you to set properties for text (characters, spaces, words, and paragraphs).

16.1 Indentation

Use the 'text-indent' property to control the indentation of the first line of a block of text. The possible values are:

- <length> e.g. 2px, -1in, 1.2cm
- <percentage> e.g. 10%, -10%, 25%
- inherit so the property is inherited from the parent.

Example 16_1. Indentation (file e16_1.html)

```
<html><head><style>
p {text-indent : 50px;}
div {text-indent : -10%;}
td {text-indent : 3cm;}
</style></head><body>
<p>This is the paragraph. This is the
paragraph. This is the paragraph. This is the
paragraph. This is the paragraph.
<div>This is the division block. This is the
division block. This is the division block.
This is the division block. </div>
<table border><tr>
<td>This is text in the first cell. This is
text in the first cell.
```

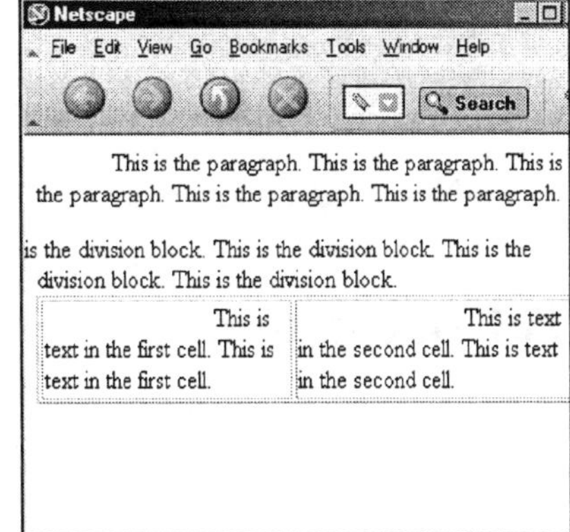

Figure 16.1

```
<td> This is text in the second cell. This is text in the second cell.
</table></body></html>
```

Note the effect a negative indentation has on the division paragraph.

16.2 Alignment

Use the 'text-align' property to control the alignment of a block of text. The possible values are:

- left | right | center | justify
- <string> to determine the character(s) used for vertical alignment. Applies to table cells; e.g. text-align: "."
- inherit so the property is inherited from the parent.

Example 16_2. Alignment (file e16_2.html)

```
<html><head><style>
p {text-align : justify;}
div {text-align : right;}
td {text-align : ".";}
</style></head><body>
<p>This is the paragraph. This is the paragraph.
This is the paragraph. This is the paragraph.
This is the paragraph.
<div>This is the division block. This is the
division block. This is the division block.
This is the division block. </div>
<table border>
<tr><td>-12.68
<tr><td>100.68
<tr><td>-12.68
<tr><td>100,000.68
</table></body></html>
```

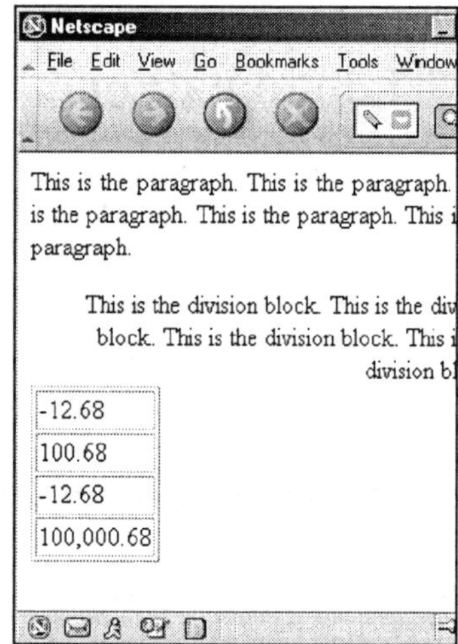

Figure 16.2

Note that browsers do not yet implement the <string> alignment.

16.3 Decoration

Use the 'text-decoration' property to control the decoration (underline, line-through, etc.) of a block of text. The possible values are:

- none | underline | overline | line-through | blink
- inherit so the property is inherited from the parent.

Example 16_3. Decoration (file e16_3.html)

```
<html><head><style>
p {text-decoration : blink;}
a:link {text-decoration : none;}
span {text-decoration : overline;}
em {text-decoration : underline;}
b {text-decoration : line-through;}
</style></head><body>
<p> text-decoration : blink;</p><br>
<a href="#"> text-decoration : none;</a>
<p><div>division<span> overline </span>
<em> underline </em><b> line-through </b>
</div></body></html>
```

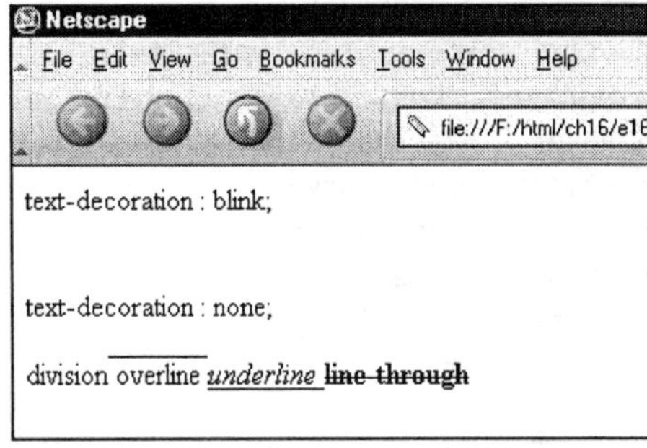

Figure 16.3

Note that Internet Explorer does not yet implement the `"blink"` value for the `'text-decoration'` property.

16.4 Shadows

Use the `'text-shadow'` property to attach shadows to a block of text. The possible values are:

- `none`
- `inherit` so the property is inherited from the parent.
- A list of comma-delimited shadow descriptions (the stack of shadows):
  - `<color><length_x><length_y><length_r>`
  - `<length_x><length_y><length_r><color>`

    where:
    - `<length_x>` and `<length_y>` represent the position of the shadow relative to the block (the offset)
    - `<length_r>` represents the blur radius
    - `<color>` represents the color of the shadow

For example:

```
text-shadow : red 10px 10px;                (right-bottom)
text-shadow : -10px -10px 5px yellow;       (left-up, blurred)
text-shadow : 5px 5px,-5px –5px;            (right-bottom and left-up)
```

Example 16_4. Shadows (file e16_4.html)

```
<html><head><style>
p {text-shadow : red 10px 10px;}
h1 {text-shadow : -10px -10px 5px yellow;}
a:hover {text-shadow : 5px 5px,-5px –5px;}
</style></head><body>
<p>This is the paragraph</p>
<h1>This is the heading 1</h1>
<a>This is the link</p>
</body></html>
```

Note that browsers do not yet implement this property.

16.5 Letter spacing

Use the 'letter-spacing' property to add *extra space* between adjacent characters. The possible values are:

- normal
- <length>
- inherit so the property is inherited from the parent.

For example:

```
letter-spacing : 0.2em
letter-spacing : 1px
letter-spacing : 2pt;
letter-spacing : 0.5cm;
```

Example 16_5. Letter spacing (file e16_5.html)

```
<html><head><style>
p {letter-spacing : 10px;}
h1 {letter-spacing : +0.2em; color : red}
a {letter-spacing : 0.5cm;}
div {letter-spacing : 2mm;}
button {letter-spacing : 2pt;}
</style></head><body>
<p>this is the paragraph</p>
<h1>this is the heading 1</h1><br>
<a href="#">this is the link</a><p>
<button>this is the <h1>button</h1></button>
<div>this is the division block</div>
</body></html>
```

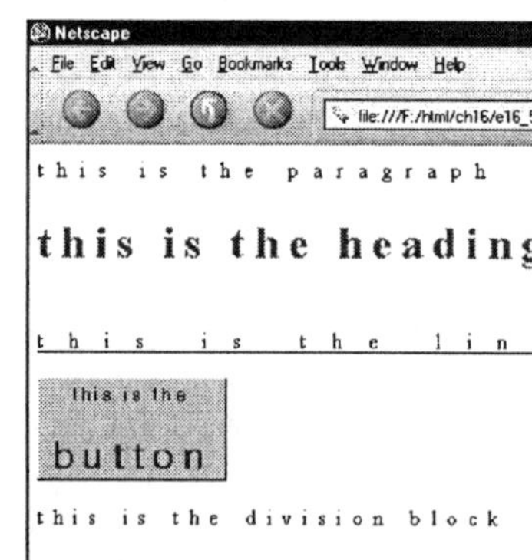

Figure 16.4

16.6 Word spacing

Use the 'word-spacing' property to add *extra space* between adjacent words. The possible values are:

- normal
- <length>
- inherit so the property is inherited from the parent.

For example:

```
word-spacing : -0.2ex
word-spacing : 2cm
```

Example 16_6. Word spacing (file e16_6.html)

```
<html><head><style>
p {word-spacing : 10px;}
h1 {word-spacing : +0.2em; color : red}
a {word-spacing : 0.5cm;}
div {word-spacing : 2mm;}
button {word-spacing : 2pt;}
</style></head><body>
<p>this is the paragraph</p>
<h1>this is the heading 1</h1><br>
<a href="#">this is the link</a><p>
<button>this is the <h1>button</h1></button>
<div>this is the division block</div>
</body></html>
```

Figure 16.5

16.7 Capitalization

Use the 'text-transform' property to control the capitalization of a block of text. The possible values are:

- none
- capitalize to capitalize the first character of each word.
- uppercase to capitalize all characters.
- lowercase to decapitalize all characters.
- inherit so the property is inherited from the parent.

For example:

```
text-transform : capitalize
text-transform : uppercase
```

Example 16_7. Capitalization (file e16_7.html)

```
<html><head><style>
p {text-transform : capitalize; color : red;}
h3 {text-transform : uppercase;}
a {text-transform : lowercase;}
</style></head><body>
<p>every word of this paragraph will be rendered capitalized</p>
<h3>the text of this heading is uppercase</h3><br>
<a href="#">This Link Is Lowercase</a><p>
</body></html>
```

Figure 16.6

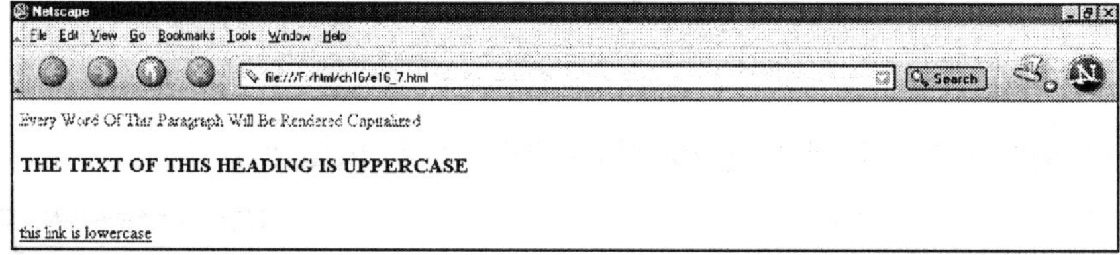

16.8 White spaces

Use the 'white-space' property to control the white spaces inside a block of text. The possible values are:

- normal to replace a sequence of white spaces with a space character.
- pre so white spaces are considered.
- nowrap so line breaks are not considered.
- inherit so the property is inherited from the parent.

For example:

```
white-space : pre
white-space : nowrap
```

Example 16_8. White spaces (file e16_8.html)

```
<html><head>
<style>
p {white-space : nowrap;}
div {white-space : pre;}
</style>
</head><body>
<p>This is a single line. This is a single
line. This is a single line. This is a
single line. This is a single line. This is
a single line. </p>
```

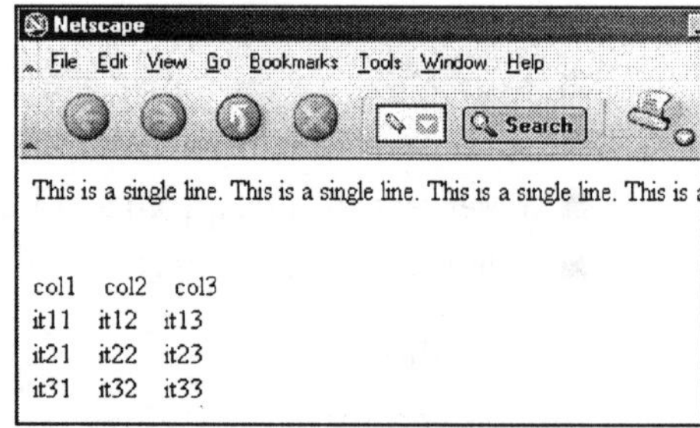

Figure 16.7

```
<div>
col1  col2  col3
it11  it12  it13
it21  it22  it23
it31  it32  it33
</div>
</body></html>
```

16.9 Review of Chapter 16

At the end of Chapter 16 you should know:

- CSS has several properties to control the appearance of text.
- The 'text-indent' property determines the indentation of the first line of a block of text.
- The 'text-align' property determines the alignment of a block of text.
- The 'text-decoration' property determines the text decoration (underline, overline, line-through, or blink).
- The 'text-shadow' property attaches a shadow to text.
- The 'letter-spacing' property determines the extra space between two adjacent letters.
- The 'word-spacing' property determines the extra space between two adjacent words.
- The 'text-transform' property determines the capitalization of a block of text (uppercase, lowercase, none, or capitalize).
- The 'white-space' property determines how the white spaces are considered (pre, nowrap, or normal).

Chapter 17

Boxes in CSS

17.1 The Box concept in CSS

In CSS, each HTML element has an associated box. The box has four parts:

- `content` - the actual content of the element
- `padding` - the area between the content and the border
- `border` - the edge of the element
- `margin` - the area between the element and similar adjacent elements

In CSS, you can set properties related to these parts. The picture below illustrates the specific terminology and the geometric relationship between each part.

Figure 17.1

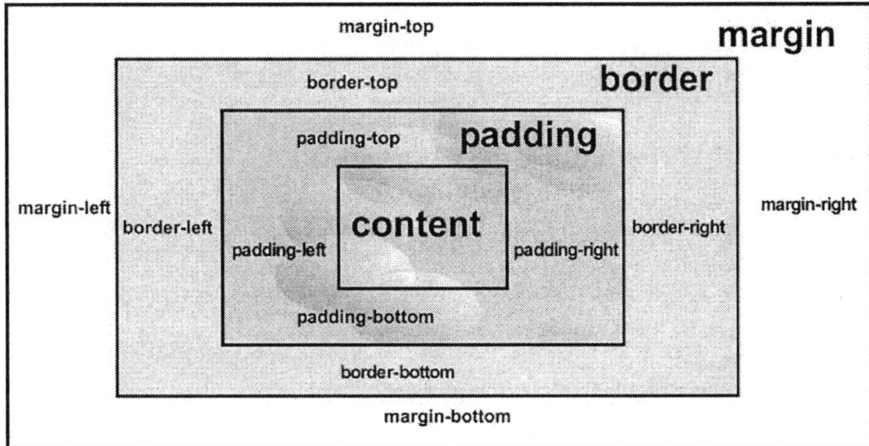

Notes

- The margin is transparent.
- The border has an associated background color.
- The padding and the content share the background property defined for the element.
- The margin, border, and padding each have a top, right, bottom, and left sub-parts, for which you can set individual properties.

17.2 Padding

The padding is the area between the content and the border. The single characteristic you can set for the padding element is `size`. There are 5 width properties (four that correspond to the four sub-parts and one that corresponds to the overall padding area):

- `padding-top`
- `padding-right`
- `padding-bottom`
- `padding-left`
- `padding`

The possible values for these properties are:

- `<length>` to specify a fixed width; only 0 or positive values are accepted.
- `<percentage>` to specify the width relative to the parent element.
- `inherit` so the property is inherited from the parent.

The `padding-top`, `padding-right`, `padding-bottom`, and `padding-left` properties each accept only one value.

Example 17_1. Padding (file e17_1.html)

```
<html><head><style>
p {padding-top : 10px; padding-right : 20px; padding-bottom : 30px; padding-left :
40px; background : red;}
blockquote {padding-top : 0.5in;padding-right : 10%; padding-bottom : 5ex;
padding-left : 0; background : yellow;}
div {padding-top : 1cm; padding-right : 5mm; padding-bottom : 2pt; padding-left :
2pc; background : #ADD8E6;}
</style></head><body>
<p>This is the paragraph. The distances between the content and the borders are:
top:10px, right:20px, bottom:30px, left:40px</p>
```

```
<blockquote>This is the blockquote. The distances between the content and the
borders are:
top:0.5in, right:10%, bottom:5ex, left:0
</blockquote>
<div>This is the division block. The distances between the content and the borders are:
top:1cm, right:5mm, bottom:2pt, left:2pc</div>
</body></html>
```

Figure 17.2

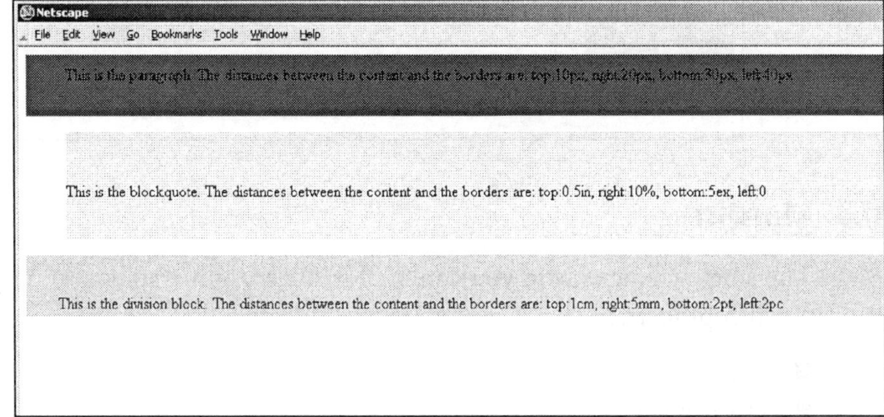

The `padding` property can accept a list (space-delimited) of 1, 2, 3, or 4 values. For example:

- `1px` top=right=bottom=left=1px
- `1px 2px` right=left=1px, top=bottom=2px
- `1px 2px 3px` top=1px, left=right=2px, bottom=3px
- `1px 2px 3px 4px` top=1px, right=2px, bottom=3px, left=4px

Example 17_2. Shorthands for padding (file e17_2.html)

```
<html><head><style>
p {padding : 50px; background : red;}
ol {padding : 1mm 2mm 3mm 4mm; background : yellow;}
span {padding : 10px 20px 30px; background : cyan;}
td {padding : 10pt 2pc; background : magenta;}
</style></head><body>
<p>This is the paragraph. <span> This is the span inside of the paragraph. </span>
This is the paragraph. </p>
<ol>The List<li>Item 1<li>Item 2</ol>
<table><tr><td>c11<td>c12<tr><td>c21<td>c22</table>
</body></html>
```

Figure 17.3

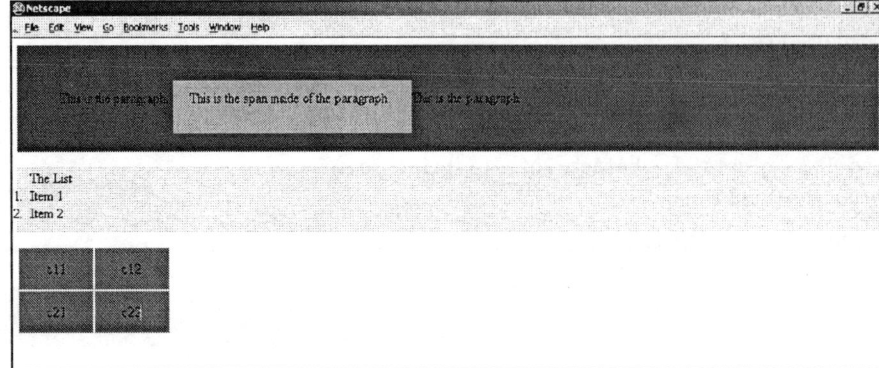

17.3 Margin

The single characteristic you can set for the margin element is `size`. There are 5 width properties:

- `margin-top`
- `margin-right`
- `margin-bottom`
- `margin-left`
- `margin`

The possible values for these properties are:

- `<length>` to specify a fixed width
- `<percentage>` to specify a width relative to the parent element
- `auto`

Notes

- The values may be either positive or negative.
- Each of the `margin-top`, `margin-right`, `margin-bottom`, and `margin-left` attributes accepts only one value.

Example 17_3. Margin (file e17_3.html)

```
<html><head><style>
p {margin-top : 1em; margin-right : 2em; margin-bottom : 3em; margin-left : 4em;
background : red;}
blockquote {margin-top : 1in; margin-right : 10%; margin-bottom : 5ex; margin-left :
-30px; background : yellow;}
```

```
div {margin-top : 1cm; margin-right : 5mm; margin-bottom : 2pt;margin-left : 2pc;
background : magenta;}
</style></head><body>
<p> This is the first paragraph.</p>
<blockquote> This is the blockquote.</blockquote>
<div>This is the division block.</div>
</body></html>
```

Figure 17.4

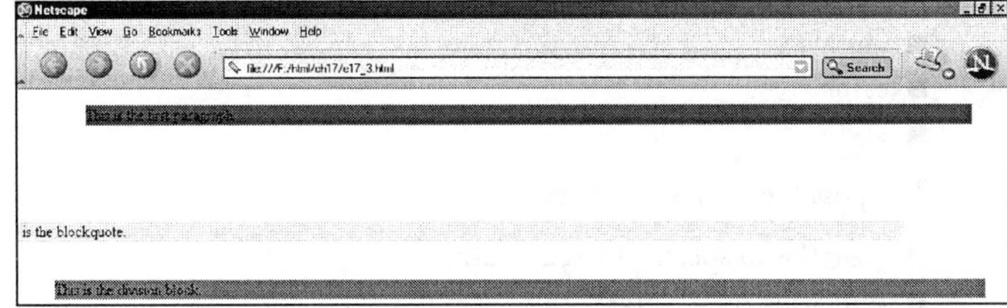

Note the effect of a negative value on the `blockquote` element (`margin-left:-30px`).

The `margin` property can accept a list (space delimited) of 1, 2, 3, or 4 of values:

- `1px` top=right=bottom=left=1px
- `1px 2px` right=left=1px, top=bottom=2px
- `1px 2px 3px` top=1px, left=right=2px, bottom=3px
- `1px 2px 3px 4px` top=1px, right=2px, bottom=3px, left=4px

Example 17_4. Shorthands for margin (file e17_4.html)

```
<html><head><style>
blockquote {margin : 1cm 2cm 3cm 4cm; background : magenta;}
div {margin : 50pt; background : olive;}
span {margin : 200px 50px; background : silver;}
</style></head><body>
<div> This is the division block.</div>
<blockquote>This is the blockquote.<span>This is the span inside of the
blockquote.</span>
This is the blockquote.</blockquote>
</body></html>
```

Figure 17.5

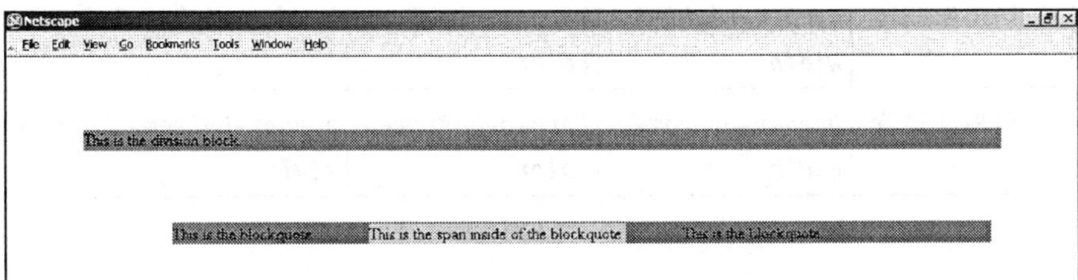

Note that a phenomenon called *collapsing* appears between the vertical margins of two adjacent boxes.

17.4 Border

There are three characteristics you can set for the border element:

- `width`
- `color`
- `style`

The possible values for `<width>` are:

- `<length>` to specify a fixed width
- `thin | medium | thick`
- `inherit`

The possible values for `color` are:

- `<color>`
- `inherit`

The possible values for `<style>` are:

- `none | hidden | dotted | dashed | solid | double | groove | ridge | inset | outset`
- `inherit`

By combining the 4 possible parts of the border element (`border-top`, `border-right`, `border-bottom`, `border-left`, `border`) with all possible characteristics (`width`, `color`, `style`, or `all`) you obtain 20 possible properties that can be set for the border element, as specified in the next table:

	WIDTH	COLOR	STYLE	ALL
BORDER-TOP	***border-top-width***	***border-top-color***	***border-top-style***	border-top
BORDER-RIGHT	***border-right-width***	***border-right-color***	***border-right-style***	border-right
BORDER-BOTTOM	***border-bottom-width***	***border-bottom-color***	***border-bottom-style***	border-bottom

	WIDTH	COLOR	STYLE	ALL
BORDER-LEFT	***border-left-width***	***border-left-color***	***border-left-style***	border-left
BORDER	border-width	border-color	border-style	border

Note that all the ***highlighted*** properties accept only a single value, while all the others accept lists of values as explained below.

Example 17_5 demonstrates the effect the `style` of the border has on rendering buttons, text fields, and table cells.

Example 17_5. Border style (file e17_5.html)

```
<html><head><style>
* {margin : 5px;}
.none {border-style : none;}
.hidden {border-style : hidden;}
.dotted {border-style : dotted;}
.dashed {border-style : dashed;}
.solid {border-style : solid;}
.double {border-style : double;}
.groove {border-style : groove;}
.ridge {border-style : ridge;}
.inset {border-style : inset;}
.outset {border-style : outset;}
</style></head><body>
<form>
<button class="none">none</button><button class="hidden">hidden</button>
<button class="dotted">dotted</button><button class="dashed">dashed</button>
<button class="solid">solid</button><button class="double">double</button>
<button class="groove">groove</button><button class="ridge">ridge</button>
<button style="inset">inset</button><button style="outset">outset</button>
<br><input class="none" value="none"><input class="hidden" value="hidden">
<input class="dotted" value="dotted"><input class="dashed" value="dashed">
<input class="solid" value="solid"><input class="double" value="double">
<input class="groove" value="groove"><input class="ridge;" value="ridge">
<input class="inset" value="inset"><input class="outset" value="outset">
</form>
<table><tr><td class="none">none<td class="hidden">hidden
<td class="dotted">dotted<td class="dashed">dashed
<td class="solid">solid<td class="double">double
<td class="groove">groove<td class="ridge">ridge
<td class="inset">inset<td class="outset">outset
</table></body></html>
```

Figure 17.6

Example 17_6 demonstrates the effect the color of the border has on rendering buttons, text fields, and table cells.

Example 17_6. Border color (file e17_6.html)

```
<html><head><style>
* {margin : 5px; border-style : solid;}
button {color : blue; background : yellow;}
td {color : white; background : silver;}
.aqua {border-color : aqua;}
.white {border-color : white;}
.lime {border-color : lime;}
.purple {border-color : purple;}
</style></head><body>
<form>
<button class="aqua">aqua</button><button class="white">white</button>
<button class="lime">lime</button><button class="purple">purple</button>
<br><input class="aqua" value="aqua"><input class="white" value="white"><br>
<input class="lime" value="lime"><input class="purple" value="purple">
</form>
<table><tr><td class="aqua">aqua<td class="white">white
<td class="lime">lime<td class="purple">purple
</table></body></html>
```

Figure 17.7

Note that the rule

```
* {margin : 5px; border-style : solid;}
```

causes a solid-style border to be rendered for all elements, including <body>, <form>, and <table>.

Example 17_7 demonstrates the effect the width of the border has on rendering buttons, text fields, and table cells.

Example 17_7. Border width (file e17_7.html)

```
<html><head><style>
* {margin : 5px;}
button {border-color : red;}
input {background : yellow; border-style : solid;}
td {border-style : double;}
</style></head><body><form>
<button style="border-width : thin">thin</button>
<button style="border-width : medium">medium</button>
<button style="border-width : thick">thick</button>
<button style="border-width : 0">zero</button>
<button style="border-width : 5px">5px</button>
<br><input style="border-width : thin" value="thin">
<input style="border-width : medium" value="medium">
<input style="border-width : thick" value="thick">
<input style="border-width : 0" value="zero">
<input style="border-width : 10pt" value="10pt">
</form><table><tr>
<td style="border-width : thin">thin
<td style="border-width : medium">medium
<td style="border-width : thick">thick
<td style="border-width : 0">zero
<td style="border-width : 3mm">3mm
</table></body></html>
```

Figure 17.8

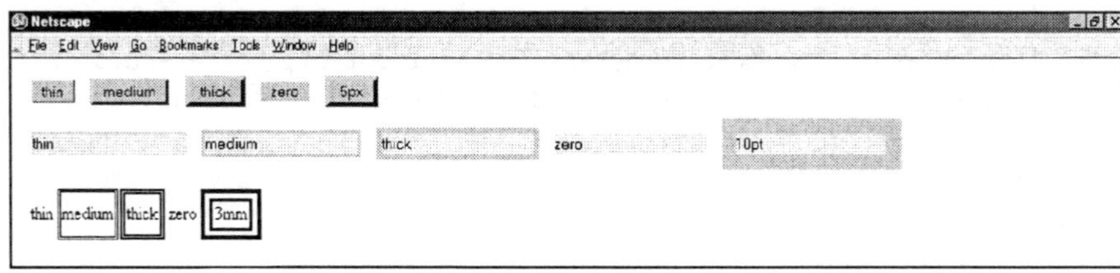

In Example 17_8, the boxes are defined using attributes for all four sides of the box.

Example 17_8. Border sides (file e17_8.html)

```
<html><head><style>
.all {border-top-width:2mm; border-top-style:solid; border-top-color:red;
border-right-width:4pt; border-right-style:double; border-right-color:blue;
border-bottom-width:2px; border-bottom-style:dotted; border-bottom-color:green;
border-left-width:1em; border-left-style:outset; border-left-color:yellow;}
</style></head><body>
<p class="all"> This is the paragraph. This is the paragraph.
This is the paragraph. This is the paragraph. </p>
<blockquote class="all">This is the blockquote.<b class="all">Bold Text inside of
the blockquote</b>This is the blockquote.</blockquote>
</body></html>
```

Figure 17.9

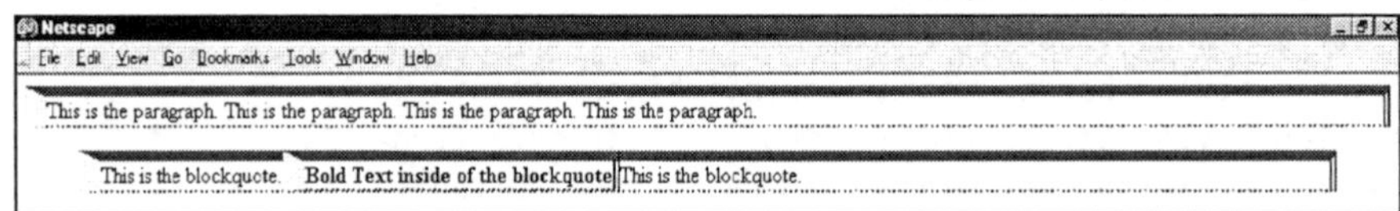

The border-width, border-color, and border-style properties accept a space-delimited list of 1, 2, 3, or 4 such values:

- 1px top=right=bottom=left=1px
- 1px 2px right=left=1px, top=bottom=2px
- 1px 2px 3px top=1px, left=right=2px, bottom=3px
- 1px 2px 3px 4px top=1px, right=2px, bottom=3px, left=4px

In Example 17_9, the boxes are defined using lists of values.

Example 17_9. The border lists of values (file e17_9.html)

```
<html><head><style>
.one {border-width:2mm; border-style:solid; border-color:red;}
.two {border-width:2mm 4mm; border-style:inset outset; border-color:red blue;}
.three {border-width:2mm 4mm 6mm; border-style:solid dashed dotted;
border-color:red green blue;}
.four {border-width:2mm 4mm 6mm 8mm; border-style:solid double groove ridge;
border-color:cyan magenta lime purple;}
</style></head><body>
<p class="one">one 3mm solid red</p>
<blockquote class="two">two 2mm 4mm inset outset red blue
<b class="three"> three 2mm 4mm 6mm solid dashed dotted red green blue </b>
This is the blockquote.</blockquote>
<h3 class="four">four 2mm 4mm 6mm 8mm solid double groove ridge cyan magenta lime
purple</h3>
</body></html>
```

Figure 17.10

Each of the `border`, `border-top`, `border-right`, `border-bottom`, and `border-left` properties accepts a space-delimited list of values using the syntax:

```
<width> <style> <color>
```

In Example 17_10, the boxes are defined using shorthands.

Example 17_10. The border shorthands (file e17_10.html)

```
<html><head><style>
p {border : 5px solid red;}
h3 {border : 2px outset blue;}
span {border : 0.2in double yellow;}
</style></head><body>
<h3>This is the heading 3: 2px outset blue</h3>
<p>The paragraph: 5px solid red <span>The span: 0.2in dotted yellow </span> The
paragraph </p>
</body></html>
```

Figure 17.11

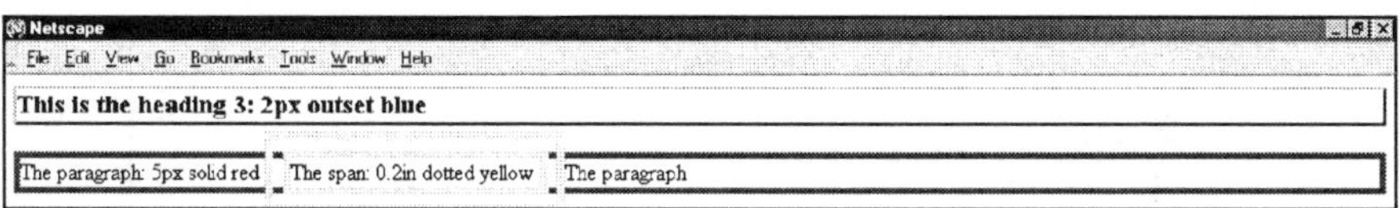

17.5 Cursors

You can attach a different kind of cursor to each box (element). To do this, use the `'cursor'` property. The possible values are *comma-separated lists of cursor identifiers and/or URLs*. The browser will use the first available cursor identifier from the list. Figure 17_12 illustrates the cursor identifiers available and their associated images:

Figure 17.12

default
help
wait
default
crosshair
text
n-resize s-resize
w-resize e-resize
nw-resize se-resize
ne-resize sw-resize
move
n-resize
pointer

Other possible values for the cursor identifiers are:

- `auto` – the displayed cursor depends on the current context
- `URL` – the URL of an Internet resource (e.g. `"example.cur"`)

Example 17_11. Cursors (file e17_11.html)

```
<html><head></head>
<body style="cursor : default;">
Default cursor.
<p style="cursor : help;">Help Cursor.</p>
<i style="cursor : wait;">Wait Cursor.</i>
<b style="cursor : crosshair;">Crosshair Cursor.</b>
<h3 style="cursor : text;">Text Cursor.</h3>
<h4 style="cursor : ne-resize;">ne-resize Cursor.</h4>
<div style="cursor : w-resize;">w-resize Cursor.</div>
<span style="cursor : move;">Move Cursor.</move>
<a href="#" style="cursor : sw-resize;">sw-resize Cursor.</a>
<img src=logo.gif style="cursor : n-resize;">
<ul style="cursor : nw-resize;">nw-resize Cursor.
<li>first item<li>second item
</ul></body></html>
```

Figure 17.13

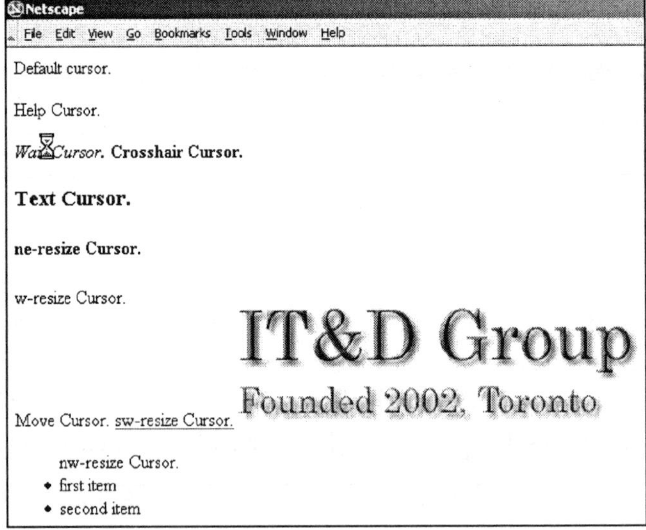

Notes

- Be aware that browsers do not implement all the possible values recommended by CSS2.
- By default, browsers associate a different cursor with different elements (e.g. a `"text"` cursor is attached to a text field, a `"pointer"` cursor is attached to a link, etc.).

17.6 The 'overflow' property

The 'overflow' property specifies what happens to the content of a block-level element when the content doesn't fit into the space allocated for the element. The possible values for the 'overflow' property are:

- visible - the content is *not clipped* and *will be rendered outside* of the box element (the default value)
- hidden - the content is *clipped* and *cannot be scrolled*
- scroll - the content is *clipped* but *can be scrolled*
- auto - this value is *browser-dependent*
- inherit - the value is *inherited* from the parent element

Example 17_12. 'overflow' (file e17_12.html)

```
<html><head></head><body>
<div style="border : 1px solid blue; width : 100px;
height : 50px; overflow : hidden; color : blue;">
This div block has overflow : hidden.
</div>
<p>
<div style="border : 1px solid red; width : 100px;
height : 50px; overflow : visible; color : red;">
This div block has overflow : visible.
</div>
<p>
<div style="border : 1px solid black; width : 200px;
height : 100px; overflow : scroll; color : black;">
This div block has overflow : scroll.
<img src="newyork.jpg">
</div></body></html>
```

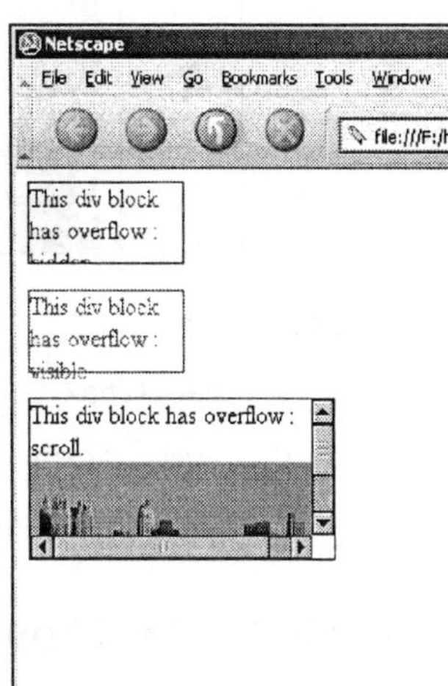

Figure 17.14

Notes

- Internet Explorer can use two other similar properties:
  - overflow-x - specify an overflow behavior along x-axis only
  - overflow-y - specify an overflow behavior along y-axis only
- The possible values for these two properties are the same as the values of the 'overflow' property.
- If the overflow property is not set, the default value ('visible') is used.

17.7 Clipping

The 'clip' property allows you to make only a portion of the box attached to a *positioned* elements visible. The possible values are:

- rect(top right bottom left)
- auto (all the boxes attached to an element are visible; the default value)

where *top* and *bottom* are integers representing distances in pixels from the top margin of the box, while *right* and *left* are integers representing distances in pixels from the left margin of the box (see Figure 17.15).

Figure 17.15

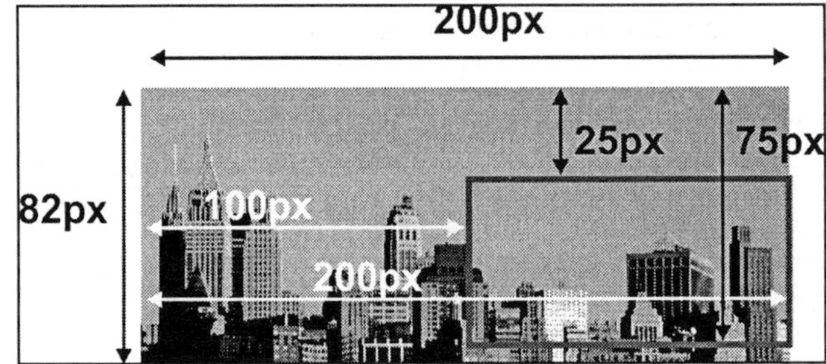

Example:

```
clip : rect(25px 200px 75px 100px);"
```

Although in CSS2, only the rect function is available to define a clipping area, it is possible other shapes may be recommended in the next versions of CSS.

Example 17_13. Clipping (file e17_13.html)

```
<html><head></head>
<body>
The normal image:<img src="newyork.jpg"><br>
The clipped image:<img style="position : absolute;
clip : rect(25px 200px 75px 100px);"
src="newyork.jpg">
</body></html>
```

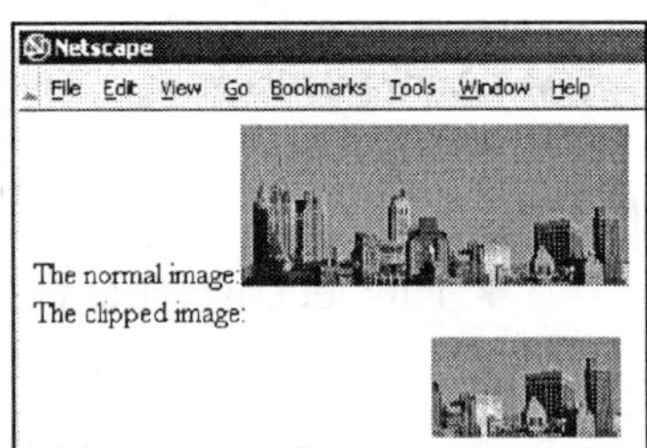

Figure 17.16

Note

◆ To make the image element positioned, I used "position : absolute;" (see Chapter 18 CSS Positioning).

17.8 The 'visibility' property

The 'visibility' property specifies whether or not the box attached to an element is visible. The possible values are:

- `visible` - the box is visible
- `hidden` - the box is not visible, but space is allocated
- `collapse` - allows adjacent non-visible element to collapse
- `inherit` - is inherited from the parent (is the default value)

Notes

- Be aware that the browser will allocate space for the element in any case.
- If you want the browser not to allocate any space for an element box, you should use the 'display' property instead.

Example 17_14. 'visibility' (file e17_14.html)

```
<html><head></head>
<body>
Normal text.
<div style="visibility : hidden">
Hidden text.
<p style="visibility : visible">
Visible paragraph inside of a hidden
div block.
<h3 style="visibility : inherit">
Inherit heading.
Hidden text.
</div>
Normal text.
</body></html>
```

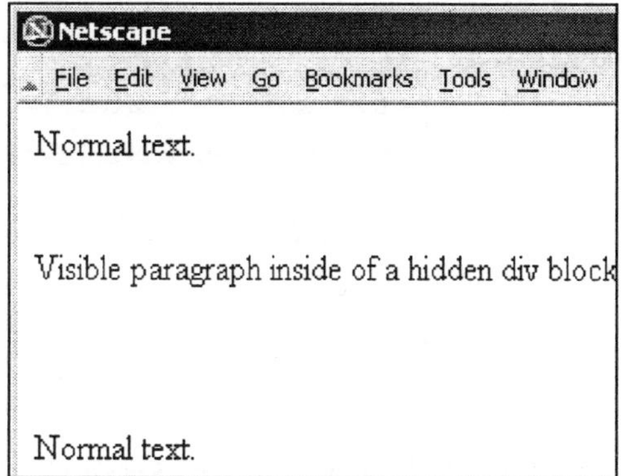

Figure 17.17

17.9 The 'background-color' property

The 'background-color' property allows you to set up the background color of the box. The possible values are valid CSS colors specifications. For example:

- `blue`
- `rgb(100,200,0)`
- `"#00ff00"`
- `"transparent"` (the default value)

Example 17_15. 'background-color' (file e17_15.html)

```
<html><head></head><body style="background-color:yellow">
Normal text on yellow background.
<i style="background-color:lightgreen">italic text on lightgreen background.</i>
<h3 style="background-color:red">Heading 3 on red background.</h3>
<table border style="background-color:lightblue">
<tr><td>table on lightblue background.<td>c12
<tr style="background-color:green"><td>row on green background.
<td style="background-color:magenta">cell on magenta background.
</table>
<ul style="background-color:#f0f0f0">List on #f0f0f0 background.
<li>item 1.
<li style="background-color:lightgreen">item on lightgreen background.
</ul>
<form>
<input type="text" size="30" style="background-color:lightblue" value="textfield
with lightblue background">
<input type="button" value="Red Button" style="background-color:red">
</form></body></html>
```

Figure 17.18

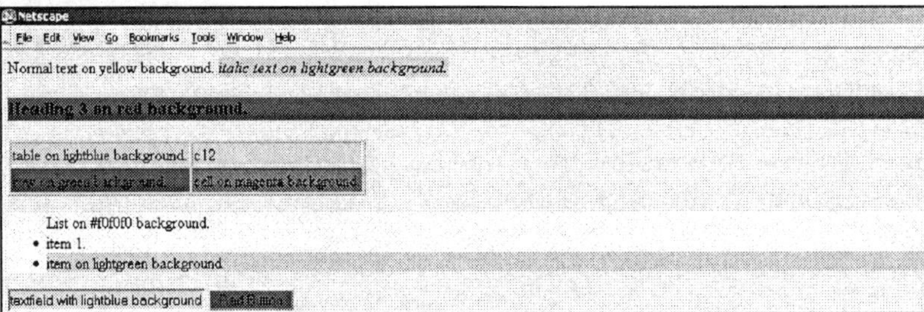

17.10 The 'background-image' property

The 'background-image' property allows you to set the background image of the box. The possible values are URLs that point to valid image files (gif, jpeg, png). If this property is present and the image can be downloaded, this property is used in favor of the background-color property. For example:

- url(image.gif)
- url(http://www.itdgroup.com/bg/im2.jpg)

Example 17_16. 'background-image' (file e17_16.html)

```
<html><head></head>
<body style="background-image:url(none.jpg);background-color:yellow;">
Normal text.
```

```
<i style="background-image:url(bg2.gif)">italic text.</i>
<h3 style="background-image:url(bg3.gif)">Heading 3.</h3>
<table border style="background-image:url(bg4.gif)">
<tr><td>table c11.<td>c12
<tr style="background-image:url(bg3.gif)"><td>c22.
<td style="background-image:url(bg5.gif)">cell 22.
</table>
<ul style="background-image:url(bg6.jpg)">List.
<li>item 1.
<li style="background-image:url(bg7.gif)">item 2.
</ul><form>
<input type="text" size="30" style="background-image:url(bg1.jpg)"
value="textfield">
<input type="button" value="Button" style="background-image:url(bg2.gif)">
</form></body></html>
```

Figure 17.19

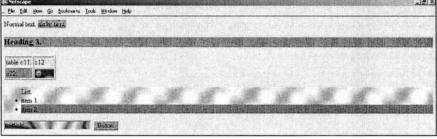

Notes

- For this example, the background image indicated for the body element doesn't exist, so the background color is used instead.
- To be completely functional, this example requires the background images to exist in the same directory as the HTML file.

17.11 The 'background-position' property

The 'background-position' property allows you to specify the top and the left of the background image relative to the top and the left of the element box. The possible values are:

- `<percentage>`
- `<length>`
- `left | center | right` (for horizontal direction)
- `top | center | bottom` (for vertical direction)

If one of these values is given, that value applies to both the vertical and horizontal directions. If two values are given, the first value applies to the horizontal direction, and the second value applies to the vertical direction. Examples:

- `30px 50px`
- `10%`
- `left bottom`

Example 17_17. 'background-position' (file e17_17.html)

```
<html><head><style>
body * {border:1px solid red;background-image:url(bg.gif);}
</style></head>
<body style="background-image:url(none.jpg); background-color:yellow;
background-position : 0px;">
Normal text.
<i style="background-position:0px;">italic text.</i>
<h3 style="background-position:10px;">Heading 3.</h3>
<table border style="background-position:-10px 10%;">
<tr><td>table c11.<td>c12
<tr style="background-position:5%;"><td>c22.
<td style="background-position:5% -5%;">cell 22.
</table>
<ul style="background-position:0%;">List.
<li>item 1.
<li style="background-position:1cm;">item 2.
</ul><form>
<input type="text" size="30" style="background-position:10px;" value="textfield">
<input type="button" value="Button" style="background-position:5px bottom;">
</form></body></html>
```

Figure 17.20

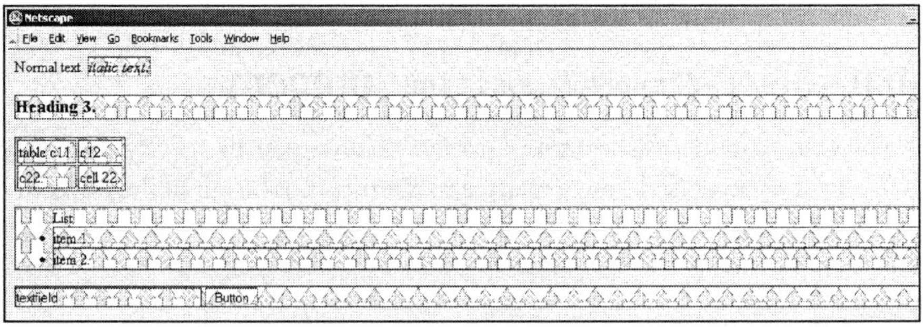

17.12 The 'background-position-x' property

The 'background-position-x' property is similar to background-position. It applies to the horizontal direction in Internet Explorer *only*.

17.13 The 'background-position-y' property

The 'background-position-y' property is similar to background-position. It applies to the vertical direction in Internet Explorer *only*.

17.14 The 'background-repeat' property

The 'background-repeat' property allows you to specify how the background image is repeated. The possible values are:

- `no-repeat` - only one instance of the image is rendered
- `repeat` - the image is repeated both horizontally and vertically
- `repeat-x` - the image is repeated only horizontally
- `repeat-y` - the image is repeated only vertically

Example 17_18. 'background-repeat' (file e17_18.html)

```
<html><head>
<style>body * {background-image:url(bg.gif);}</style>
</head><body>Normal text.
<i style="background-repeat:no-repeat;">no-repeat.</i>
<h3 style="background-repeat:repeat-x;">repeat-x.</h3>
<ul style="background-repeat:repeat-y;">repeat-y.
<li>item 1.
<li style="background-repeat:repeat;">repeat.<br>repeat (next line)
</ul>
<form><input type="text" size="30" style="background-repeat:repeat-x;"
value="repeat-x repeat-x">
<input type="button" value="Button no-repeat"
style="background-repeat:no-repeat;"></form></body></html>
```

Figure 17.21

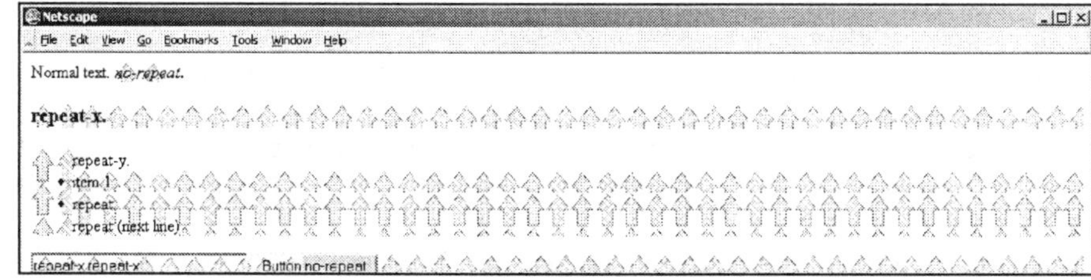

17.15 The 'background-attachment' property

The 'background-attachment' property allows you to specify whether or not the background image scrolls with the document. The possible values are:

- fixed - the image is fixed relative to the view-port
- scroll - the image is fixed relative to the document, and the two will be scrolled together (the default value)

Example 17_19. 'background-attachment' (file e17_19.html)

```
<html><head><style>
body * {background-image:url(bg.gif);}
</style></head><body>
Normal text.
<div style="background-attachment:fixed;width : 200px;
height : 100px; overflow : scroll;">
This div block has overflow : scroll and
background-attachment : fixed.
<img src="newyork.jpg">
</div>
<div style="background-attachment:scroll;width :
200px; height : 100px; overflow : scroll;">
This div block has overflow : scroll and
background-attachment : scroll.
<img src="newyork.jpg">
</div></body></html>
```

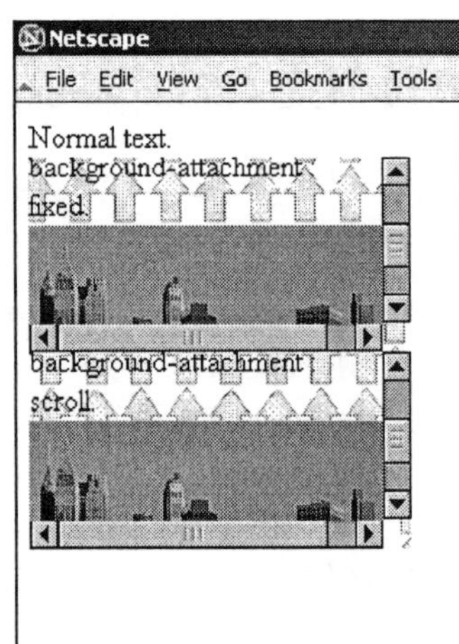

Figure 17.22

17.16 The 'background' property

The 'background' property is a shortcut that can be used to set the background image properties. The syntax is:

```
<background-attachment> <background_color> <background_image> <background_po-
sition> < background_repeat>
```

Example 17_20. 'background' (file e17_20.html)

```
<html><head></head>
<body style="background:fixed yellow url(bg4.gif) 10px repeat-y;">
Normal text.
<h3 style="background:fixed blue url(bg.gif) 5cm repeat-x;">
This is a heading 3. The background is "fixed blue url(bg.gif) 5cm repeat-x".
</h3>
<ul style="background:fixed red url(bg5.gif) no-repeat;">
```

```
<li>item 1
<li>item 2
</ul>
</body></html>
```

Figure 17.23 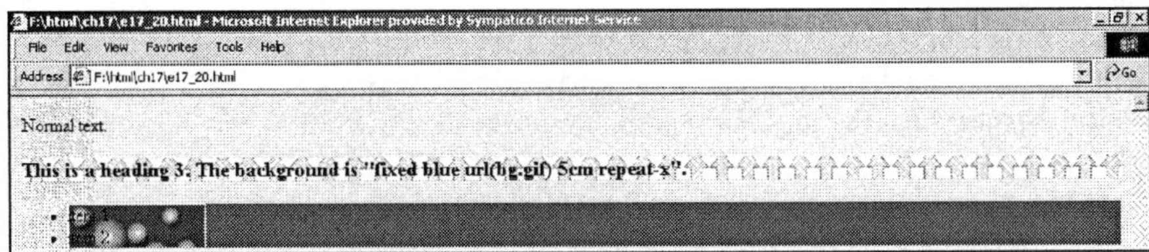

It is possible for both the `background-color` and the `background-image` to be rendered simultaneously.

17.17 The `'line height'` property

The `'line-height'` property can be set for a:

- *block-level element* to define the *minimum* height for each inline element contained in the block-level element
- *in-line element* to define the *exact* height for that element

The possible values for the `'line-height'` property are:

- `normal` - the default value
- `<number>` - represents a multiplier used to determine the actual value
- `<length>` - represents the actual value
- `<percentage>` - represents a multiplier used to determine the actual value

Notes

- ◆ When multipliers are used, the actual value of the `line-height` is the product of the multiplier and the largest font size.
- ◆ `<length>` must be followed by a unit.
- ◆ Negative values are not allowed.

Example 17_21. `'line height'` (file e17_21.html)

```
<html>
<head></head>
<body>
<ul style="line-height:0.5mm;">
<li>item 1
```

```
<li>item 2
<li>item 3
</ul>
<p style="line-height:300%;">This paragraph has a line-height
equals to 200%.</p>
Normal text.<br>Normal text.<br>Normal text.
<div style="line-height:2.25;">This division block has
a line-height equals to 1.5</div>
</body>
</html>
```

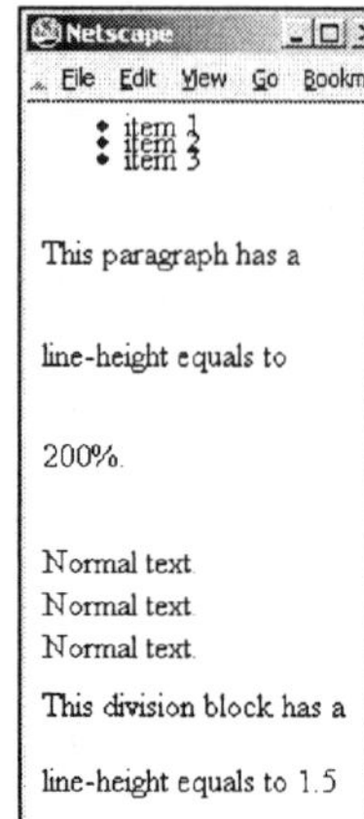

Figure 17.24

17.18 Review of Chapter 17

At the end of Chapter 17 you should know:

- In CSS, each HTML element generates a box.
- A box has four parts: content, padding, border, and margin.
- The padding, border, and margin each have four sub-parts: top, right, bottom, and left.
- For the padding area, you can control only the width (the background of this area is the same as the content).
- For the margin area, you can control only the width (this area is transparent).
- For the border area, you can define a color, a border style and a width.
- To define the properties of a box, you can use shorthands like `padding`, `margin`, `border-color`, `border-style`, `border-width`, and `border`.

Chapter 18

CSS Positioning

18.1 CSS Positioning

The purpose of this chapter is to explain the default algorithm a browser uses to render the elements of a web page and how you can change this implicit behavior with CSS.

When the layout of the web page is generated, the browser analyses:

- The *document tree* of elements
- The *type* of the elements (in-line or block-level)
- The *floating* objects
- The *positioned* objects

The next sections present these aspects in detail.

18.2 The box model

The main concept in rendering a web page is the box concept. Each element of a web page (including the `<body>` element itself and any regular text) generates a *box*. Boxes can be nested and have rendering properties determined by the HTML file from which they are generated.

The boxes model organizes the HTML elements (boxes) into a tree (the *document tree*). The *root* element doesn't have a parent and has only a single child: the `<body>` element. The *leaves* of the tree are simple fragments of text that do not have any children. Example 18_1 shows how you can visualize the document tree.

Example 18_1. The document tree (file e18_1.html)

```
<html><head><title>Boxes</title>
<style>
* {border-style : solid;
border-width:1px; margin : 5px;}
body * {background : yellow;}
body * * {background : cyan;}
body {border-color:red;}
</style></head><body>
normal text <b>bold <i> bold and italic
</i> bold again </b> normal text
<p>paragraph</p>
normal text<em> emphasize </em>
before image<img src="smile.gif"
height="50">after image
<form>Form<input value="text field">
End Form</form>
<h2>heading 2</h2>
<ol>list<li>a<li>b</ol>
before table
<table>
<tr><td>cell 11<td>cell 12
<tr><td>cell 21<td>cell 22
</table>after table
<span>text in span</span>
<div>text in div 1
<div>text in div 2</div></div>
</body></html>
```

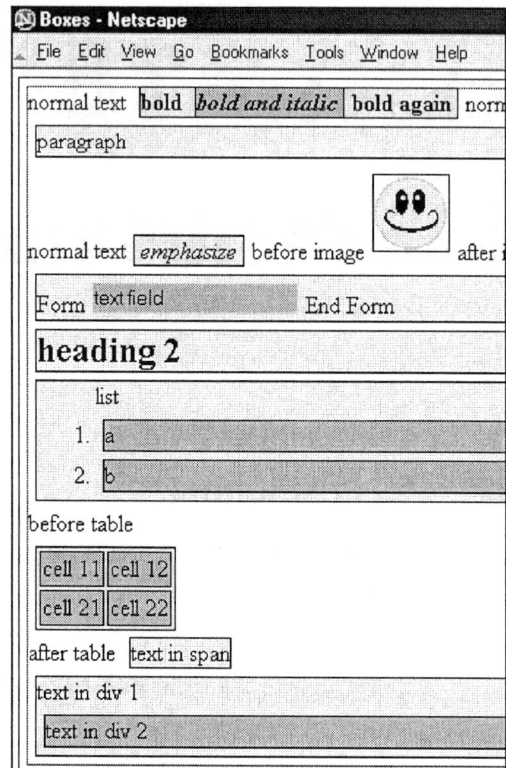

Figure 18.1

Notes

- The rule {border-style : solid; border-width:1px; margin : 5px;} creates a solid border one pixel thick for each HTML element except the leaves (regular text).
- The outermost box (black) represents the root element corresponding to the HTML document.
- The red box represents the <body> element.
- Inside the <body> element, there are leaves (regular text like "normal text") and other boxes corresponding to other HTML elements.
- Some boxes are rendered one after another (many on the same line). These are called **in-line boxes** and correspond to HTML in-line elements (e.g. <b>, <i>, <em>, <img>, and <input>).
- Some boxes are rendered one under another (only one on each line). These are called **block boxes** and correspond to HTML block-level elements (<p>, <h2>, <form>, and <div>).

◆ Special attention should be given to boxes corresponding to `<ol>`, `<ul>` and `<table>` elements.

The formatting algorithm presented above is called *normal flow*. This normal flow can be changed by *floated* and *positioned* elements (see section 18.4 Floating boxes and section 18.7 Positioning elements).

18.3 The `'display'` property

The `'display'` property applies to all HTML elements and determines both the *in-line* and *block* level behavior. The possible values are:

- `inline` to set the box type to inline
- `block` to set the box type to block
- `none` to eliminate the element from the rendering process

Note that other possible values exist for tables and lists, each having a special comportment in the rendering process.

Example 18_2. All elements are inline (file e18_2.html)

Let's add the following line into the style sheet of Example 18_1 to change the behavior of all elements to *inline*:

```
* {display : inline;}
```

Observe the changes in Figure 18.2:

Figure 18.2

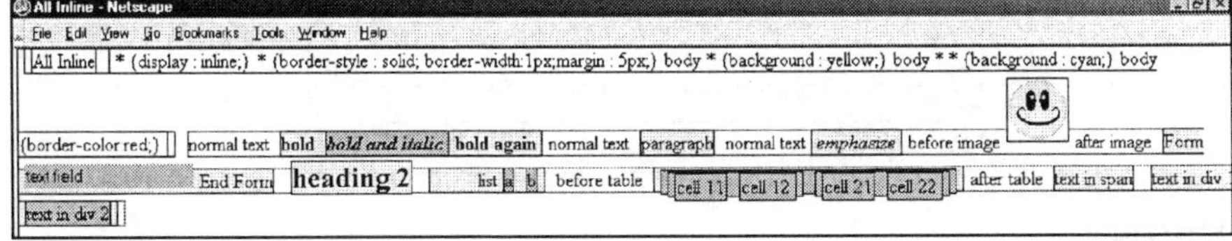

Notes

◆ All elements that belong to the <body> element are displayed inside the red box. The browser tries to render the entire <body> element on a single line. Because there are too many elements to be rendered on a single line, the line-type box continues onto the next lines.

◆ Netscape Navigator 7.1 generates another line-type box for the <head> element, including the `<title>` and the `<style>` content.

◆ Be aware that the display of this page can vary from browser to browser.

Example 18_3. All elements are block-level (file e18_3.html)

Next, let's insert the following line into the style sheet of Example 18_1 to add a new rule that changes the behavior of all elements to *block-level*:

```
* {display : block;}
```

Observe the changes in Figure 18.3:

Figure 18.3

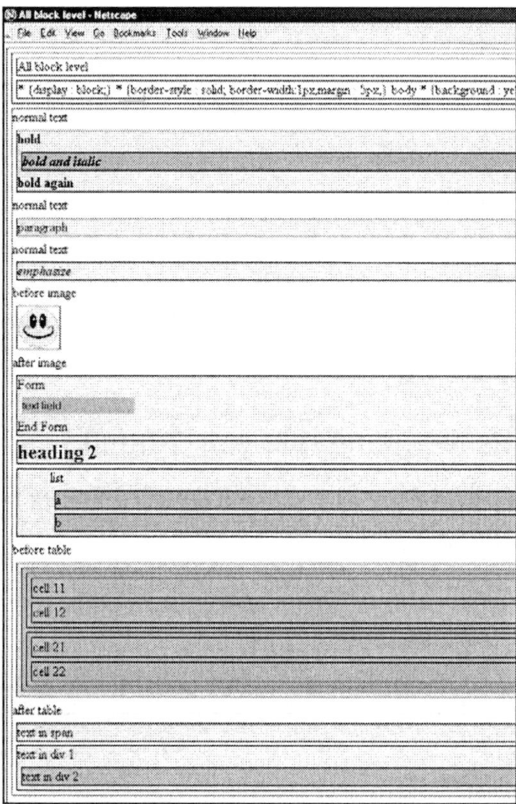

Notes

- A block box is generated for each element.
- Each element starts in a new line-type box.
- Netscape Navigator 7.1 also generates block boxes for the `<head>`, `<title>`, and `<style>` elements.

Also, note that the designer should exercise caution when changing the default behavior of an element from in-line to block-level or vice versa because rendering varies from browser to browser.

Example 18_4. The 'none' value of the 'display' property (file e18_4.html)

Let's insert the following new rule into the style sheet of Example 18_1 to change the value of the 'display' property of some elements to 'none':

```
form, ol, table {display : none;}
```

Observe the changes in Figure 18.4:

Figure 18.4

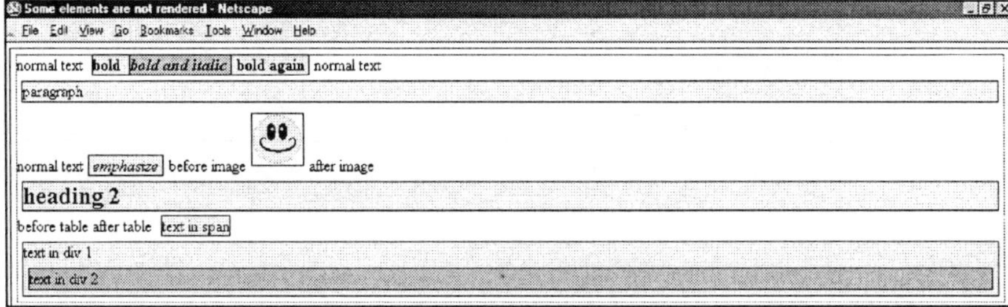

Note that none of the <form>, <ol>, or <table> elements (including their sub-elements) are rendered.

18.4 Floating boxes

The normal flow of element rendering can be changed if there are *floating* objects. The floating objects can be defined using HTML code with the align attribute (e.g. <img align="right">) for the HTML elements that accept it, or by CSS code using the 'float' property attached to any element. The possible values of this property are:

- none to generate a box that is not floated
- right to generate a box that is floated to the right
- left to generate a box that is floated to the left

Example 18_5. Floating boxes (file e18_5.html)

Let's analyze what happens if an element is declared a floating element. To do this, add the two following rules to the style sheet of Example 18_1 (also see the comment blocks for explanations):

```
img {float : right;}    /*this rule declares all images as right floating
objects*/
```

```
ol {float : left;}      /*this rule declares all ordered lists as left
floating objects*/
```

Observe the changes in Figure 18.5:

Figure 18.5

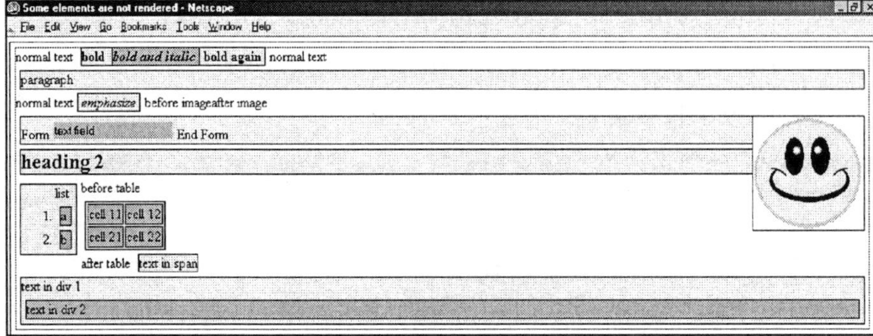

Notes

- When a floating object is met, the following things happens:

  1. The normal flow is stopped, and the browser puts a virtual marker to indicate the point where the normal flow was stopped.

  2. The floating object is rendered in the specified position (right or left), starting on the next line with the default or specified dimensions.

  3. The normal flow continues from the virtual marker, and all the remaining objects are rendered using all the empty space left after rendering the floating object.

- It is possible for the box corresponding to a floating object to overlap with the boxes of adjacent objects. Note that only the boxes overlap, not the contents.
- The `<ol>` element can be declared a floating object in CSS only, because HTML doesn't accept an `align` attribute for this element.

18.5 The stack of floating boxes

If many adjacent objects are floated in the same direction, a *stack* of floating objects can appear (the floating objects are rendered on the same line one after another).

Example 18_6. The stack of floating objects (file e18_6.html)

```
<html><head><style>
* {border-style : solid;
border-width:1px;margin : 5px;}
body * {background : yellow;}
body * * {background : cyan;}
body {border-color:red;}
```

```
</style></head><body>
normal text<em> emphasize </em>
before image <img src="smile.gif" style="float: right;"> after image
before list <ol style="float: left;">list<li>a<li>b</ol> after list
before table<table style="float: right;">
<tr><td>cell 11<td>cell 12
<tr><td>cell 21<td>cell 22
</table>after table
<span>text in span</span>
<div>text in div 1<div>text in div 2</div></div>
<h2>heading 2</h2>
normal text</body></html>
```

Figure 18.6

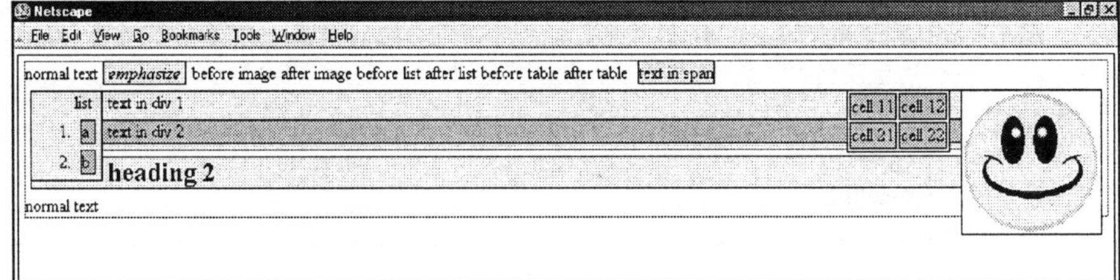

Notes

- The <img> and the <table> elements are floated and stacked on the right side.
- The <ol> element is floated on the left side.
- All the other elements are rendered in the remaining free space.

18.6 The `'clear'` property

The `'clear'` property can be attached to block-level objects to render them in a single-line box. In this case, no content (including floating objects) is added on the left side or on the right side.

The possible values are:

- `none`
- `left` so the left side of the element will be cleared
- `right` so the right side of the element will be cleared
- `both` so both sides of the element will be cleared

Example 18_7. The 'clear' property (file e18_7.html)

For example, the <h2> element in Example 18_6 is a block-level element that has the floating <ol> element on the left side and the <img> and <table> floating elements on the right side. To clear the left side, change the line

```
<h2>heading 2</h2>
```

to

```
<h2 style="clear: left;">heading 2</h2>
```

Observe the changes in Figure 18.7:

Figure 18.7

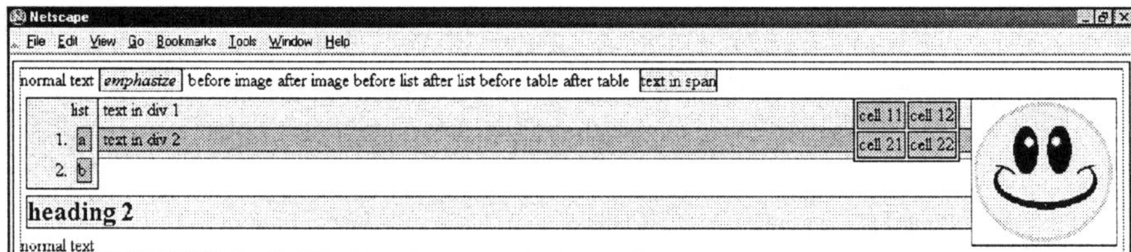

Notes

- The top edge of the <h2> box is moved below the bottom edge of the <ol> box.
- The right side of the <h2> element is not yet cleared (the <img> floating box overlaps it).
- The 'clear' property can be attached to a floating object to render it on a single line.

18.7 Positioning elements

CSS allows you to define exactly where an element should be rendered. To do this, use the 'position' property that can be attached to any element. The possible values are:

- `static` corresponding to the normal flow; this is the default value.
- `relative` so the element participates in the normal flow but is rendered with an *offset* relative to its normal position; after this translation, the element can overlap the other elements.
- `absolute` so the element is eliminated from the normal flow and is rendered with an *offset* relative to the first positioned parent element.
- `fixed` so the element is eliminated from the normal flow and is rendered with an *offset* relative to the view-port; its position remains the same when the content of the page is scrolled using the navigation bars.

Notes

- An element is positioned when the `'position'` property is set to any value other than `static`
- The edges of the box corresponding to the positioned element are defined by the following properties:
  - `top`
  - `right`
  - `bottom`
  - `left`
- The possible values for these properties are:
  - `<length>` for fixed dimensions.
  - `<percentage>` for dimensions relative to the dimensions of the parent box.
  - `auto` for values determined by the normal flow.
  - `inherit` for values inherited from the parent block.

18.8 Relative positioning

To define a relative position for an element, attach the following style to the element:

```
position : relative
```

and set the values for the `top`, `right`, `bottom`, and `left` properties.

Example 18_8. Relative positioning (file e18_8.html)

```
<html><head><style>
body {font-size : 1cm;}
.up {position : relative; top : -10px;}
.down {position : relative; top : +10px;}
</style></head><body>
This <span class="up">text</span> is <span
class="down">oscillating</span>!</body></html>
```

Figure 18.8

18.9 Absolute positioning

To define an absolute position for an element, attach the following style to the element:

```
position : absolute
```

and set the values for the `top`, `right`, `bottom`, and `left` properties.

Example 18_9. Absolute positioning (file e18_9.html)

```
<html><head><style>
body {font-size : 1cm;}
*[id] {border-style : double;}
#one {position : absolute; top : 40px; left : 40px;}
#two {position : absolute; top : 80px; left : 80px;}
#three {position : absolute; top : 120px; left : 120px;}
</style></head><body>
This <span id="one">is</span> an <span id="two">absolute</span> positioned <span
id="three">text.</span>
</body></html>
```

Figure 18.9

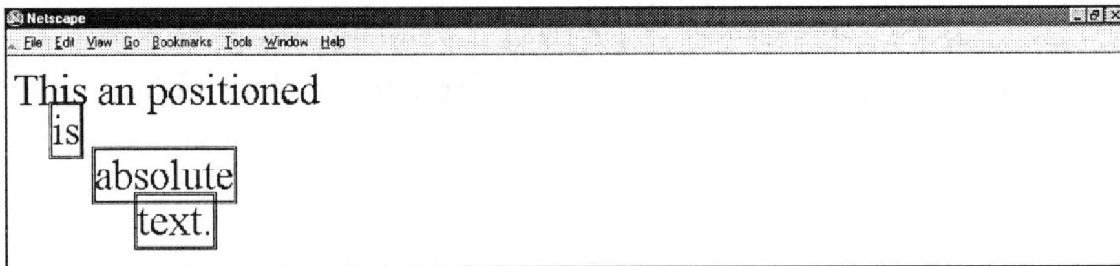

In Example 18_10, the `<span>` element contains a period '.'. The two images are positioned relative to that period.

Example 18_10. The positioned element (file e18_10.html)

```
<html><head></head><body>
The position of the two images will be
determined relative to the period at the end
of this sentence, regardless of where it is
rendered
<span style="position : absolute;">
.
<img src="smile.gif" style="position :
absolute; left : 50px; top : 50px;">
<img src="smile.gif" style="position :
absolute; left : 100px top : 100px;">
</span></body></html>
```

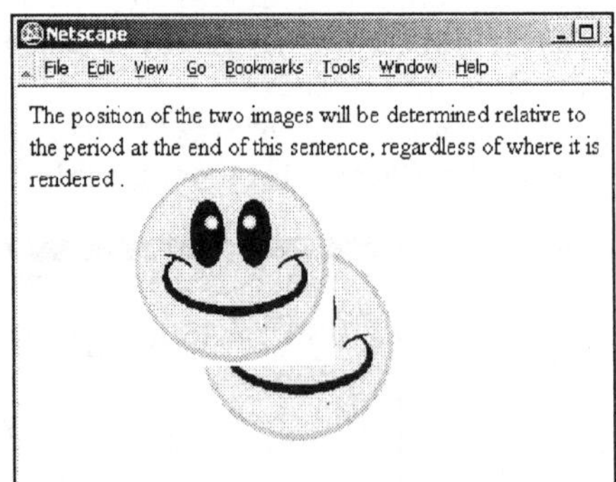

Figure 18.10

18.10 Fixed positioning

To define a fixed position element, attach the following style to the element:

```
position : fixed
```

and set the values for the `top`, `right`, `bottom`, and `left` properties.

Example 18_11. Fixed positioning (file e18_11.html)

```
<html><head><style>
</style></head><body>
line 1<br>line 2<br>line 3<br>line 4<br>line 5<br>line
6<br>line 7<br>line 8<br>line 9<br>line 10<br>
line 11<br>line 12<br>line 13<br>line 14<br>line
15<br>line 16<br>line 17<br>line 18<br>line 19<br>line
20
<img src="smile.gif" style="position : fixed; top :
50px; left : 50px">
</body></html>
```

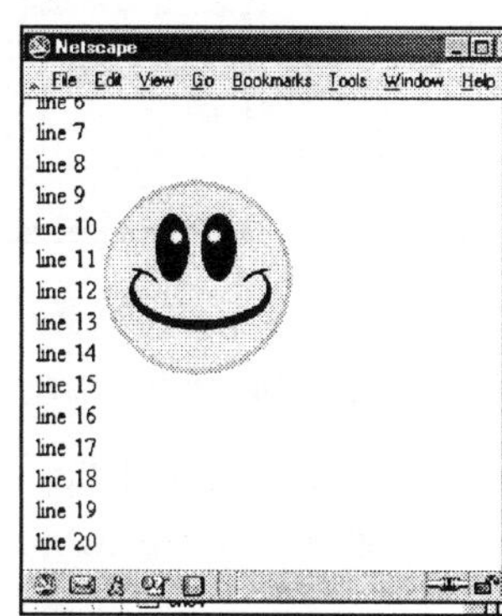

Figure 18.11

18.11 The stack of layers

If you change the normal flow of a web page using floating boxes or using absolute, relative or fixed boxes, it is possible for these boxes to overlap. As a result, a stack of boxes (elements or layers) appears. By default, the boxes are rendered in the order they are inserted into the document, each one being rendered over top of the preceding ones.

Example 18_12. The default stack of layers (file e18_11.html)

```
<html><head><style>
* {border-style : solid; border-width : 1px;}
</style></head><body>
Number 1<table><tr><td>c11<td>c12<tr><td>c21<td>c22</table>
<img src="logo.gif">
<ol style="position : absolute; top : 150px; left: 150px; background :
yellow;">Number 4<li>Item 1<li>Item 2<li>Item 3</ol>
<h1 align="center" style="position : relative; top : 20px; left: 50px; background :
pink;">Number 5</h1>
<div style="position : absolute; top : 200px; left: 250px; background :
cyan;">Number 6
<div style="position : relative; left: -20px; background : silver;">Number 7</div>
```

```
<div style="position : relative; left: -10px; top : -10px; background :
silver;">Number 8</div>
Number 6</div></body></html>
```

Figure 18.12

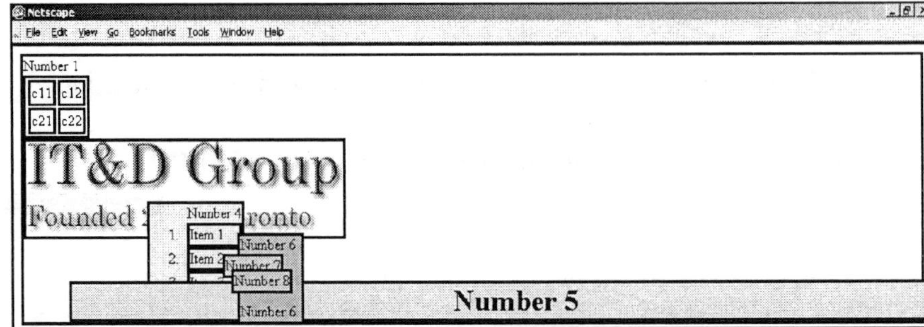

To change the stack level for an element (box), use the 'z-index' property. The possible values are:

- auto the default value
- <integer> to determine the stack level relative to the *parent* element

The boxes with a bigger stack level will be rendered over the boxes with a smaller stack level, inside the same parent.

Example 18_13. Custom made stack of layers (file e18_13.html)

```
<html><head><style>
* {border-style : solid; border-width : 1px;}
</style></head><body>
Number 1<table><tr><td>c11<td>c12<tr><td>c21<td>c22</table>
<img src="logo.gif" style="position : relative; z-index : 6;">
<ol style="position : absolute; top : 150px; left: 150px; background : yellow;
z-index : 5;">Number 4<li>Item 1<li>Item 2<li>Item 3</ol>
<h1 align="center" style="position : relative; top : 20px; left: 50px; background :
pink; z-index : 4;">Number 5</h1>
<div style="position : absolute; top : 200px; left: 250px; background : cyan;
z-index : 1";>
Number 6
<div style="position : relative; left: -20px; background : silver; z-index :
8;">Number 7</div>
<div style="position : relative; left: -10px; top : -10px; background : silver;
z-index : 7;">Number 8</div>
Number 6</div></body></html>
```

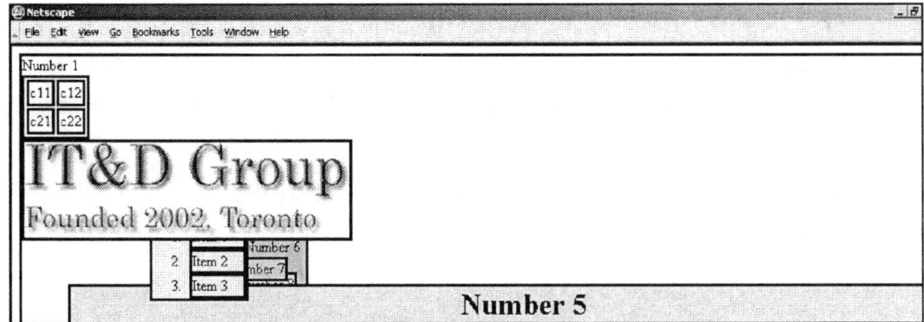

Figure 18.13

Notes

- Most of the elements are children of the <body> element, and the stack of layers is rendered using the stack level assigned to each child.
- Although the Number 7 division block has the biggest stack level (8), it is not rendered on top of all the others. This is because this division block is inside another division block (Number 6 division block). Its stack level is relative to its parent and not relative to the <body> element. Its parent has a stack level equal to 1 and is rendered below all its sibling elements.

18.12 Review of Chapter 18

At the end of Chapter 18 you should know:

- CSS positioning determines the rules for rendering the document.
- In the rendering process, the document tree of elements, the type of each element, the floating elements (if present), and the positioned elements (if present) are all important.
- In the normal flow, the in-line elements are rendered one after another (on a single line) and the block-level elements are rendered one under another (only one element on a line).
- The `'display'` property determines the behavior of an element as `inline` or `block`
- The `'float'` property determines the behavior of a floating element as `right`, `left`, or `none`
- The `'clear'` property clears a side of a block-level element (`left`, `right`, `both`) of floating elements.
- To position an element, set the `'position'` property to `relative`, `absolute` or `fixed`, but not to `static`

- The properties `top`, `right`, `bottom`, and `left` set the position of the positioned element.
- If floating or positioned elements exist, an overlap of the elements' boxes can appear.
- To change the order in which this overlapping is rendered, use the `'z-index'` property.

Chapter 19

Tables in CSS

19.1 Regular HTML tables

Tables require special attention in CSS because they are organized structures. A table is a container for rows, which in turn are containers for cells. Therefore, the `<td>` and `<th>` elements are children of `<tr>` elements, and the `<tr>` elements in turn are children of a `<table>` element. Tables can be nested, so a `<table>` element can be the child of a `<td>` or `<th>` element. When the `<table>` element is rendered, it generates a block-level box by default.

19.2 CSS tables

CSS allows you to attach a table behavior to any structure that is organized similarly to a table. This is possible using the 'display' property, which can have specific values for tables:

- table — to attach a table behavior to an element
- table-row — to attach a table row behavior to an element
- table-cell — to attach a table cell behavior to an element

Example 19_1. A CSS table (file e19_1.html)

```
<html><head>
<style>
* {border-width : 1px;border-style : solid;
padding : 5px;margin : 5px;}
div {display : table;}
```

```
div div {display : table-row;}
div div span {display : table-cell;}
</style></head><body>
<div>
<div><span>c11</span><span>c12</span></div>
<div><span>c21</span><span>c22</span></div>
<div><span>c31</span><span>c32</span></div>
</div>
</body></html>
```

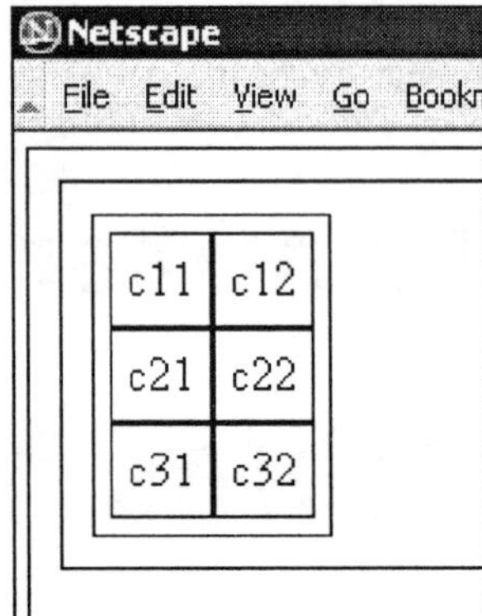

Figure 19.1

Notes

- The table structure is based on generic <div> and <span> blocks.
- The 'display' property changes the default behavior for these elements.
- Borders are used to better show the tree structure of the whole page.
- Be aware that some browsers may render this page differently.

19.3 Advanced HTML tables

In HTML, you can add sections to a table using the <caption> element for the table caption, the <thead> and <tfoot> elements to add a header and a footer, and one or more <tbody> elements to define body sections. Also, you can use the <colgroup> and <col> elements to define column attributes.

19.4 Advanced CSS tables

To define a table structure having sections, use the following possible values of the 'display' property:

- table-row-group — corresponds to <tbody> elements
- table-header-group — corresponds to <thead> elements
- table-footer-group — corresponds to <tfoot> elements
- table-column-group — corresponds to <colgroup> elements
- table-column — corresponds to <col> elements
- table-caption — corresponds to <caption> elements

For the <caption> element (or for a CSS caption element) the 'caption-side' property allows you to define where the table caption will be rendered. The possible values are:

bottom | left | right | top (the default value)

Example 19_2. An advanced CSS table (file e19_2.html)

```
<html><head>
<style>
* {border-width : 1px;border-style : solid;padding : 5px;margin : 5px;}
div.table {display : table;}
div.row {display : table-row;}
div.cell {display : table-cell;}
div.caption {display : table-caption; caption-side : right;}
div.c1 {width : 100px; text-align : right; background : cyan;}
div.c2 {width : 150px; text-align : center;}
div.thg {display : table-header-group; color : red;}
div.trg {display : table-row-group; font-style : italic;}
div.tfg {display : table-footer-group; color : blue;}
</style></head><body>
<div class="table">
<div class="caption">This is the caption</div>
<div class="thg"><div class="row"><div class="cell c1">c11</div><div class="cell
c2">c12</div></div></div>
<div class="trg"><div class="row"><div class="cell c1">c21</div><div class="cell
c2">c22</div></div></div>
<div class="tfg"><div class="row"><div class="cell c1">c31</div><div class="cell
c2">c32</div></div></div>
</div>
</body></html>
```

Figure 19.2

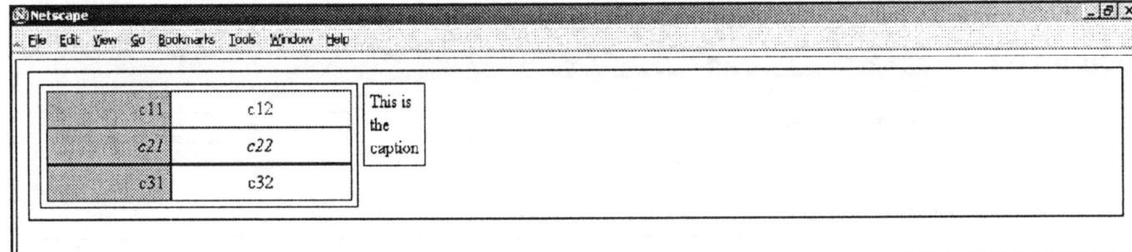

Notes

- The table structure is based only on <div> elements.
- The column structure is defined by two classes: "c1" and "c2".
- Be aware that some browsers could render this page differently.

19.5 Column properties

There are several properties than can be applied to the <col> elements of a table:

- `border` to define the border width, style, and color. The possible values are: <length> <border-style> <color>
- `background` to define the background color. The possible values are: <color>
- `width` to define the column width. The possible values are: <length>
- `visibility` to define how the column is rendered. The possible values are: hide | hidden | inherit | show | visible

Example 19_3. Column properties (file e19_3.html)

```
<html><head>
<style>
* {border : 1px solid red;}
col.c1 {font-style : italic; background : yellow; }
col.c2 {visibility : hidden;}
col.c3 {width : 150px; color : blue;}
</style></head><body>
<table>
<colgroup>
<col width="50" class="c1">
<col width="100" class="c2">
<col class="c3">
</colgroup>
<tr><td>c11<td>c12<td>c13
<tr><td>c21<td>c22<td>c23
</table>
</body></html>
```

Figure 19.3

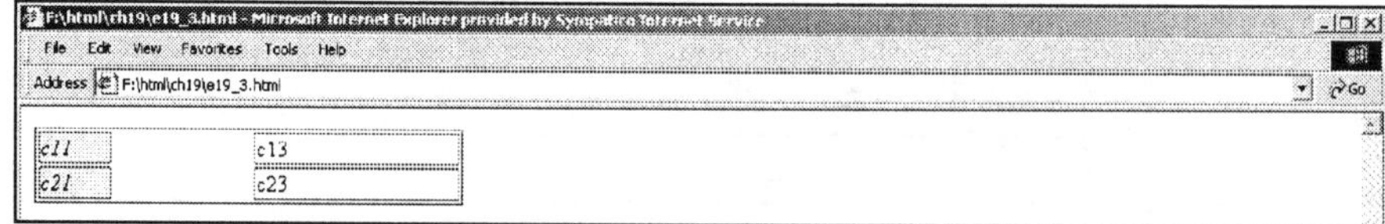

Notes

- An HTML table was used in the previous example.
- The browser reserved space for the hidden element.
- Be aware that some browsers could render this page differently.

19.6 Table layout

Browsers render a table according the value of the 'table-layout' property. The possible values are:

- auto (the default value). First, the table data is read, then the row and cell data is completely rendered using the minimum necessary space.
- fixed First, the table rows and cells are rendered using the specified values for width and height, then the table data is rendered using the existing space.

Example 19_4. Table layout (file e19_4.html)

```
<html><head><style>
table.cl {table-layout : auto;}
table.c2 {table-layout : fixed;}
table td {width : 50px;}
table tr {height : 50px;}
</style></head><body>
<table class="cl" border>
<tr><td>This is the cell c11
<td>before<img src="tree.gif">after
<td style="font-size : 30pt;">Big Text
<tr><td>Second Row, First Cell<td>This is cell c22
<td>The last cell of the table
</table>
<table class="c2" border>
<tr><td>This is the cell c11
<td>before<img src="tree.gif">after
<td style="font-size : 30pt;">Big Text
<tr><td>Second Row, First Cell<td>This is cell c22
<td>The last cell of the table
</table></body></html>
```

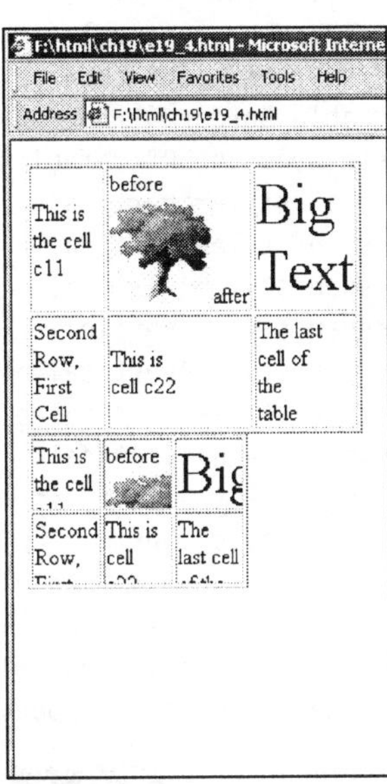

Figure 19.4

Notes

- The first table has an auto layout, and the second has a fixed layout.
- The exact dimensions of the tables are defined using the width property for the table cells and the height property for the table rows.
- The cell content for the fixed layout table is cropped to the actual cell dimensions.
- Be aware that some browsers could render this page differently.

19.7 Vertical alignment

The 'vertical-align' property allows you to set the vertical alignment between several in-line elements that belong to the same parent (e.g. the same table cell). The possible values are:

- baseline | top | bottom | middle | sub | super | text-top | text-bottom
- <length> or <percentage>

Example 19_5. Vertical alignment (file e19_5.html)

```
<html><head><style>
* {border : 1px solid red; margin 5px;}
</style></head><body>
<table border><tr height="100" style="font-size : 17pt;">
<td height="50">default<img src="tree.gif">
<span style="vertical-align : baseline;">baseline</span>
<span style="vertical-align : text-bottom;">text-bottom</span>
<span style="vertical-align : text-top;">text-top</span>
<span style="vertical-align : middle;">middle</span>
<span style="vertical-align : sub;">sub</span>
<span style="vertical-align : super;">super</span>
<span style="vertical-align : top;">top</span>
<img src="tree.gif" style="vertical-align : top;">
<span style="vertical-align : bottom;">bottom</span>
<img src="tree.gif" style="vertical-align : bottom;">
<span style="vertical-align : 320%;">320%</span>
<span style="vertical-align : -30px;">-30px</span>
</td></tr></table></body></html>
```

Figure 19.5

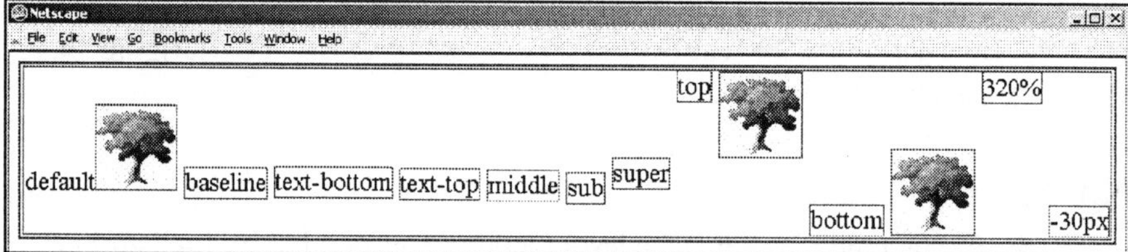

Notes

- The elements are rendered relative to the baseline of the parent.
- The top elements are top-aligned with the highest element.
- The bottom elements are bottom-aligned with the lowest element.
- When applied to a parent element, the 'vertical-align' property is inherited by all the children elements.

19.8 Horizontal alignment

The 'text-align' property allows you to set the horizontal alignment for the content relative to the element box. This property can also be attached to the <col> or <table> element. When applied to a parent element, the 'text-align' property is inherited by all the child elements. The possible values are:

- center | justify | left | right
- <string> (only for table cells; e.g. text-align : ".")

Example 19_6. Horizontal alignment (file e19_6.html)

```
<html><head><style>
* {border : 1px solid red; margin 5px;}
</style></head><body>
<table>
<colgroup><col width="300" style="text-align : right;">
<col width="300"></colgroup>
<tr><td>col:right<td>default</tr>
<tr style="text-align : center;"> <td>col:right;tr:center<td>tr:center</tr>
</table></body></html>
```

Figure 19.6

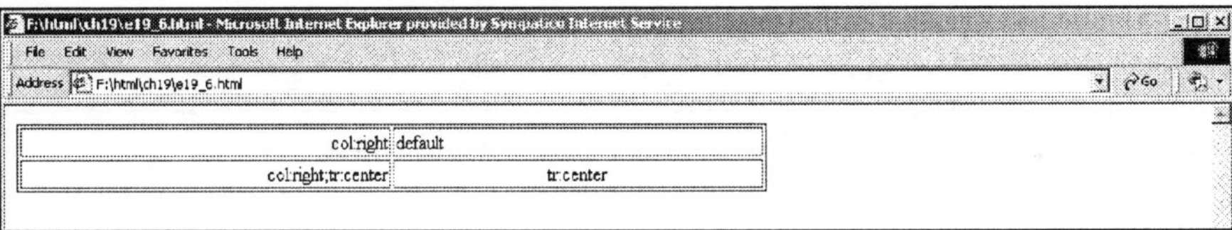

Notes

- The default value is left.
- The <col> setting has a greater priority than the <tr> setting.

19.9 Borders for table cells

CSS allows you to define the style, width and color for the table elements, similar to any kind of boxes. To do this, use the border-style, border-width, border-color, or border properties.

Example 19_7. Border style (file e19_7.html)

```
<html><head><style>
.none {border-style : none;}
.hidden {border-style : hidden;}
.dotted {border-style : dotted;}
.dashed {border-style : dashed;}
.solid {border : 5px solid red;}
.double {border-style : double;}
.groove {border-style : groove;}
.ridge {border-style : ridge;}
.inset {border-style : inset;}
.outset {border-style : outset;}
table {border : 2px solid blue;}
tr {border : 2px solid green;}
</style></head><body>
<table><tr><td class="none">none
<td class="hidden">hidden
<td class="dotted">dotted
<td class="dashed">dashed
<td class="solid">5px, solid, red
<tr><td class="double">double
<td class="groove">groove
<td class="ridge">ridge
<td class="inset">inset
<td class="outset">outset</table>
</body></html>
```

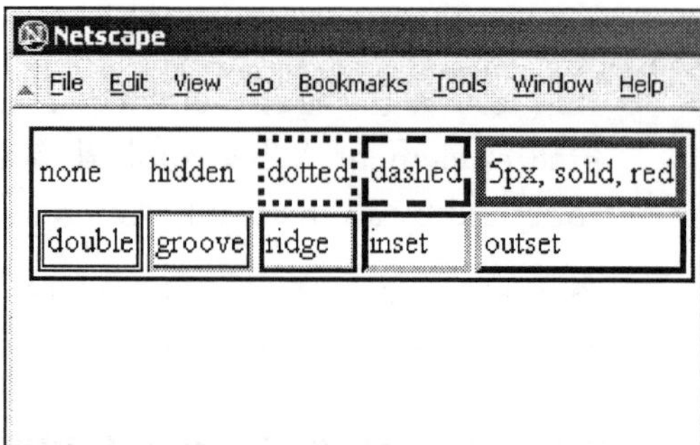

Figure 19.7

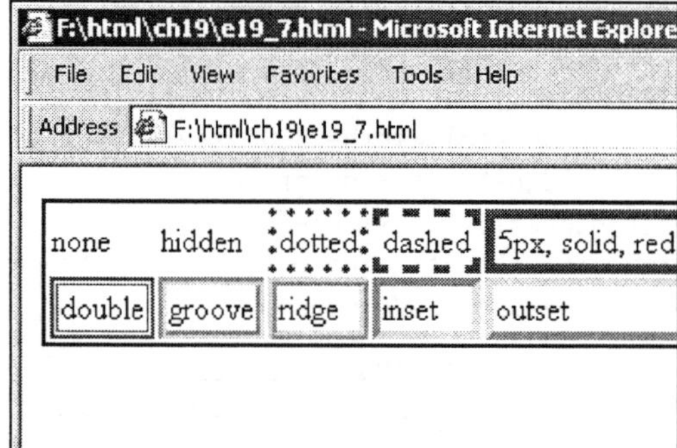

Figure 19.8

Notes

- The <tr> elements are rendered without a border.
- The style defined for <tr> elements applies to the <td> elements (only in Internet Explorer).
- The style defined for a <table> element doesn't apply to its children.

19.10 Border spacing

The 'border-spacing' property determines the distance between the borders of two adjacent cells. The possible values are:

- <length> *horizontal_distance=vertical_distance*
- <length> <length> *horizontal_distance vertical_distance*

Example 19_8. Border spacing (file e19_8.html)

```
<html><head><style>
table {border : 1px solid blue;}
td {border : 1px solid red;}
</style></head><body>
<table cellspacing="10">
<tr><td>c11<td>c12<td>c13<tr><td>c21<td>c22<td>c23
</table>
<table style="border-spacing : 10px 20px;">
<tr><td>c11<td>c12<td>c13<tr><td>c21<td>c22<td>c23
</table></body></html>
```

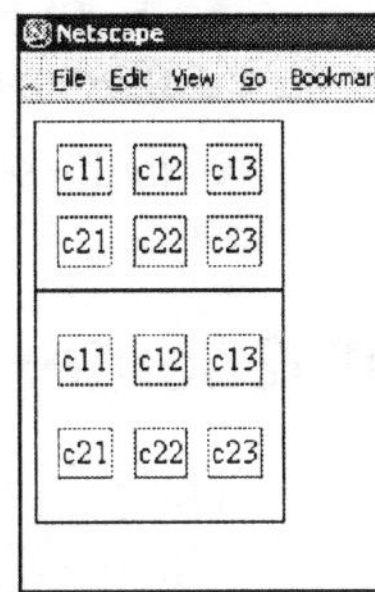

Figure 19.9

Notes

- The distance between two adjacent cells in the first table was set using the HTML `cellspacing` attribute of the `<table>` element, but that distance in the second table was set using the `border-spacing` property.
- The `border-spacing` property allows you to specify different spacing values horizontally and vertically.

19.11 Empty cells

The property `'empty-cells'` determines if an empty cell is rendered with a border. The possible values are:

- `show` to render an empty cell with a border
- `hide` to render an empty cell without a border

Example 19_9. Empty cells (file e19_9.html)

```
<html><head><style>
* {border : 1px solid red;}
</style></head><body>
<table>
<tr><td>c11<td><td> 
<tr><td>c21<td>c22<td>
<tr><td>c31<td>c32<td>c33
</table>
<table style="empty-cells : show;">
<tr><td>c11<td><td>
<tr><td>c21<td>c22<td>
<tr><td>c31<td>c32<td>c33
</table>
</body></html>
```

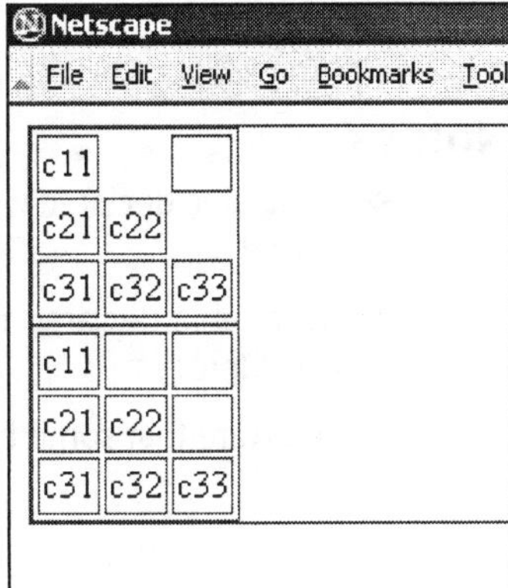

Figure 19.10

Notes

- The first table is a regular HTML table with empty cells (note that an ` ` character was used to create a border for cell `c13`, even though it was rendered empty).
- In the second table, a border was rendered for all empty cells.

19.12 Border collapse

The property `'border-collapse'` determines the border model of the table cells. The possible values are:

- `collapse` to define a *collapsing* border model
- `separated` to define a *separated* border model

Example 19_10. Border collapse (file e19_10.html)

```
<html><head><style>
* {border : 1px solid red; margin : 10px; padding : 10px;}
</style></head><body>
<table style="border-collapse : collapse; border-spacing :
cellspacing="10">
<tr><td>c11<td>c12<td>c13
<tr><td>c21<td>c22<td>c23
<tr><td>c31<td>c32<td>c33
</table>
<table style="border-collapse : separate; border-spacing :
cellspacing="10">
<tr><td>c11<td>c12<td>c13
<tr><td>c21<td>c22<td>c23
<tr><td>c31<td>c32<td>c33
</table>
</body></html>
```

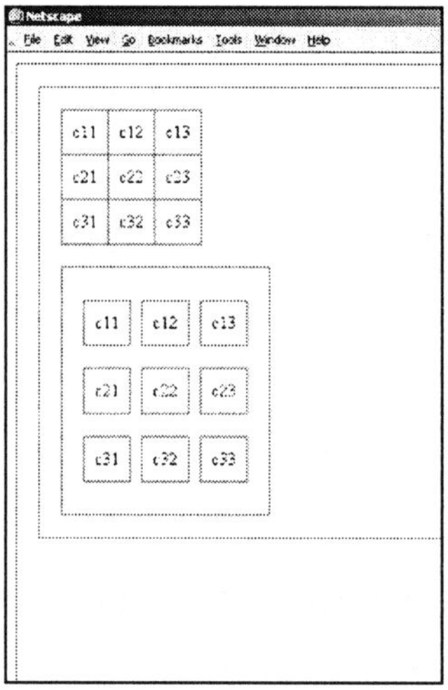

Figure 19.11

Notes

- For a table declared with a `collapse` border-style, the inter-cell space and margins are collapsed.
- For a table declared with a `separate` border-style, the inter-cell space and margins are considered.
- Be aware that some browsers could render this page differently.

19.13 Review of Chapter 19

- Tables are considered special elements in CSS.
- By default, tables are block-level elements.
- There are three values of the 'display' property that allow you to set for an element a behavior as a table (table), table row (table-row) or table cell (table-cell).
- If you have structures similar with a table, then you can identify the body of the table with the value table-row-group of the 'display' property, the header with table-header-group, the footer with table-footer-group, and the caption with table-caption.
- The position of the table caption can be set using the 'caption-side' property.
- The table-column-group and the table-column values of the 'display' property corresponds to the <colgroup> and <col> elements.
- There are four properties you can set for the <col> element of a table: 'border', 'background', 'width', and 'visibility'.
- The layout of a table is determined by the value of the 'table-layout' property (auto or fixed).
- The 'vertical-align' property allows you to set the vertical alignment of in-line elements belonging to the same parent element.
- The 'text-align' property allows you to set the horizontal alignment for the content relative to an element box.
- The borders of a table can be set using the 'border-style', 'border-width', 'border-color', or 'border' properties.
- The property 'border-spacing' determines the distance between the borders of two adjacent cells of a table.
- The property 'empty-cells' determines if the empty cells are rendered with or without a border.
- The property 'border-collapse' determines the border model used to render the table cells.

Chapter 20

Generated content and lists in CSS

20.1 Generated content

CSS allows you to automatically *generate content* that doesn't belong to the document tree. The code that determines the generated content is placed in the CSS style sheets inside of the same file or in the external files. You can use generated content to personalize the appearance of the web page and to create custom-made lists.

20.2 Pseudo-elements

You can add the generated content *before or after* an element is generated. *Pseudo-elements* allow you to specify when to automatically generate content. The pseudo-elements you can use are:

- `E:before` to generate content *before* the E element
- `E:after` to generate content *after* the E element

20.3 The `'content'` property

The `'content'` property allows you to specify what content will be automatically generated. The possible values for this property are *space delimited lists* of:

- `<string>` to insert any text

- `<URL>` to insert an Internet resource; e.g. `url(tree.gif)`
- `<counter>` to insert a counter for a list
- `attr(A)` to insert the value of the A attribute
- `open-quote | close-quote | no-open-quote | no-close-quote` (see section 20.4 Quotation marks)

Notes

- ◆ The default value of the `'content'` property is an empty string.
- ◆ To insert a forced new line (similar to the `<br>` element) use the `"\A"` escape sequence.

To automatically generate content, use the pseudo-elements in conjunction with the `'content'` property.

Example 20_1. Generated content (file e20_1.html)

```
<html><head><style>
:before {content : "<>"; color : red;}
:after {content : "</>"; color : red;}
table, form {display : block;}
</style></head><body>
Normal Text.
<h3>This is a Header 3.</h3>
<p> This is a Paragraph. <i>Italic Text</i>
<blockquote>This is a Blockquote.</blockquote>
<form>
TextField:<input type="text"><br>
Submit Button:<input type="submit">
</form>
<table><tr><td>c11<td>c12<tr><td>c21<td>c22</table>
<ul>Unordered List:<li>Item 1.<li>Item 2.</ul>
Normal Text.</body></html>
```

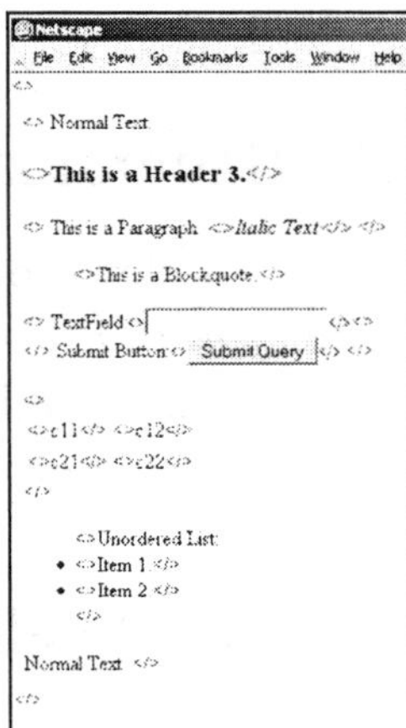

Figure 20.1

Notes

- ◆ This example has generated content before and after each element.
- ◆ The string `"<>"` is generated before each element, and the string `"</>"` is generated after each element.
- ◆ The browser used in Figure 20.2 (Netscape Navigator 7.1) doesn't generate any content for table and form elements without declaring them as block-level boxes.

The following example creates a document tree using CSS-generated content.

Example 20_2. A document tree (file e20_2.html)

```
<html><head>
<style>
body * {display : block; position : relative;
left : 50px;}
body:before {content : "<body>"; color : red;}
body:after {content : "</body>"; color : red;}
h3:before {content : "<h3>"; color : pink;}
h3:after {content : "</h3>"; color : pink;}
p:before {content : "<p>"; color : green;}
p:after {content : "</p>"; color : green;}
i:before {content : "<i>"; color : cyan;}
i:after {content : "</i>"; color : cyan;}
blockquote:before {content : "<blockquote>";
color : magenta;}
blockquote:after {content : "</blockquote>";
color : magenta;}
form:before {content : "<form>"; color :
purple;}
form:after {content : "</form>"; color :
purple;}
input:before {content : "<input type="
attr(type) ">"; color : purple;}
input:after {content : "</input>"; color :
purple;}
table:before {content : "<table>"; color :
orange;}
table:after {content : "</table>"; color :
orange;}
tr:before {content : "<tr>"; color : orange;}
tr:after {content : "</tr>"; color : orange;}
td:before {content : "<td>"; color : orange;}
td:after {content : "</td>"; color : orange;}
ul:before {content : "<ul>"; color : blue;}
ul:after {content : "</ul>"; color : blue;}
li:before {content : "<li>"; color : blue;}
li:after {content : "</li>"; color : blue;}
</style></head><body>
Normal Text.
<h3>This is a Header 3.</h3>
<p> This is a Paragraph. <i>Italic Text</i>
<blockquote>This is a Blockquote.</blockquote>
<form>
TextField:<input type="text">
Submit Button:<input type="submit">
```

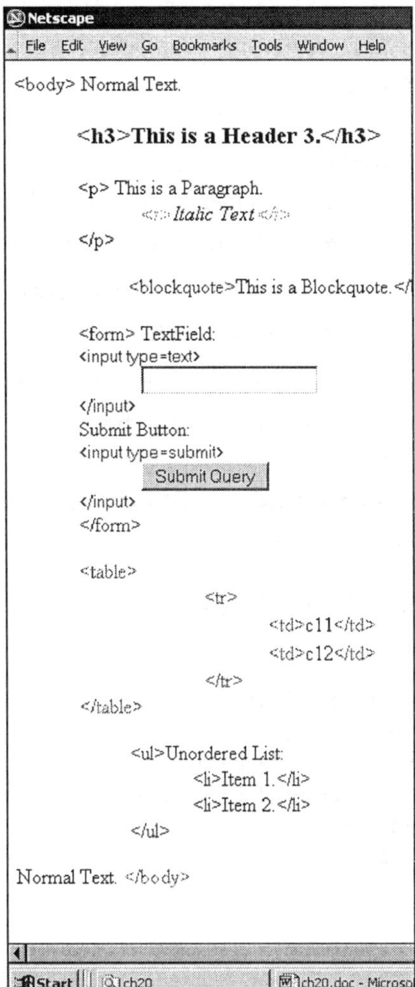

Figure 20.2

```
</form>
<table><tr><td>c11<td>c12</table>
<ul>Unordered List:<li>Item 1.<li>Item 2.</ul>
Normal Text.
</body></html>
```

Notes

- All elements are declared block-level.
- To obtain a tree structure, all elements are positioned relative to their parent elements.
- The starting and ending tags are generated for each element.
- The values of the `type` attributes are generated for each `<input>` element.

Example 20_3 shows how to insert images into a web page using the CSS-generated content method.

Example 20_3. Inserting images (file e20_3.html)

```
<html><head>
<style>
body:before {content : url(logo.gif);}
body:after {content : url(arrow.gif);}
ul:before {content : url(tree.gif);}
</style></head><body>
Normal Text.
<h3>This is a Header 3.</h3>
<ul>Unordered List:<li>Item 1.<li>Item 2.</ul>
Normal Text.
</body></html>
```

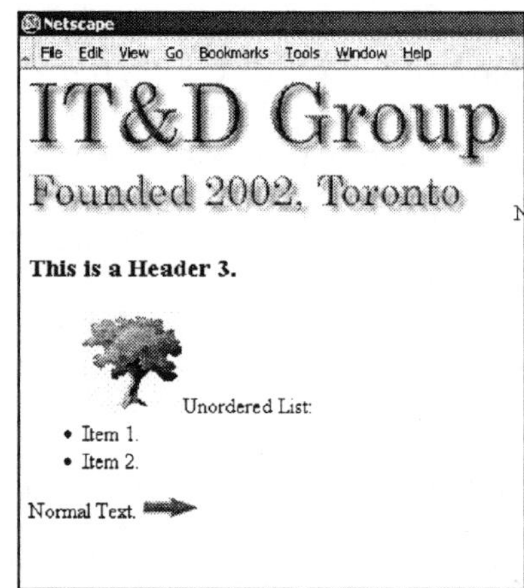

Figure 20.3

Notes

- In this example, an image is inserted before and after the body document.
- The "`tree.gif`" image is inserted before the unordered list.

20.4 Quotation marks

CSS allows you to define *quotation marks* for any element. To do this, a two-step procedure is required:

1. First, the quotation marks must be defined. To define a set of quotation marks, use a selector and the `'quotes'` property. The possible values are `none` or a space-delimited list of pairs:
   - `<string1> <string2>` to define each level of quotation (`<string1>` for the *open quotation mark* and `<string2>` for the *close quotation mark*).
2. Then the quotation marks can be inserted using the `:before` or `:after` pseudo-elements with the `'content'` property set to one of these four values:
   - `open-quote | close-quote | no-open-quote | no-close-quote`

Example 20_4. Quotation marks (file e20_4.html)

```
<html><head>
<style>
q {quotes : '"' '"'; color : purple;}
q>q {quotes : "'" "'"; color : red;}
q>q>q {quotes : "<" ">"; color : blue}
q:before {content : open-quote;}
q:after {content : close-quote;}
</style></head><body>
Normal Text.
<q>This is the first level.<q>This is the second level.<q>This is the third
level.</q>This is the second level.</q>This is the first level</q>
Normal Text.
</body></html>
```

Figure 20.4

Netscape

Normal Text " This is the first level ' This is the second level <This is the third level > This is the second level ' This is the first level " Normal Text

Notes

- To define a string, you can use single (') or double (") quotation marks.
- You can use escape sequences to define quotation mark characters:
  - `"\00AB"` for «
  - `"\00BB"` for »
  - `"\2018"` for `

  - "\2019" for ’
  - "\201C" for “
  - "\201D" for ”

- Quotation marks can be attached to any element.
- Quotation marks can be specified for each language.

Example 20_5. Language quotation marks (file e20_5.html)

```
<html><head><style>
blockquote:lang(en) {quotes : "\201C" "\201D";}
blockquote:lang(fr) {quotes : "\00AB" "\00BB";}
blockquote:before {content : open-quote;}
blockquote:after {content : close-quote;}
td, a {quotes : "[" "]";}
td:before, a:before {content : open-quote;}
td:after, a:after {content : close-quote;}
</style></head><body>
Normal Text.
<blockquote lang="en">This is an English
blockquote.</blockquote>
<blockquote lang="fr">This is a French
blockquote.</blockquote>
<table><tr><td>c11</td><td>c12</td><tr><td>c21</td>
<td>c22</td></table>
<a href="#">This is a link.</a>
<br>Normal Text.
</body></html>
```

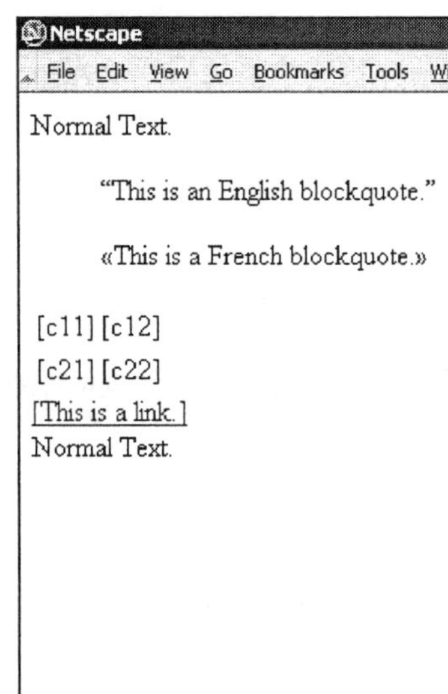

Figure 20.5

20.5 List-item elements

CSS allows you to create new types of lists and to define the visual formatting of the lists. You can make custom-made lists if you set the value of the '`display`' property of an element to `list-item`.

In the next example, lists are created from paragraphs and table cells.

Example 20_6. List-item elements (file e20_6.html)

```
<html><head><style>
* {border : 1px solid red; margin : 5px;}
td,p {display : list-item;}
</style></head><body>
Normal Text.
```

```
<p>paragraph 1</p>
<p>paragraph 2</p>
<p>paragraph 3</p>
<table>
<tr><td>c11<td>c12<td>c13
<tr><td>c21<td>c22<td>c23
</table>
<p>paragraph 4</p>
Normal Text.
</body></html>
```

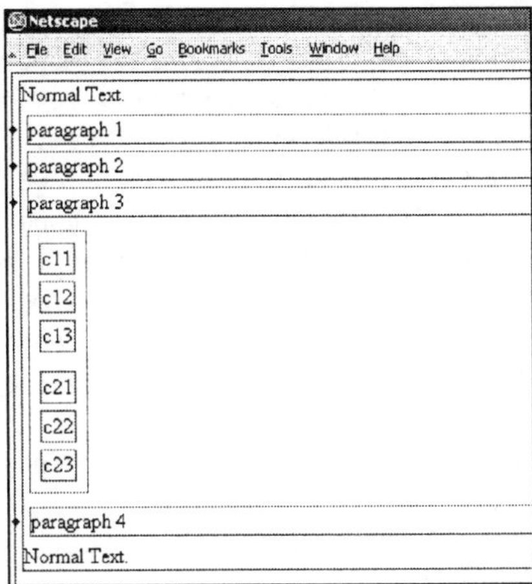

Figure 20.6

20.6 The 'list-style-type' property

The 'list-style-type' property allows you to define the leading symbol that is rendered for each list item. The possible values are:

- disc | circle | square
- decimal | decimal-leading-zero
- lower-roman | upper-roman
- lower-greek
- lower-alpha | upper-alpha
- lower-latin | upper-latin
- Hebrew | Armenian | Georgian
- cjk-ideographic | hiragana | katakana | hiragana-iroha | katakana-iroha
- none

Example 20_7. The list-style-type property (file e20_7.html)

```
<html><head></head><body>
<table><tr>
<td><ul style="list-style-type : disc;">disc<li>First<li>Second</ul>
<ul style="list-style-type : circle;">circle<li>First<li>Second</ul>
<ul style="list-style-type : square;">square<li>First<li>Second</ul>
<td><ol style="list-style-type : decimal;">decimal<li>Item 1<li>Item 2</ol>
<ol style="list-style-type : decimal-leading-zero;">decimal-leading-zero<li>Item
1<li>Item 2</ol>
<ol style="list-style-type : lower-roman;">lower-roman<li>Item 1<li>Item 2</ol>
```

```
<td><ol style="list-style-type : upper-roman;">upper-roman<li>Item 1<li>Item 2</ol>
<ol style="list-style-type : lower-greek;">lower-greek<li>Item 1<li>Item 2</ol>
<ol style="list-style-type : lower-alpha;">lower-alpha<li>Item 1<li>Item 2</ol>
<td><ol style="list-style-type : upper-alpha;">upper-alpha<li>Item 1<li>Item 2</ol>
<ol style="list-style-type : lower-latin;">lower-latin<li>Item 1<li>Item 2</ol>
<ol style="list-style-type : upper-latin;">upper-latin<li>Item 1<li>Item 2</ol>
<td><ol style="list-style-type : hebrew;">hebrew<li>Item 1<li>Item 2</ol>
<ol style="list-style-type : armenian;">armenian<li>Item 1<li>Item 2</ol>
<ol style="list-style-type : georgian;">georgian<li>Item 1<li>Item 2</ol>
<td><ol style="list-style-type : cjk-ideografic;">cjk-ideografic<li>Item 1<li>Item
2</ol>
<ol style="list-style-type : hiragana;">hiragana<li>Item 1<li>Item 2</ol>
<ol style="list-style-type : katakana;">katakana<li>Item 1<li>Item 2</ol>
<td><ol style="list-style-type : hiragana-iroha;">hiragana-iroha<li>Item 1<li>Item
2</ol>
<ol style="list-style-type : katakana-iroha;">katakana-iroha<li>Item 1<li>Item
2</ol>
<ol style="list-style-type : none;">none<li>Item 1<li>Item 2</ol>
</table></body></html>
```

Figure 20.7

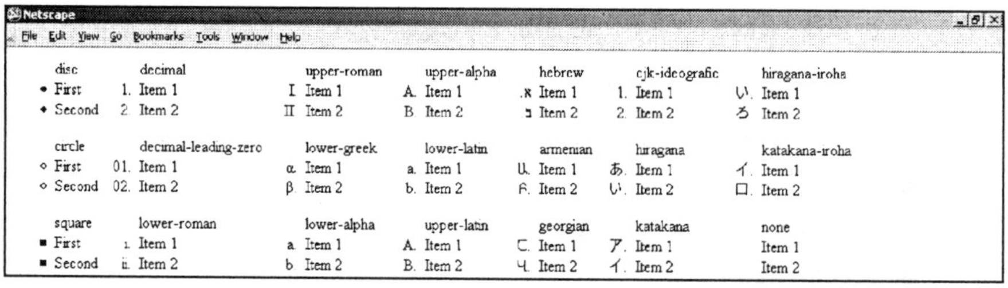

20.7 The 'list-style-image' property

The 'list-style-image' property allows you to define a leading image that is rendered for each list item. The possible values are:

- <url> e.g. url("http://www.itdgroup.com/images/im1.gif")
- none

Example 20_8. The list-style-image property (file e20_8.html)

```
<html><head></head>
<body>
<ul style="list-style-image : url(star.gif);">
star.gif<li>First<li>Second</ul>
<ul style="list-style-image : url(square.gif);">square.gif
<li>First<li>Second</ul>
<ul style="list-style-image : url(cross.gif);">
```

```
cross.gif<li>First<li>Second</ul>
<ul style="list-style-image : none;">
none<li>First<li>Second</ul>
</body></html>
```

Figure 20.8

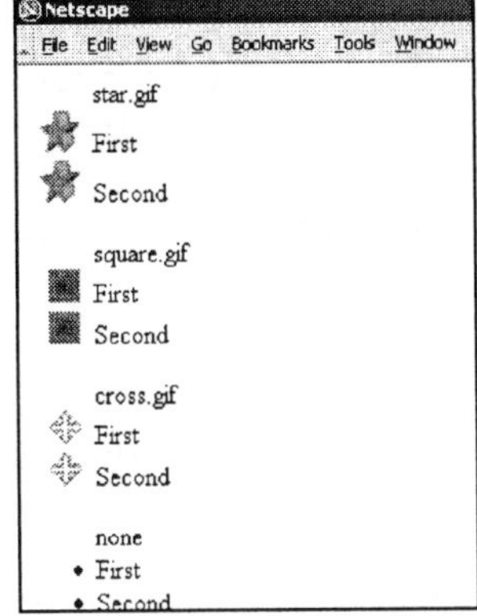

20.8 The 'list-style-position' property

The 'list-style-position' property allows you to define the position (inside or outside of the list item box) for the leading symbol/image that is rendered for each list item. The possible values are:

- inside
- outside (the default value)

Example 20_9. The list-style-position property (file e20_9.html)

```
<html><head><style>
body * {border : 1px solid red; margin : 5px;}
</style></head><body>
<ol style="list-style-type : decimal; list-style-position : inside;">
Inside<li>First<li>Second</ol>
<ul style="list-style-type : square; list-style-position : outside;">
Outside<li>First<li>Second</ul>
<ul style="list-style-image : url(star.gif); list-style-position :
inside;">Inside<li>First<li>Second</ul>
</body></html>
```

Figure 20.9

20.9 The 'list-style' property

The 'list-style' property is a shorthand for the three previously presented properties. The possible values are:

- <list-style-type> <list-style-position> <list-style-image>

Example 20_10. The list-style property (file e20_10.html)

```
<html><head></head><body>
<ol style="list-style : decimal inside;">
Decimal Inside<li>First<li>Second</ol>
<ul style="list-style : circle outside
url(cross.gif);">
Circle Outside Cross.gif<li>First<li>Second</ul>
<ul style="list-style : url(xx.gif) square;">
xx.gif square<li>First<li>Second</ul>
</body></html>
```

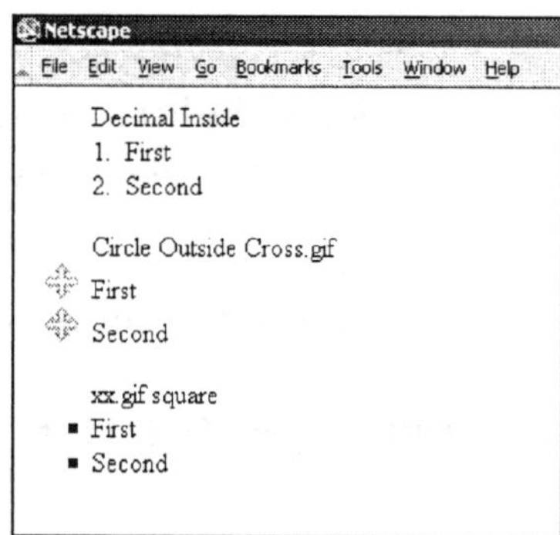

Figure 20.10

Notes

- If the image file exists, the image will be rendered.
- If the image file is missing, the leading symbol will be rendered.

20.10 Review of Chapter 20

- CSS allows you to automatically generate content that is not included in the regular <body> element.
- To add generated content, use the :before and :after pseudo-elements in conjunction with the 'content' property.

- The possible values for the 'content' property are *space delimited lists* of: <string>, <URL>, <counter>, attr(A)
- To define a set of quotation marks, use a selector and the 'quotes' property, then set the value of the 'content' property to open-quote | close-quote | no-open-quote | no-close-quote
- You can make custom-made lists if you set the value of the 'display' property of an element to list-item
- The 'list-style-type' property allows you to define the leading symbol that is rendered for each list item.
- The 'list-style-image' property allows you to define a leading image that is rendered for each list item.
- The 'list-style-position' property allows you to define the position (inside or outside of the list item box) for the leading symbol/image that is rendered for each list item.
- The 'list-style' property is a shorthand used to set the properties for a list element.

Chapter 21

XML

21.1 What is XML?

XML stands for e**X**tensible **M**arkup **L**anguage. XML was design to add new facilities to existing web technologies. XML is a *hierarchical data structure* stored in text format files, using a markup language. Let's explain in short what this means:

- XML is a markup language, similar to SGML (Standard Generalized Markup Language) and HTML.
- XML uses a text file format, which makes XML a cross-platform technology, independent of software and hardware.
- XML was designed to describe and to carry data *similar to a database.*
- XML is a hierarchical structure based on the parent-child relationship.

21.2 Similarities between HTML, CSS and XML

There are several similarities between HTML, CSS, and XML:

- All were designed to create web technologies.
- All use text files and therefore are cross-platform, software and hardware independent.

21.3 Differences between HTML, CSS and XML

There are many differences between HTML, CSS and XML:

- HTML and XML are markup languages; CSS is not a markup language.
- HTML was design to carry *data* (what you want to display) and *layout* (how you want to display it) information.
- CSS was exclusively designed to improve the *layout* (presentation) information.
- XML was designed to carry *data structure* and *data*, but not layout (presentation) information.
- Browsers try to render every part of an HTML file, regardless of errors or incorrect coding, but they ignore or generate errors for miscoded CSS or XML files.
- HTML and CSS are *not* case sensitive, but XML *is* case sensitive.
- In HTML, the elements are *predefined*; in XML, the elements are *defined by the developer*.

21.4 Using HTML, CSS and XML together

To display a web page you need:

- *Data* (to specify what information will be displayed)
- *Layout or presentation* (to specify how the information will be displayed)

A few solutions can be derived from here:

1. HTML contains both data and layout information and is a complete solution for web pages (see Chapters 1-13 for examples).
2. HTML can be used in conjunction with CSS if you want to refine the presentation of data contained in the HTML files (see Chapters 14-20 for examples).
3. XML (containing data) can be used in conjunction with CSS (containing layout information) to create a complete web solution (as illustrated in this chapter).
4. XML (containing data) can be used in conjunction with other XML file (containing layout information) to create a complete web and XML solution (see Chapter 23 XSL, XSLT and XPath for examples).

21.5 The first XML example

Here is an example of an XML file and how Netscape 7.1 renders it.

Example 21_1. The first XML example (file e21_1.xml)

```
<invoice id="123">
<date>June 13, 2003</date>
<company type="from">Company A</company>
<!--this is a comment-->
<company type="to">Company B</company>
<price currency="A'b'C">1234.56
      <gst currency='A"b"C' val="60.05"/>
</price>
<payed/>
</invoice>
```

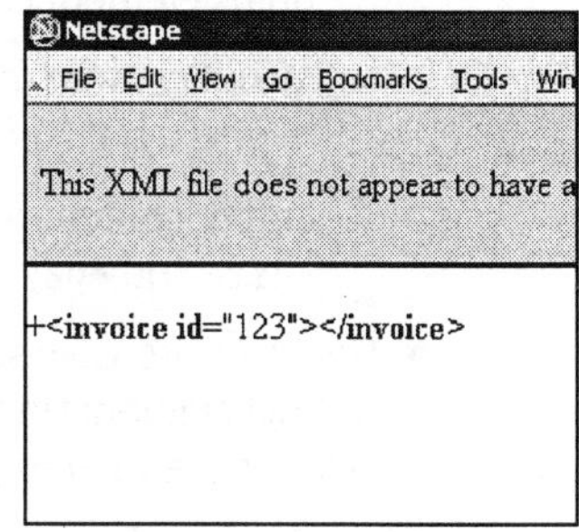

Figure 21.1

```
Netscape
File Edit View Go Bookmarks Tools Window Help
This XML file does not appear to have any style information associated with it. The document tree is shown below.
-<invoice id="123">
   <date>June 13, 2003</date>
   <company type="from">Company A</company>
   <!--this is a comment-->
   <company type="to">Company B</company>
 - <price currency="A'b'C">
     1234.56
     <gst currency="A"b"C" val="60.05"/>
   </price>
   <payed/>
</invoice>
```

Figure 21.2

```
Netscape
File Edit View Go Bookmarks Tools Window Help
This XML file does not appear to have any style inform
-<invoice id="123">
   <date>June 13, 2003</date>
   <company type="from">Company A</company>
   <!--this is a comment-->
   <company type="to">Company B</company>
 + <price currency="A'b'C"></price>
   <payed/>
</invoice>
```

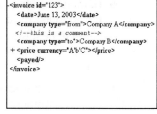

Figure 21.3

Notes

- The file extension should be `.xml` so the browser can understand the file contains XML data (e.g. `e21_1.xml`).
- The browser informs the user that the XML file doesn't have any style information (layout) associated with it and then renders the document tree.
- The document tree can be expanded or condensed using the + and – buttons rendered to the left of the **expandable** elements (elements that have children).
- There is a single element that contains all the other elements. This is the **root element**. In our example, the root element is `<invoice>`

- All elements have one of these types of content:
  - **Simple content** (pure text). In this case they are **leaves** (they don't have any children) of the document tree. In our example, the `<date>`, and `<company>` elements have simple content.
  - **Element content** (contains other elements). In our example, the `<invoice>` element holds element content.
  - **Mixed content** (contains pure text and other elements). In our example, the `<price>` element holds mixed content.
  - **Empty content** (contains nothing). These are empty elements. In our example, the `<gst>` and `<payed>` elements are empty.
- Elements are case-sensitive, so `<invoice>`, `<Invoice>` and `<INVOICE>` represent totally distinct elements in XML. The ending tag must be coded with the same sequence of character as the opening tag.
- All elements have an ending tag. The only exception is empty elements, where the single tag must contain a final / (e.g. `<payed/>`).
- All elements must be properly nested. For example:
  `<a>text<b>text</a>text</b>` is not properly nested, but
  `<a>text<b>text</b>text</a>` is.
- Elements can have one attribute or many attributes separated by spaces. The values of the attributes must be single-quoted or double-quoted. It is preferable to use double quotation if the attribute value contains a single-quoted fragment (e.g. `currency="A'b'C"`). Use single quotation if the attribute value contains a double-quoted fragment (e.g. `currency='A"b"C'`).
- Element names should start with a **letter** and continue with **letters**, **numbers**, and/or **underscore** symbols "_" (e.g. `<invoice>`, `<item_cod>`, `<phone_number_1>`, etc.). Do not use as element names `<xml>`, `<Xml>`, `<XML>`, ... because they are reserved for XML purposes.
- Comments can be inserted using the HTML syntax. For example:
  `<!--this is a comment-->`

21.6 Well-formedness

An XML document that conforms to the rules explained in the previous section is called a *well-formed* XML document. If the document is not well-formed, the browser parser identifies the first possible mistake and renders an error message in the browser window.

Example 21_2. Well-formedness (file e21_2.xml)

```
<invoice id="123">
<date>June 13, 2003</DATE>
<company type="from">Company A</company>
<!--this is a comment-->
<company type="to">Company B</company>
<price currency="A'b'C">1234.56
      <gst currency='A"b"C' val="60.05"/>
</price>
<payed/></invoice>
```

Figure 21.4

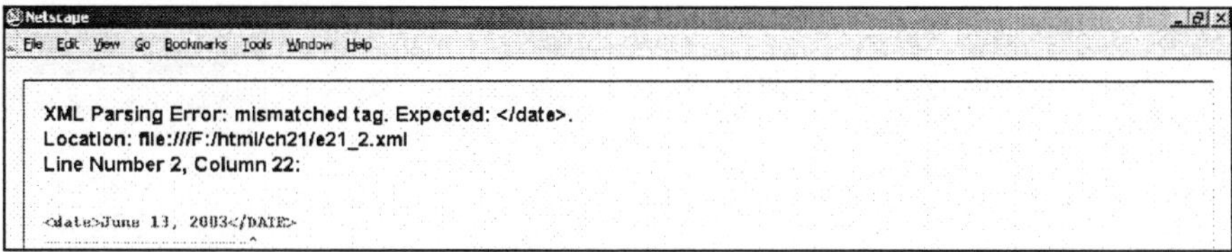

Netscape
File Edit View Go Bookmarks Tools Window Help
XML Parsing Error: mismatched tag. Expected: </date>.
Location: file:///F:/html/ch21/e21_2.xml
Line Number 2, Column 22:
<date>June 13, 2003</DATE>

Note the opening tag <date> doesn't match with the ending tag </DATE>.

21.7 XML data islands in Netscape

XML data islands are sections written in XML and inserted into non-XML files. An XML data island can be inserted directly into an HTML web page inside of the <body> element. Netscape renders the text of each element without any formatting style.

Example 21_3. XML data islands in Netscape (file e21_3.html)

```
<html><head></head>
<body>
Text before the Data Island.
<invoice id="123">
<date>June 13, 2003</date>
<company type="from">Company A</company>
<!--this is a comment-->
<company type="to">Company B</company>
<price currency="A'b'C">1234.56
            <gst currency='A"b"C' val="60.05"/>
</price>
<payed/>
</invoice>Text after the Data Island.
</body></html>
```

Figure 21.5

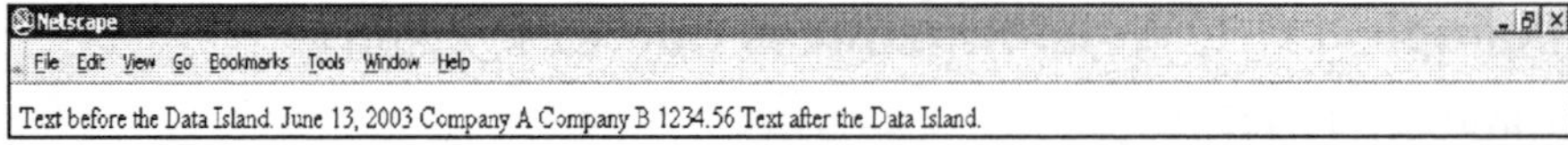

Note that only the text elements are rendered. The attributes' values are not rendered.

To add layout information and to extract all the information contained by the data island, use CSS, as in the following example.

Example 21_4. Formatting XML data islands with CSS (file e21_4.html)

```
<html><head><style>
invoice * {display : list-item;}
invoice:before {content : "Invoice: " attr(id);}
date:before {content : "Date:"}
date {font : italic 10pt Arial;}
company {font-weight : bold;}
company[type="from"]:before {content : "From: "}
company[type="to"]:before {content : "To: "}
price:before {content : "Price: "}
gst:before {content : "GST: " attr(val);}
payed:before {content : "Payed."}
</style></head>
<body>
Text before the Data Island.<br>
<invoice id="123">
      <date>June 13, 2003</date>
      <company type="from">Company A</company>
      <!--this is a comment-->
      <company type="to">Company B</company>
      <price currency="A'b'C">1234.56
            <gst currency='A"b"C' val="60.05"/>
      </price>
      <payed/>
</invoice>
<br>Text after the Data Island.
</body></html>
```

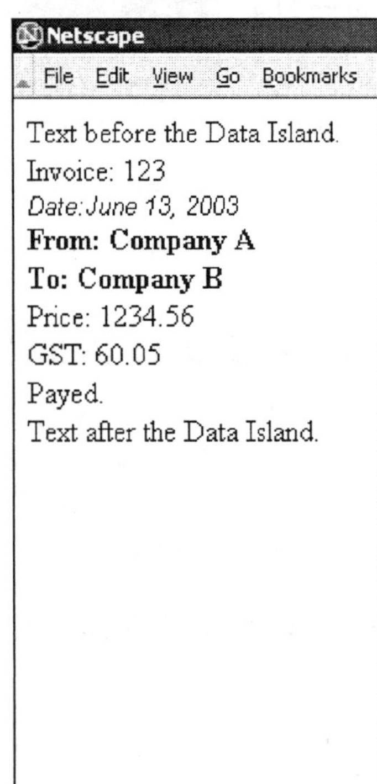

Figure 21.6

21.8 Data islands in Internet Explorer

Internet Explorer has facilities to render XML data islands. Data islands can be inserted directly into the HTML file, or they can be inserted into an external file.

Four steps are required to complete this task:

1. Insert an <xml>…</xml> block into the <body> element of the web page and set its id attribute to an identifier (e.g. id="invs").
2. Insert the XML data into the <xml>…</xml> block.
3. Use a <table> element to render the XML data. To bind the XML data to the table, use the datasrc attribute set to the identifier defined in step 1 (e.g. datasrc="#invs").
4. For each XML element you want to render, insert the following construction into a <tr> element:
   <td><span datafld="xml_element_name"></span></td>

Example 21_5. XML data islands in Internet Explorer. (file e21_5.html)

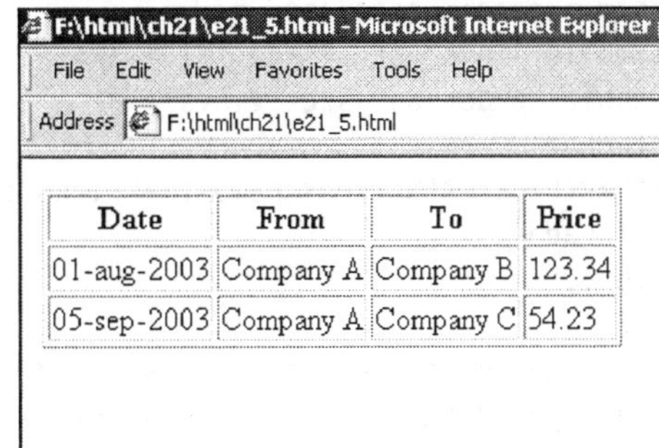

Figure 21.7

```
<html><head></head><body>
<xml id="invs">
<invoices>
      <invoice id="001">
            <date>01-aug-2003</date>
            <from>Company A</from>
            <to>Company B</to>
            <price>123.34</price>
      </invoice>
      <invoice id="002">
            <date>05-sep-2003</date>
            <from>Company A</from>
            <to>Company C</to>
            <price>54.23</price>
      </invoice>
</invoices>
</xml>
<table border datasrc="#invs">
<thead><tr><th>Date<th>From<th>To<th>Price</tr></thead>
<tbody>
      <tr><td><span datafld="date"></span></td>
      <td><span datafld="from"></span></td>
      <td><span datafld="to"></span></td>
      <td><span datafld="price"></span></td></tr>
</tbody>
</table>
</body></html>
```

Notes

- In this example, the XML data island represents a sequence of invoices having the `<invoices>` element as the root element.
- For each `<invoice>` element, a corresponding row is added to the table.
- Each `<span>...</span>` element included in the `<td>...</td>` is an empty element that is connected to a sub-element of the `<invoice>` element.
- You can add as many XML data islands as you need into a web page, each identified by a unique identifier that can correspond to an HTML table.

If the XML data is inserted into an external file, a few changes are required. However, the technique of binding XML data to an HTML table remains the same.

Example 21_6. XML data in external files (files e21_6.html, data.xml)

```
<html><head></head><body>
<xml id="invs" src="data.xml"></xml>
<table border datasrc="#invs">
<thead>
<tr><th>Date<th>From<th>To<th>Price</tr>
</thead>
<tbody>
<tr>
<td><span datafld="date"></span></td>
<td><span datafld="from"></span></td>
<td><span datafld="to"></span></td>
<td><span datafld="price"></span></td>
</tr>
</tbody>
</table>
</body></html>
```

```
<invoices>
<invoice id="001">
      <date>01-aug-2003</date>
      <from>Company A</from>
      <to>Company B</to>
      <price>123.34</price>
</invoice>
<invoice id="002">
      <date>05-sep-2003</date>
      <from>Company A</from>
      <to>Company C</to>
      <price>54.23</price>
</invoice>
</invoices>
```

Figure 21.8

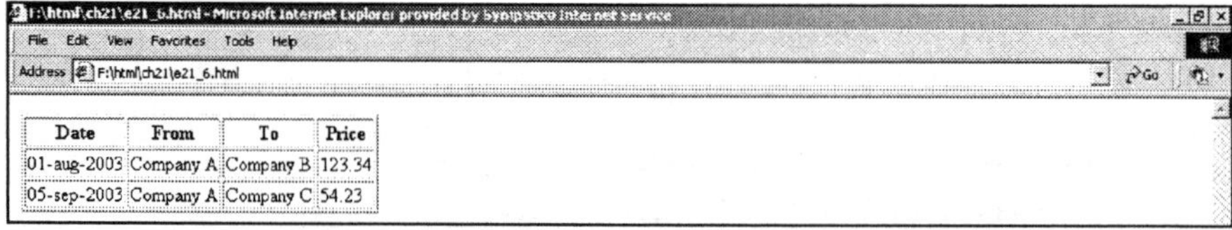

Date	From	To	Price
01-aug-2003	Company A	Company B	123.34
05-sep-2003	Company A	Company C	54.23

Notes

- Internet Explorer renders this example identically to Example 21_5.
- The single difference is that the `<xml>...</xml>` block is empty, and the `<xml>` element contains the new attribute `src` pointing to the `.xml` file name containing the data (e.g. `src="data.xml"`).

21.9 XML and CSS

Although both Netscape and Internet Explorer accept XML data islands, these solutions are not cross-platform. They are distinct and dedicated solutions for these two browsers.

A cross-platform solution can be obtained by attaching a CSS file to the XML file. In this way, the data contained in the XML file will be rendered using the layout described by the CSS file.

Example 21_7. XML and CSS (files e21_7.xml, layout.css)

```
/* layout.css */
invoice {display : block; border : 1px solid red; margin : 5px;}
invoice * {display : block;}
invoice:before {content : "Invoice: " attr(id);}
date:before {content : "Date:"}
date {font : italic 10pt Arial;}
company {font-weight : bold;}
company[type="from"]:before {content : "From: "}
company[type="to"]:before {content : "To: "}
total:before {content : "Total: " attr(currency) " "}
gst:before {content : "GST: " attr(currency) " " attr(val);}
payed:before {content : "Payed."}

<?xml-stylesheet type="text/css" href="layout.css"?>
<invoices>
<invoice id="123">
            <date>June 13, 2003</date>
            <company type="from">Company A</company>
            <!--this is a comment-->
            <company type="to">Company B</company>
            <total currency="USD">100.00
                  <gst currency='USD' val="7.00"/>
            </total>
            <payed/>
</invoice>
<invoice id="456">
            <date>August 14, 2004</date>
            <company type="from">Company A</company>
            <!--this is file e21_7.xml-->
            <company type="to">Company C</company>
            <total currency="CAD">1234.56
                  <gst currency='CAD' val="60.05"/>
            </total>
</invoice>
</invoices>
```

Figure 21.9

Netscape
File Edit View Go Bookmarks Tools Window Help
Invoice: 123
Date: June 13, 2003
From: Company A
To: Company B
Total: USD 100.00
GST: USD 7.00
Payed.
Invoice: 456
Date: August 14, 2004
From: Company A
To: Company C
Total: CAD 1234.56
GST: CAD 60.05

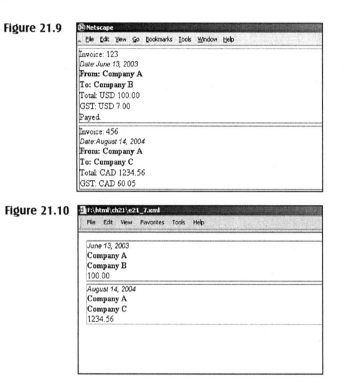

Figure 21.10

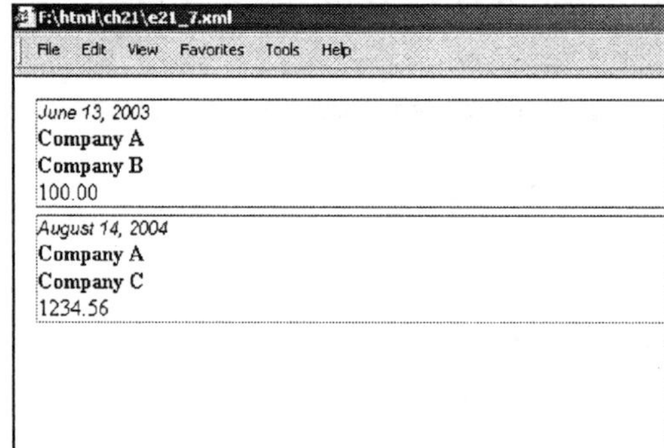

Notes

- The first line in the XML file:
  `<?xml-stylesheet type="text/css" href="layout.css"?>`

is a **processing directive** that informs the browser that this XML file has associated presentation information that will be used to render the data. Two attributes are used to specify the type of the style sheet (`type="text/css"`) and the file where the presentation information is stored (`href="layout.css"`).

- As you can see, Internet Explorer cannot automatically generate content and cannot access the information stored in attributes, so use attributes with care.

21.10 XML declaration

It is recommended that an XML document have an XML declaration in the very first line using the syntax:

```
<?xml version="1.0" encoding="ISO-8859-2" standalone="yes" ?>
```

where:

- `version` attribute is *required* and specifies the XML version used in the document.

- `encoding` attribute is *optional* and specifies the character set used in the document. The possible values are the character set identifiers (e.g. "UTF-8" – the default value, "UTF-16", "ISO-8859-2", etc.).
- `standalone` attribute is *optional* and specifies whether the XML document can be completely validated using DTD rules contained in the document (see Chapter 22 DTD). The possible values are "yes" and "no".

Example 21_8. XML declaration (file e21_8.xml)

```
<?xml version="1.0" encoding="ISO-8859-2"
standalone="yes" ?>
<facture>
<produit>souris</produit>
<produit>moniteur</produit>
<produit>base de donées</produit>
<produit>lecteur de disques</produit>
<produit>jeu électronique</produit>
</facture>
```

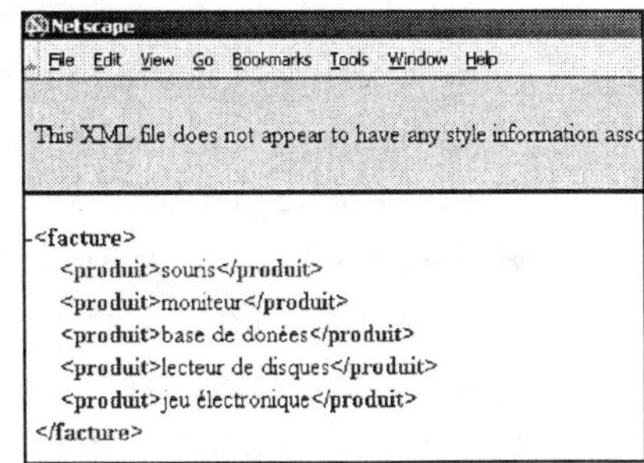

Figure 21.11

21.11 Review of Chapter 21

- HTML was designed to carry data and layout information.
- CSS was designed exclusively for layout information.
- XML was designed to carry data.
- In HTML the element names are predefined, but in XML the designer defines the element names.
- XML can be defined as a *hierarchical data structure* stored in text format files, using a markup language.
- XML is a cross-platform technology, independent of software and hardware.
- An XML document is *well-formed* if:
  - There is a single element that contains all the other elements. This is the *root element.*
  - All the elements have either *simple content* (pure text), *element content* (containing other elements), *mixed content* (containing pure text and other elements), or *empty content* (containing nothing).
  - Element names are case-sensitive.
  - All elements have an ending tag.
  - All elements are properly nested.

  - Elements have one attribute or many attributes separated by spaces. The values of the attributes are single-quoted or double-quoted.
  - Comments are inserted using HTML syntax.
- XML *data islands* are sections written in XML and inserted into non-XML files.
- Netscape renders the text of each element of a data island without any formatting style.
- Internet Explorer has facilities to render XML data islands in a tabular format. To do this, use an `<xml>...</xml>` element and a `<table>...<table>` element. The `<xml>` element has the `id` attribute set to a value that is referenced by the `datasrc` attribute of the `<table>` element. Each `<td>` element has a `<span>` element with the `datafld` attribute set to an element name from the `<xml>` block.
- The XML data can be rendered using the layout information contained by a CSS file. To do this, use a processing directive like: `<?xml-stylesheet type="text/css" href="layout.css"?>`
- It is recommended that an XML document have an XML declaration in the first line using the syntax: `<?xml version="1.0" encoding="ISO-8859-2" standalone="yes" ?>`

Chapter 22

DTD

22.1 What is DTD?

DTD stands for Document Type Definition. DTD represents a section in an XML document and/or in an external file where the rules the XML document must comply with are presented. These rules contain markup declarations for elements, attributes, entities, and notations.

An XML document is *valid* if:

- the XML document has an associated DTD
- the XML document complies with the constraints expressed in the DTD associated to it

The DTD associated to an XML file can be:

- *internal* when the rules are inserted directly into the same XML document
- *external* when the rules are contained in an external file
- *internal and external* when some rules are inserted directly into the XML file and other rules are contained in an external file

Generally, external files containing the DTD rules for an XML document have the extension "`.dtd`".

22.2 A DTD example

The following code expresses a very simple example for the DTD section that can be attached to an XML file:

```
<!ELEMENT invoice (item)+>
<!ATTLIST invoice id ID #REQUIRED>
<!ELEMENT item (#PCDATA)>
```

Notes

- The first line represents an **element declaration**. This declares the **root element** called `invoice`. This element must contain **at least one** `item` element.
- The second line represents an **attribute declaration**. This declares a **required** attribute for the invoice element, called `id`, having the **ID type**.
- The third line represents an **element declaration**. This declares that the `item` element contains only **parsed data** (data than can be interpreted by the parser application as markup symbols).

22.3 Internal DTD section

The DTD section contains the rules an XML document must comply with to be a valid document. This section can be inserted directly into the XML document. To do this, use a *doctype declaration*, as presented in the following example:

```
<!DOCTYPE invoice [
<!ELEMENT invoice (item)+>
<!ATTLIST invoice id ID #REQUIRED>
<!ELEMENT item (#PCDATA)>
]>
```

Notes

- The DTD section is included between square brackets "[" and "]".
- The first line declares `invoice` as the root element for the XML document.

Example 22_1. Internal DTD (file e22_1.xml)

```
<!DOCTYPE invoice [
<!ELEMENT invoice (item)+>
<!ATTLIST invoice id ID #REQUIRED>
<!ELEMENT item (#PCDATA)>
]>
<invoice id="i001">
```

```
<item>screwdriver</item>
<item>hammer</item>
<item>pliers</item>
</invoice>
```

Now, let's create now a well-formed but invalid XML document. To do this, insert a `<total>` element that is not declared in the DTD section.

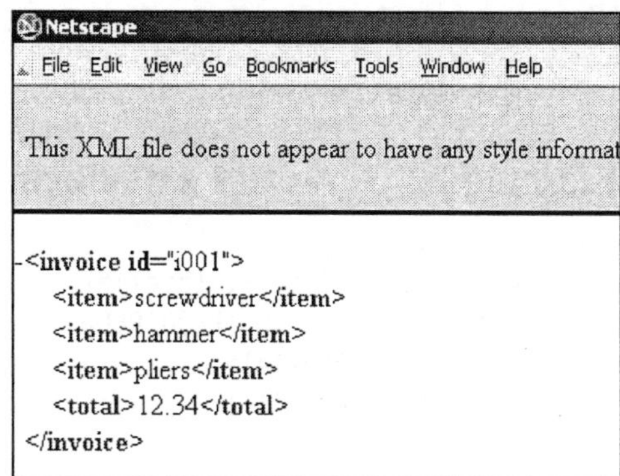

Figure 22.1

Example 22_2. An invalid XML document (file e22_2.xml)

```
<!DOCTYPE invoice [
<!ELEMENT invoice (item)+>
<!ATTLIST invoice id ID #REQUIRED>
<!ELEMENT item (#PCDATA)>
]>
<invoice id="i001">
<item>screwdriver</item>
<item>hammer</item>
<item>pliers</item>
<total>12.34</total>
</invoice>
```

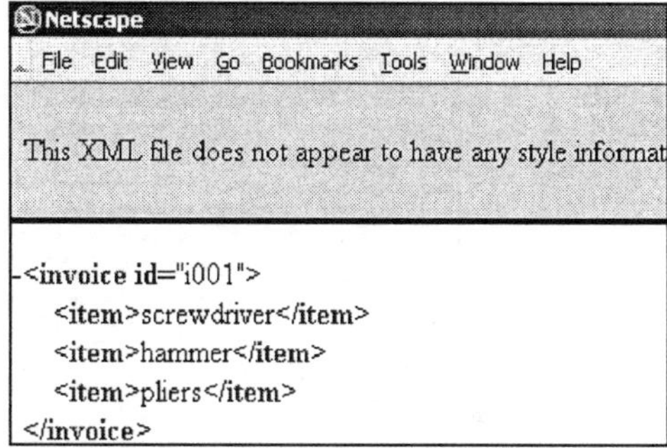

Figure 22.2

As you can see in Figure 22.2, Netscape checks only for *well-formedness* but not for *validity* of the XML file. Internet Explorer does the same. If you open the XML file with the XMLSPY application, you'll get the message: "This file is not valid. Mandatory element `'item'` expected in place of `'total'`."

Figure 22.3

To make the document valid, we can change the DTD section to include rules for the 'total' element.

Example 22_3. A valid XML document (file e22_3.xml)

```
<!DOCTYPE invoice [
<!ELEMENT invoice (item+, total)>
<!ATTLIST invoice id ID #REQUIRED>
<!ELEMENT item (#PCDATA)>
<!ELEMENT total (#PCDATA)>
]>
<invoice id="i001">
<item>screwdriver</item>
<item>hammer</item>
<item>pliers</item>
<total>12.34</total>
</invoice>
```

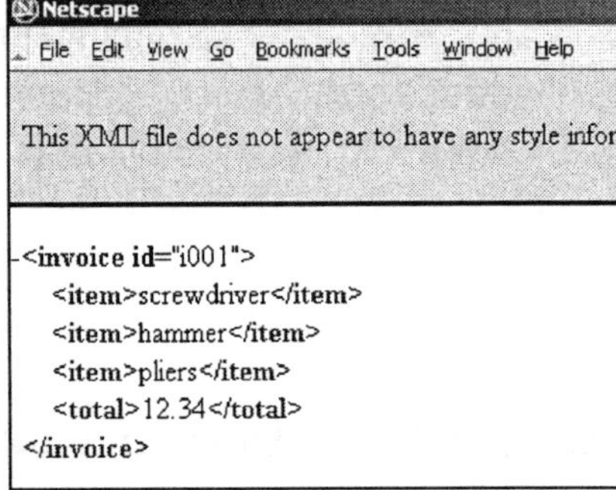

Figure 22.4

Figure 22.5

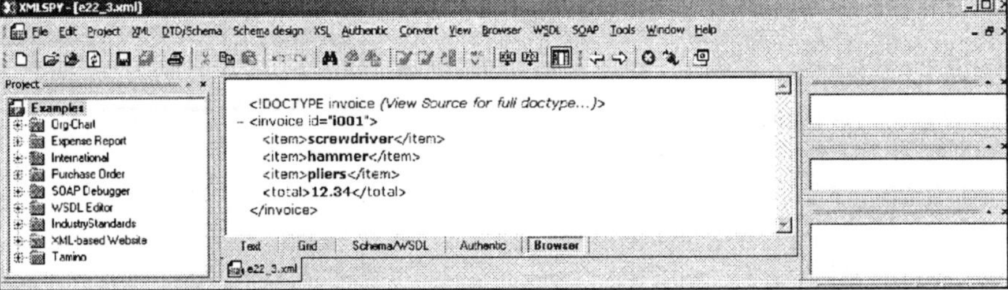

When asked to render the document in the browser, XMLSPY checks for *well-formedness* and for *validity*. As you can see, Example 22_3 passes both these tests.

22.4 External DTD section

The DTD section can be placed in an external file. In this way, many XML documents can be tested to comply with the restrictions expressed by DTD declarations.

To attach the DTD file to an XML document, insert a DOCTYPE declaration with one of the following syntaxes into the XML document:

```
<DOCTYPE root_element_name SYSTEM "DTD_file_URL">
```

or

```
<DOCTYPE root_element_name PUBLIC "public_ID" "DTD_file_URL">
```

Notes

- In the first case, the XML document is validated using the specified DTD file.
- In the second case, a direct access to the DTD file is not required, but the application that validates the XML document must recognize the "`public_ID`". This public identifier is unique for standard DTD files on the web.

Example 22_4. External DTD section (files e22_4.xml, e22_4.dtd)

```
<!--e22_4.xml-->
<!DOCTYPE invoice SYSTEM "e22_4.dtd">
<invoice id="i001">
<item>screwdriver</item>
<item>hammer</item>
<item>pliers</item>
<total>12.34</total>
</invoice>
```

```
<!ELEMENT invoice (item+, total)>
<!ATTLIST invoice id ID #REQUIRED>
<!ELEMENT item (#PCDATA)>
<!ELEMENT total (#PCDATA)>
```

Figure 22.6

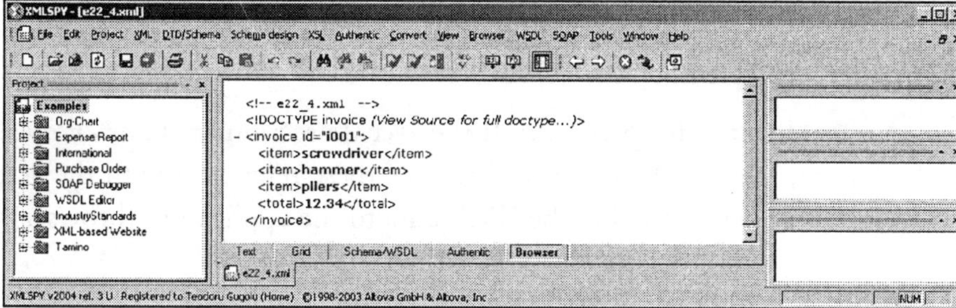

22.5 Internal and external DTD sections

The DTD sections required to validate an XML document can be inserted partially into the document and partially into an external DTD file, as presented in the following example. To do this, use the syntax:

```
<!DOCTYPE invoice SYSTEM "external_DTD_file_URL" [
insert the internal DTD section here
]>
```

Example 22_5. Internal and external DTD sections (files e22_5.xml, e22_5.dtd)

```
<!--e22_5.xml-->
<!DOCTYPE invoice SYSTEM "e22_5.dtd" [
<!ELEMENT invoice (item+, total)>
<!ATTLIST invoice id ID #REQUIRED>
]>
```

```
<invoice id="i001">
<item>screwdriver</item>
<item>hammer</item>
<item>pliers</item>
<total>12.34</total>
</invoice>
```

```
<!--e22_5.dtd-->
<!ELEMENT item (#PCDATA)>
<!ELEMENT total (#PCDATA)>
```

Figure 22.7

22.6 Declaring elements with #PCDATA content

To declare an element, use the syntax:

```
<!ELEMENT element_name (element_content)>
```

To declare an element with #PCDATA content, use the syntax:

```
<!ELEMENT element_name (#PCDATA)>
```

#PCDATA stands for *plain text*. If the #PCDATA section contains *entity references* (e.g. "<", ">"), the parser will replace these references with the actual data (e.g. "<", ">") before passing the XML data to the application (browser).

Example 22_6. #PCDATA (file e22_6.xml)

```
<!--e22_6.xml-->
<!DOCTYPE invoice [
<!ELEMENT invoice (#PCDATA)>
]>
<invoice>
This is #PCDATA.
&lt;h3&gt;Heading 3&lt;/h3&gt;
This is plain text.
</invoice>
```

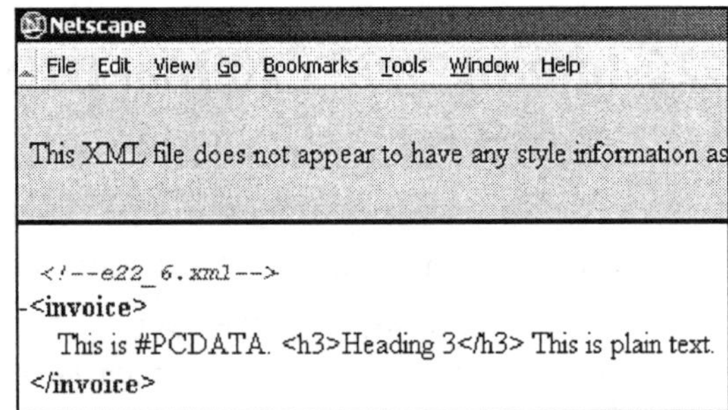

Figure 22.8

Note

- If an element is declared as having #PCDATA, you cannot use **markup symbols** inside of the element, so the next example is invalid as shown by XMLSPY.

Example 22_7. `#PCDATA` and markup symbols (file e22_7.xml)

```
<!--e22_7.xml-->
<!DOCTYPE invoice [
<!ELEMENT invoice (#PCDATA)>
]>
<invoice>
This is #PCDATA.
<h3>Heading 3</h3>
This is plain text.
</invoice>
```

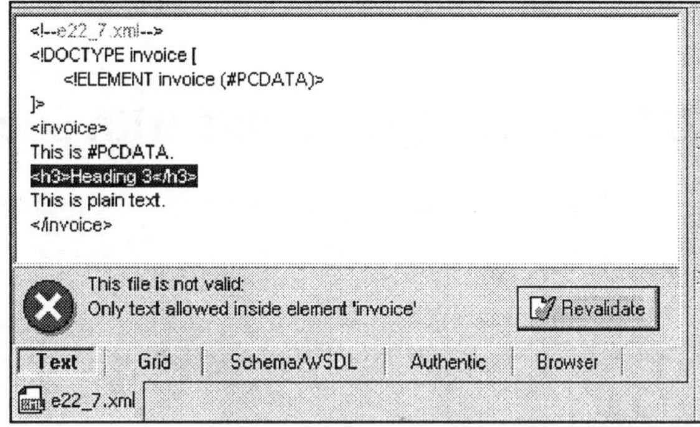

Figure 22.9

22.7 Declaring elements with child content

To declare an element as being the child of another element, use the syntax:

```
<!ELEMENT element_name (child_element_name)>
```

Example 22_8. Child elements (file e22_8.xml)

```
<!--e22_8.xml-->
<!DOCTYPE invoices [
<!ELEMENT invoices (invoice)>
<!ELEMENT invoice (item)>
<!ELEMENT item (description)>
<!ELEMENT description (#PCDATA)>
]>
<invoices>
      <invoice>
            <item>
                  <description>
                  Pliers
                  </description>
            </item>
      </invoice>
</invoices>
```

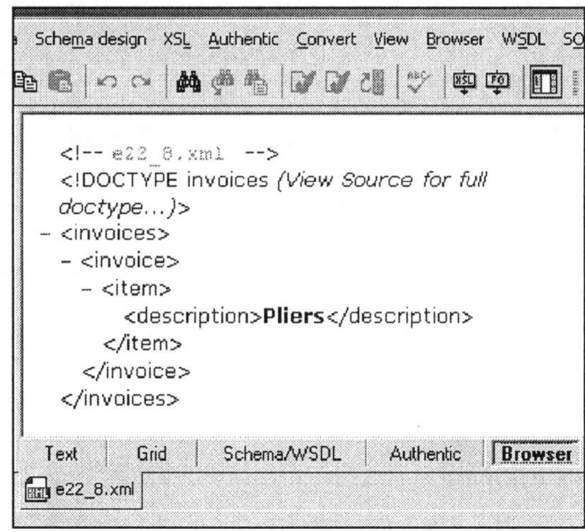

Figure 22.10

Let's explain this example. The root element in this example is `invoices`. This element must contain a single child element called `invoice`. The `invoice` element must contain a single child element called `item`. The `item` element can contain a single child element called `description`. Finally, the `description` element has a `#PCDATA` content.

22.8 Declaring elements with sequence content

If the content of an element is a sequence of child elements, use the syntax:

```
<!ELEMENT element_name (child_1, child_2, ...)>
```

Example 22_9. Sequence content (file e22_9.xml)

```
<!--e22_9.xml-->
<!DOCTYPE invoices [
<!ELEMENT invoices (invoice)>
<!ELEMENT invoice (invoice_id, date, items)>
<!ELEMENT items (item)>
<!ELEMENT item (item_id, quantity, price)>
<!ELEMENT invoice_id (#PCDATA)>
<!ELEMENT date (#PCDATA)>
<!ELEMENT total (#PCDATA)>
<!ELEMENT item_id (#PCDATA)>
<!ELEMENT quantity (#PCDATA)>
<!ELEMENT price (#PCDATA)>
]>
<invoices>
      <invoice>
            <invoice_id>001</invoice_id>
            <date>April 9, 2004</date>
            <items>
                  <item>
                        <item_id>12345</item_id>
                        <quantity>10</quantity>
                        <price>12.76</price>
                  </item>
            </items>
      </invoice>
</invoices>
```

Figure 22.11

Let's explain this example. The root element in this example is `invoices`. This element must contain a single child element called `invoice`. The `invoice` element must contain three children in this order: `invoice_id`, `date` and `items`. The `items` element must contain a single child called `item`. The `item` element must contain three children in this order: `item_id`, `quantity` and `price`. All the other elements have `#PCDATA` content.

22.9 Declaring elements with choice list content

If the content of an element is only one element from a list of possible elements, use the syntax:

```
<!ELEMENT element_name (child_1 | child_2 | ...)>
```

The elements that belongs to the list of possible choices are separated by "|" symbols.

Example 22_10. Choice list content (file e22_10.xml)

```
<!--e22_10.xml-->
<!DOCTYPE items [
	<!ELEMENT items (item+)>
	<!ELEMENT item (item_id | description | short_description)>
	<!ELEMENT description (english | french)>
	<!ELEMENT item_id (#PCDATA)>
	<!ELEMENT english (#PCDATA)>
	<!ELEMENT french (#PCDATA)>
	<!ELEMENT short_description (#PCDATA)>
]>
<items>
	<item>
		<item_id>12345</item_id>
	</item>
	<item>
		<description>
			<english>Exercise book</english>
		</description>
	</item>
	<item>
		<description>
			<french>Cahier des exercices</french>
		</description>
	</item>
	<item>
		<short_description>Booklet</short_description>
	</item>
</items>
```

Let's explain this example. The root element is `items`. The `items` element contains at least one `item` element. Each `item` element contains either an `item_id` element, a `description` element or a `short_description` element. The `description` element contains either an `english` element or a `french` element. All other elements have `#PCDATA` content.

Figure 22.12

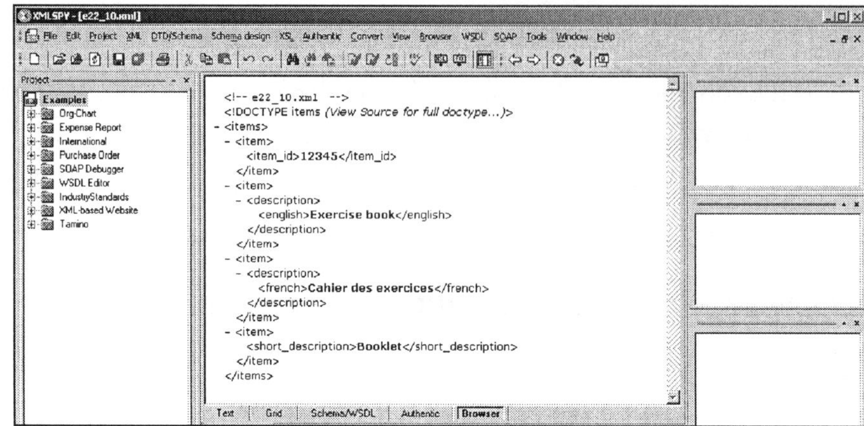

22.10 Declaring elements with repetition suffixes

To specify how many times a child element can appear in a row, use the *repetition suffixes* presented below:

- "?" zero or one time
- "*" zero or more times
- "+" one or more times

Example 22_11. Repetition suffixes (file e22_11.xml)

```
<!--e22_11.xml-->
<!DOCTYPE invoice [
      <!ELEMENT invoice (invoice_id, date?, contact_person*, items)>
      <!ELEMENT items (item+)>
      <!ELEMENT item (item_id, description?, quantity, price)>
      <!ELEMENT invoice_id (#PCDATA)>
      <!ELEMENT date (#PCDATA)>
      <!ELEMENT contact_person (#PCDATA)>
      <!ELEMENT item_id (#PCDATA)>
      <!ELEMENT description (#PCDATA)>
      <!ELEMENT quantity (#PCDATA)>
      <!ELEMENT price (#PCDATA)>
]>
<invoice>
      <invoice_id>001</invoice_id>
      <contact_person>Julia Bart</contact_person>
      <contact_person>Jimm Roberts</contact_person>
      <items>
            <item>
```

```
                <item_id>12345</item_id>
                <quantity>10</quantity>
                <price>25.99</price>
            </item>
            <item>
                <item_id>54321</item_id>
                <description>Rubber Boat</description>
                <quantity>1</quantity>
                <price>234.45</price>
            </item>
    </items>
</invoice>
```

Figure 22.13

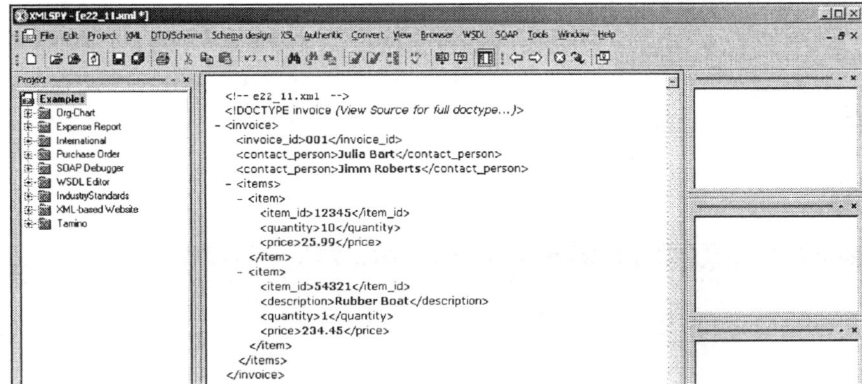

22.11 Declaring content with grouping rules

When declaring an element's content, you can create groups delimited by "(" and ")". You can use groups in *sequences*, include them in *choice lists* or attach *repetition suffixes* to them.

Example 22_12. Grouping (file e22_12.xml)

```
<!--e22_12.xml-->
<!DOCTYPE invoices [
<!ELEMENT invoices (invoice*)>
<!ELEMENT invoice (invoice_id, ((from, to) | (to, from))?, items, (total,
currency)*)>
<!ELEMENT items (item+)>
<!ELEMENT item (item_id, price)>
<!ELEMENT invoice_id (#PCDATA)>
<!ELEMENT from (#PCDATA)>
<!ELEMENT to (#PCDATA)>
<!ELEMENT total (#PCDATA)>
```

```
<!ELEMENT currency (#PCDATA)>
<!ELEMENT item_id (#PCDATA)>
<!ELEMENT price (#PCDATA)>
]>
<invoices>
<invoice>
<invoice_id>001</invoice_id>
<to>Company B</to>
<from>Company A</from>
<items><item><item_id>12345</item_id><price>12.99</price></item></items>
</invoice>
<invoice>
<invoice_id>001</invoice_id>
<items><item><item_id>12345</item_id><price>12.99</price></item></items>
<total>12.99</total>
<currency>CAD</currency>
<total>10.00</total>
<currency>USD</currency>
</invoice>
</invoices>
```

Figure 22.14

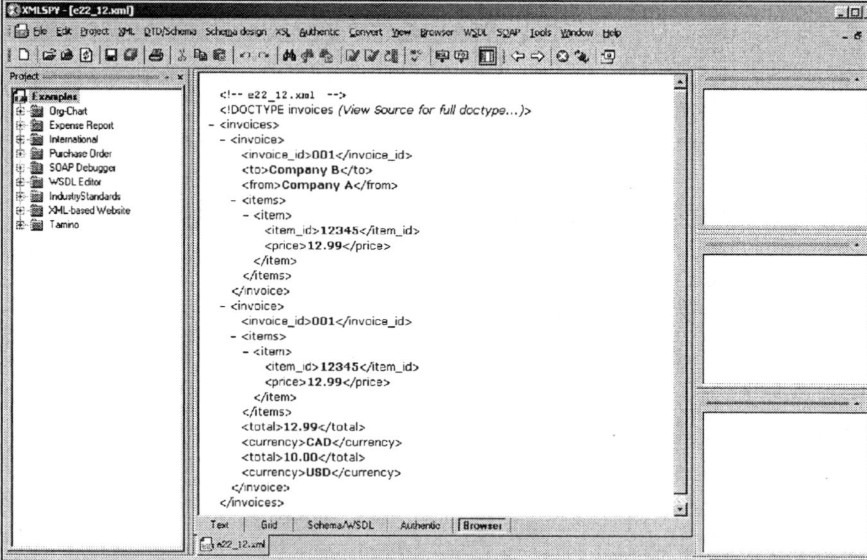

22.12 Declaring elements with mixed content

An element has *mixed content* if the element can contain both plaintext (`#PCDATA`) elements and other elements. To declare an element having mixed content, use the syntax:

```
<!ELEMENT element_name (#PCDATA | child | child...)*>
```

Example 22_13. Mixed content (file e22_13.xml)

```
<!--e22_13.xml-->
<!DOCTYPE invoice [
      <!ELEMENT invoice (#PCDATA | item)*>
      <!ELEMENT item (id, qty, price)>
      <!ELEMENT price (#PCDATA | value)*>
      <!ELEMENT id (#PCDATA)>
      <!ELEMENT qty (#PCDATA)>
      <!ELEMENT value (#PCDATA)>
]>
<invoice>
Invoice Id=001
Line 1.
<item>
            <id>12345</id>
            <qty>12</qty>
            <price>
      USD=<value>100.00</value>
      CAD=<value>130.00</value>
            </price>
      </item>
Line 2.
<item>
            <id>12345</id>
            <qty>12</qty>
            <price>$99.99</price>
      </item>
End of the Invoice Id=001
</invoice>
```

```
<!-- e22_13.xml -->
<!DOCTYPE invoice (View Source for full d
- <invoice>
    Invoice Id=001 Line 1.
  - <item>
      <id>12345</id>
      <qty>12</qty>
    - <price>
        USD=
        <value>100.00</value>
        CAD=
        <value>130.00</value>
      </price>
    </item>
    Line 2.
  - <item>
      <id>12345</id>
      <qty>12</qty>
      <price>$99.99</price>
    </item>
    End of the Invoice Id=001
  </invoice>
Text | Grid | Schema/WSDL | Authentic
e22_13.xml
```

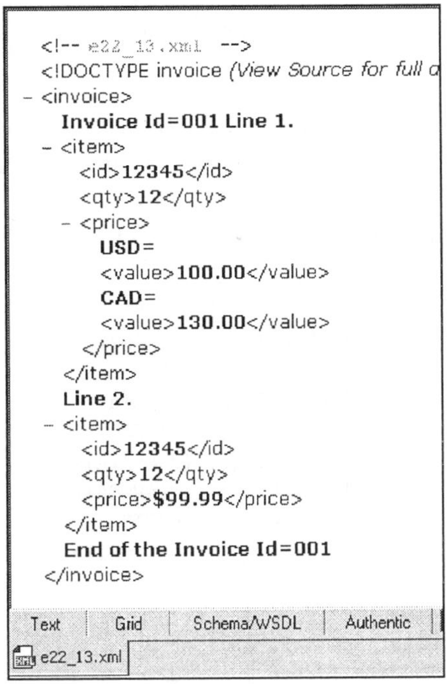

Figure 22.15

Notes

- The root element has mixed content (a combination of `#PCDATA` and `item` elements, in any order).
- The `price` element has mixed content (a combination of `#PCDATA` and `value` elements in any order).

- The `item` element is declared as a sequence of `id`, `qty`, and `price` elements.
- All other elements have `#PCDATA` content.

22.13 Declaring elements with empty or any content

To declare an element with empty content, use the syntax:

```
<!ELEMENT element_name EMPTY>
```

To declare an element with any possible content (any declared elements or any `#PCDATA`), use the syntax:

```
<!ELEMENT element_name ANY>
```

Be aware that elements declared with `ANY` content don't have a strict content model, so try to avoid using them.

Example 22_14. EMPTY and ANY contents (file e22_14.xml)

```
<!--e22_14.xml-->
<!DOCTYPE invoice [
      <!ELEMENT invoice ANY>
      <!ELEMENT item ANY>
      <!ELEMENT id (#PCDATA)>
      <!ELEMENT total (#PCDATA)>
      <!ELEMENT qty (#PCDATA)>
      <!ELEMENT price (#PCDATA)>
      <!ELEMENT paid EMPTY>
      <!ELEMENT shipped EMPTY>
]>
<invoice>
Date: April 9, 2004
Invoice Id:<id>001</id>
Total: <total>$105.34</total>
      <item>Line 1.
      <id>12345</id>
            <qty>5</qty>
            <price>12.34</price>
            <shipped/>
      </item>
      <item>Line 2.
      <id>12345</id>
            <qty>10</qty>
            <price>2.99</price>
      </item>
      <paid/>
      <shipped/>
</invoice>
```

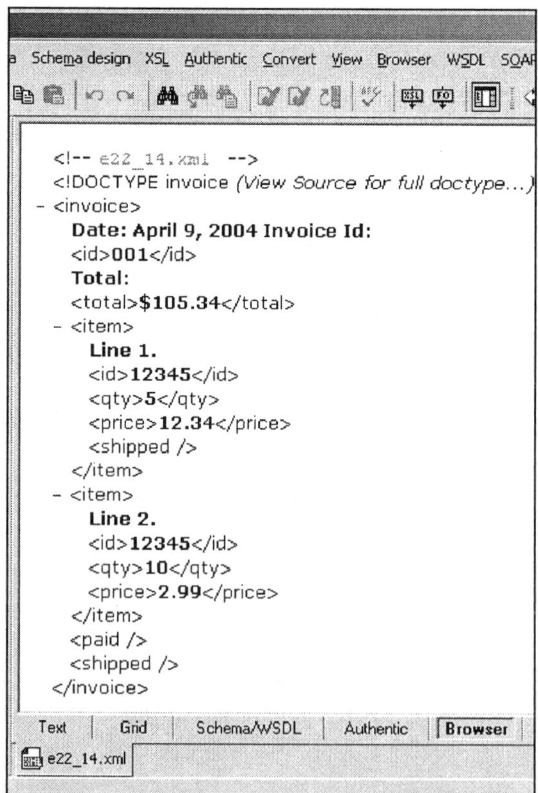

Figure 22.16

Notes

- The root element `invoice` and the `item` element are declared having `ANY` content. These elements can contain `#PCDATA` or any other elements declared in the DTD section.
- The `paid` and `shipped` elements are declared `EMPTY` elements.
- The `id` and `shipped` elements appear as children of the `invoice` and `item` elements.

22.14 XML Nmtokens and XML Names

An *XML Nmtoken* (name token) can be any combination of `letters`, `digits`, `'.'`, `'-'`, `'_'`, or `':'`. No space characters are allowed.

Examples of XML Nmtokens are:

- `12345`
- `.xyz`
- `-abc`
- `a1.b-c_d:1f`

An *XML Name* satisfies these restrictions:

- Starts with a letter, `'_'` or `':'`
- Continues with an XML Nmtoken
- No space characters are allowed

Examples of XML Names are:

- `a_1`
- `_p1`
- `:abc`
- `a1.b-c_d:1f`

22.15 Attribute declaration

To declare one or more attributes for an XML element, use the syntax:

```
<!ATTLIST element_name      attribute_name attribute_type attribute_default
                            attribute_name attribute_type attribute_default
                            ...
>
```

The *attribute_type* can be:

- CDATA - the attribute value is any string of characters
- ID - the attribute value is a unique XML Name
- IDREF - the attribute value is equal to the value of an attribute of ID type
- IDREFS - the attribute value is a space-delimited list of attribute values of ID types
- ENTITY - the attribute value is equal to the name of an ENTITY
- ENTITIES - the attribute value is a space delimited list of names of ENTITIES
- NMTOKEN - the attribute value is an XML Nmtoken
- NMTOKENS - the attribute value is a space-delimited list of Nmtokens
- (Nmtoken | Nmtoken |...) - the attributes value must be one of the Nmtokens presented in the enumeration

The *attribute_default* can be:

- #REQUIRED - the attribute value must be present for each instance of the element
- #IMPLIED - the attribute value can be present but is not required
- #FIXED attribute_value - the attribute value must have the value defined by *attribute_value*
- attribute_value - this represents the *default value* of the attribute

The *value of an attribute* is a string delimited by double (") or single (') quotes. Inside of this string the '<' and '&' characters are not allowed. The '&' character is allowed only if it is a part of a *reference* (e.g. '<').

22.16 Declaring CDATA attributes

If you declare an attribute with the CDATA type, the value of this attribute can be any string of characters. This type is used when no restriction can be applied to the attribute values.

Example 22_15. CDATA type attributes (file e22_15.xml)

```
<!--e22_15.xml-->
<!DOCTYPE invoice [
      <!ELEMENT invoice (item+)>
      <!ELEMENT item EMPTY>
      <!ATTLIST invoice
            id CDATA #REQUIRED
            date CDATA #IMPLIED
            from CDATA #FIXED "Company A"
            to CDATA "Company B"
      >
      <!ATTLIST item
            id CDATA #REQUIRED
            qty CDATA "1"
            desc CDATA #IMPLIED
            price CDATA #REQUIRED
            currency CDATA #FIXED "USD"
      >
]>
<invoice id="001" date="April 10, 2004" to="Company C">
<item id="12345" price="10.99"/>
<item id="54321" qty="2" desc="pliers 5 inch" price="9.12" currency="USD"/>
</invoice>
```

Figure 22.17

Notes

- The root element (`invoice`) contains empty `item` elements.
- The `invoice` element has four attributes (`id`, `date`, `from`, and `to`).
- The `item` element has five attributes (`id`, `qty`, `desc`, `price`, and `currency`).

22.17 Declaring ID, IDREF and IDREFS attributes

If you declare an attribute with the `ID` type, the values of this attribute must be *unique* among all values of the attributes declared as `ID` type.

If an attribute is declared with the `IDREF` type, then the value of this attribute must be equal to the value of another attribute of the same or another element declared with the `ID` type.

If an attribute is declared with the `IDREFS` type, the value of this attribute must be a *space-delimited list* of values of other attributes of the same or other elements declared with the `ID` type.

Note

◆ The attribute values of ID, IDREF and IDREFS types must be XML Name values.

Example 22_16. ID, IDREF and IDREFS (file e22_16.xml)

```
<!--e22_16.xml-->
<!DOCTYPE accounting [
<!ELEMENT accounting (inventory,
invoices, sales)>
<!ELEMENT inventory (inventory_item+)>
<!ELEMENT invoices (invoice+)>
<!ELEMENT invoice (item+)>
<!ELEMENT sales EMPTY>
<!ELEMENT inventory_item EMPTY>
<!ELEMENT item EMPTY>
<!ATTLIST inventory_item
            id ID #REQUIRED
            qty CDATA #IMPLIED
            price CDATA #IMPLIED
>
<!ATTLIST item
            id IDREF #REQUIRED
            qty CDATA "1"
            price CDATA #REQUIRED
>
<!ATTLIST sales ids IDREFS #REQUIRED >
]>
<accounting>
<inventory>
<inventory_item id="i123" />
<inventory_item id="i234" />
<inventory_item id="i345" />
</inventory>
<invoices>
<invoice>
<item id="i123" qty="2" price="1.23" />
</invoice>
<invoice>
<item id="i234" price="13.99" />
<item id="i345" qty="2" price="1.23" />
</invoice>
</invoices>
<sales ids="i123 i345" />
</accounting>
```

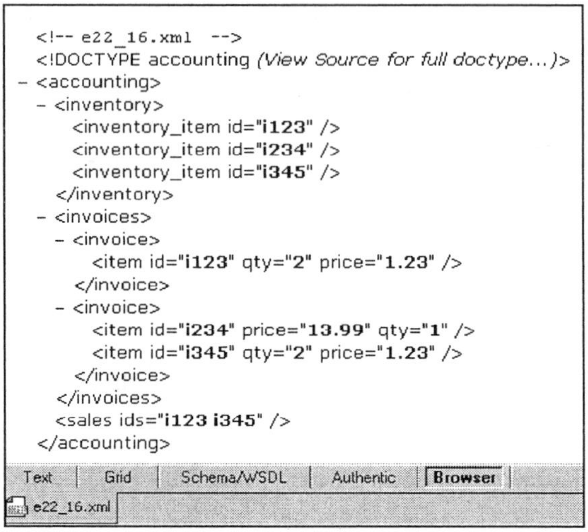

```
  <!-- e22_16.xml -->
  <!DOCTYPE accounting (View Source for full doctype...)>
- <accounting>
  - <inventory>
      <inventory_item id="i123" />
      <inventory_item id="i234" />
      <inventory_item id="i345" />
    </inventory>
  - <invoices>
    - <invoice>
        <item id="i123" qty="2" price="1.23" />
      </invoice>
    - <invoice>
        <item id="i234" price="13.99" qty="1" />
        <item id="i345" qty="2" price="1.23" />
      </invoice>
    </invoices>
    <sales ids="i123 i345" />
  </accounting>
Text | Grid | Schema/WSDL | Authentic | Browser
e22_16.xml
```

Figure 22.18

Notes

- This example refers to a hypothetical accounting system.
- The root element is `accounting` and contains three elements: `inventory`, `invoices`, and `sales`
- The `inventory` element contains at least one `inventory_item` element with an `ID` type attribute called `id`
- The `invoices` element contains at least one `invoice` element.
- The `invoice` element contains at least one `item` element. This `item` element has an `IDREF` type attribute called `id`. The values of this attribute must be one of the values of the `id` attribute of the `inventory_item` element.
- The `sales` element is an `EMPTY` element with an `IDREFS` type attribute called `ids`. The value of this attribute must be a space-delimited list of `id` attribute values of the `inventory_item` element. The purpose of the `sales` element is to keep track of the items that are on sale.

22.18 Declaring NMTOKEN and NMTOKENS attributes

If an attribute is declared with the `NMTOKEN` type, the value of this attribute must be a valid XML Nmtoken.

If an attribute is declared with the `NMTOKENS` type, the value of this attribute must be a space-delimited list of valid XML Nmtokens.

Example 22_17. NMTOKEN and NMTOKENS (file e22_17.xml)

```
<!--e22_17.xml-->
<!DOCTYPE inventory [
      <!ELEMENT inventory (item+)>
      <!ELEMENT item EMPTY>
      <!ATTLIST item
            id NMTOKEN #REQUIRED
            quantities NMTOKENS #IMPLIED
            prices NMTOKENS #IMPLIED
>
]>
<inventory>
      <item id="123" quantities="10"
      prices="3.99 3.49"/>
      <item id="-XP.234_06" quantities="200 25" prices="12.56 7.76 5.50"/>
      <item id=":345-a_bc.xyz" quantities="1234 231" prices="7.99"/>
</inventory>
```

Figure 22.19

Notes

- The root element is `inventory` and contains at least one `EMPTY item` element.
- The `item` element has one required `NMTOKEN` type attribute (`id`) and two other `NMTOKENS` type attributes (`quantities` and `prices`).
- The `quantities` attribute is a list consisting of **quantity on hand** and **quantity on order** (for example).
- The `prices` attribute is a list consisting of **regular price**, **sale price** and **clearance price** (for example).

22.19 Declaring attributes with the enumeration type

If the possible values of an attribute can be enumerated using a list, declare that attribute with the *enumeration type*. Each element of the list is a valid XML Nmtoken. The list elements are separated by '|' characters.

The following example shows another possible way to set up a DTD section for a hypothetical inventory system.

Notes

- The root element is `inventory`. This element contains at least one `item` element.
- The `item` element is described by a sequence of three elements: `id`, `qty` (at least one), and `price` (at least one).
- The `qty` element has an enumerated type attribute called `type` set to the default value `"on_hand"`
- The `price` element has an enumerated type attribute called `currency` set to the default value `"USD"`

Example 22_18. Enumeration type attributes (file e22_18.xml)

```
<!--e22_18.xml-->
<!DOCTYPE inventory [
<!ELEMENT inventory (item+)>
<!ELEMENT item (id, qty+, price+)>
<!ELEMENT id (#PCDATA)>
<!ELEMENT qty (#PCDATA)>
<!ELEMENT price (#PCDATA)>
<!ATTLIST qty type (on_hand | on_orders) "on_hand">
<!ATTLIST price currency (USD | CAD | ROL) "USD">
]>
<inventory>
<item>
```

```
<id>123</id>
<qty type="on_hand">100</qty>
<qty type="on_orders">12</qty>
<price currency="USD">10.00</price>
<price currency="CAD">13.99</price>
</item>
<item>
<id>234</id>
<qty>540</qty>
<price currency="USD">10.00</price>
</item>
</inventory>
```

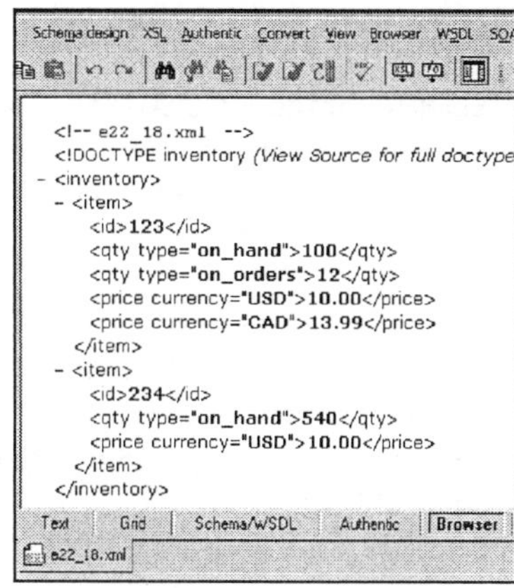

Figure 22.20

22.20 Entity References

To declare an *entity reference*, use the syntax:

```
<!ENTITY entity_name entity_value>
```

where *entity_value* is a string delimited by double (") or single (') quotes. To insert the value of an entity reference into the document, use the syntax:

```
&entity_name;
```

There are a few entity references that are predefined in XML:

```
<!ENTITY lt "<">
<!ENTITY gt ">">
<!ENTITY amp "&">
<!ENTITY apos "'">
<!ENTITY quot '"'>
```

Notes

- You can insert an entity reference anywhere a string is allowed.
- You can use an entity reference inside of another entity reference.
- You cannot use a reference entity to automatically generate DTD sections. Use a **parameter entity** instead (see section 22.22 Parameter entities).

Example 22_19. Entity references (file e22_19.xml)

```
<!--e22_19.xml-->
<!DOCTYPE invoice [
<!ELEMENT invoice (#PCDATA | item)*>
<!ELEMENT item (id, qty, price)>
```

```
<!ELEMENT id (#PCDATA)>
<!ELEMENT qty (#PCDATA)>
<!ELEMENT price (#PCDATA)>
<!ENTITY us "USD">
<!ATTLIST price currency CDATA "&us;">
<!ENTITY ca "CAD">
<!ENTITY a "aa">
<!ENTITY b "bb-&a;-bb">
<!ENTITY header "Invoice 001">
<!ENTITY footer "Due Date: April 12, 2004">
<!ENTITY special_item "<price>&ca;
11.99</price>">
]>
<invoice>
&header;
<item>
<id>&b;</id>
<qty>12345</qty>
<price currency="&ca;">12.50</price>
</item>
<item>
<id>12345&a;54321</id>
<qty>10</qty>
&special_item;
</item>
&footer;
</invoice>
```

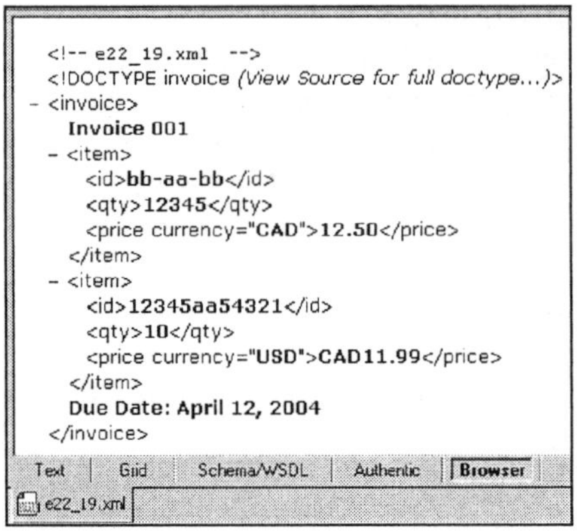

```
<!-- e22_19.xml -->
<!DOCTYPE invoice (View Source for full doctype...)>
- <invoice>
    Invoice 001
  - <item>
      <id>bb-aa-bb</id>
      <qty>12345</qty>
      <price currency="CAD">12.50</price>
    </item>
  - <item>
      <id>12345aa54321</id>
      <qty>10</qty>
      <price currency="USD">CAD11.99</price>
    </item>
    Due Date: April 12, 2004
  </invoice>
Text | Grid | Schema/WSDL | Authentic | Browser
e22_19.xml
```

Figure 22.21

Notes

- The parser resolves any entity reference before sending data to the application (browser).
- The entity reference can contain markup elements if the document obtained after the replacement of all entity references is well-formed and valid.

22.21 External entities

You can declare an entity that references an external file. This file can be a parsed text file, like an XML file, or an unparsed non-text file, like an image file.

To define an entity reference to an externally parsed file, use the syntax:

```
<!ENTITY external_entity_name SYSTEM file_URL>
```

To insert the external parsed file into the XML document, use the syntax:

```
&external_entity_name;
```

To define an entity reference to an external, unparsed non-text file (e.g an image file), use the syntax presented in the following example:

```
<!ENTITY logo_image "logo.gif" SYSTEM NDATA gif>
```

You can reference it in a context like this:

```
<!ELEMENT img EMPTY>
<!ATTLIST img src ENTITY #REQUIRED>
<img src="logo_image" />
```

Example 22_20. External entities (files e22_20.xml, data.xml)

```
<!--e22_20.xml-->
<!DOCTYPE invoice [
<!ELEMENT invoice (item+)>
<!ELEMENT item (id, qty, price)>
<!ELEMENT id (#PCDATA)>
<!ELEMENT qty (#PCDATA)>
<!ELEMENT price (#PCDATA)>
<!ENTITY external_item SYSTEM "data.xml">
]>
<invoice>
<item>
      <id>12345</id>
      <qty>2</qty>
      <price>USD 12.99</price>
</item>
&external_item;
</invoice>

<!-- data.xml -->
<item>
      <id>54321</id>
      <qty>200</qty>
      <price>CAD 0.56</price>
</item>
```

Figure 22.22

22.22 Parameter entities

As mentioned before, you cannot use an entity reference to automatically generate DTD sections. You can use a *parameter entity* instead.

To declare a *parameter entity*, use the syntax:

```
<!ENTITY % parameter_entity_name entity_value>
```

where *entity_value* is a string delimited by double (") or single (') quotes. To insert the previously declared value of the parameter entity into *the DTD section*, use the syntax:

```
%parameter_entity_name;
```

To define a parameter entity to an external DTD section, use the syntax:

```
<!ENTITY % external_dtd_section SYSTEM file_URL>
```

To insert the external DTD section into *the DTD section* of an XML document, use the syntax:

```
%external_dtd_section;
```

Example 22_21. Parameter entities (files e22_21.xml, external.dtd)

```
<!--e22_21.xml-->
<!DOCTYPE accounting [
      <!ELEMENT accounting (inventory, invoice+)>
      <!ELEMENT inventory (inventory_item+)>
      <!ELEMENT invoice (invoice_item+)>
      <!ENTITY % external_dtd SYSTEM "external.dtd">
      %external_dtd;
      ]>
<accounting>
<inventory>
      <inventory_item>
            <id>12345</id>
            <qty>1000</qty>
            <price>5.89</price>
      </inventory_item>
</inventory>
<invoice>
      <invoice_item>
            <id>12345</id>
            <qty>10</qty>
            <price>8.49</price>
      </invoice_item>
</invoice>
</accounting>
```

```
<!-- e22_21.xml -->
<!DOCTYPE accounting (View Source for full doctype...)>
- <accounting>
  - <inventory>
    - <inventory_item>
        <id>12345</id>
        <qty>1000</qty>
        <price>5.89</price>
      </inventory_item>
    </inventory>
  - <invoice>
    - <invoice_item>
        <id>12345</id>
        <qty>10</qty>
        <price>8.49</price>
      </invoice_item>
    </invoice>
  </accounting>
Text | Grid | Schema/WSDL | Authentic | Browser
e22_21.xml
```

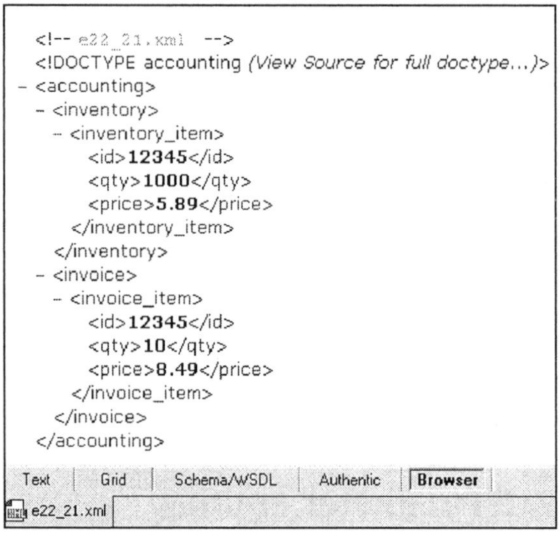

Figure 22.23

```
<!--external.dtd-->
<!ENTITY % children "id, qty, price">
<!ELEMENT inventory_item (%children;)>
<!ELEMENT invoice_item (%children;)>
<!ENTITY % pcd "#PCDATA">
```

```
<!ELEMENT id (%pcd;)>
<!ELEMENT qty (%pcd;)>
<!ELEMENT price (%pcd;)>
```

Note that internal DTD sections do not allow parameter entities to be used in markup declarations. Instead, use external DTD sections.

22.23 Review of Chapter 22

- DTD stands for Document Type Definition
- DTD represents a section in an XML document and/or in an external file that contains the rules the XML document must comply with to be valid.
- The DTD section describing the rules can be inserted internally (in the XML document), externally (in a separate file), or both (internally and externally) in the same time.
- To attach the DTD file to an XML document, insert a DOCTYPE declaration.
- To declare an element, use the syntax: `<!ELEMENT element_name (element_content)>`
- The *element_content* can be `#PCDATA` (parsed text), child content, a sequence, a choice list, a group, mixed content, any content or empty content.
- To specify how many times in a row a group can appear, use the *repetition suffixes*: `"?"`, `"*"` and `"+"`
- The XML Nmtoken and XML Name are identifiers used in XML.
- To declare one or more attributes for an XML element, use the syntax:
- `<!ATTLIST element_name attribute_name attribute_type attribute_default ...>`
- The *attribute_type* can be: `CDATA`, `ID`, `IDREF`, `IDREFS`, `ENTITY`, `ENTITIES`, `NMTOKEN`, `NMTOKENS`, or `(Nmtoken | Nmtoken |...)`
- The *attribute_default* can be: `#REQUIRED`, `#IMPLIED`, `#FIXED` *attribute_value*, or *attribute_default_value*
- To declare an *entity reference*, use the syntax: `<!ENTITY entity_name entity_value>`. To insert the value of an entity reference into the document, use the syntax `&entity_name;`
- You can declare an entity that references an external file.
- To declare a *parameter entity*, use the syntax: `<!ENTITY % parameter_entity_name entity_value>`. To insert the parameter entity into *the DTD section*, use the syntax: `%parameter_entity_name;`

Chapter 23

XSL, XSLT and XPath

23.1 XSL

In this chapter, we'll present another technique for rendering XML data in a browser. This technique is based on XML style sheets and is called XSL.

XSL stands for e**X**tensible **S**tylesheet **L**anguage. XSL is divided in XSLT and XSL-FO. XSLT is presented in this chapter. XSL-FO (Formating Objects) is not yet implemented by browsers and is beyond the scope of this book.

23.2 XSLT

XSLT stands for e**X**tensible **S**tylesheet **L**anguage **T**ransformation. An XSLT application transforms an XML file (the input) into another XML file (the output) using the instructions contained in the XSLT file.

Newer browsers come with a built-in XSLT application, which loads XML files and generates (X)HTML files that can be rendered properly by browsers. Transforming XML files into (X)HTML files is the main scope of this chapter.

23.3 XPath

As mentioned above, XML is a *hierarchical data structure* stored in text files using a markup language. Using the information contained in the XML file, the XML(XSLT) application builds a *document tree* based on element names, element data, and the relationships (parent/child) between elements. The generic name for the document tree elements is *node*. There are seven kinds of nodes in an XML document tree:

- The root node
- Element nodes
- Text nodes
- Attribute nodes
- Comment nodes
- Processing instruction nodes
- Namespace nodes

XPath is a technique that allows you to identify a *set of nodes* in the XML document tree. Then, using the XSLT templates, you can apply a set of transformations to this set of nodes.

23.4 The chapter's XML data

In this chapter, we'll use the same XML data for all examples. This data contains the sale invoices of a fictitious company. The root (document) *element* is `<invoices>`. This element is a child of the root node (document root) denoted by `"/"`. The element nodes are `<invoices>`, `<invoice>`, `<date>`, `<company>`, `<total>`, `<gst>`, `<paid>`, `<item>`, `<id>`, `<desc>`, `<qty>`, and `<price>`. Some elements have attributes. The `<paid/>` element is an empty element and is optional. For instructional purposes, text nodes in the following examples are represented in bold style and comment nodes are represented in italic style (the XML file are pure text files). In XSLT, an element can have attributes as its children, but attributes are not considered to have any parents.

```
<!--This is e23.xml file-->
<invoices>
<invoice id="002">
      <!--first invoice-->
      <date>13-aug-2003</date>
      <company type="from">Company A</company>
      <company type="to">Company B</company>
      <total currency="USD">16.68<gst currency='USD' val="1.02"/></total>
      <paid/>
      <item>
            <id>54321</id>
            <desc>item a</desc>
            <qty>2</qty>
            <price currency="USD">10.10</price>
```

```
        </item>
        <item>
              <id>235</id>
              <desc>item c</desc>
              <qty>-10</qty>
              <price currency="USD">-0.57</price>
        </item>
  </invoice>
  <invoice id="001">
        <date>1-aug-2003</date>
        <company type="from">Company A</company>
        <company type="to">Company C</company>
        <total currency="USD">13.11<gst currency='USD' val="0.798"/></total>
        <!--not paid-->
        <item>
              <id>235</id>
              <desc>item c</desc>
              <qty>20</qty>
              <price currency="USD">0.57</price>
        </item>
  </invoice>
  <invoice id="003">
        <date>10-sep-2004</date>
        <company type="from">Company A</company>
        <company type="to">Company D</company>
        <total currency="CAD">41.4<gst currency='CAD' val="2.52"/></total>
        <paid/>
        <item>
              <id>123</id>
              <desc>item d</desc>
              <qty>2</qty>
              <price currency="CAD">1.50</price>
        </item>
        <item>
              <id>234</id>
              <desc>item e</desc>
              <qty>100</qty>
              <price currency="CAD">0.25</price>
        </item>
        <item>
              <id>235</id>
              <desc>item c</desc>
              <qty>10</qty>
              <price currency="CAD">0.80</price>
        </item>
  </invoice>
  </invoices>
```

23.5 XSLT file structure

An XSLT file is a pure text file having the `.xsl` extension. It is used to transform one XML file into another XML file. Generally, browsers have an XSLT processor that can load an XML file, make transformations according to an XSLT style-sheet file, and then render the file in the browser window.

An XSLT file is also an XML file and must be well-formed. The document (root) element is <xsl:stylesheet>. This element has two useful attributes:

`version="1.0"` specifies the version of XSL used in the document (this attribute is required).

`xmlns:xsl="http://www.w3.org/1999/XSL/Transform"` defines the prefix `"xsl"` for all elements that belong to the XSLT name space. You can change the `"xsl"` prefix to any other identifier you like.

Each element in the XSLT file has the syntax: <xsl:element_name>. The style sheet is defined inside of the <xsl:stylesheet></xsl:stylesheet> block.

XSLT is a *rule-based style-sheet* similar to CSS, but using a totally different syntax. In XSLT, a rule is defined by a template. The template syntax is:

```
<xsl:template match="XPath-expression">
<!--here are the rules-->
</xsl:template>
```

where the body of the template contains the rules of transformations of the nodes that belong to the node-set defined by the XPath expression of the `match` attribute.

For example, the template:

```
<xsl:template match="/">
<xsl:apply-templates/>
</xsl:template>
```

is applied to the root node and determines that the pre-defined templates (if they exist) will be called and executed.

Each of the following examples is based on an XML file containing the same data as file `e22.xml`, with an XSLT style-sheet attached. To attach an XSLT style-sheet file (`"transform1.xsl"`) to an XML file (`"e23_1.xml"`), include in the XML file (`"e23_1.xml"`) a processing instruction like this:

```
<?xml-stylesheet type="text/xsl" href="transform1.xsl"?>
```

This attaches an XSL style-sheet to the "e23_1.xml" file, with the transformation rules defined in the file "transform1.xsl".

Example 23_1. First XSLT (files e23_1.xml, transform1.xsl)

```
<?xml-stylesheet type="text/xsl" href="transform1.xsl"?>
<!--This is file e23_1.xml and uses file transform1.xsl to render data-->
<!--The following data is copied from file e23.xml -->
<invoices>
<invoice id="002">
      <!--first invoice-->
      <date>13-aug-2003</date>
      <company type="from">Company A</company>
<xsl:stylesheet version="1.0" xmlns:xsl="http://www.w3.org/1999/XSL/Transform">
<!--this is the XSLT file transform1.xsl-->
<xsl:template match="/">
<html><body>
<h3>Hello from XSLT!</h3>
<xsl:apply-templates/>
</body></html>
</xsl:template>
</xsl:stylesheet>
```

Figure 23.1

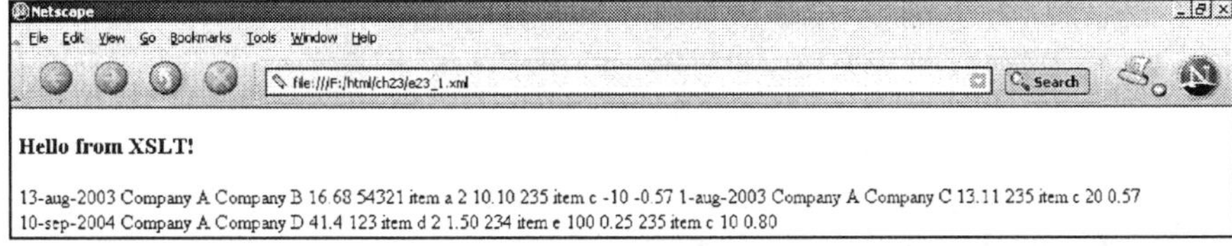

Notes

- The XSLT file `transform1.xsl` contains a single template that matches to the document root. The content of this template generates the elements required by a standard web page. The message "Hello from XSLT!" and the XSLT element `<xsl:apply-templates/>` (which calls the **pre-defined templates**) are both inserted into the `<body>` element of this web page.
- The pre-defined template for the root node determines that the text content of each element is to be inserted into the output file.
- The pre-defined template adds no value of the attributes to the output.
- Each element that doesn't belong to the `xsl` space (e.g. `<html>`, `<body>` and `<h3>`) is copied identically to the output without any special treatment from the XSLT processor.
- Finally, the browser renders the output file as illustrated in Figure 23.1.

23.6 Extracting all information from an XML file: Method 1.

The following example shows the first method by which all information contained in an XML file can be extracted, formatted and rendered by a browser.

This method uses a recursive calling of the `<apply-templates>` elements, each call meaning a further step into the document tree.

Example 23_2. Method 1 (files e23_2.xml, transform2.xsl)

```
<?xml-stylesheet type="text/xsl" href="transform2.xsl"?>
<!--This is file e23_2.xml and uses file transform2.xsl to render data-->
<!--The following data is copied from file e23.xml-->
<invoices>
<invoice id="002">
      <!--first invoice-->
      <date>13-aug-2003</date>
      <company type="from">Company A</company>
```

Note that in the following text box, line numbers are added for reference purposes only. Do not include them in the source file.

```
<xsl:stylesheet version="1.0"
xmlns:xsl="http://www.w3.org/1999/XSL/Transform">
<!--this is the XSLT file: transform2.xsl-->

<xsl:template match="/">
<html><body>Here starts the root node!
<xsl:apply-templates select="invoices"/>
</body></html>
</xsl:template>

<xsl:template match="invoices">
<br/>Here starts the root element!
<xsl:apply-templates select="invoice"/>
</xsl:template>

<xsl:template match="invoice">
<br/>Here starts the invoice element!
id: <xsl:value-of select="@id"/><br/>
date: <xsl:value-of select="date"/><br/>
<xsl:apply-templates select="company"/>
total: <xsl:apply-templates select="total"/><br/>
gst: <xsl:apply-templates select="total/gst"/><br/>
<xsl:apply-templates select="paid"/><br/>
<xsl:value-of select="comment()"/>
```

```
<table border="1">
<xsl:apply-templates select="item"/>
</table>
</xsl:template>

<xsl:template match="item">
<tr>
<xsl:apply-templates select="id"/>
<xsl:apply-templates select="desc"/>
<xsl:apply-templates select="qty"/>
<xsl:apply-templates select="price"/>
</tr>
</xsl:template>

<xsl:template match="id|desc|qty">
<td><xsl:value-of select="text()"/></td>
</xsl:template>

<xsl:template match="price">
<td><xsl:value-of select="@currency"/></td>
<td><xsl:value-of select="text()"/></td>
</xsl:template>

<xsl:template match="total">
<xsl:value-of select="@currency"/><xsl:value-of select="text()"/>
</xsl:template>

<xsl:template match="total/gst">
<xsl:value-of select="@currency"/><xsl:value-of select="@val"/>
</xsl:template>

<xsl:template match="paid">This invoice is paid.</xsl:template>

<xsl:template match="company">
<xsl:value-of select="@type"/><xsl:text>
</xsl:text><xsl:value-of select="text()"/><br/>
</xsl:template>

</xsl:stylesheet>
```

Figure 23.2

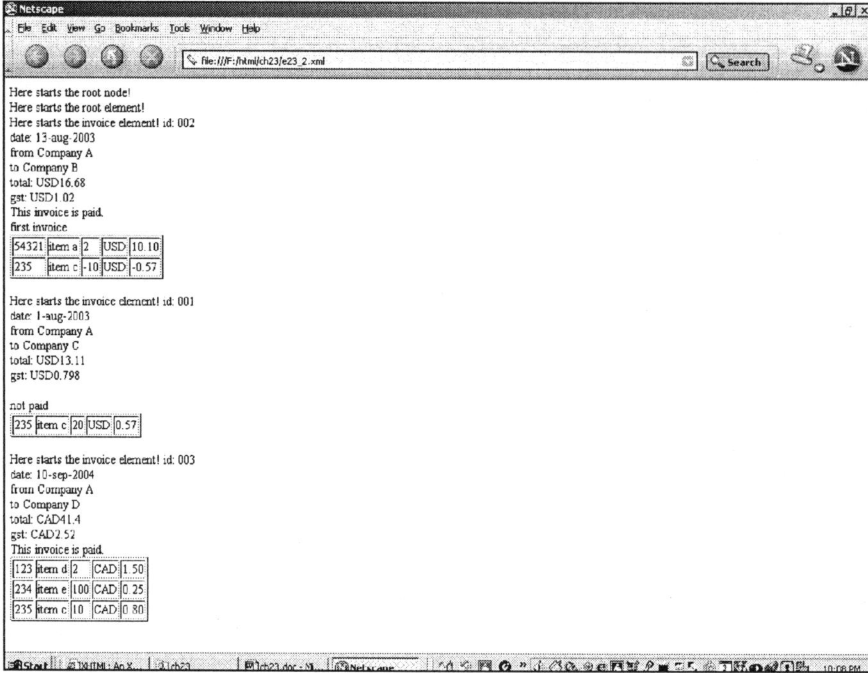

Let's explain this example:

- Line 1 declares "xsl" as the prefix for the elements belonging to the "http://www.w3.org/1999/XSL/Transform" name space.
- Lines 3-7 declare the starting template that matches to the root node. The content of this template inserts the <html> and <body> elements of a regular web page, a message, and a call to execute the template that matches to the <invoices> element, which is a child of the root node.
- Lines 8-11 describe the template that matches to the <invoices> element. This template contains only a message and a call for the template that matches to the <invoice> element, which is a child of the <invoices> element.
- Lines 12-24 describe the template that matches to the <invoice> element. Line 13 inserts a message. Line 14 adds the value of the id attribute of the <invoice> element to the output. Line 15 extracts the value of the <date> element and adds it to the output. Lines 16-19 call the templates dedicated to the <company>, <total>, <gst> (a child of the <total> element), and <paid> elements. Line 20 adds any *comments* of the <invoice> element into the output. Lines 21 and 23 create a <table> element for each invoice. Line 22 calls the template that matches to each <item> element, which are children of the <invoice> element.

- Lines 25-32 describe the template that matches to the <item> elements. Lines 26 and 31 open and close a <tr> element. Lines 27-30 call templates that match to the <id>, <desc>, <qty>, and <price> elements, which are children of the <item> elements.
- Lines 33-35 describe the template that matches to any of the <id>, <desc> or <qty> elements. In any of these cases, the value of the text node is inserted into a table cell and is copied to the output.
- Lines 36-39 describe the template that matches to any <price> element. The value of the `currency` attribute (line 37) and the value of the <price> element (line 38) are each inserted into a table cell and added to the output.
- Lines 40-42 describe the template that matches to the <total> element. The value of the `currency` attribute is concatenated with a *space* character and with the value of the <total> element, then added to the output.
- Lines 43-45 describe the template that matches to the <gst> elements, which are children of the <total> elements. The values of the `currency` and `val` attributes are concatenated and added to the output.
- Line 46 describes the template that matches to the <paid> element. In this case, only a message is added to the output.
- Finally, lines 47-49 describe the template that matches to the <company> elements. The value of the `type` attribute, a *space* character and the value of the text node of the <company> element are concatenated and then added to the output.

Notes

- To call a template, use the syntax:
  ```
  <xsl:apply-templates select="XPath-expression"/>
  ```
- To extract the text node of the current element, use syntax:
  ```
  <xsl:value-of select="text()"/>
  ```
- To extract the value of an attribute of the current element, use the syntax:
  ```
  <xsl:value-of select="@attribute_name"/>
  ```
- To extract the comments of the current element, use the syntax:
  ```
  <xsl:value-of select="comment()"/>
  ```
- To insert a space character, use the syntax:
  ```
  <xsl:text> </xsl:text>
  ```

23.7 Extracting all information from an XML file: Method 2.

The following example shows the second method by which information contained by an XML file can be extracted, formatted and rendered by a browser.

This method uses nested <xsl:for-each> XSLT elements that permit the elements that belong to a node-set to loop over.

Example 23_3. Method 2 (files e23_3.xml, transform3.xsl)

```
<?xml-stylesheet type="text/xsl" href="transform3.xsl"?>
<!--This is file e23_3.xml and uses file transform3.xsl to render data-->
<!--The following data is copied from file e23.xml-->
<invoices>
<invoice id="002">
      <!--first invoice-->
      <date>13-aug-2003</date>
      <company type="from">Company A</company>
<xsl:stylesheet version="1.0" xmlns:xsl="http://www.w3.org/1999/XSL/Transform">
<!--this is the XSLT file: transform3.xsl-->

<xsl:template match="/">
      <html><body>Here starts the root node!
      <xsl:for-each select="invoices">
            <br/>Here starts the root element!
            <xsl:for-each select="invoice">
                  <br/>Here starts the invoice element!
                  id: <xsl:value-of select="@id"/><br/>
                  date: <xsl:value-of select="date"/><br/>
                  <xsl:for-each select="company">
                        <xsl:value-of select="@type"/>
                        <xsl:text> </xsl:text>
                        <xsl:value-of select="text()"/><br/>
                  </xsl:for-each>
                  total:
                  <xsl:for-each select="total">
                        <xsl:value-of select="@currency"/>
                        <xsl:value-of select="text()"/>
                  </xsl:for-each>
                  <br/>gst:
                  <xsl:for-each select="total/gst">
                        <xsl:value-of select="@currency"/>
                        <xsl:value-of select="@val"/>
                  </xsl:for-each>
                  <xsl:for-each select="paid">
```

```
                <br/>This invoice is paid.
                </xsl:for-each>
                <br/><xsl:value-of select="comment()"/>
                <table border="1">
                <xsl:for-each select="item">
                      <tr>
                      <td><xsl:value-of select="id"/></td>
                      <td><xsl:value-of select="desc"/></td>
                      <td><xsl:value-of select="qty"/></td>
                      <xsl:for-each select="price">
                              <td><xsl:value-of select="@currency"/></td>
                              <td><xsl:value-of select="text()"/></td>
                      </xsl:for-each>
                </tr>
                </xsl:for-each>
                </table>
           </xsl:for-each>
      </xsl:for-each>
      </body></html>
</xsl:template>

</xsl:stylesheet>
```

Notes

- Browsers render this example similarly to Example 23_2.
- In this example, no template is called.
- To reach each element of the document tree, a sequence of nested <xsl:for-each> elements is used.
- To extract information from an element, the same <xsl:value-of> element is used as in Example 23_2.
- The syntax for the <xsl:for-each> element is:

```
<xsl:for-each select="XPath-expression">
      <!--here are the rules and/or other for-each elements-->
      </xsl:for-each>
```

23.8 Attribute-element conversion

Let's suppose we want to export the invoice with `id="003"` from the XML file and import it into a new accounting system that accepts XML files without attribute elements.

To keep all information contained in the attribute values, we'll generate a sub-element with the same name as the attribute name and the text node value equal to the attribute value.

Example 23_4. Attribute-element conversion (files e23_4.xml, transform4.xsl)

```
<?xml-stylesheet type="text/xsl" href="transform4.xsl"?>
<!--This is file e23_4.xml and uses file transform4.xsl to render data-->
<!--The following data is copied from file e23.xml-->
<invoices>
<invoice id="002">
      <!--first invoice-->
      <date>13-aug-2003</date>
      <company type="from">Company A</company>

<xsl:stylesheet version="1.0" xmlns:xsl="http://www.w3.org/1999/XSL/Transform">
<!--this is the XSLT file transform4.xsl-->
<xsl:output method="xml"/>
<xsl:template match="/">
      <invoice>
            <xsl:for-each select="/invoices/invoice[@id='003']">
                  <xsl:element name="id">
                  <xsl:value-of select="@id"/>
                  </xsl:element>
                  <xsl:for-each select="company">
                  <company>
                        <xsl:element name="type">
                                          <xsl:value-of select="@type"/>
                        </xsl:element>
                        <xsl:element name="name">
                                    <xsl:value-of select="text()"/>
                        </xsl:element>
                  </company>
                  </xsl:for-each>
                  <xsl:for-each select="item">
                        <item>
                        <id><xsl:value-of select="id"/></id>
                        <desc><xsl:value-of select="desc"/></desc>
                        <xsl:for-each select="price">
                                    <price>
                                    <xsl:element name="currency">
                                                <xsl:value-of select="@currency"/>
                                    </xsl:element>
                                    <xsl:value-of select="text()"/>
```

```
                        </price>
                    </xsl:for-each>
                    </item>
               </xsl:for-each>
          </xsl:for-each>
     </invoice>
</xsl:template>
</xsl:stylesheet>
```

The output is contained in the XSL file "`Output.xml`" and is rendered by Netscape, as shown in Figure 23.3:

```
This XML file does not appear to have any style inform
- <invoice>
    <id>003</id>
  - <company>
      <type>from</type>
      <name>Company A</name>
    </company>
  - <company>
      <type>to</type>
      <name>Company D</name>
    </company>
  - <item>
      <id>123</id>
      <desc>item d</desc>
    - <price>
        <currency>CAD</currency>
        1.50
      </price>
    </item>
  - <item>
      <id>234</id>
      <desc>item e</desc>
    - <price>
        <currency>CAD</currency>
        0.25
      </price>
    </item>
  - <item>
      <id>235</id>
      <desc>item c</desc>
    - <price>
        <currency>CAD</currency>
        0.80
      </price>
    </item>
  </invoice>
```

Figure 23.3

Notes

- The syntax used to transform an attribute into an element is:
  `<xsl:element name="new_element_name">`
  `<xsl:value-of select="@attribute_name"/>`
  `</xsl:element>`

- The XPath used to select only the invoice with `id="003"` is:
  `"/invoices/invoice[@id='003']"`
  and contains the predicate `[@id='003']` that matches only for the invoice having the attribute `id='003'`

- The top-level element:
  `<xsl:output method="xml"/>`
  declares the output as an XML file.

- To obtain the output files, you need an application capable of transforming an XML file into another XML file using an XSLT style-sheet file, e.g. SAXON, XALAN, or XMLSPY.

23.9 Element-attribute conversion

Let's suppose we want to export the invoice with `id="003"` from the XML file and import it into a new accounting system that accepts invoices with `<item>` elements having no children. All the information required by an item should be attached to an attribute of the `<item>` element.

The syntax to attach an attribute to the current element is:

```
<xsl:attribute name="attribute_name">
```

```
<xsl:value-of select="expression"/>
</xsl:attribute>
```

Example 23_5. Element-attribute conversion (files e23_5.xml, transform5.xsl)

```
<?xml-stylesheet type="text/xsl" href="transform5.xsl"?>
<!--This is file e23_5.xml and uses file transform5.xsl to render data-->
<!--The following data is identically copied from file e23.xml-->
<invoices>
<invoice id="002">
      <!--first invoice-->
      <date>13-aug-2003</date>
      <company type="from">Company A</company>
```

```
<xsl:stylesheet version="1.0" xmlns:xsl="http://www.w3.org/1999/XSL/Transform">
<!--this is the XSLT file transform5.xsl-->
<xsl:output method="xml"/>
<xsl:template match="/">
      <invoice>
            <xsl:for-each select="/invoices/invoice[@id='003']">
            <xsl:for-each select="item">
                  <item>
                        <xsl:attribute name="id">
                                 <xsl:value-of select="id"/>
                        </xsl:attribute>
                        <xsl:attribute name="desc">
                                 <xsl:value-of select="desc"/>
                        </xsl:attribute>
                        <xsl:attribute name="qty">
                                 <xsl:value-of select="qty"/>
                        </xsl:attribute>
                        <xsl:for-each select="price">
                                 <xsl:attribute name="currency">
                                          <xsl:value-of select="@currency"/>
                                 </xsl:attribute>
                                 <xsl:attribute name="val">
                                          <xsl:value-of select="text()"/>
                                 </xsl:attribute>
                        </xsl:for-each>
                  </item>
            </xsl:for-each>
            </xsl:for-each>
      </invoice>
</xsl:template>
</xsl:stylesheet>
```

The output is contained in the XSL file `"Output2.xml"` and is rendered by Netscape as shown in Figure 23.4:

Figure 23.4

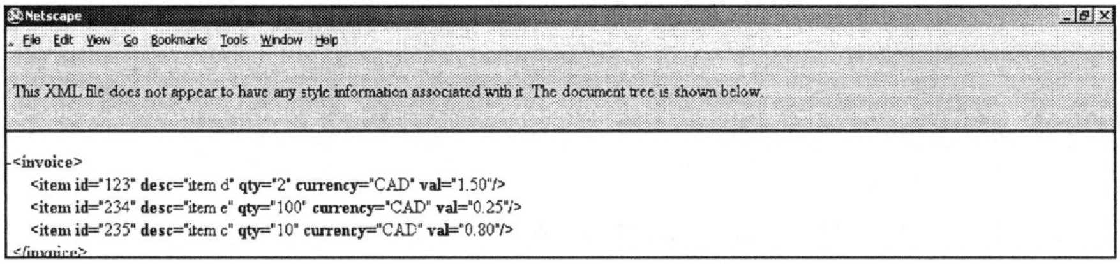

Netscape

File Edit View Go Bookmarks Tools Window Help

This XML file does not appear to have any style information associated with it. The document tree is shown below.

```
-<invoice>
   <item id="123" desc="item d" qty="2" currency="CAD" val="1.50"/>
   <item id="234" desc="item e" qty="100" currency="CAD" val="0.25"/>
   <item id="235" desc="item c" qty="10" currency="CAD" val="0.80"/>
</invoice>
```

23.10 XSLT sorting

To sort data according to a criterion, use the `<xsl:sort>` element as a child of the `<xsl:template>` or `<xsl:for-each>` element. The syntax for the `<xsl:sort>` element is:

```
<xsl:sort
            select = "sort-criteria-expression"
            data-type = "text" | "number"
            lang = "language-expression"
            order = "ascending" | "descending"
            case-order = "upper-first" | "lower-first"
/>
```

Example 23_6. XSLT sorting (files e23_6.xml, transform6.xsl)

```
<?xml-stylesheet type="text/xsl" href="transform6.xsl"?>
<!--This is file e23_6.xml and uses file transform6.xsl to render data-->
<!--The following data is copied from file e23.xml-->
<invoices>
<invoice id="002">
      <!--first invoice-->
      <date>13-aug-2003</date>
      <company type="from">Company A</company>

<xsl:stylesheet version="1.0" xmlns:xsl="http://www.w3.org/1999/XSL/Transform">
<!--this is the XSLT file transform6.xsl-->
<xsl:template match="/">
      <html><body>
      The most sold items!
      <table border="1">
      <xsl:for-each select="/invoices/invoice/item">
      <xsl:sort select="qty" data-type="number" order="descending"/>
            <tr>
            <td><xsl:value-of select="id"/></td>
            <td><xsl:value-of select="desc"/></td>
```

```
                <td><xsl:value-of select="qty"/></td>
                <td><xsl:value-of select="price"/></td>
                </tr>
        </xsl:for-each>
        </table>
        </body></html>
</xsl:template>
</xsl:stylesheet>
```

Figure 23.5

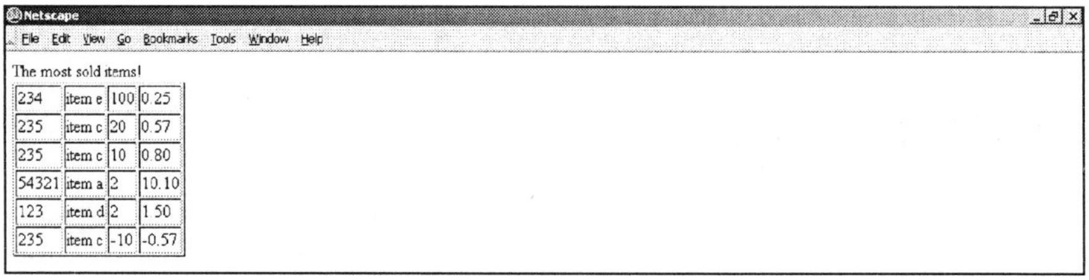

Netscape

File Edit View Go Bookmarks Tools Window Help

The most sold items!

234	item e	100	0.25
235	item c	20	0.57
235	item c	10	0.80
54321	item a	2	10.10
123	item d	2	1.50
235	item c	-10	-0.57

23.11 XSLT functions

There are many *functions* you can use in XSLT. Here are some of them:

- `position()` returns the position (number) of the current node in the current node-set.
- `last()` returns the position (number) of the last node in the current node-set.
- `concat(string1, string2, …)` returns the concatenation string of the arguments.
- `number(string)` converts the string argument to a number

Read only variables can be declared using the syntax:

```
<xsl:variable name="variable_name">
            <xsl:value-of select="expression"/>
            </xsl:variable>
```

and can be used later using the syntax:

```
"{$variable_name}"
```

Example 23_7. XSLT functions (files e23_7.xml, transform7.xsl)

```
<?xml-stylesheet type="text/xsl" href="transform7.xsl"?>
<!--This is file e23_7.xml and uses file transform7.xsl to render data-->
<!--The following data is copied from file e23.xml-->
<invoices>
<invoice id="002">
        <!--first invoice-->
        <date>13-aug-2003</date>
        <company type="from">Company A</company>
```

```
<xsl:stylesheet version="1.0"
xmlns:xsl="http://www.w3.org/1999/XSL/Transform">
<!--this is the XSLT file transform7.xsl-->
<xsl:template match="/">
      <html><body>
      XSLT Functions<br/>
      <table border="1">
      <tr><td>Line Number</td><td>Item Id</td><td>Item Description</td>
      <td>Quantity</td><td>Unit Price</td><td>Currency</td>
      <td>Sub-total</td><td>Item Image</td></tr>
      <xsl:for-each select="/invoices/invoice[@id='003']/item">
      <tr>
      <td><xsl:value-of select="concat(position(), ' of ',last())"/></td>
      <td><xsl:value-of select="id"/></td>
      <td><xsl:value-of select="desc"/></td>
      <td><xsl:value-of select="qty"/></td>
      <td><xsl:value-of select="price"/></td>
      <xsl:for-each select="price">
      <td><xsl:value-of select="@currency"/></td>
      </xsl:for-each>
      <td><xsl:value-of select="number(qty)*number(price)"/></td>
      <td align="center">
            <xsl:variable name="source">
            <xsl:value-of select="concat(id,'.gif')"/>
            </xsl:variable>
            <img src="{$source}"/>
      </td>
      </tr>
      </xsl:for-each>
      </table>
      </body></html>
</xsl:template>
</xsl:stylesheet>
```

Figure 23.6

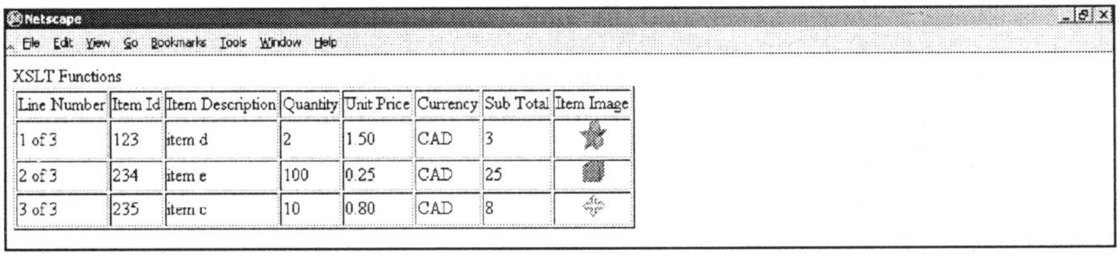

Netscape

File Edit View Go Bookmarks Tools Window Help

XSLT Functions

Line Number	Item Id	Item Description	Quantity	Unit Price	Currency	Sub Total	Item Image
1 of 3	123	item d	2	1.50	CAD	3	
2 of 3	234	item e	100	0.25	CAD	25	
3 of 3	235	item c	10	0.80	CAD	8	

Notes

- The "source" variable gets a value equal to the concatenation of the "id" value of the current item and the extension ".gif"
- In order for this example to work, three image files ("123.gif", "234.gif", and "235.gif") must be in the same directory as the file e23_7.xml.

23.12 XSLT `if`

XSLT only allows you to insert content into the output if a condition is met. The syntax you can use is:

```
<xsl:if test="condition">
...
</xsl:if>
```

If a *condition* is true, the content of the <xsl:if> element is inserted into the output.

Example 23_8. XSLT `if` (files e23_8.xml, transform8.xsl)

```
<?xml-stylesheet type="text/xsl" href="transform8.xsl"?>
<!--This is file e23_8.xml and uses file transform8.xsl to render data-->
<!--The following data is copied from file e23.xml-->
<invoices>
<invoice id="002">
        <!--first invoice-->
        <date>13-aug-2003</date>
        <company type="from">Company A</company>
```

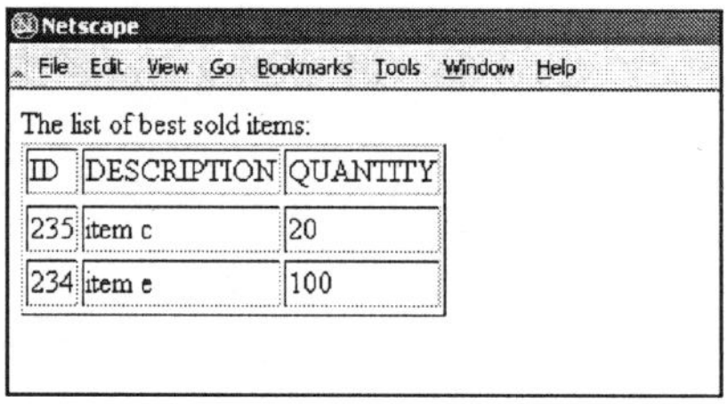

```
<xsl:stylesheet version="1.0"
xmlns:xsl="http://www.w3.org/1999/XSL/Transform">
<!--this is the XSLT file transform8.xsl-->
<xsl:template match="/">
        <html><body>
        The list of best sold items:<br/>
        <table border="1">
        <tr><td>ID</td><td>DESCRIPTION</td><td>QUANTITY</td></tr>
        <xsl:for-each select="/invoices/invoice/item">
        <tr><xsl:if test="qty>10">
        <td><xsl:value-of select="id"/></td>
        <td><xsl:value-of select="desc"/></td>
        <td><xsl:value-of select="qty"/></td>
        </xsl:if></tr>
        </xsl:for-each>
        </table></body></html>
</xsl:template>
</xsl:stylesheet>
```

Netscape
File Edit View Go Bookmarks Tools Window Help

The list of best sold items:

ID	DESCRIPTION	QUANTITY
235	item c	20
234	item e	100

Figure 23.7

Notes

- The <xsl:if> element has a `test` condition that filters items sold in quantities greater than 10.

◆ To create a `test` **condition**, you can use any of the following operators:

- `=` equal to
- `!=` not equal to
- `<` less than
- `>` greater than
- `<=` less than or equal to
- `>=` greater than or equal to

23.13 XSLT choose

The <xsl:choose> element allows you to refine conditional structures in XSLT. The syntax is:

```
<xsl:choose>
      <xsl:when test="condition1"> content1 </xsl:when>
      <xsl:when test="condition2"> content2 </xsl:when>
      ...
      <xsl:otherwise> content </xsl:otherwise>
</xsl:choose>
```

Notes

- If **condition1** is true, only **content1** is inserted into the output.
- If **condition1** is false, **condition2** is tested. If **condition2** is true, only **content2** is inserted into the output, and so on.
- If all conditions defined by `test` attributes are false, and the <xsl:otherwise> element is present, the **content** of this element is inserted into the output.
- The <xsl:otherwise> element is optional.

Example 23_9. XSLT choose (files e23_9.xml, transform9.xsl)

```
<xsl:stylesheet version="1.0"
xmlns:xsl="http://www.w3.org/1999/XSL/Transform">
<!--this is the XSLT file transform9.xsl-->
<xsl:template match="/">
      <html><body>
      The list of best sold items:<br/>
      <table border="1">
      <tr><td>ID</td><td>DESCRIPTION</td></tr>
      <xsl:for-each select="/invoices/invoice/item">
      <tr>
      <xsl:choose>
```

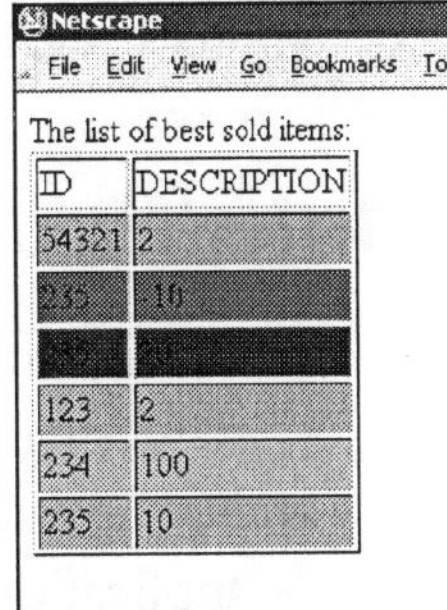

Figure 23.8

```
            <xsl:when test="qty&lt;0">
                  <td bgcolor="#ff0000"><xsl:value-of select="id"/></td>
                  <td bgcolor="#ff0000"><xsl:value-of select="qty"/></td>
            </xsl:when>
            <xsl:when test="qty&lt;15">
                  <td bgcolor="#00ff00"><xsl:value-of select="id"/></td>
                  <td bgcolor="#00ff00"><xsl:value-of select="qty"/></td>
            </xsl:when>
            <xsl:when test="qty&lt;25">
                  <td bgcolor="#0000ff"><xsl:value-of select="id"/></td>
                  <td bgcolor="#0000ff"><xsl:value-of select="qty"/></td>
            </xsl:when>
            <xsl:otherwise>
                  <td bgcolor="#aaaaaa"><xsl:value-of select="id"/></td>
                  <td bgcolor="#aaaaaa"><xsl:value-of select="qty"/></td>
            </xsl:otherwise>
      </xsl:choose>
      </tr>
      </xsl:for-each>
      </table></body></html>
</xsl:template>
</xsl:stylesheet>

<?xml-stylesheet type="text/xsl" href="transform9.xsl"?>
<!--This is file e23_9.xml and uses file transform9.xsl to render data-->
<!--The following data is copied from file e23.xml-->
<invoices>
<invoice id="002">
      <!--first invoice-->
      <date>13-aug-2003</date>
      <company type="from">Company A</company>
```

Notes

- The text of the qty element is tested, and the background color of the cells is set.
- To use the '<' symbol in the test condition, you must use the reference '<'

23.14 Review of Chapter 23

- XSL stands for e**X**tensible **S**tylesheet **L**anguage. This is another technique for rendering XML data in a browser.
- XSLT stands for e**X**tensible **S**tylesheet **L**anguage **T**ransformation. An XSLT application transforms an XML file (the input) into another XML file (the output) using the instructions contained in the XSLT file.

- An XSLT file is also an XML file and must be well-formed. The document (root) element is <xsl:stylesheet>.
- XPath is a technique that allows you to identify a *set of nodes* in the XML document tree.
- In XSLT, a rule is defined by a template. The template syntax is:
  ```
  <xsl:template match="XPath-expression"><!--here are the rules-->
  </xsl:template>
  ```
- To attach the "transform1.xsl" XSLT style-sheet file to the XML file, use a processing instruction like this: <?xml-stylesheet type="text/xsl" href="transform1.xsl"?>
- The XSLT element <xsl:apply-templates/> calls the *pre-defined templates*. The *pre-defined templates* insert only the text nodes into the output.
- To call a template, use the syntax:
  ```
  <xsl:apply-templates select="XPath-expression"/>
  ```
- To extract the text node of the current element, use syntax:
  ```
  <xsl:value-of select="text()"/>
  ```
- To extract the value of an attribute of the current element, use the syntax:
  ```
  <xsl:value-of select="@attribute_name"/>
  ```
- To extract the comments of the current element, use the syntax:
  ```
  <xsl:value-of select="comment()"/>
  ```
- To insert a space character, use the syntax: <xsl:text> </xsl:text>
- Using nested <xsl:for-each> XSLT elements, you can loop on the elements that belong to a node-set.
- The syntax for the <xsl:for-each> element is:
  ```
  <xsl:for-each select="XPath-expression"><!--rules--></xsl:for-each>
  ```
- The syntax used to transform an attribute into an element is:
  ```
  <xsl:element name="name"><xsl:value-of select="@attribute"/></xsl:name>
  ```
- The syntax to attach an attribute to the current element is:
  ```
  <xsl:attribute name="attr_name"><xsl:value-of select="expression"/>
  </xsl:attribute>
  ```
- To sort data according to a criterion, use the <xsl:sort> element as a child of the <xsl:template> or <xsl:for-each> element.
- There are many *functions* you can use in XSLT.
- The <xsl:if> and the <xsl:choose> elements allow you to define conditional structures in XSLT.

Chapter 24

XHTML

24.1 XHTML

XHTML stands for E**X**tensible **H**yper**T**ext **M**arkup **L**anguage. XHTML is the new generation of HTML, which conforms to the XML technology. As such, XHTML has facilities inherited from both these markup languages:

- Like HTML, XHTML can be used to create web pages. There are some minor differences, but all the capabilities of regular HTML are maintained in XHTML.
- Like XML, XHTML can be used with all XML applications. The code is more strict but also more stable and clean.

Note that in order for an XHTML page to be rendered correctly, a browser must support XHTML. To maintain reverse compatibility with older browsers, XHTML files must be coded with care (see following sections of this chapter for details).

24.2 XML declaration

To declare an XHTML file as an XML file, the first line should contain an XML declaration having the syntax:

```
<?xml version="1.0" encoding="UTF-8"?>
```

Notes

- The XML declaration is recommended but not required.
- The XML declaration can generate some problems in rendering the XHTML document with non-XHTML browsers.
- Use this XML declaration if your XHTML file uses a character encoding other than the default UTF-8 or UTF-16 and you don't have a <meta> element to specify the character encoding used by the XHTML page.

24.3 DOCTYPE declaration

XHTML files must contain a DOCTYPE declaration. There are 3 possibilities for this required declaration:

1. *XHTML 1.0 Strict*: In this case, you cannot use *deprecated* HTML 4.01 elements (<applet>, <basefont>, <center>, <dir>, <font>, <isindex>, <menu>, <s>, <strike>, and <u>) nor *obsolete* HTML 4.01 elements (<listing>, <plaintext>, and <xmp>). The syntax is:

```
<!DOCTYPE html
        PUBLIC "-//W3C//DTD XHTML 1.0 Strict//EN"
        "http://www.w3.org/TR/xhtml1/DTD/xhtml1-strict.dtd">
```

2. *XHTML 1.0 Transitional*: In this case, you can use the *deprecated* elements but not the *obsolete* ones. The syntax is:

```
<!DOCTYPE html
        PUBLIC "-//W3C//DTD XHTML 1.0 Transitional//EN"
        "http://www.w3.org/TR/xhtml1/DTD/xhtml1-transitional.dtd">
```

3. *XHTML 1.0 Frameset*: In this case, you can use <frameset> and <frame> elements. The syntax is:

```
<!DOCTYPE html
        PUBLIC "-//W3C//DTD XHTML 1.0 Frameset//EN"
        "http://www.w3.org/TR/xhtml1/DTD/xhtml1-frameset.dtd">
```

Notes

- Any of these DOCTYPE declarations declare "html" as the root element of the XHTML file and a "PUBLIC" identifier that references a DTD file containing the rules to which the XHTML file must conform.
- Place the DOCTYPE declaration on the first line of the XHTML file if the XML declaration is missing, or immediately after the XML declaration if this exists.
- The DOCTYPE declaration must be placed before the "html" root element of the XHTML file.

24.4 Metadata

In case you decide not to include an XML declaration in your XHTML file, it is recommended that you include a <meta> tag declaring the character set used by the document. Use the following syntax:

```
<meta http-equiv="Content-Type" content="text/html;charset=UTF-8" />
```

Note that you can include both if you like.

24.5 The XHTML document root

An XHTML file must have "html" as the document root. The document root must have the XHTML namespace declared as shown in here:

```
<html xmlns="http://www.w3.org/1999/xhtml">
```

The document root must contain only two elements: <head> and <body>.

Using all the information presented so far, we can build a minimal standard XHTML file, as illustrated in the following example.

Example 24_1. The standard XHTML document (file e24_1.html)

```
<?xml version="1.0" encoding="UTF-8"?>
<!DOCTYPE html
   PUBLIC "-//W3C//DTD XHTML 1.0 Transitional//EN"
   "http://www.w3.org/TR/xhtml1/DTD/xhtml1-transitional.dtd">
<html xmlns="http://www.w3.org/1999/xhtml">
<head><title>The standard XHTML document</title>
<meta http-equiv="Content-Type" content="text/html;charset=UTF-8" />
</head><body>
This is a standard XHTML document!
</body></html>
```

Figure 24.1

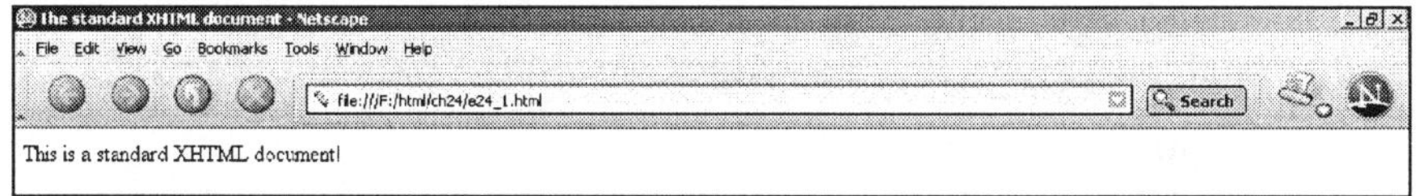

Note

- The extension of an XHTML file can be ".html" or ".xhtml". To maintain compatibility with older browsers, use the ".html" extension.

24.6 XHTML elements

There are several rules that apply to XHTML elements:

1. XHTML document must be *well-formed.* This means that the XHTML elements must be completely nested one inside of another. Overlapping the element tags is forbidden. For example, `<b><i>text</b></i>` is incorrect and should be re-coded as `<b><i>text</i></b>`.
2. XHTML is a *case-sensitive* language. The names of the XHTML elements must be coded in lower case. For example, `<HTML>` elements will be considered to be incorrect or belonging to another name space. This tag must be re-coded as `<html>`.
3. All non-empty XHTML elements must have an opening and an ending tag using the syntax `<element_name>content</element_name>`. These rules apply especially to those non-empty elements that have an optional ending tag in HTML. For example:
   a) `<body> content </body>`
   b) `<colgroup> content </colgroup>`
   c) `<dd> content </dd>`
   d) `<dt> content </dt>`
   e) `<head> content </head>`
   f) `<html> content </html>`
   g) `<li> content </li>`
   h) `<option> content </option>`
   i) `<p> content </p>`
   j) `<tbody> content </tbody>`
   k) `<td> content </td>`
   l) `<tfoot> content </tfoot>`
   m) `<th> content </th>`
   n) `<thead> content </thead>`
   o) `<tr> content </tr>`
4. All empty elements must conform to one of the following syntaxes:
   - `<empty_element_name/>` (recommended by W3C)
   - `<empty_element_name />` (recommended for older browsers)
   - `<empty_elemnt_name></empty_element_name>`

Here is a list of all the empty elements in XHTML 4.01 and how you can re-code them in XHTML:

```
<area/>          <img/>
<base/>          <input/>
<basefont/>      <isindex/>
<br/>            <link/>
<col/>           <meta/>
<frame/>         <param/>
<hr/>
```

Example 24_2. XHTML elements (file e24_2.html)

```
<?xml version="1.0" encoding="UTF-8"?>
<!DOCTYPE html
   PUBLIC "-//W3C//DTD XHTML 1.0 Transitional//EN"
   "http://www.w3.org/TR/xhtml1/DTD/xhtml1-transitional.dtd">
<html xmlns="http://www.w3.org/1999/xhtml">
<head><title>The standard XHTML document</title>
<meta http-equiv="Content-Type" content="text/html;charset=UTF-8" />
</head><body>
<table>
<tr><td>c11</td><td>c12</td></tr>
<tr><td>c21</td><td>c22</td></tr>
</table>
<basefont size="+5" face="fantasy" color="#00ff00" />
This text is in Fantasy font.<br/>
<hr/ >
<form>
<input type="text" />
</form>
<hr />
<img src="arrow.gif" id="arrow.gif" />
</body></html>
```

Figure 24.2

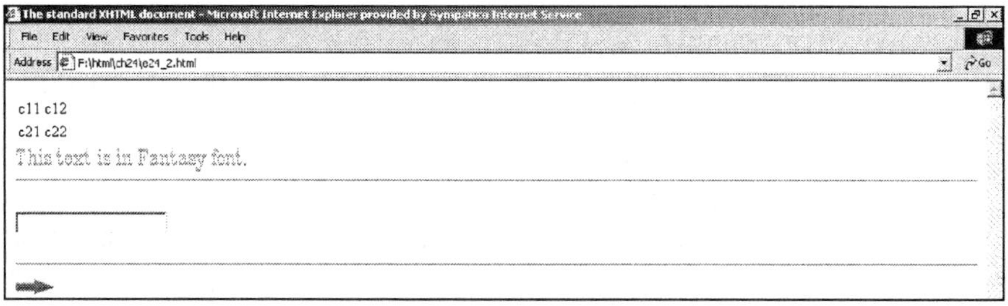

24.7 XHTML attributes

There are several rules that apply to XHTML attributes:

1. Attribute names must be coded in lower case.
2. The values of the enumerated attributes (having predefined values) must be in lower case. For example:

   ```
   <input type="text" value="Initial Text" />
   ```
3. Attribute values must be quoted using single (') or double (") quotation marks.
4. Line breaks and multiple white space characters should be avoided within attribute values.
5. Attribute minimization is forbidden. The following syntax must be used:
   - `checked="checked"` for `<input>` elements
   - `compact="compact"` for `<dl>`, `<ol>`, `<ul>`, `<menu>`, `<dir>` elements
   - `declare="declare"` for `<object>` elements
   - `defer="defer"` for `<script>` elements
   - `disabled="disabled"` for `<button>`, `<input>`, `<optgroup>`, `<option>`, `<select>`, and `<textarea>` elements
   - `ismap="ismap"` for `<img>` and `<input>` elements
   - `multiple="multiple"` for `<select>` elements
   - `nohref="nohref"` for `<area>` elements
   - `noresize="noresize"` for `<frame>` elements
   - `noshade="noshade"` for `<hr>` elements
   - `nowrap="nowrap"` for `<td>` and `<th>` elements
   - `readonly="readonly"` for `<input>` and `<textarea>` elements
   - `selected="selected"` for `<option>` elements

   For example:

   ```
   <input type="checkbox" value="yes" name="cb1" checked="checked" />
   ```
6. In HTML 4.01, the `name` attribute is used to add an identifier to the `<a>`, `<applet>`, `<frame>`, `<iframe>`, `<image>`, and `<map>` elements. These elements are then referenced using these identifiers. W3C recommends using the `id` attribute in favor of the `name` attribute. To keep your XHTML web page compatible with older browsers, it is recommended that you include both the `name` and `id` attributes, as in the following example:

   ```
   <img src="newyork.gif" id="im1" name="im1" />
   ```

7. If you use the `lang` attribute for an element, you must also add the `xml:lang` attribute, as in the following example (the value of `xml:lang` attributes take precedence):

```
<div lang="en" xml:lang="en">This is an XHTML division block!</div>
```

Example 24_3. XHTML attributes (file e24_3.html)

```
<?xml version="1.0" encoding="UTF-8"?>
<!DOCTYPE html
   PUBLIC "-//W3C//DTD XHTML 1.0 Transitional//EN"
   "http://www.w3.org/TR/xhtml1/DTD/xhtml1-transitional.dtd">
<html xmlns="http://www.w3.org/1999/xhtml">
<head><title>XHTML attributes</title>
<meta http-equiv="Content-Type" content="text/html;charset=UTF-8" />
</head><body>
<form>
<input type="text" value="Initial Text" readonly="readonly" />
<input type="checkbox" value="yes" name="cbl" checked="checked" />
</form>
<img src="arrow.gif" id="iml" name='iml' />
<div lang="fr" xml:lang="fr">&Agrave; propos, pr&eacute;cision, mat&eacute;riel,
ma&icirc;trise, il peut &ecirc;tre tr&egrave;s difficile </div>
</body></html>
```

Figure 24.3

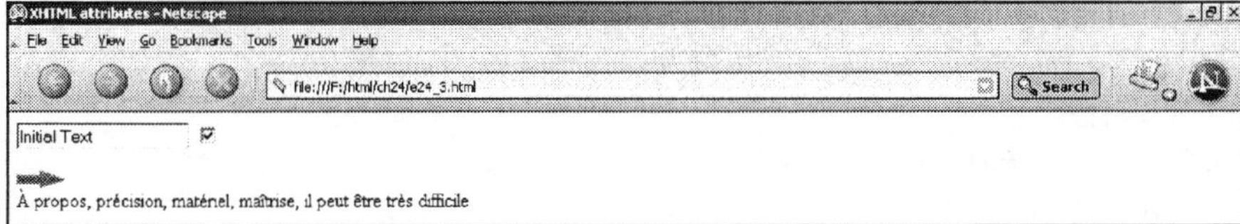

24.8 XHTML and CSS

There are several rules that apply to XHTML files that use CSS:

- Property names and property values must be coded in lower case.
- If CSS is inserted into an external file, an XML style-sheet declaration must be added using the syntax:

```
<?xml-stylesheet href="style_sheet_URL" type="text/css"?>
```

- If CSS is inserted into the XHTML file, an XML style-sheet declaration must be added using the syntax:

```
<?xml-stylesheet href="#internal_style_sheet_id" type="text/css"?>
```

The "internal_style_sheet_id" identifier is the "id" attribute value attached to the <style> element that is generally inserted into the <head> element. For example:

```
<style id="internal_style_sheet_id" type="text/css">
p {coclor : red;}
</style>
```

Example 24_4. XHTML and CSS (files e24_4.html, styles.css)

```
<?xml version="1.0" encoding="UTF-8"?>
<?xml-stylesheet href="styles.css" type="text/css"?>
<?xml-stylesheet href="#internal" type="text/css"?>
<!DOCTYPE html
   PUBLIC "-//W3C//DTD XHTML 1.0 Transitional//EN"
   "http://www.w3.org/TR/xhtml1/DTD/xhtml1-transitional.dtd">
<html xmlns="http://www.w3.org/1999/xhtml">
<head><title>XHTML and CSS</title>
<meta http-equiv="Content-Type" content="text/html;charset=UTF-8" />
<link rel="stylesheet" type="text/css" href="styles.css" />
<style id="internal" type="text/css">
p {color : red;}
</style>
</head><body>
This is a normal text block.
<p>This paragraph has a style defined in the document's head element and in an
external file.</p>
<div>This division element has a style defined in an external style sheet
file.</div>
This is a normal text block.
</body></html>

/* this is the styles.css file */
p {font-style : italic;}
div {color : blue;}
```

Figure 24.4

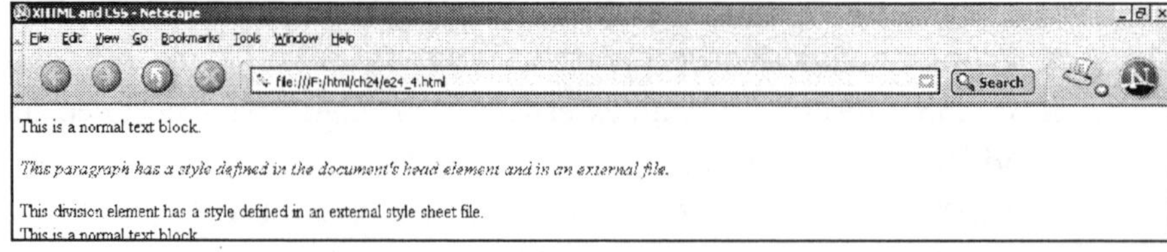

24.9 XHTML and Script elements

There are several rules that apply to XHTML files that use JavaScript code:

1. It is recommended that you use external script documents.
2. In XHTML, the `<style>` and `<script>` elements are declared as having `#PCDATA` content. That means:
   a. any "<" and "&" characters will be interpreted as the beginning of a markup element, and
   b. any "<" and "&" character sequences will be interpreted as entity references to "<" and "&" characters.
3. You can use `<style>` or `<script>` elements as in HTML if they do not contain "<", "&", "<" or "&" characters.
4. If your `<style>` or `<script>` elements contain at least one of the "<", "&", "<" or "&" characters, use a `CDATA` section to avoid an expansion of these entities. Be aware that some browsers do not recognize the `CDATA` sections. A recommended solution is illustrated in the following example (use JavaScript comment syntax "//" to comment "<![CDATA[" and "]]>" lines):

```
<script type="text/javascript"> //<![CDATA[
function f3(){
if (1<2) {alert("message");}
}
//]]>
</script>
```

In this way, the file remains an XML file and the "<" character is interpreted as a "less than" operator and not as the beginning of a markup element.

Example 24_5. XHTML and Script elements (files e24_5.html, script.js)

```
<?xml version="1.0" encoding="UTF-8"?>
<!DOCTYPE html
   PUBLIC "-//W3C//DTD XHTML 1.0 Transitional//EN"
   "http://www.w3.org/TR/xhtml1/DTD/xhtml1-transitional.dtd">
<html xmlns="http://www.w3.org/1999/xhtml">
<head><title>XHTML and Script elements</title>
<meta http-equiv="Content-Type" content="text/html;charset=UTF-8" />
<script type="text/javascript">
//<![CDATA[
```

```
function f1(){if (1<2) {alert("You clicked button 1!");}}
//]]>
</script>
<script src="script.js"></script>
</head><body><form>
<input type="button" name="b1" id="b1" value="b1" onClick="f1();" />
<input type="button" name="b2" id="b2" value="b2" onClick="f2();" />
</form></body></html>
//this is script.js file
function f2()
{alert("You clicked button 2!");}
```

Figure 24.5

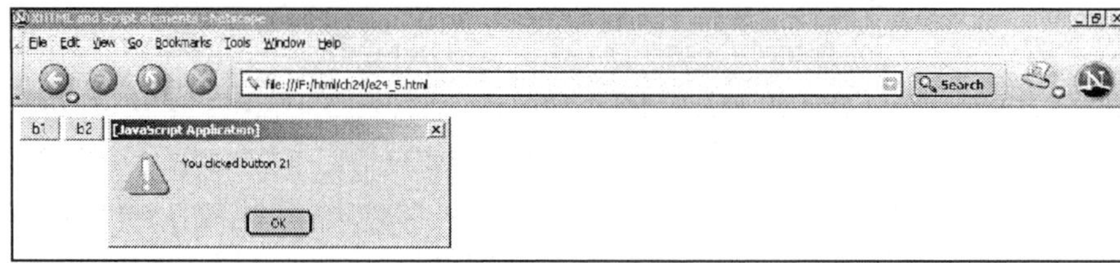

If you change the extension of e24.html from ".html" to ".xml" and open it in Internet Explorer, you'll see that the file is well-formed, and that the CDATA is interpreted as an XML element:

Figure 24.6

```
<?xml version="1.0" encoding="UTF-8" ?>
<!DOCTYPE html (View Source for full doctype...)>
- <html xmlns="http://www.w3.org/1999/xhtml">
  - <head>
      <title>XHTML and Script elements</title>
      <meta http-equiv="Content-Type" content="text/html;charset=UTF-8" />
    - <script type="text/javascript" xml:space="preserve">
        //
      - <![CDATA[
          function f1(){if (1<2) {alert("You clicked button 1!");}}
          //
        ]]>
      </script>
      <script src="script.js" xml:space="preserve" />
    </head>
  - <body>
    - <form method="get" enctype="application/x-www-form-urlencoded">
        <input type="button" name="b1" id="b1" value="b1" onClick="f1();" />
        <input type="button" name="b2" id="b2" value="b2" onClick="f2();" />
      </form>
    </body>
  </html>
```

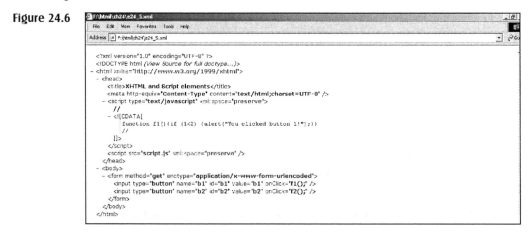

Note also a few changes made automatically by Internet Explorer.

24.10 XHTML and other name spaces

XHTML allows you to insert fragments coded in name spaces other than XML name spaces, but it is not recommended that you do so. For example, you can insert MathML into an XHTML file using syntax like this:

```
<math xmlns=http://www.w3.org/1998/Math/MathML>
<!--here is the math element content-->
</math>
```

Also, you can insert XHTML code into any other XML document using syntax like this:

```
<div xmlns=http://www.w3.org/1998/xtml>
<!--here is the div element content-->
</div>
```

Example 24_6. XHTML and MathML (file e24_6.xhtml)

```
<?xml version="1.0"?>
<!DOCTYPE html PUBLIC "-//W3C//DTD XHTML 1.1 plus MathML 2.0//EN"
        "http://www.w3.org/TR/MathML2/dtd/xhtml-math11-f.dtd">
<html xmlns="http://www.w3.org/1999/xhtml">
<head><title>XHTML and MathML</title></head>
<body>
This is a fraction:
<math xmlns="http://www.w3.org/1998/Math/MathML">
      <mfrac>
            <mi>a</mi>
            <mi>b</mi>
      </mfrac>
</math>
</body></html>
```

Figure 24.7

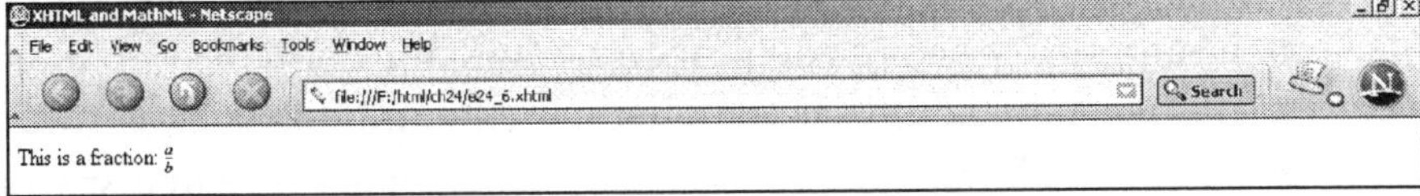

To obtain a working example, we used:

- A `DOCTYPE` declaration like this:
  `<!DOCTYPE html PUBLIC "-//W3C//DTD XHTML 1.1 plus MathML 2.0//EN"`
  `"http://www.w3.org/TR/MathML2/dtd/xhtml-math11-f.dtd">`
- The file extension `".xhtml"`
- Netscape 7.1

24.11 Review of Chapter 24

- XHTML stands for **EX**tensible **H**yper**T**ext **M**arkup **L**anguage. XHTML is the new generation of HTML, which conforms to the XML technology.
- To declare an XHTML file as an XML file, the first line should contain an XML declaration having the syntax: `<?xml version="1.0" encoding="UTF-8"?>`
- The XML declaration is recommended but not required.
- XHTML files must contain a `DOCTYPE` declaration.
- An XHTML file must have `"html"` as the document root.
- The document root must have the XHTML namespace declared as shown in the syntax: `<html xmlns="http://www.w3.org/1999/xhtml">`
- XHTML documents must be *well-formed.*
- XHTML is a *case-sensitive* language.
- All non-empty XHTML elements must have an opening and an ending tag.
- All empty elements must conform to one of the following syntaxes: `<empty_element_name/>` or `<empty_element_name />`
- Attribute names must be coded in lower case.
- The values of the enumerated attributes (having predefined values) must be in lower case.
- Attribute values must be quoted using single (') or double (") quotation marks.
- Attribute minimization is forbidden.
- CSS property names and property values must be coded in lower case.
- It is recommended that you use external script documents.
- XHTML allows you to insert fragments coded in name spaces other than XML name spaces.

Appendix A

HTML 4.01 elements and attributes

Legend:

D (Deprecated), L (Loose DTD), F (Frameset DTD), E (Empty), * (#REQUIRED)

Name	Attributes	Start Tag	End Tag	Empty	Deprecated	DTD
a	accesskey charset cords href hreflang name rel rev shape tabindex target type					
abbr						
acronym						
address						
applet	align alt archive code codebase height* hspace name object vspace width*				D	L
area	accesskey alt* cords href nohref shape tabindex target		F	E		
b						
base	href target		F	E		
basefont	color face size*		F	E	D	L

Name	Attributes	Start Tag	End Tag	Empty	Depre-cated	DTD
bdo						
big						
block-quote	cite					
body	alink background bgcolor link text vlink	O	O			
br	clear		F	E		
button	accesskey disabled name tabindex type value					
caption	align					
center					D	L
cite						
code						
col	align char charoff span valign width		F	E		
colgrou p	align char charoff span valign width		O			
dd			O			
del	cite datetime					
dfn						
dir	compact				D	L
div	align					
dl	compact					
dt			O			
em						
fieldset						
font	color face size				D	L
form	accept-charset accept action* enctype method name target					

Name	Attributes	Start Tag	End Tag	Empty	Deprecated	DTD
frame	frameborder longdesc marginheight marginwidth name noresize scrolling src		F	E		F
frameset	cols rows					F
h1	align					
h2	align					
h3	align					
h4	align					
h5	align					
h6	align					
head	profile	O	O			
hr	align noshade size width		F	E		
html	version	O	O			
i						
iframe	align frameborder height longdesc marginheight marginwidth name scrolling src width					L
img	align alt* border height hspace ismap longdesc name src* usemap vspace width		F	E		
input	accept accesskey align alt checked disabled ismap maxlength name readonly size src tabindex type usemap value		F	E		
ins	cite datetime					
isindex	prompt		F	E	D	L
kbd						
label	accesskey for					
legend	accesskey align					

Name	Attributes	Start Tag	End Tag	Empty	Deprecated	DTD
li	type value		O			
link	charset href hreflang media rel rev target type		F	E		
map	name*					
menu	compact				D	L
meta	content* http-equiv name scheme		F	E		
noframes						F
noscript						
object	align archive border classid codebase codetype data declare height hspace name standby tabindex type usemap vspace width					
ol	compact start type					
optgroup	disabled label*					
option	disabled label selected value		O			
p	align		O			
param	name* type value valuetype		F	E		
pre	width					
q	cite					
s					D	L
samp						
script	charset defer language src type*					
select	disabled multiple name size tabindex					
small						
span						

Name	Attributes	Start Tag	End Tag	Empty	Deprecated	DTD
strike					D	L
strong						
style	media type*					
sub						
sup						
table	align bgcolor border cellpadding cellspacing frame rules summary width					
tbody	align char charoff valign	O	O			
td	abbr align axis bgcolor char charoff colspan headers height nowrap rowspan scope valign width		O			
textarea	accesskey cols* disabled name readonly rows* tabindex					
tfoot	align char charoff valign		O			
th	abbr align axis bgcolor char charoff colspan headers height nowrap rowspan scope valign width		O			
thead	align char charoff valign		O			
title						
tr	align bgcolor char charoff valign		O			
tt						
u					D	L
Ul	compact type					
var						

Notes

- The class and style attributes apply to all elements except base, basefont, head, html, meta, param, script, style, title
- The dir attributes apply to all elements except applet, base, basefont, bdo, br, frame, frameset, iframe, param, script
- The id attributes apply to all elements except base, head, html, meta, script, style, title
- The lang attributes apply to all elements except applet, base, basefont, br, frame, frameset, iframe, param, script
- The title attributes apply to all elements except base, basefont, head, html, meta, param, script, style, title

Appendix B

CSS2 properties and values

Name	Values	Initial value
'azimuth'	<angle> [left-side | far-left | left | center-left | center | center-right | right | far-right | right-side] || behind leftwards | rightwards | inherit	center
'background'	'background-color' || 'background-image' || 'background-repeat' || 'background-attachment' || 'background-position' inherit	
'background-attachment'	scroll | fixed | inherit	scroll
'background-color'	<color> transparent | inherit	transparent
'background-image'	<uri> none | inherit	none
'background-position'	[<percentage> | <length>]{1,2} [top | center | bottom] || [left | center | right] inherit	0% 0%
'background-repeat'	repeat | repeat-x | repeat-y | no-repeat | inherit	repeat

Name	Values	Initial value
'border'	'border-width' || 'border-style' || <color> inherit	
'border-collapse'	collapse | separate | inherit	collapse
'border-color'	<color>{1,4} transparent | inherit	
'border-spacing'	<length> <length>? inherit	0
'border-style'	<border-style>{1,4} inherit	
'border-top' 'border-right' 'border-bottom' 'border-left'	'border-top-width' || 'border-style' || <color> inherit	
'border-top-color' 'border-right-color' 'border-bottom-color' 'border-left-color'	<color> inherit the value of the 'color' property	
'border-top-style' 'border-right-style' 'border-bottom-style' 'border-left-style'	<border-style> inherit	none
'border-top-width' 'border-right-width' 'border-bottom-width' 'border-left-width'	<border-width> inherit	medium

Name	Values	Initial value
'border-width'	<border-width>{1,4} inherit	
'bottom'	<length> <percentage> auto | inherit	auto
'caption-side'	top | bottom | left | right | inherit	top
'clear'	none | left | right | both | inherit	none
'clip'	<shape> auto | inherit	auto
'color'	<color> inherit	
'content'	[<string> | <uri> | <counter> | attr(X) | open-quote | close-quote | no-open-quote | no-close-quote]+ inherit empty	string
'counter-increment'	[<identifier> <integer>?]+ none inherit	none
'counter-reset'	[<identifier> <integer>?]+ none inherit	none
'cue'	'cue-before' || 'cue-after' inherit	
'cue-after'	<uri> none | inherit	none
'cue-before'	<uri> none | inherit	none

<table>
<tr><th>Name</th><th>Values</th><th>Initial value</th></tr>
<tr><td>'cursor'</td><td>[<uri> ,]* [auto | crosshair | default | pointer | move | e-resize | ne-resize | nw-resize | n-resize | se-resize | sw-resize | s-resize | w-resize| text | wait | help]
inherit</td><td>auto</td></tr>
<tr><td>'direction'</td><td>ltr | rtl | inherit</td><td>ltr</td></tr>
<tr><td>'display'</td><td>inline | block | list-item | run-in | compact | marker | table | inline-table | table-row-group | table-header-group | table-footer-group | table-row | table-column-group | table-column | table-cell | table-caption | none | inherit</td><td>inline</td></tr>
<tr><td>'elevation'</td><td><angle>
below | level | above | higher | lower | inherit</td><td>level</td></tr>
<tr><td>'empty-cells'</td><td>show | hide | inherit</td><td>show</td></tr>
<tr><td>'float'</td><td>left | right | none | inherit</td><td>none</td></tr>
<tr><td>'font'</td><td>['font-style' || 'font-variant' || 'font-weight']? 'font-size' [/
'line-height']? 'font-family'caption | icon | menu | message-box | small-caption | status-bar
inherit</td><td></td></tr>
<tr><td>'font-family'</td><td>[[<family-name> | <generic-family>],]* [<family-name> | <generic-family>]
inherit</td><td></td></tr>
<tr><td>'font-size'</td><td><absolute-size>
<relative-size>
<length>
<percentage>
inherit</td><td>medium</td></tr>
<tr><td>'font-size-adjust'</td><td><number>
none | inherit</td><td>none</td></tr>
</table>

Name	Values	Initial value
'font-stretch'	normal | wider | narrower | ultra-condensed | extra-condensed | condensed | semi-condensed | semi-expanded | expanded | extra-expanded | ultra-expanded | inherit	normal
'font-style'	normal | italic | oblique | inherit	normal
'font-variant'	normal | small-caps | inherit	normal
'font-weight'	normal | bold | bolder | lighter | 100 | 200 | 300 | 400 | 500 | 600 | 700 | 800 | 900 | inherit	normal
'height'	<length> <percentage> auto | inherit	auto
'left'	<length> <percentage> auto | inherit	auto
‘letter-spacing’	normal <length> inherit	normal
‘line-height’	normal <number> <length> <percentage> inherit	normal
‘list-style’	‘list-style-type’ || ‘list-style-position’ || ‘list-style-image’ inherit	
‘list-style-image’	<uri> none | inherit	none
‘list-style-position’	inside | outside | inherit	outside

Name	Values	Initial value
'list-style-type'	disc | circle | square | decimal | decimal-leading-zero | lower-roman | upper-roman | lower-greek | lower-alpha | lower-latin | upper-alpha | upper-latin | georgian | cjk-ideographic | hiragana | katakana | hiragana-iroha | katakana-iroha | none inherit	disc
'margin'	<margin-width>{1,4} inherit	
'margin-top' 'margin-right' 'margin-bottom' 'margin-left'	<margin-width> inherit	0
'marker-offset'	<length> auto | inherit	auto
'marks'	crop || cross none inherit	none
'max-height'	<length> <percentage> none | inherit	none
'max-width'	<length> <percentage> none | inherit	none
'min-height'	<length> <percentage> inherit	0
'min-width'	<length> <percentage> inherit	
'orphans'	<integer> inherit	2

Name	Values	Initial value
'outline'	'outline-color' || 'outline-style' || 'outline-width' inherit	
'outline-color'	<color> invert | inherit	invert
'outline-style'	<border-style> inherit	none
'outline-width'	<border-width> inherit	medium
'overflow'	visible | hidden | scroll | auto | inherit	visible
'padding'	<padding-width>{1,4} inherit	
'padding-top' 'padding-right' 'padding-bottom' 'padding-left'	<padding-width> inherit	0
'page'	<identifier> auto	auto
'page-break-after'	auto | always | avoid | left | right | inherit	auto
'page-break-before'	auto | always | avoid | left | right | inherit	auto
'page-break-inside'	avoid | auto | inherit	auto
'pause'	[<time> | <percentage>]{1,2} inherit	
'pause-after'	<time> <percentage> inherit	
'pause-before'	<time> <percentage> inherit	

<table>
<tr><th>Name</th><th>Values</th><th>Initial value</th></tr>
<tr><td>'pitch'</td><td><frequency>
x-low | low | medium | high | x-high | inherit
medium</td><td></td></tr>
<tr><td>'pitch-range'</td><td><number>
inherit</td><td>50</td></tr>
<tr><td>'play-during'</td><td><uri> mix? repeat?
auto | none | inherit</td><td>auto</td></tr>
<tr><td>'position'</td><td>static | relative | absolute | fixed | inherit</td><td>static</td></tr>
<tr><td>'quotes'</td><td>[<string> <string>]+
none
inherit</td><td></td></tr>
<tr><td>'richness'</td><td><number>
inherit</td><td>50</td></tr>
<tr><td>'right'</td><td><length>
<percentage>
auto | inherit</td><td>auto</td></tr>
<tr><td>'size'</td><td><length>{1,2}
auto | portrait | landscape |
inherit</td><td>auto</td></tr>
<tr><td>'speak'</td><td>normal | none | spell-out | inherit</td><td>normal</td></tr>
<tr><td>'speak-header'</td><td>once | always | inherit</td><td>once</td></tr>
<tr><td>'speak-numeral'</td><td>digits | continuous | inherit</td><td>continuous</td></tr>
<tr><td>'speak-punctuation'</td><td>code | none | inherit</td><td>none</td></tr>
<tr><td>'speech-rate'</td><td><number>
x-slow | slow | medium | fast | x-fast | faster |
slower | inherit
medium</td><td></td></tr>
<tr><td>'stress'</td><td><number>
inherit</td><td>50</td></tr>
<tr><td>'table-layout'</td><td>auto | fixed | inherit</td><td>auto</td></tr>
</table>

<table>
<tr><th>Name</th><th>Values</th><th>Initial value</th></tr>
<tr><td>'text-align'</td><td>left | right | center | justify
<string>
inherit</td><td></td></tr>
<tr><td>'text-decoration'</td><td>none
underline || overline || line-through || blink
inherit</td><td>none</td></tr>
<tr><td>'text-indent'</td><td><length>
<percentage>
inherit</td><td>0</td></tr>
<tr><td>'text-shadow'</td><td>none
[<color> || <length> <length><length>? ,]*
[<color> || <length> <length> <length>?]
inherit</td><td>none</td></tr>
<tr><td>'text-transform'</td><td>capitalize | uppercase | lowercase |
none | inherit</td><td>none</td></tr>
<tr><td>'top'</td><td><length>
<percentage>
auto | inherit</td><td>auto</td></tr>
<tr><td>'unicode-bidi'</td><td>normal | embed | bidi-override |
inherit</td><td>normal</td></tr>
<tr><td>'vertical-align'</td><td>baseline | sub | super | top | text-top | middle |
bottom | text-bottom
<percentage>
<length>
inherit</td><td>baseline</td></tr>
<tr><td>'visibility'</td><td>visible | hidden | collapse |
inherit</td><td>inherit</td></tr>
<tr><td>'voice-family'</td><td>[[<specific-voice> | <generic-voice>],]*
[<specific-voice> | <generic-voice>]
inherit</td><td></td></tr>
</table>

Name	Values	Initial value
'volume'	<number> <percentage> silent | x-soft | soft | medium | loud | x-loud | inherit	medium
'white-space'	normal | pre | nowrap | inherit	normal
'widows'	<integer> inherit	2
'width'	<length> <percentage> auto | inherit	auto
'word-spacing'	normal <length> inherit	normal
'z-index'	auto | <integer> | inherit	auto

Appendix C

Color Names

Color Name	Hexadecimal
AliceBlue	#F0F8FF
AntiqueWhite	#FAEBD7
Aqua	#00FFFF
Aquamarine	#7FFFD4
Azure	#F0FFFF
Beige	#F5F5DC
Bisque	#FFE4C4
Black	#000000
BlanchedAlmond	#FFEBCD
Blue	#0000FF
BlueViolet	#8A2BE2
Brown	#A52A2A
BurlyWood	#DEB887
CadetBlue	#5F9EA0
Chartreuse	#7FFF00
Chocolate	#D2691E
Coral	#FF7F50

Color Name	Hexadecimal
GhostWhite	#F8F8FF
Gold	#FFD700
GoldenRod	#DAA520
Gray	#808080
Green	#008000
GreenYellow	#ADFF2F
HoneyDew	#F0FFF0
HotPink	#FF69B4
IndianRed	#CD5C5C
Indigo	#4B0082
Ivory	#FFFFF0
Khaki	#F0E68C
Lavender	#E6E6FA
LavenderBlush	#FFF0F5
LawnGreen	#7CFC00
LemonChiffon	#FFFACD
LightBlue	#ADD8E6

Color Name	Hexadecimal	Color Name	Hexadecimal
CornflowerBlue	#6495ED	LightCoral	#F08080
Cornsilk	#FFF8DC	LightCyan	#E0FFFF
Crimson	#DC143C	LightGoldenRod Yellow	#FAFAD2
Cyan	#00FFFF	LightGrey	#D3D3D3
DarkBlue	#00008B	LightGreen	#90EE90
DarkCyan	#008B8B	LightPink	#FFB6C1
DarkGoldenRod	#B8860B	LightSalmon	#FFA07A
DarkGray	#A9A9A9	LightSeaGreen	#20B2AA
DarkGreen	#006400	LightSkyBlue	#87CEFA
DarkKhaki	#BDB76B	LightSlateBlue	#8470FF
DarkMagenta	#8B008B	LightSlateGray	#778899
DarkOliveGreen	#556B2F	LightSteelBlue	#B0C4DE
Darkorange	#FF8C00	LightYellow	#FFFFE0
DarkOrchid	#9932CC	Lime	#00FF00
DarkRed	#8B0000	LimeGreen	#32CD32
DarkSalmon	#E9967A	Linen	#FAF0E6
DarkSeaGreen	#8FBC8F	Magenta	#FF00FF
DarkSlateBlue	#483D8B	Maroon	#800000
DarkSlateGray	#2F4F4F	MediumAqua Marine	#66CDAA
DarkTurquoise	#00CED1	MediumBlue	#0000CD
DarkViolet	#9400D3	MediumOrchid	#BA55D3
DeepPink	#FF1493	MediumPurple	#9370D8
DeepSkyBlue	#00BFFF	MediumSeaGreen	#3CB371
DimGray	#696969	MediumSlateBlue	#7B68EE
DodgerBlue	#1E90FF	MediumSpring Green	#00FA9A
Feldspar	#D19275	MediumTurquoise	#48D1CC

Color Name	Hexadecimal		Color Name	Hexadecimal
FireBrick	#B22222		MediumVioletRed	#C71585
FloralWhite	#FFFAF0		MidnightBlue	#191970
ForestGreen	#228B22		MintCream	#F5FFFA
Fuchsia	#FF00FF		MistyRose	#FFE4E1
Gainsboro	#DCDCDC		Moccasin	#FFE4B5
NavajoWhite	#FFDEAD		SandyBrown	#F4A460
Navy	#000080		SeaGreen	#2E8B57
OldLace	#FDF5E6		SeaShell	#FFF5EE
Olive	#808000		Sienna	#A0522D
OliveDrab	#6B8E23		Silver	#C0C0C0
Orange	#FFA500		SkyBlue	#87CEEB
OrangeRed	#FF4500		SlateBlue	#6A5ACD
Orchid	#DA70D6		SlateGray	#708090
PaleGoldenRod	#EEE8AA		Snow	#FFFAFA
PaleGreen	#98FB98		SpringGreen	#00FF7F
PaleTurquoise	#AFEEEE		SteelBlue	#4682B4
PaleVioletRed	#D87093		Tan	#D2B48C
PapayaWhip	#FFEFD5		Teal	#008080
PeachPuff	#FFDAB9		Thistle	#D8BFD8
Peru	#CD853F		Tomato	#FF6347
Pink	#FFC0CB		Turquoise	#40E0D0
Plum	#DDA0DD		Violet	#EE82EE
PowderBlue	#B0E0E6		VioletRed	#D02090
Purple	#800080		Wheat	#F5DEB3
Red	#FF0000		White	#FFFFFF
RosyBrown	#BC8F8F		WhiteSmoke	#F5F5F5
RoyalBlue	#4169E1		Yellow	#FFFF00
SaddleBrown	#8B4513		YellowGreen	#9ACD32
Salmon	#FA8072			

Appendix D

Character Entities

	"!"	!
"	"""	"
	"#"	#
	"$"	$
	"%"	%
&	"&"	&
	"'"	'
	"("	(
	")"	)
	"*"	*
	"+"	+
	","	,
	"-"	-
	"."	.
	"/"	/
	"0"	0
	"9"	9
<	"<"	<
	"="	=
>	">"	>
	"?"	?
	"@"	@
	"A"	A
	"Z"	Z
	"["	[
	"\"	\
	"]"	]
	"^"	^
	"_"	_
	"`"	'
	"a"	a
	"z"	z
	"{"	{
	"|"	|
	"}"	}
	"~"	~

	""	□
	"€"	□
	""	□
	"‚"	‘
	"ƒ"	ƒ
	"„"	„
	"…"	…
	"†"	†
	"‡"	‡
	"ˆ"	ˆ
	"‰"	‰
	"Š"	Š
	"‹"	‹
	"Œ"	Œ
	""	□
	"Ž"	□
	""	□
	""	□
	"‘"	‘
	"’"	’
	"“"	“
	"”"	”
	"•"	
	"–"	–
	"—"	—
	"˜"	˜
	"™"	™
	"š"	š
	"›"	›

	"œ"	œ
	""	□
	"ž"	□
	"Ÿ"	Ÿ
	" "	
¡	"¡"	¡
¢	"¢"	¢
£	"£"	£
¤	"¤"	¤
¥	"¥"	¥
¦	"¦"	
§	"§"	§
¨	"¨"	¨
©	"©"	©
ª	"ª"	ª
«	"«"	«
¬	"¬"	¬
	""	
®	"®"	®
¯	"¯"	¯
°	"°"	°
±	"±"	±
²	"²"	^{2}
³	"³"	^{3}
´	"´"	´
µ	"µ"	µ
¶	"¶"	¶
·	"·"	·
¸	"¸"	¸

¹	"¹"	¹
º	"º"	º
»	"»"	»
¼	"¼"	¼
½	"½"	½
¾	"¾"	¾
¿	"¿"	¿
À	"À"	À
Á	"Á"	Á
Â	"Â"	Â
Ã	"Ã"	Ã
Ä	"Ä"	Ä
Å	"Å"	Å
Æ	"Æ"	Æ
Ç	"Ç"	Ç
È	"È"	È
É	"É"	É
Ê	"Ê"	Ê
Ë	"Ë"	Ë
Ì	"Ì"	Ì
Í	"Í"	Í
Î	"Î"	Î
Ï	"Ï"	Ï
Ð	"Ð"	Ð
Ñ	"Ñ"	Ñ
Ò	"Ò"	Ò
Ó	"Ó"	Ó
Ô	"Ô"	Ô
Õ	"Õ"	Õ

Ö	"Ö"	Ö
×	"×"	×
Ø	"Ø"	Ø
Ù	"Ù"	Ù
Ú	"Ú"	Ú
Û	"Û"	Û
Ü	"Ü"	Ü
Ý	"Ý"	Ý
Þ	"Þ"	Þ
ß	"ß"	ß
à	"à"	à
aacute;	"á"	á
â	"â"	â
ã	"ã"	ã
ä	"ä"	ä
å	"å"	å
æ	"æ"	æ
ç	"ç"	ç
è	"è"	è
é	"é"	é
ê	"ê"	ê
ë	"ë"	ë
ì	"ì"	ì
í	"í"	í
î	"î"	î
ï	"ï"	ï
ð	"ð"	ð
ñ	"ñ"	ñ
ò	"ò"	ò

ó	"ó"	ó
ô	"ô"	ô
õ	"õ"	õ
ö	"ö"	ö
÷	"÷"	÷
ø	"ø"	ø
ù	"ù"	ù

ú	"ú"	ú
û	"û"	û
ü	"ü"	ü
ý	"ý"	ý
þ	"þ"	þ
ÿ	"ÿ"	ÿ

Appendix E

References

1. *HTML 4.01 Specification* (http://www.w3.org/TR/html401/)
2. *Cascading Style Sheets, Level 2, CSS2 Specification* (http://www.w3.org/TR/REC-CSS2/)
3. *Extensible Markup Language (XML) 1.0* (http://www.w3.org/TR/REC-xml/)
4. *XHTML™ 1.0 The Extensible HyperText Markup Language* (http://www.w3.org/TR/xhtml1/)

Index

A

B

C

D

E

O

P

Q

R

S

T

U

V

W

X

Z